Language Development
A Reader for Teachers

BRENDA MILLER POWER
University of Maine

RUTH SHAGOURY HUBBARD
Lewis & Clark College

Merrill,
an imprint of Prentice Hall
Englewood Cliffs, New Jersey   *Columbus, Ohio*

Library of Congress Cataloging-in-Publication Data

Language development : A reader for classroom teachers / [edited by] Brenda Miller Power,
Ruth Shagoury Hubbard.

      p. cm.

    Includes bibliographical references and index.

    ISBN 0-13-191032-9 (pbk.)

    1. Children—Language. 2. Language acquisition. 3. Sociolinguistics.   I. Power,
Brenda Miller. II. Hubbard, Ruth Shagoury

  LB1139.L3L3239 1996

  401'.93—dc20

95-32102
CIP

Cover art: Marjory Dressler
Editor: Bradley J. Potthoff
Production Editor: Louise N. Sette
Design Coordinator: Julia Zonneveld Van Hook
Text Designer: Ed Horcharik
Cover Designer: Tammy Grabrian Johnson
Production Manager: Deidra M. Schwartz
Electronic Text Management: Marilyn Wilson Phelps, Matthew Williams, Karen L. Bretz,
   Tracey Ward

This book was set in Revival 565 and Swiss 721 BT by Prentice Hall and was printed and
bound by R.R. Donnelley & Sons Company. The cover was printed by Phoenix Color Corp.

Printed in the United States of America

10 9 8 7 6 5 4 3

ISBN: 0-13-191032-9

Prentice-Hall International (UK) Limited, *London*
Prentice-Hall of Australia Pty. Limited, *Sydney*
Prentice-Hall of Canada, Inc., *Toronto*
Prentice-Hall Hispanoamericana, S. A., *Mexico*
Prentice-Hall of India Private Limited, *New Delhi*
Prentice-Hall of Japan, Inc., *Tokyo*
Simon & Schuster Asia Pte. Ltd., *Singapore*
Editora Prentice-Hall do Brasil, Ltda., *Rio de Janeiro*

For our children

Meghan, Nathaniel, Cory, and Deanna

Who taught us the rules of language and schools, and then cheerfully broke most of them.

Preface

There is something fascinating, almost magical, about the ability to speak. Though it is a common miracle, played out each day, we are a long way from understanding the mysteries of language. Human speech has very special properties that allow us to communicate at a rate 3 to 10 times faster than we could otherwise. Linguists have spent decades trying to unlock the codes of communication. There is more to language than speech, however, and anthropologists have spent just as much time considering the links between culture and perception. Teachers must have the skills of both to understand and build on the language of their students. Through understanding students' language, teachers hold the key to understanding their learning.

TEXT FOCUS

This reader is designed to take teachers into the domains of linguists and anthropologists. We believe it's important to read the studies of researchers who have shaped our understanding of how we develop language and how we use it to communicate meaning. But it's equally important to take that knowledge into the world of the classroom, examining how we can use language as a tool for genuine learning, for sharing understanding with others, and for delighting in the magic of language. We have included many studies of language from classrooms, written by teachers. These stories help us all understand how language develops and changes over time—and how this knowledge can help us change classroom practice for the better.

To take the dialogue further, we invited four language researchers to tell us more about the process of their work—and beyond their published research to what they are working on now, what motivates their research, and how they link it to their teaching lives. Our interviews with Courtney Cazden, Shirley Brice Heath, Deborah Tannen, and Gordon Wells encourage us to engage in a "passion for the ordinary," exploring closely what is occurring all around us.

In *A Map of the World*, Jane Hamilton writes about a 2-year-old child, Lizzie, who is just learning to speak:

> She was just beginning to speak in short sentences. She was at the juncture in her baby-hood when it was possible she knew everything worth knowing. She understood the texture of her family; she understood the territory and rage and love, although she couldn't say much more than *ball* and *moo, I want, pretty girl*, and *bad dog*. As her language shaped her experience and limited her ideas, she would probably lose most of her wisdom for a time. . . . Lizzie, at two, was on the brink, between stations. It was tempting to think that if only they could speak, infants could take us back to their beginning, to the forces of their becoming; they could tell us about patience, about waiting and waiting in the dark.[1]

The pieces in this reader can help give us a language to speak about language. We can understand that feeling a toddler has of losing knowledge for a time. Some of these readings will challenge you—as they have challenged us—to rethink some of your most cherished beliefs about language, learning, and culture. Learning about language has taught us much about patience, about waiting and listening closely to students so we can grasp multiple meanings beneath the words they use.

TEXT ORGANIZATION

We have divided this book into three parts. These sections represent different "stations" of knowledge classroom teachers need to understand in working with students. Part I, *Historical Perspectives and Landmark Studies*, highlights the major theorists who have shaped our understanding of how language is acquired. Teachers need to know the wide range of normal language development. Too often, differences within this wide range are equated with deficiencies in schools.

Part II, *Talk in Schools*, is filled with examples of how teachers can change curriculum to support oral language development, as well as link oral language development to written language. In this section, teachers will see new ways to listen to and consider the language communities of which they are a part and also learn to assess talk in the classroom.

Finally, Part III, *Sociocultural and Personal Perspectives*, tackles some of the complex issues of language and culture. Language is a social construction that doesn't exist in a vacuum. And as our society becomes more diverse, it is even more important for teachers to understand how language use among students reflects diversity.

We have included a series of extensions at the end of each section to help you learn to analyze language in your own classroom. We believe that teachers can understand most deeply the lives and learning of their students if they are researchers within their own classrooms. While we hope you learn important concepts and theories about language within these pages, we know the best learning, about your students' "territories and rages and loves," can only come as you learn to listen to them closely and patiently. These extensions are designed to help you learn

---

[1]From *A Map of the World* by J. Hamilton, 1994, New York: Doubleday, p. 27.

to do this. We've peppered them with examples from novice teacher-researchers who like you are just learning how to analyze language. They cover everything from purchasing tape recorders to coding tape transcripts to noting the way a head is held when someone laughs.

We hope you enjoy this reader as much as we enjoyed putting it together. Our aim is to bring us all to a new place in understanding, awareness, and celebration of the language our students use.

ACKNOWLEDGMENTS

We thank Cynthia McCallister for all her work in organizing the materials, and Janet Murakami and Glennellen Pace for suggestions of helpful articles. Abigail Garthwait and Kelly Chandler were thoughtful readers of galleys. Courtney Cazden, Shirley Brice Heath, Deborah Tannen, and Gordon Wells were generous and gracious participants in interviews. James Whitney provided continuous friendly technical advice about tape recording and transcribing. The support staff at the University of Maine—especially Dianne Avery, Ethel Hill, Sue Russell and Phyllis Thibodeau—has been our lifeline at every deadline. Linda Scharp invested lots of energy in initiating this project at Merrill/Prentice Hall, and Brad Potthoff was just as thoughtful and careful in shepherding the book through to completion.

We are most indebted to the many teachers in our language development classes over the past decade. Their research and insights are infused throughout this book. We also thank our colleagues, who share our love for active, hands-on learning in language. They are too many to mention, but their enthusiasm sustains us.

We would also like to acknowledge the reviewers of this text: Kathy H. Barclay, Western Illinois University; Carole L. Bond, Memphis State University; Thomas G. Devine, University of Massachusetts–Lowell; M. Jean Greenlaw, University of North Texas; Judith P. Mitchell, Weber State University; Terry Piper, St. Mary's University/Halifax, N.S., Canada; Walter Prentice, University of Wisconsin–Superior; Jessie A. Roderick, University of Maryland; Tonja L. Root-Sirmans, Valdosta State University; and Marilou R. Sorensen, University of Utah.

Contents

Part III
Sociocultural and Personal Perspectives   187

Historical Perspectives and Landmark Studies

Children's Language Acquisition

MABEL L. RICE   *University of Kansas*

● ●

Editor's introduction

We begin with this essay because it is a comprehensive overview of landmark research in language development, the issues that continue to challenge language researchers, and implications for instruction in language. Mabel Rice presents all the terms and major findings that are informing current research in language, even as she highlights theories that are the most contentious in the field. The themes she presents are woven throughout all the readings that follow.

● ● ● ● ● ● ● ● ● ● ● ●

One of the most remarkable achievements of childhood is also one of the most commonplace. Sometime during their second year, most children begin to talk, and in apparently little time they are adept at using language to address their needs and carry on social interactions. What is remarkable about this achievement is that little or no explicit teaching seems to be necessary.

Although this observation has long fascinated philosophers, it is a relatively recent topic of major interest for developmental psychologists. The contemporary literature began to appear in the 1960s but emerged as a strong area of inquiry only during the 1970s and 1980s. The study of child language sits at an interface among linguistics, developmental psychology, sociology, anthropology, and education, and it links basic questions about the nature of human intellectual competencies to applied questions of how best to teach young children.

The purpose of this article is to provide an overview of the current questions and findings regarding children's acquisition of language so as to highlight some fundamental issues and to suggest guidelines for educational policy. It must be recognized at the outset that this area of study is among the most contentious in the developmental literature. There is little consen-sus about the most fundamental issues. The debates are lively, and the data base, although growing rapidly, is far from complete. Therefore, the interested reader is encouraged to consult more comprehensive treatments of the literature (e.g., Berko Gleason, 1985; Fletcher & Garman, 1986; Ingram, in press; Rice & Schiefelbusch, 1989; Wanner & Gleitman, 1982).

The article is divided into four sections. In the first, the language acquisition literature is summarized according to some of the major current questions. In the second section, consideration will turn to children who do not master language readily. The third section will address how to teach language to children. In the final section, suggestions for educational policy will be presented.

OVERVIEW OF LANGUAGE ACQUISITION

Language acquisition entails three components: One is the language to be acquired, or, in other words, the

Source: "Children's Language Acquisition" by M. L. Rice, 1989, *American Psychologist*, *44*:2, pp. 149–156. Copyright 1989 by the American Psychological Association.

task to be mastered; another is the child and the abilities and predispositions that he or she brings to language acquisition; and the third is the environmental setting, that is, the language that the child hears and the speaking context. Each of these components has generated considerable attention. The biggest problem, however, is to characterize how all three aspects fit together to account for the spontaneous appearance of language.

The Nature of Language

Dimensions of Communicative Competence. Language consists of four major dimensions: the sound system (phonology), the system of meanings (semantics), the rules of word formation (morphology), and the rules of sentence formation (syntax). The phonological dimension is evident in such contrasts as *bat* and *pat*, where differences in sounds constitute linguistic distinctions. Semantics refers to the expression of meanings in language and is differentiated from underlying concepts or categories, a distinction to be discussed more fully later. Morphemes are the minimal units of meaning, either words (free morphemes) or meaningful parts of words (bound morphemes). Syntax refers to sentence patterns and the arrangement of words to represent relations between them.

In addition to these dimensions, language has important social aspects. A speaker is ill-equipped to use language effectively if all he or she knows is how to formulate a grammatically correct sentence. The social setting requires adjustment of both the topic and the style of language used, and it also determines how language is interpreted. For example, in some contexts, "Is that my coat?" might be a request for information, whereas in other circumstances it might be a request for the coat or an accusation of theft.

All these aspects of language must be, and are, mastered by children. The entire package of skills is referred to as *communicative competence* (Hymes, 1972).

Theoretical Models

Linguists have focused much of their attention on the grammatical aspects of language, the morphology, syntax, and, more recently, semantics. Their goal has been to arrive at a satisfactory description of linguistic structures, both at the level of individual languages and at the level of universally shared features. They emphasize that languages do not appear in all possible forms, but the variation across human languages occurs within highly constrained bounds. Linguists hypothesize that these constraints correspond to those provided by a specialized biological program for language acquisition that is an isolated realm of competence not accounted for by more general cognitive abilities (cf. Chomsky, 1965; Goodluck, 1986; Wexler & Culicover, 1980).

Linguistic theorists have attempted to model the outcome of language acquisition, that is, the linguistic knowledge of the mature speaker. Although several models have been proposed, there is currently no consensus of support for any one of them (cf. Newmeyer, 1986). Instead, the field is in a period of rapid development, with emerging linguistic models competing with existing accounts and continual revision or updating of old models to meet new challenges, such as the emerging evidence about language growth and change over the life span.

Among the theoretical models applied to child-language data are transformational grammar, which is now several generations removed from the original model proposed by Chomsky (1957, 1981; Wexler & Culicover, 1980), case grammar (Brown, 1973; Fillmore, 1968), and lexical functionalist grammar (Bresnan, 1982). These models differ from one another in many ways, but one dimension of particular importance for studies of language acquisition is the extent to which syntax is seen as independent of semantics. The early transformation models assumed that syntax, or grammar, is an abstract, rule-governed system independent of the meanings of individual words. Case grammar, on the other hand, introduced semantic roles for noun phrases. This distinction allowed the case grammar model to capture important differences between syntactic constructions that appear to be highly similar in form. For example, in the sentences "John opened the door" and "The key opened the door," *John* and *key* are both nouns and both subjects. Yet the sentence "John opened the door with a key" reveals that there is something very different about these two subjects: *John* is an agent, and *key* is an instrument.

In the more recent lexical functionalist and government binding models, the meanings packaged in individual words are seen as carrying rich syntactic information. Verbs provide necessary information about the kinds of relationships that can be expressed and how they can be expressed in sentences. The following example, with asterisks to indicate ungrammatical sentences, is from Pinker (1989):

> John fell.
> *John fell the floor.
> John devoured something.
> *John devoured.
> John put something somewhere.
> *John put something.
> *John put somewhere.
> *John put.

A current hot issue is how children learn to avoid the ungrammatical sentences. The problem was pointed out by Baker (1979), and it rests on three observations. One is that there is no negative evidence available to children; that is, adults do not explicitly state such constraints while conversing with their children. Second, children tend to overgeneralize linguistic rules and make mistakes similar to the ungrammatical sentences listed earlier. Therefore, they must somehow learn to retreat from such errors. Finally, the constraints in a language are quite arbitrary and not readily predictable and thus seem not to be easily learnable.

What the Child Brings to Language Acquisition

The answer to the problem, as well as to other unresolved questions, lies in information about what children know about language, the sequence in which they come to learn language, and how they use language. In turn, these observations lead to inferences about the means by which children master language. Ultimately, any satisfactory model of language development must be compatible with how children learn; their ability to perceive, conceptualize, store, and access information; and their motivations. What remains unresolved is the extent to which children draw upon general learning mechanisms or language-specific learning strategies and capabilities.

Much of the literature focuses on the conceptual and social processes that bear on language development and, to a lesser extent, on the cultural influences. Of primary interest is the ability of children to form linguistic categories, abstract rules for relating the categories, and learn to adjust language to social settings.

Because language emerges when children are very young, around one year of age, and because children this age do not answer direct questions, the major source of information about children's language learning comes from what children say. Investigators carefully transcribe exactly what children say, along with the utterances of other speakers conversing with children. The advent of audio- and videotape records has been central to the contemporary literature, allowing for permanent records and careful data analysis. Most of the available transcript data are from White, middle-class, English-speaking children, usually with no or few siblings, although there are data from children learning non-English languages. The value of such data is evident in the formation of the Child Language Data Exchange System (MacWhinney & Snow, 1985), which serves as an international data exchange and transcript analysis center.

The transcript data capture children's production of linguistic forms and the settings and circumstances in which targeted forms are used. In addition, investigators explore children's comprehension of linguistic forms and grammatical rules and, as children become old enough to do so, ask children to make judgments of grammatical correctness.

Cognitive Underpinnings.   Much of the work of the 1970s focused on the earliest stage of language development, the emergence of first words and word combinations, in the belief that the beginnings of language would be most revealing of the origins of communicative competence. The findings were striking and amazingly consistent across children and languages. In effect, young children first talked about what they knew, primarily the world of objects and actions upon objects, favorite things, and people and their activities. Children's first words were not about objects of no interest to them, such as refrigerators, but instead they named bottles and favorite toys and indicated recurrence ("more"), nonexistence ("all gone"), and negation ("no"). Furthermore, English-speaking children's first sentences were simple combinations of content words, such as "more juice," "Mommy sock," and "big ball" (Bloom, 1970; Bowerman, 1973; Brown, 1973). Conspicuously absent were words without obvious content, such as the linking words or functors, for example, *is*, *to*, and *will*. These simple early sentences were characterized as "telegraphic." This feature has not turned out to be universal, however, but instead varies as a function of the language to be acquired (cf. Slobin, 1985).

Brown (1973) noted that the kinds of meanings that seemed to be central for young language learners indicated strong parallels with Piaget's model of young children's cognitive achievements during the sensorimotor period (birth to around 18 months of age). Piaget emphasized the salience of objects and actions upon objects, a salience supported by children's first words. He also proposed that toddlers formulated an abstract knowledge about the world, with a system of mental representation that included knowledge that objects exist when not in view (object permanence) and that one object can be used to obtain another (means-ends).

It was a small inductive step to hypothesize that general cognitive growth accounted for the emergence of language, a position made appealing by its congruence with the transcript data and by accounting for why children the world over, who presumably share cognitive universals, were able to learn language in a similar fashion. For the past 15 years, investigators have collected linguistic and cognitive data from children in attempts to work out the relation between cognition and language.

Contrary to Piaget's prediction, the subsequent pattern of findings did not support the model of abstract cognitive precursors to language. There is not a clear temporal order of cognitive insights first, followed by linguistic achievements. Instead, language and related non-linguistic competencies tend to appear at the same time. For example, toddlers begin to say "all gone" at roughly the same time they are solving advanced object-permanence tasks. The conclusion has been that there are very specific, rather than broad and pervasive, relations between cognitive developments and semantic developments (cf. Bates, Bretherton, & Snyder, 1988; Gopnik & Meltzoff, 1987). Furthermore, the direction is not one way. Instead, children can use words to search for or solidify general understandings as well as to search for words or word combinations to express what they have already worked out nonlinguistically. It remains, however, that at the earliest stages of acquisition, most of the successful nonlinguistic predictors of language are cognitive measures (Bates, 1979).

Even good predictors do not, however, account for all the variability. Part of the unexplained variance may be due to the fact that nonlinguistic concepts are not isomorphic with linguistic categories or rules. Instead, there is a mapping, a translation from nonlinguistic to linguistic, that is required (cf. Rice & Kemper, 1984).

The world and a child's understanding of it do not come prepackaged in a manner that transparently corresponds to language. For example, even a category as apparently obvious (to adults) as that of "cup" is not clearly given by the properties of objects. What is called a cup may or may not have a handle, may or may not be made of glass, may or may not be small. The styrofoam object that has no handles and looks like a glass is nevertheless called a cup. The repackaging of information needed for linguistic categories is apparent when considering the variability evident across languages. For example, in Dyirbal, an aboriginal language of Australia, there is a classifier category that includes women, fire, and dangerous things, a linguistic category unlike any in English and unlike any obvious nonlinguistic category of things (cf. Lakoff, 1987). The point is that semantics refers to meanings expressed in language, a mapping established by the conventions of each language.

Furthermore, not all linguistic categories or rules have obvious parallels with meanings. Instead, they seem to fall outside the sphere of the mapping problem. An example is provided by the law of particle movement in English, wherein we can say "put the hat on," "put it on," or "put on the hat," but we cannot say "put on it." Such constraints are of a formal, grammatical nature not captured in the meanings expressed. Another example is from the English question-formation rule. We can say, "Mary threw something" and transform that into the question, "What did Mary throw?," or we can say "Mary threw stones and something," but we cannot transform it into the question, "What did Mary throw stones and?" (from Goodluck, 1986). It is not likely that children could master these rules on the basis of general nonlinguistic knowledge.

The relation between cognition and language seems to be strongest at the earliest stages of language development. Even at the beginning, however, it is not the case that prelinguistic conceptual knowledge always precedes and accounts for language development. Instead, the two domains seem to develop synchronously. By school age, children are adept at using language as a way of solving conceptual problems, as a mnemonic device, and as a way of organizing mental spaces. In other words, children at first draw heavily upon concepts as a way to master language and later use language to learn new concepts.

The acquisition of word meanings is a matter of great interest given the prominence accorded to the mapping of meanings and the centrality of meanings in current linguistic models. A well-known phenomenon is the rapid spurt in number of new words learned that usually appears somewhere around 18 months, at the time of early word combinations. This is followed by an impressive rate of new word acquisition throughout the preschool years. It has been estimated that during this time children learn to comprehend more than 14,000 words (Templin, 1957), or an average of about nine new words per day. Obviously, children manage to do this without explicit word-by-word tutoring. Instead, they seem to absorb, or "map," new meanings as they encounter them in conversational interactions. They draw on an ability to "fast map" new meanings, forming a quick, initial partial understanding of a word's meaning involving a restructuring of the known word-storage space and a restructuring of the underlying conceptual domain (Carey, 1978). They are able to fast map on the basis of only one or very few encounters with a new word in a meaningful context (cf. Rice & Woodsmall, 1988). Although the phenomenon of fast mapping has been replicated across several studies, the process by which children accomplish this apparently sophisticated feat remains undetermined. It is most likely that they draw upon a quick sense of likely meanings as well as their knowledge of word-formulation rules and grammatical contexts, although the relative contribution of these variables remains to be determined. At any rate, this rapid word-learning ability is central to a preschooler's overall language development and serves as an important foundation for later reading skills.

Social Skills. Just as the early meanings of emergent language show remarkable similarity across children, so do the early social uses. From the outset, language emerges as a social tool. Toddlers use language to get the attention of others, to request actions by others, to greet, to protest, and to comment, among other functions. Children have social as well as intellectual motivations for learning language.

Language skills emerge from prelinguistic communicative needs. The social dimension controls early uses of language, and the social setting in turn provides validation and confirmation of the child's effectiveness as a communicator. Children do not use their first words in a vacuum, as an intellectual exercise. Instead, in our society their earliest vocalizations, even cries, are interpreted as meaningful and are regarded as an important indication of the emergence of a new person. Parents actively shape the social aspects of language in the explicit teaching of polite forms such as "please" and "thank you" and appropriate ways of speaking to different individuals.

The social contexts of children's development are not universal but instead demonstrate enormous variability. Therefore, there is reason for caution in espousing a strong causal role for social input in language development. Any such factors would have to be consistent with what is known about different cultures and be able to account for how various cultural practices can lead to the general similarities in emergence of language skills (cf. Heath, 1989).

Individual Variability. At one level of description, there are striking commonalities across children in language acquisition. Among them are the following: Language tends to appear at about the same age; the same sorts of meanings are encoded in early words and sentences; and basic meaning relations are mastered before formal grammatical devices. Such consistencies suggest a universal language-making capacity (Slobin, 1985).

At the same time, on another, more specific level, there is considerable variability from one child to another in the rate of language acquisition and in the manner in which particular aspects of language are mastered and combined with one another (Ferguson, 1989). For example, toddlers vary in their preference for nounlike words versus other words. Children who prefer nouns, and later expand their number of verbs, have an advantage for early mastery of grammar (Bates et al., 1988).

Universal propensities and a child's idiosyncratic style interact in the language-acquisition process. There is no one formula, pattern, sequence, or gradient applicable to each child. Instead, each child draws upon a unique mixture of biological, psychological, social, and environmental factors to arrive ultimately at the shared conventions of formal language.

What the Environment Contributes to Language Development

Obviously, children must hear language in use in order to master the system. Furthermore, it must make sense to them and somehow be important for them to acquire. Beyond these general requirements, it is difficult to specify essential features of input that must be present for a child to learn language. On the other hand, there is evidence about which features can enhance or facilitate a youngster's language development (cf. Snow, 1984).

Much has been written about the "motherese" style of adult input in White, middle-class, Western societies, in which adults and older children adjust their language input to young children. These adjustments consist of simplifications that correspond to youngsters' comprehension levels and interests. Among the features of motherese are an emphasis on the here and now, with a restricted vocabulary and much paraphrasing; simple, well-formed sentences; frequent repetitions; and a slow rate of speech with pauses between utterances and after-content words. It must be noted, however, that these features of "motherese" are not universal but instead reflect cultural practices for addressing infants and young children (Pye, 1986).

Central to the package of facilitative input style is semantically contingent speech. *Semantic contingency* refers to an immediate matching of the adult utterance to the topic or content of the child's utterances. In this scenario, a child may comment on a toy of interest, such as "ball." The adult may then repeat the child's utterance or use the child's word in an expanded comment, such as "that's a ball," or use the child's word in a question, any one of which demonstrates semantic contingency. The effectiveness of this interactive style has been replicated across a number of studies. The combination of linguistic encoding of what is of immediate interest to the child with the child's own utterances maximizes the matching of language form to communicative intent by means of joint attention.

Social interactive routines, such as book reading, are strongly supportive of language development, especially for vocabulary. Joint adult-child book reading is an activity appropriate for a wide age span, from toddlerhood through the elementary grades, and it bridges the development of oral language skills and the emergence of print literacy.

On the other hand, there are indications that some input styles may not be helpful for a child's language development. One widely cited finding is that a directive adult style, consisting of many commands, requests, directions, and instructions, is associated with a slower rate of acquisition of naming words (Nelson, 1973). There is reason for caution in interpretation, however, insofar as it is unclear whether the input style led to the delay, or delayed onset influenced the parental input patterns.

How Do the Three Factors of Language, Child, and Environment Interact?

Ultimately, the question becomes how do children extract or induct from the language they hear or see the conventional linguistic rules of their native language(s)? To argue that children call upon cognitive or social underpinnings or innate linguistic devices only introduces an intervening layer and does not resolve the basic question of *how*.

At this relatively early stage of inquiry, investigators have rightfully concentrated their efforts on the description of children's linguistic abilities and patterns of acquisition. Contemporary attempts to account for how children acquire language tend to be narrowly defined, with an exclusive emphasis on one of the three components (specific linguistic rules, child variables, or input variables). One of the more comprehensive psychological models available was proposed by Nelson (1989). He argued that language can be mastered by a general cognitive mechanism, the rare event learning mechanism (RELM), which is applicable to all complex, symbolic, rule-governed systems. He concluded that language learning is based on rare events, or isolated moments of understanding. He emphasized the cognitive processes of attention, comparison, categorization, and memory as central to language acquisition, with localized "hot spots" of intellectual realignment. In this model, language acquisition does not proceed in a steady linear progression of increasingly accurate responses but, instead, encompasses four phases: preparation, analysis, assessment, and consolidation. These phases occupy unequal and sometimes overlapping times during the acquisition process. Language acquisition is a consequence of child-constructed experience.

The RELM model deals with the interface of what the child brings to the task and what the environment offers, in terms of what we know about children's general cognitive mechanisms. What is relatively neglected is the language-specific dimension of language acquisition. It is unclear how cognitive mechanisms, powerful as they may be, help children resolve the learnability problem or arrive at language-specific knowledge. On the other hand, linguistic models espousing an innate linguistic learning device have not satisfactorily specified how such a device would work and how it interfaces with the rich network of general cognitive mechanisms available to even very young children. Resolution of these problems constitutes the most challenging of current questions about language development.

Summary of Normal Language Development

Overall, the outcomes of two decades of child-language research lead to the following picture of children's language. There is a remarkable similarity in the general acquisition sequence for language skills across language and cultures, although there is considerable individual variability in learning strategies and rate of acquisition. Children learn language as a means of talking about what they know so they can accomplish social goals important to them. Explicit language teaching from adults is not necessary. In fact, if adults try to structure and direct a child's language learning, the outcome may be interference with, instead of enhancement of, a child's language skill. Language emerges from a child's explorations of the world in a rich social setting. Although children's cognitive and social knowledge contribute to language mastery, they do not fully account for language development. Not all aspects of language have close parallels to general cognitive or social skills. The specifics of how children manage to combine their mental resources with the environmental input to master language continue to elude scholars, but much progress has been made in terms of the empirical validity of explanatory models.

IMPAIRED OR DELAYED LANGUAGE DEVELOPMENT

Not all children develop language effortlessly. Instead, some youngsters struggle to achieve linguistic competence. Their difficulty is made more poignant in a society that places a high premium on an individual's ability to express himself or herself well. Traditional teaching methods are based on the assumption that a learner can process language readily and use verbal language as a means of conveying ideas. From kindergarten through higher education to subsequent high-status roles such as those of professors and physicians, it is assumed that a learner or practitioner can understand and manipulate linguistic symbols.

If children cannot master the fundamentals of language during their preschool years, they are greatly at risk for educational achievement, particularly for reading skills. Furthermore, their limited verbal skills

affect their social skills. It is difficult for a youngster to win an argument over a desired toy if he or she cannot negotiate verbally.

Language-learning difficulties can be secondary to another handicapping condition, such as a hearing loss, limited intellectual ability, or atypical social/affective functioning. Of all handicapped children served by speech-language pathologists, more than 40% have other primary handicaps (Dublinske, 1981). The remainder have communication problems as a primary handicap (i.e., without other significant handicaps). Overall, 5% of school-age children receive services for communication handicaps (Dublinske, 1981). These children include those whose problems are with production aspects of communication, such as fluency and voice disorders. It is estimated that approximately 3% of preschoolers lag significantly behind their peers in language development, even though their general sensory, cognitive, and emotional abilities are commensurate with their cohorts (Leske, 1981). These children are referred to by a variety of labels, including *language delayed*, *language impaired*, and *specific language disability*.

The existence of children whose only significant handicap is that of language development is an interesting challenge to current models of language acquisition. If language is such a robust human-skill domain, why are some children at such risk? What is known about these children is certainly less extensive than the data base for normally developing children. The safest conclusions are about what is not true of language-disabled children. First, by definition, they do not have general intellectual limitations, as indicated by performance within the normal range, or above, on nonverbal measures of intelligence. In other words, they are defined as demonstrating a discrepancy between linguistic and general cognitive ability. This discrepancy is often not recognized by lay persons and educators, presumably because they expect a close association of linguistic and intellectual abilities. The implied erroneous causal interpretation of slow language because of slow intellect can be particularly distressing to a youngster and his or her parents.

Second, language-disabled children are not necessarily from environments with insufficient or inappropriate input, although that can sometimes be the case. It is very difficult to ascribe causal effects to environmental input, in part because communication with a child with limited skills is different from that with a more interactive or responsive youngster, and therefore unusual input patterns can be a consequence instead of a cause of the delayed language. Furthermore, the effects of unjustly attributing guilt to parents are unproductive, at best.

If not general intellect or environmental input, what does account for the difficulties of some children in acquiring language? At present, there is no consensus as to etiology (cf. Johnston, 1988; Leonard, 1979). Among the current hypotheses are specific problems in mental representation or information processing that have close parallels to language but are not crucial for performance on nonlinguistic intelligence tests (Johnston, 1988; Nelson, Kamhi, & Apel, 1987). Another candidate is a problem with on-line linguistic processing, evident in the limited ability of language-delayed preschoolers to fast map new words (Rice, 1987; Rice, Buhr, & Nemeth, 1988).

TEACHABILITY OF LANGUAGE

Although not usually necessary, in some cases language must be explicitly taught to children. For children who do not have them, language skills can enhance their social worlds, increase their learning capability, contribute significantly to their chances for academic success, and help ensure their eventual functioning as independent, self-actualizing adults. This teaching responsibility is distributed across teachers, speech/language pathologists, and parents.

In line with the three subdivisions of the first section of this article, the teachability of language depends upon the extent to which certain language skills are learnable, the characteristics of the individual learner, and the match between learner and teaching strategy. Principles of teachability are in the formative stages, and given the time demands inherent in evaluation of teaching methods, definitive conclusions will not be available immediately. With these caveats in mind, I have proposed a basic principle for each of the three components of teachability (Rice & Schiefelbusch, 1988, 1989):

1. The key dimension of language to be targeted for training is the lexicon (word meanings), especially verbs, insofar as they are the key to grammar, according to current theoretical models. Therefore, formal syntax is a secondary training target.

2. Children bring a wide variety of intellectual, perceptual, social, and motor competencies to language learning. Their teachability depends upon a synergistic balance of interacting skills and knowledge bases.

3. Teaching new language skills requires the use of converging strategies to enhance the aspects of the environment relevant to linguistic mapping in a manner that matches a learner's style of language learning with the targeted linguistic skill.

CONCLUSIONS AND APPLICATIONS

Naive intuitions about children's language development greatly underestimate the complexities of the achievement, the significance of the accomplishment for related areas of development, and the child's strong but apparently effortless contribution to the acquisition process. As adults, our language facility is so intimately ingrained in our thinking and social functioning that it is difficult to imagine the perspective of the language-learning youngster. We routinely assume that children understand what is said to them and that children mean what they say. We bring our assumptions to our plans for caring for and educating young children. In our culture, verbal communication is the primary means of managing the behavior of children and gaining access to their minds. With this in mind, there are two major conclusions.

First, for normally developing preschoolers (including infants and toddlers), it is important to remember that one of the ways in which these children are qualitatively different from school-age children is that they have not mastered the fundamentals of language. Although much of English grammar is mastered by age five, and kindergarten children can readily follow simple verbal instructions displaced by time and space, preschool children are still working on these skills. Language development is a primary educational objective for preschoolers. The best way to encourage development of language is to provide many opportunities for a child to interact with objects and events and other children. Children's play is a primary source of language enrichment. Adult-directed teaching drills are not appropriate. In other words, most children do not need to be taught language, but they do need opportunities to develop language. The role of the adult in language facilitation is to follow the child's interests, paraphrase what the child says with simple elaborations, and interact in a conversational manner about objects and events on which the child's attention is focused. Also, children do not always need to respond in order to learn new language skills. They can benefit greatly by the opportunity to absorb the conversations of others. At the same time, they do need opportunities to practice expressing words and sentences when they are ready to do so. An easy way to allow for opportunities is to provide pauses in conversations with children; in other words, for adults to refrain from doing all the talking.

Second, some children do need to be taught. Furthermore, a deficiency in language skill should not automatically be equated with limited intelligence, sensory handicaps, poor parental skills, or impoverished environmental circumstances. Careful assessment of the child and the family by trained professionals will be required to identify causal factors. Language teaching requires specialized strategies designed to meet the needs of individual children. Given that these children have not been able to benefit from ordinary communicative situations, it is unlikely that they will profit from placement in a typical preschool classroom, without directed focusing on targeted language forms. Instead, an appropriate preschool is one designed to enhance language, in which the teacher input is adjusted to the children's comprehension levels, communication opportunities are socially engineered in the context of meaningful play activities, and specific linguistic skills are targeted as goals for individual children (cf. Fey 1986). Furthermore, special adjustments to the school curriculum, in which a specific focus on language is provided, are likely to be needed throughout the secondary level as a child makes the transition from oral to written language, from language to express what is known to the use of language as a mental tool for acquiring new knowledge.

Overall, the study of children's language acquisition provides insight into fundamental human mental abilities, contributes to formal models of linguistic knowledge, provides a challenge to accounts of how children learn and how adults can teach, and reminds us of the priority of the social/communicative nature of human existence.

REFERENCES

Baker, C. L. (1979). Syntactic theory and the projection problem. *Linguistic Inquiry, 10,* 533–581.

Bates, E. (1979). *The emergence of symbols.* New York: Academic Press.

Bates, E., Bretherton, I., & Snyder, L. (1988). *From first words to grammar.* Cambridge, England: Cambridge University Press.

Belmont, J. M. (1989). Cognitive strategies and strategic learning. *American Psychologist, 44,* 142–148.

Berko Gleason, J. B. (1985). *The development of language.* Columbus, OH: Charles E. Merrill.

Bloom, L. (1970). *Language development: Form and function in emerging grammar.* Cambridge, MA: MIT Press.

Bowerman, M. (1973). *Early syntactic development: A cross-linguistic study with special reference to Finnish.* Cambridge, England: Cambridge University Press.

Bresnan, J. (Ed.). (1982). *The mental representation of grammatical relations.* Cambridge, MA: MIT Press.

Brown, R. (1973). *A first language: The early stages.* Cambridge, MA: Harvard University Press.

Carey, S. (1978). The child as word learner. In M. Halle, G. Miller, & J. Bresnan (Eds.). *Linguistic theory and psychological reality* (pp. 264–293). Cambridge, MA: The MIT Press.

Chomsky, N. (1957). *Syntactic structures.* The Hague, the Netherlands: Mouton Publishers.

Chomsky, N. (1965). *Aspects of the theory of syntax.* Cambridge, MA: MIT Press.

Chomsky, N. (1981). *Lectures on government and binding.* Dordrecht, Holland: Foris.

Dublinske, S. (1981). Action: School services. *Language, Speech, and Hearing Services in Schools, 12,* 192–200.

Ferguson, C. (1989). Individual differences in language learning. In M. L. Rice & R. L. Schiefelbusch (Eds.), *Teachability of language.* Baltimore: Brookes.

Fey, M. E. (1986). *Language intervention with young children.* San Diego: College Hill.

Fillmore, C. J. (1968). The case for case. In E. Bach & R. T. Harms (Eds.), *Universals in linguistic theory* (pp. 1–90). New York: Holt, Rinehart, & Winston.

Fletcher, P., & Garman, M. (Eds.) (1986). *Language acquisition: Studies in first language development.* London: Cambridge University Press.

Goodluck, H. (1986). Language acquisition and linguistic theory. In P. Fletcher & M. Garman (Eds.), *Language acquisition: Studies in first language development* (pp. 49–68). London: Cambridge University Press.

Gopnik, A., & Meltzoff, A. N. (1987). Language and thought in the young child: Early semantic developments and their relationships to object permanence, means-ends understanding, and categorization. In K. Nelson & A. Van Kleeck (Eds.), *Children's language* (Vol. 6, pp. 191–212). Hillsdale, NJ Erlbaum.

Heath, S. B. (1989). The learner as cultural member. In M. L. Rice & R. L. Schiefelbusch (Eds.), *Teachability of language.* Baltimore: Brookes.

Hymes, D. (1972). On communicative competence. In J. B. Pride & J. Holmes (Eds.), *Sociolinguistics* (pp. 269–285). Harmondsworth, Middlesex, England: Penguin.

Ingram, D. (in press). *First language acquisition: Method, description, and explanation.* London: Cambridge University Press.

Johnston, J. R. (1988). Specific language disorders in children. In N. Lass, L. McReynolds, J. Northern, & D. Yoder (Eds.), *Handbook of speech-language pathology and audiology* (pp. 697–727). Philadelphia: B. C. Decker.

Lakoff, G. (1987). *Women, fire, and dangerous things: What categories reveal about the mind.* Chicago: University of Chicago Press.

Leonard, L. B. (1979). Language impairment in children. *Merrill-Palmer Quarterly, 25*(3), 205–232.

Leske, M. C. (1981). Speech prevalence estimates of communicative disorders in the U.S. *ASHA, 23,* 229–237.

MacWhinney, B., & Snow, C. (1985). The child language data exchange system. *Journal of Child Language, 12,* 271–296.

Nelson, K. (1973). Structure and strategy in learning to talk. *Monographs of the Society for Research in Child Development, 38*(1–2, Serial No. 149).

Nelson, K. E. (1989). Strategies for first language teaching. In M. L. Rice & R. L. Schiefelbusch (Eds.), *Teachability of language.* Baltimore: Brookes.

Nelson, K. E., Kamhi, A. G., & Apel, K. (1987). Cognitive strengths and weaknesses in language-impaired children: One more look. *Journal of Speech and Hearing Disorders, 52,* 36–43.

Newmeyer, F. J. (1986). *Linguistic theory in America.* New York: Academic Press.

Pinker, S. (1989). Resolving a learnability paradox in the acquisition of the verb lexicon. In M. L. Rice & R. L. Schiefelbusch (Eds.), *Teachability of language.* Baltimore: Brookes.

Pye, C. (1986). Quiché Mayan speech to children. *Journal of Child Language, 13,* 85–100.

Rice, M. L. (1987, July). *Preschool children's fast mapping of words: Robust for most, fragile for some.* Paper presented at the International Congress for the Study of Child Language, Lund, Sweden.

Rice, M. L., Buhr, J., & Nemeth, M. (1988). *Fast mapping abilities of language-delayed preschoolers.* Unpublished manuscript.

Rice, M. L., & Kemper, S. (1984). *Child language and cognition: Contemporary issues.* Baltimore: University Park Press.

Rice, M. L., & Schiefelbusch, R. L. (1988, June). *Principles of language teachability.* Paper presented at the National Institute of Child Health and Human Development Conference on Biobehavioral Foundations of Language Development, Washington, DC.

Rice, M. L., & Schiefelbusch, R. L. (Eds.). (1989). *Teachability of language.* Baltimore: Brookes.

Rice, M. L., & Woodsmall, L. (1988). Lessons from television: Children's word learning when viewing. *Child Development, 59,* 420–429.

Slobin, D. I. (1985). *The cross-linguistic study of language acquisition* (Vols. 1 & 2). Hillsdale, NJ: Erlbaum.

Snow, C. E. (1984). Parent-child interaction and the development of communicative ability. In R. L. Schiefelbusch & J. Pickar (Eds.), *Communicative competence: Acquisition and intervention* (pp. 69–108). Baltimore: University Park Press.

Templin, M. C. (1957). *Certain language skills in children.* Minneapolis: University of Minnesota Press.

Wanner, E., & Gleitman, L. R. (Eds.). (1982). *Language acquisition: The state of the art.* London: Cambridge University Press.

Wexler, K., & Culicover, P. W. (1980). *Formal principles of language acquisition.* Cambridge, MA: MIT Press.

On Inner Speech

Lev Semenovich Vygotsky

Editor's introduction

The social context of language, and of thinking itself, is at the heart of Lev Vygotsky's influential work. Vygotsky, a Russian educator-turned-psychologist, explored ways children use language to interact with their world. In the following excerpt from *Thought and Language*, Vygotsky lays out his underlying theory that even our private thought and language are originally shaped through the ways we learn to interact with others. An internalization of private, or "inner," speech was a key concept in his work, one that differed sharply from the theories of his contemporary, Jean Piaget. Both men see strong links between developing language and cognitive abilities, but their theories and analyses of data couldn't be more different and remain a source of debate among child development experts.

We must probe still deeper and explore the plane of inner speech lying beyond the semantic plane. We shall discuss here some of the data of the special investigation we have made of it. The relationship of thought and word cannot be understood in all its complexity without a clear understanding of the psychological nature of inner speech. Yet, of all the problems connected with thought and language, this is perhaps the most complicated, beset as it is with terminological and other misunderstandings.

The term *inner speech*, or *endophasy*, has been applied to various phenomena, and authors argue about different things that they call by the same name. Originally, inner speech seems to have been understood as verbal memory. An example would be the silent recital of a poem known by heart. In that case, inner speech differs from vocal speech only as the idea or image of an object differs from the real object. It was in this sense that inner speech was understood by the French authors who tried to find out how words were reproduced in memory—whether as auditory, visual, motor, or synthetic images. We shall see that word memory is indeed one of the constituent elements of inner speech but not all of it.

In a second interpretation, inner speech is seen as truncated external speech—as "speech minus sound" (Mueller) or "subvocal speech" (Watson). Bekhterev defined it as a speech reflex inhibited in its motor part. Such an explanation is by no means sufficient. Silent "pronouncing" of words is not equivalent to the total process of inner speech.

The third definition is, on the contrary, too broad. To Goldstein (1927, 1932) the term covers everything that precedes the motor act of speaking, including

Source: Thought and Language (pp. 130–138) by L. S. Vygotsky (translated and edited by E. Hanfman and G. Vakar), 1962, Cambridge, MA: M.I.T. Press. Copyright 1962 by Massachusetts Institute of Technology. Reprinted by permission of publisher.

Wundt's "motives of speech" and the indefinable, non-sensory, and nonmotor specific speech experience—i.e., the whole interior aspect of any speech activity. It is hard to accept the equation of inner speech with an inarticulate inner experience in which the separate identifiable structural planes are dissolved without trace. This central experience is common to all linguistic activity, and for this reason alone Goldstein's interpretation does not fit that specific, unique function that alone deserves the name of inner speech. Logically developed, Goldstein's view must lead to the thesis that inner speech is not speech at all but rather an intellectual and affective-volitional activity, since it includes the motives of speech and the thought that is expressed in words.

To get a true picture of inner speech, one must start from the assumption that it is a specific formation, with its own laws and complex relations to the other forms of speech activity. Before we can study its relation to thought, on the one hand, and to speech, on the other, we must determine its special characteristics and function.

Inner speech is speech for oneself; external speech is for others. It would indeed be surprising if such a basic difference in function did not affect the structure of the two kinds of speech. Absence of vocalization per se is only a consequence of the specific nature of inner speech, which is neither an antecedent of external speech nor its reproduction in memory but is, in a sense, the opposite of external speech. The latter is the turning of thought into words, is materialization and objectification. With inner speech, the process is reversed: Speech turns into inward thought. Consequently, their structures must differ.

The area of inner speech is one of the most difficult to investigate. It remained almost inaccessible to experiments until ways were found to apply the genetic method of experimentation. Piaget (1926) was the first to pay attention to the child's egocentric speech and to see its theoretical significance, but he remained blind to the most important trait of egocentric speech—its genetic connection with inner speech—and this warped his interpretation of its function and structure. We made that relationship the central problem of our study and thus were able to investigate the nature of inner speech with unusual completeness. A number of considerations and observations led us to conclude that egocentric speech is a stage of development preceding inner speech: Both

fulfill intellectual functions, their structures are similar; egocentric speech disappears at school age, when inner speech begins to develop. From all this we infer that one changes into the other.

If this transformation does take place, then egocentric speech provides the key to the study of inner speech. One advantage of approaching inner speech through egocentric speech is its accessibility to experimentation and observation. It is still vocalized, audible speech, i.e., external in its mode of expression, but at the same time inner speech in function and structure. To study an internal process it is necessary to externalize it experimentally, by connecting it with some outer activity; only then is objective functional analysis possible. Egocentric speech is, in fact, a natural experiment of this type.

This method has another great advantage: Since egocentric speech can be studied at the time when some of its characteristics are waning and new ones forming, we are able to judge which traits are essential to inner speech and which are only temporary, and thus to determine the goal of this movement from egocentric to inner speech—i.e., the nature of inner speech.

Before we go on to the results obtained by this method, we shall briefly discuss the nature of egocentric speech, stressing the differences between our theory and Piaget's. Piaget contends that the child's egocentric speech is a direct expression of the egocentrism of his thought, which in turn is a compromise between the primary autism of his thinking and its gradual socialization. As the child grows older, autism recedes and socialization progresses, leading to the waning of egocentrism in his thinking and speech.

In Piaget's conception, the child in his egocentric speech does not adapt himself to the thinking of adults. His thought remains entirely egocentric; this makes his talk incomprehensible to others. Egocentric speech has no function in the child's realistic thinking or activity—it merely accompanies them. And since it is an expression of egocentric thought, it disappears together with the child's egocentrism. From its climax at the beginning of the child's development, egocentric speech drops to zero on the threshold of school age. Its history is one of involution rather than evolution. It has no future.

In our conception, egocentric speech is a phenomenon of the transition from interpsychic to intrapsychic functioning, i.e., from the social, collective activity of the child to his more individualized activity—a pattern of development common to all the higher psychological functions. Speech for oneself originates through differentiation from speech for others. Since the main course of the child's development is one of gradual individualization, this tendency is reflected in the function and structure of his speech.

Our experimental results indicate that the function of egocentric speech is similar to that of inner speech: It does not merely accompany the child's activity, it serves mental orientation, conscious understanding, it helps in overcoming difficulties; it is speech for oneself, intimately and usefully connected with the child's thinking. Its fate is very different from that described by Piaget. Egocentric speech develops along a rising, not a declining, curve; it goes through an evolution, not an involution. In the end, it becomes inner speech.

Our hypothesis has several advantages over Piaget's: It explains the function and development of egocentric speech and, in particular, its sudden increase when the child faces difficulties which demand consciousness and reflection—a fact uncovered by our experiments and which Piaget's theory cannot explain. But the greatest advantage of our theory is that it supplies a satisfying answer to a paradoxical situation described by Piaget himself. To Piaget, the quantitative drop in egocentric speech as the child grows older means the withering of that form of speech. If that were so, its structural peculiarities might also be expected to decline; it is hard to believe that the process would affect only its quantity, and not its inner structure. The child's thought becomes infinitely less egocentric between the ages of 3 and 7. If the characteristics of egocentric speech that make it incomprehensible to others are indeed rooted in egocentrism, they should become less apparent as that form of speech becomes less frequent; egocentric speech should approach social speech and become more and more intelligible. Yet what are the facts? Is the talk of a 3 year old harder to follow than that of a 7 year old? Our investigation established that the traits of egocentric speech which make for inscrutability are at their lowest point at 3 and at their peak at 7. They develop in a reverse direction to the frequency of egocentric speech. While the latter keeps falling and reaches zero at school age, the structural characteristics become more and more pronounced.

This throws a new light on the quantitative decrease in egocentric speech, which is the cornerstone of Piaget's thesis.

What does this decrease mean? The structural peculiarities of speech for oneself and its differentiation from external speech increase with age. What is it then that diminishes? Only one of its aspects: vocalization. Does this mean that egocentric speech as a whole is dying out? We believe that it does not, for how then could we explain the growth of the functional and structural traits of egocentric speech? On the other hand, their growth is perfectly compatible with the decrease of vocalization—indeed, clarifies its meaning. Its rapid dwindling and the equally rapid growth of the other characteristics are contradictory in appearance only.

To explain this, let us start from an undeniable, experimentally established fact. The structural and functional qualities of egocentric speech become more marked as the child develops. At 3, the difference between egocentric and social speech equals zero; at 7, we have speech that in structure and function is totally unlike social speech. A differentiation of the two speech functions has taken place. This is a fact—and facts are notoriously hard to refute.

Once we accept this, everything else falls into place. If the developing structural and functional peculiarities of egocentric speech progressively isolate it from external speech, then its vocal aspect must fade away; and this is exactly what happens between 3 and 7 years. With the progressive isolation of speech for oneself, its vocalization becomes unnecessary and meaningless and, because of its growing structural peculiarities, also impossible. Speech for oneself cannot find expression in external speech. The more independent and autonomous egocentric speech becomes, the poorer it grows in its external manifestations. In the end it separates itself entirely from speech for others, ceases to be vocalized, and thus appears to die out.

But this is only an illusion. To interpret the sinking coefficient of egocentric speech as a sign that this kind of speech is dying out is like saying that the child stops counting when he ceases to use his fingers and starts adding in his head. In reality behind the symptoms of dissolution lies a progressive development, the birth of a new speech form.

The decreasing vocalization of egocentric speech denotes a developing abstraction from sound, the child's new faculty to "think words" instead of pronouncing them. This is the positive meaning of the sinking coefficient of egocentric speech. The downward curve indicates development toward inner speech.

We can see that all the known facts about the functional, structural, and genetic characteristics of egocentric speech point to one thing: It develops in the direction of inner speech. Its developmental history can be understood only as a gradual unfolding of the traits of inner speech.

We believe that this corroborates our hypothesis about the origin and nature of egocentric speech. To turn our hypothesis into a certainty, we must devise an experiment capable of showing which of the two interpretations is correct. What are the data for this critical experiment?

Let us restate the theories between which we must decide. Piaget believes that egocentric speech stems from the insufficient socialization of speech and that its only development is decrease and eventual death. Its culmination lies in the past. Inner speech is something new brought in from the outside along with socialization. We believe that egocentric speech stems from the insufficient individualization of primary social speech. Its culmination lies in the future. It develops into inner speech.

To obtain evidence for one or the other view, we must place the child alternately in experimental situations encouraging social speech and in situations discouraging it, and see how these changes affect egocentric speech. We consider this an *experimentum crucis* for the following reasons.

If the child's egocentric talk results from the egocentrism of his thinking and its insufficient socialization, then any weakening of the social elements in the experimental setup, any factor contributing to the child's isolation from the group, must lead to a sudden increase in egocentric speech. But if the latter results from an insufficient differentiation of speech for oneself from speech for others, then the same changes must cause it to decrease.

We took as the starting point of our experiment three of Piaget's own observations. (1) Egocentric speech occurs only in the presence of other children engaged in the same activity, and not when the child is alone, i.e., it is a collective monologue. (2) The child is under the illusion that his egocentric talk, directed to nobody, is understood by those who surround him. (3) Egocentric speech has the character of external speech: It is not inaudible or whispered. These are certainly not chance peculiarities. From the child's own point of view, egocentric speech is not yet separated from social speech. It occurs under the subjective and objective conditions of social speech and may be considered a correlate of the insufficient isolation of the child's individual consciousness from the social whole.

In our first series of experiments (Vygotsky, Luria, Leontiev and Levina, unpublished; Vygotsky and Luria, 1930), we tried to destroy the illusion of being understood. After measuring the child's coefficient of egocentric speech in a situation similar to that of Piaget's experiments, we put him into a new situation: either with deaf-mute children or with children speaking a foreign language. In all other respects the setup remained the same. The coefficient of egocentric speech dropped to zero in the majority of cases, and in the rest to one-eighth of the previous figure, on the average. This proves that the illusion of being understood is not a mere epiphenomenon of egocentric speech but is functionally connected with it. Our results must seem paradoxical from the point of view of Piaget's theory: The weaker the child's contact is with the group—the less the social situation forces him to adjust his thoughts to others and to use social speech—the more freely should the egocentrism of his thinking and speech manifest itself. But from the point of view of our hypothesis, the meaning of these findings is clear: Egocentric speech, springing from the lack of differentiation of speech for oneself from speech for others, disappears when the feeling of being understood, essential for social speech, is absent.

In the second series of experiments, the variable factor was the possibility of collective monologue. Having measured the child's coefficient of egocentric speech in a situation permitting collective monologue, we put him into a situation excluding it—in a group of children who were strangers to him, or by himself at a separate table in a corner of the room; or he worked quite alone, even the experimenter leaving the room. The results of this series agreed with the first results. The exclusion of the group monologue caused a drop in the coefficient of egocentric speech, though not such a striking one as in the first case—seldom to zero and, on the average, to one-sixth of the original figure. The different methods of precluding collective monologue were not equally effective in reducing the coefficient of egocentric speech. The trend, however, was obvious in all the variations of the experiment. The exclusion of the collective factor, instead of giving full freedom to egocentric speech, depressed it. Our hypothesis was once more confirmed.

In the third series of experiments, the variable factor was the vocal quality of egocentric speech. Just outside the laboratory where the experiment was in progress, an orchestra played so loudly, or so much noise was made, that it drowned out not only the voices of others but the child's own; in a variant of the experiment, the child was expressly forbidden to talk loudly and allowed to talk only in whispers. Once again the coefficient of egocentric speech went down, the relation to the original figure being 5:1. Again the different methods were not equally effective, but the basic trend was invariably present.

The purpose of all three series of experiments was to eliminate those characteristics of egocentric speech that bring it close to social speech. We found that this always led to the dwindling of egocentric speech. It is logical, then, to assume that egocentric speech is a form developing out of social speech and not yet separated from it in its manifestation, although already distinct in function and structure.

The disagreement between us and Piaget on this point will be made quite clear by the following example: I am sitting at my desk talking to a person who is behind me and whom I cannot see; he leaves the room without my noticing it, and I continue to talk, under the illusion that he listens and understands. Outwardly, I am talking with myself and for myself, but psychologically my speech is social. From the point of view of Piaget's theory, the opposite happens in the case of the child: His egocentric talk is for and with himself; it only has the appearance of social speech, just as my

speech gave the false impression of being egocentric. From our point of view, the whole situation is much more complicated than that: Subjectively, the child's egocentric speech already has its own peculiar function—to that extent, it is independent from social speech; yet its independence is not complete because it is not felt as inner speech and is not distinguished by the child from speech for others. Objectively, also, it is different from social speech but again not entirely, because it functions only within social situations. Both subjectively and objectively, egocentric speech represents a transition from speech for others to speech for oneself. It already has the function of inner speech but remains similar to social speech in its expression.

The investigation of egocentric speech has paved the way to the understanding of inner speech.

REFERENCES

Bekhterev, V. *General Principles of Human Reflexology.* New York: International Publishers, 1932.

Goldstein, K. "Ueber Aphasie." Abh.aus.d.Schs. Arch.F. Neurol. U. Psychiat. Heft 6, 1927.

Goldstcin, K. "Die Pathologischen Tatsachen in ihrer Bedeutung fuer das Problem der Sprache." Kongr. D. Ges. Psychology, 12, 1932.

Piaget, J. *La Representation de Monde Chez L'Enfant.* Paris, F. Alcan, 1926.

Watson, J. *Psychology from the Standpoint of a Behaviorist,* Philadelphia and London, G. B. Lippincott, 1919.

The Language and Thought of the Child

JEAN PIAGET

• •

Editor's introduction

The Swiss psychologist Jean Piaget is considered one of the giants of twentieth century child development research and theory. His work in the area of child-language research emphasizes the egocentrism of children's speech, a factor that is disputed by other researchers, even as early as Vygotsky in the 1930s. Despite these many critiques, his influence in the field of language acquisition and the development of cognitive processes has been enormous.

We have chosen a brief excerpt from his controversial study focusing on egocentrism in child language and thought. It was originally published in French in 1923.

• • • • • • • • • • • •

CONCLUSIONS

Having defined, so far as was possible, the various categories of the language used by our two children, it now remains for us to see whether it is not possible to establish certain numerical constants from the material before us. We wish to emphasize at the very outset the artificial character of such abstractions. The number of unclassifiable remarks, indeed, weighs heavily in the statistics. In any case, a perusal of the list of Lev's first 50 remarks, which we shall give as an example for those who wish to make use of our method, should give a fair idea of the degree of objectivity belonging to our classification. But these difficulties are immaterial. If among our results some are definitely more constant than others, then we shall feel justified in attributing to these a certain objective value.

The Measure of Egocentrism

Among the data we have obtained there is one, incidentally of the greatest interest for the study of child logic, which seems to supply the necessary guarantee

of objectivity: we mean the proportion of egocentric language to the sum of the child's spontaneous conversation. Egocentric language is, as we have seen, the group made up by the first three of the categories we have enumerated—*repetition, monologue,* and *collective monologue.* All three have this in common: that they consist of remarks that are not addressed to anyone, or not to anyone in particular, and that they evoke no reaction adapted to them on the part of anyone to whom they may chance to be addressed. Spontaneous language is therefore made up of the first seven categories, *i.e.,* of all except *answers.* It is therefore the sum total of all remarks, *minus* those which are made as an answer to a question asked by an adult or a child. We have eliminated this heading as being subject to chance circumstances; it is sufficient for a child to have come in contact with many adults or

Source: The Language and Thought of the Child (3rd ed., pp. 34–40) by J. Piaget, 1959, London: Routledge & Kegan Paul Ltd. Copyright 1959 by Routledge & Kegan. Reprinted by permission of publisher.

with some talkative companion, to undergo a marked change in the percentage of his answers. Answers given, not to definite questions (with interrogation mark) or commands, but in the course of the dialogue, *i.e.*, propositions answering to other propositions, have naturally been classed under the heading *information and dialogue*, so that there is nothing artificial about the omission of questions from the statistics which we shall give. The child's language *minus* his answers constitutes a complete whole in which intelligence is represented at every stage of its development.

The proportion of egocentric to other spontaneous forms of language is represented by the following fractions:

$$\frac{Eg.\,L}{Sp.L} = 0.47 \text{ for Lev,} \quad \frac{Eg.L}{Sp.L} = 0.43 \text{ for Pie.}$$

(The proportion of egocentric language to the sum total of the subject's speech, including answers, is 39 percent for Lev and 37 percent for Pie.) The similarity of result for Lev and Pie is a propitious sign, especially as what difference there is corresponds to a marked difference of temperament. (Lev is certainly more egocentric than Pie.) But the value of the result is vouched for in yet another way.

If we divide the 1400 remarks made by Lev during the month in which his talk was being studied into sections of 100 sentences, and seek to establish for each section the ratio

$$\frac{Eg.L.}{Sp.L.}$$

the fraction will be found to vary only from 0.40 to 0.57, which indicates only a small maximum deviation. On the contrary, the *mean variation*, *i.e.*, the average of the deviations between each value and the arithmetical average of these values, is only 0.04, which is really very little.

If Pie's 1500 remarks are submitted to the same treatment, the proportions will be found to vary between 0.31 and 0.59, with an average variation of 0.06. This greater variability is just what we should expect from what we know of Pie's character, which at first sight seems more practical, better adapted than

Lev's, more inclined to collaboration (particularly with his bosom friend Ez). But Pie every now and then indulges in fantasies which isolate him for several hours, and during which he soliloquizes without ceasing.

. . . Moreover . . . these two coefficients do actually represent the average for children between the ages of 7 and 8. The same calculation based on some 1500 remarks in quite another classroom yielded the result of 0.45 (a. v. = 0.05).

This constancy in the proportion of egocentric language is the more remarkable in view of the fact that we have found nothing of the kind in connection with the other coefficients which we have sought to establish. We have, it is true, determined the proportion of socialized factual language (*information* and *questions*) to socialized nonfactual language (*criticism, commands,* and *requests*). But this proportion fluctuates from 0.72 to 2.23 with a mean variation 0.71 for Lev (as compared with 0.04 and 0.06 as the coefficients of egocentrism), and between 0.43 and 2.33 with a mean variation of 0.42 for Pie. Similarly, the relation of egocentric to socialized factual language yields no coefficient of any constancy.

Of all this calculation let us bear only this in mind, that our two subjects of 6½ have each an egocentric language which amounts to nearly half of their total spontaneous speech.

The following table summarizes the functions of the language used by both these children:

	Pie	Lev
1. Repetition	2	1
2. Monologue	5	15
3. Collective Monologue	30	23
4. Adapted Information	14	13
5. Criticism	7	3
6. Commands	15	10
7. Requests	13	17
8. Answers	14	18
Egocentric Language	37	39
Spontaneous Socialized Language	49	43
Sum of Socialized Language	63	61
Coefficient of Egocentrism	0.43	0.47
	∓0.06	∓0.04

We must once more emphasize the fact that in all these calculations the number of remarks made by children to adults is negligible. By omitting them we raise the coefficient of egocentrism to about 0.02, which is within the allowed limits of deviation. In the future, however, we shall have completely to eliminate such remarks from our calculations, even if it means making a separate class for them. We shall, moreover, observe this rule in the next chapter where the coefficient of egocentrism has been calculated solely on the basis of remarks made between children.

Conclusion

What are the conclusions we can draw from these facts? It would seem that up to a certain age we may safely admit that children think and act more egocentrically than adults, that they share each other's intellectual life less than we do. True, when they are together they seem to talk to each other a great deal more than we do about what they are doing, but for the most part they are only talking to themselves. We, on the contrary, keep silent far longer about our action, but our talk is almost always socialized.

Such assertions may seem paradoxical. In observing children between the ages of 4 and 7 at work together in the classes of the *Maison des Petits*, one is certainly struck by silences, which are, we repeat, in no way imposed nor even suggested by the adults. One would expect, not indeed the formation of working groups, since children are slow to awake to social life, but a hubbub caused by all the children talking at once. This is not what happens. All the same, it is obvious that a child between the ages of 4 and 7, placed in the conditions of spontaneous work provided by the educational games of the *Maison des Petits*, breaks silence far oftener than does the adult at work, and seems at first sight to be continuously communicating his thoughts to those around him.

Egocentrism must not be confused with secrecy. Reflection in the child does not admit of privacy. Apart from thinking by images or autistic symbols which cannot be directly communicated, the child up to an age, as yet undetermined but probably somewhere about seven, is incapable of keeping to himself the thoughts which enter his mind. He says everything. He has no verbal continence. Does this mean that he socializes his thought more than we do? That is the whole question, and it is for us to see to whom the child really speaks. It may be to others. We think on the contrary that, as the preceding study shows, it is

first and foremost to himself, and that speech, before it can be used to socialize thought, serves to accompany and reinforce individual activity. Let us try to examine more closely the difference between thought which is socialized but capable of secrecy, and infantile thought which is egocentric but incapable of secrecy.

The adult, even in his most personal and private occupation, even when he is engaged in any inquiry which is incomprehensible to his fellow beings, thinks socially, has continually in his mind's eye his collaborators or opponents, actual or eventual, at any rate members of his own profession to whom sooner or later he will announce the result of his labors. This mental picture pursues him throughout his task. The task itself is henceforth socialized at almost every stage of its development. Invention eludes this process, but the need for checking and demonstrating calls into being an inner speech addressed throughout to a hypothetical opponent, whom the imagination often pictures as one of flesh and blood. When, therefore, the adult is brought face to face with his fellow beings, what he announces to them is something already socially elaborated and therefore roughly adapted to his audience, *i.e.*, it is comprehensible. Indeed, the further a man has advanced in his own line of thought, the better able is he to see things from the point of view of others and to make himself understood by them.

The child, on the other hand, placed in the conditions which we have described, seems to talk far more than the adult. Almost everything he does is to the tune of remarks such as "I'm drawing a hat," "I'm doing it better than you," etc. Child thought, therefore, seems more social, less capable of sustained and solitary research. This is so only in appearance. The child has less verbal continence simply because he does not know what it is to keep a thing to himself. Although he talks almost incessantly to his neighbors, he rarely places himself at their point of view. He speaks to them for the most part as if he were alone, and as if he were thinking aloud. He speaks, therefore, in a language which disregards the precise shade of meaning in things and ignores the particular angle from which they are viewed, and which above all is always making assertions, even in argument, instead of justifying them. Nothing could be harder to understand than the notebooks which we have filled with the conversation of Pie and Lev. Without full commentaries, taken down at the same time as the children's remarks, they would be incomprehensible. Everything is indicated by allusion, by pronouns and demonstrative articles—"he, she, the, mine, him, etc."—which can mean anything in turn, regardless of the demands of clarity or even of intelligibility. In a word, the child hardly ever even asks himself whether he has been understood. For him, that goes without saying, for he does not think about others when he talks. He utters a "collective monologue." His language only begins to resemble that of adults when he is directly interested in making himself understood; when he gives orders or asks questions. To put it quite simply, we may say that the adult thinks socially, even when he is alone, and that the child under 7 thinks egocentrically, even in the society of others.

Language and the Mind

NOAM CHOMSKY

Editor's introduction

This article by Noam Chomsky represents some of the most accessible explanations of his complex theories, theories that have revolutionized the study of language development over the past 40 years. Chomsky disputed Piaget's base of empirical/biological evidence, instead working from highly technical structural models of language development. This essay highlights many of Chomsky's key contributions to the field, including his refutation of B. F. Skinner's behaviorist theories, the concept of "surface" and "deep" structures in language, and the definition of transformational grammar.

How does the mind work? To answer this question we must look at some of the work performed by the mind. One of its main functions is the acquisition of knowledge. The two major factors in acquisition of knowledge, perception and learning, have been the subject of study and speculation for centuries. It would not, I think, be misleading to characterize the major positions that have developed as outgrowths of classical rationalism and empiricism. The rationalist theories are marked by the importance they assign to *intrinsic* structures in mental operations—to central processes and organizing principles in perception, and to innate ideas and principles in learning. The empiricist approach, in contrast, has stressed the role of experience and control by environmental factors.

The classical empiricist view is that sensory images are transmitted to the brain as impressions. They remain as ideas that will be associated in various ways, depending on the fortuitous character of experience. In this view a language is merely a collection of words, phrases, and sentences, a habit system, acquired acci-

dentally and extrinsically. In the formulation of Williard Quine, knowledge of a language (and, in fact, knowledge in general) can be represented as "a fabric of sentences variously associated to one another and to nonverbal stimuli by the mechanism of conditioned response." Acquisition of knowledge is only a matter of the gradual construction of this fabric. When sensory experience is interpreted, the already established network may be activated in some fashion. In its essentials, this view has been predominant in modern behavioral science, and it has been accepted with little question by many philosophers as well.

The classical rationalist view is quite different. In this view the mind contains a system of "common notions" that enable it to interpret the scattered and incoherent data of sense in terms of objects and their

Source: "Language and the Mind" by N. Chomsky, 1968, *Psychology Today, I*(9), pp. 48–51, 66–68. Copyright 1968 by *Psychology Today.* Reprinted by permission of publisher.

relations, cause and effect, whole and part, symmetry, gestalt properties, functions, and so on. Sensation, providing only fleeting and meaningless images, is degenerate and particular. Knowledge, much of it beyond immediate awareness, is rich in structure, involves universals, and is highly organized. The innate general principles that underlie and organize this knowledge, according to Leibniz, "enter into our thoughts, of which they form the soul and the connection . . . although we do not at all think of them."

This "active" rationalist view of the acquisition of knowledge persisted through the romantic period in its essentials. With respect to language, it achieves its most illuminating expression in the profound investigations of Wilhelm von Humboldt. His theory of speech perception supposes a generative system of rules that underlies speech production as well as its interpretation. The system is generative in that it makes infinite use of finite means. He regards a language as a structure of forms and concepts based on a system of rules that determine their interrelations, arrangement, and organization. But these finite materials can be combined to make a never-ending product.

In the rationalist and romantic tradition of linguistic theory, the normal use of language is regarded as characteristically innovative. We construct sentences that are entirely new to us. There is no substantive notion of "analogy" or "generalization" that accounts for this creative aspect of language use. It is equally erroneous to describe language as a "habit structure" or as a network of associated responses. The innovative element in normal use of language quickly exceeds the bounds of such marginal principles as analogy or generalization (under any substantive interpretation of these notions). It is important to emphasize this fact because the insight has been lost under the impact of the behaviorist assumptions that have dominated speculation and research in the twentieth century.

In Humboldt's view, acquisition of language is largely a matter of maturation of an innate language capacity. The maturation is guided by internal factors, by an innate "form of language" that is sharpened, differentiated, and given its specific realization through experience. Language is thus a kind of latent structure in the human mind, developed and fixed by exposure to specific linguistic experience. Humboldt believes that all languages will be found to be very similar in their grammatical form, similar not on the surface but in their deeper inner structures. The innate organizing principles severely limit the class of possible languages, and these principles determine the properties of the language that is learned in the normal way.

The active and passive views of perception and learning have been elaborated with varying degrees of clarity since the seventeenth century. These views can be confronted with empirical evidence in a variety of ways. Some recent work in psychology and neurophysiology is highly suggestive in this regard. There is evidence for the existence of central processes in perception, specifically for control over the functioning of sensory neurons by the brain-stem reticular system. Behavioral counterparts of this central control have been under investigation for several years. Furthermore, there is evidence for innate organization of the perceptual system of a highly specific sort at every level of biological organization. Studies of the visual system of the frog, the discovery of specialized cells responding to angle and motion in the lower cortical centers of cats and rabbits, and the somewhat comparable investigations of the auditory system of frogs—all are relevant to the classical questions of intrinsic structure mentioned earlier. These studies suggest that there are highly organized, innately determined perceptual systems that are adapted closely to the animal's "life space" and that provide the basis for what we might call "acquisition of knowledge." Also relevant are certain behavioral studies of human infants, for example, those showing the preference for faces over other complex stimuli.

These and other studies make it reasonable to inquire into the possibility that complex intellectual structures are determined narrowly by innate mental organization. What is perceived may be determined by mental processes of considerable depth. As far as language learning is concerned, it seems to me that a rather convincing argument can be made for the view that certain principles intrinsic to the mind provide invariant structures that are a precondition for linguistic experience. In the course of this article I would like to sketch some of the ways such conclusions might be clarified and firmly established.

There are several ways linguistic evidence can be used to reveal properties of human perception and learning. In this section we consider one research strategy that might take us nearer to this goal.

Let us say that in interpreting a certain physical stimulus a person constructs a "percept." This percept represents some of his conclusions (in general, unconscious) about the stimulus. To the extent that we can characterize such percepts, we can go on to investigate the mechanisms that relate stimulus and percept. Imagine a model of perception that takes stimuli as inputs and arrives at percepts as "outputs." The model might contain a system of beliefs, strategies for interpreting stimuli, and other factors, such as the organization of memory. We would then have a perceptual model that might be represented graphically, as in Figure 1.

Consider next the system of beliefs that is a component of the perceptual model. How was this acquired? To study this problem, we must investigate a second model, which takes certain data as input and gives as "output" (again, internally represented) the system of beliefs operating in the perceptual model. This second model, a model of learning, would have its own intrinsic structure, as did the first. This structure might consist of conditions on the nature of the system of beliefs that can be acquired, of innate inductive strategies, and again, of other factors such as the organization of memory (see Figure 2).

Under further conditions, which are interesting but not relevant here, we can take these perceptual and learning models as theories of the acquisition of knowledge, rather than of belief. How then would the models apply to language? The input stimulus to the perceptual model is a speech signal, and the percept is a representation of the utterance that the hearer takes the signal to be and of the interpretation he assigns to it. We can think of the percept as the structural description of a linguistic expression which contains certain phonetic, semantic, and syntactic information.

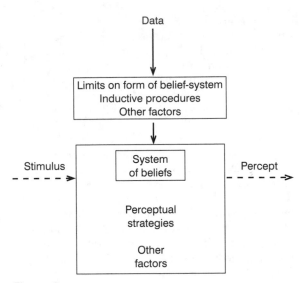

Figure 2
One's system of beliefs, a part of the perception model, is acquired from data as shown above.

Most interesting is the syntactic information, which best can be discussed by examining a few typical cases.

The following three sentences seem to be the same syntactic structure.

1. I told John to leave
2. I expected John to leave
3. I persuaded John to leave

Each contains the subject *I*, and the predicate of each consists of a verb (*told, expected, persuaded*), a noun phrase (*John*), and an embedded predicate phrase (*to leave*). This similarity is only superficial, however—a similarity in what we may call the "surface structure" of the sentences, which differ in important ways when we consider them with somewhat greater care.

The differences can be seen when the sentences are paraphrased or subjected to certain grammatical operations, such as the conversion from active to passive forms. For example, in normal conversation the sentence "I told John to leave" can be roughly paraphrased as:

1a. What I told John was to leave

But the other two sentences cannot be paraphrased as:

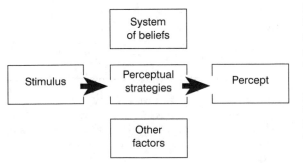

Figure 1
Each physical stimulus, after interpretation by the mental processes, will result in a percept.

2a. *What I expected John was to leave

3a. *What I persuaded John was to leave

Sentence (2) can be paraphrased as:

2b. It was expected by me that John would leave

But the other two sentences cannot undergo a corresponding formal operation, yielding:

1b. *It was told by me that John would leave

or

3b. *It was persuaded by me that John would leave

Sentences (2) and (3) differ more subtly. In (3) *John* is the direct object of *persuade*, but in (2) *John* is not the direct object to *expect*. We can show this by using these verbs in slightly more complex sentences:

4. I expected the doctor to examine John

5. I persuaded the doctor to examine John

If we replace the embedded proposition *the doctor to examine John* with its passive form *John to be examined by the doctor*, the change to the passive does not, in itself, change the meaning. We can accept as paraphrases "I expected the doctor to examine John" and

4. I expected John to be examined by the doctor

But we cannot accept as paraphrases "I persuaded the doctor to examine John" and

5a. I persuaded John to be examined by the doctor

The parts of these sentences differ in their grammatical functions. In "I persuaded John to leave" *John* is both the object of *persuade* and the subject of *leave*. These facts must be represented in the percept since they are known, intuitively, to the hearer of the speech signal. No special training or instruction is necessary to enable the native speaker to understand these examples, to know which are "wrong" and which "right," although they may all be quite new to him. They are interpreted by the native speaker instantaneously and

uniformly, in accordance with structural principles that are known tacitly, intuitively, and unconsciously.

These examples illustrate two significant points. First, the surface structure of a sentence, its organization into various phrases, may not reveal or immediately reflect its deep syntactic structure. The deep structure is not represented directly in the form of the speech signal; it is abstract. Second, the rules that determine deep and surface structure and their interrelation in particular cases must themselves be highly abstract. They are surely remote from consciousness, and in all likelihood they cannot be brought to consciousness.

A study of such examples, examples characteristic of all human languages that have been carefully studied, constitutes the first stage of the linguistic investigation outlined above, namely the study of the percept. The percept contains phonetic and semantic information related through the medium of syntactic structure. There are two aspects of this syntactic structure. It consists of a surface directly related to the phonetic form, and a deep structure that underlies the semantic interpretation. The deep structure is represented in the mind and rarely is indicated directly in the physical signal.

A language, then, involves a set of semantic-phonetic percepts, of sound-meaning correlations, the correlations being determined by the kind of intervening syntactic structure just illustrated. The English language correlates sound and meaning in one way, Japanese in another, and so on. But the general properties of percepts, their forms and mechanisms, are remarkably similar for all languages that have been carefully studied.

Returning to our models of perception and learning, we can now take up the problem of formulating the system of beliefs that is a central component in perceptual processes. In the case of language, the "system of beliefs" would now be called the "generative grammar," the system of rules that specifies the sound-meaning correlation and generates the class of structural descriptions (percepts) that constitute the language in question. The generative grammar, then, represents the speaker-hearer's knowledge of his language. We can use the term *grammar of a language* ambiguously, as referring not only to the speaker's internalized, subconscious knowledge but to the professional linguist's representation of this internalized and intuitive system of rules as well.

How is this generative grammar acquired? Or, using our learning model, what is the internal structure of the device that could develop a generative grammar?

We can think of every normal human's internalized grammar as, in effect, a theory of his language. This theory provides a sound-meaning correlation for an infinite number of sentences. It provides an infinite set of structural descriptions; each contains a surface structure that determines phonetic form and a deep structure that determines semantic content.

In formal terms, then, we can describe the child's acquisition of language as a kind of theory construction. The child discovers the theory of his language with only small amounts of data from that language. Not only does his "theory of the language" have an enormous predictive scope, but it also enables the child to reject a great deal of the very data on which the theory has been constructed. Normal speech consists, in large part, of fragments, false starts, blends, and other distortions of the underlying idealized forms. Nevertheless, as is evident from a study of the mature use of language, what the child learns is the underlying ideal theory. This is a remarkable fact. We must also bear in mind that the child constructs this ideal theory without explicit instruction, that he acquires this knowledge at a time when he is not capable of complex intellectual achievements in many other domains, and that this achievement is relatively independent of intelligence or the particular course of experience. These are facts that a theory of learning must face.

A scientist who approaches phenomena of this sort without prejudice or dogma would conclude that the acquired knowledge must be determined in a rather specific way by intrinsic properties of mental organization. He would then set himself the task of discovering the innate ideas and principles that make such acquisition of knowledge possible.

It is unimaginable that a highly specific, abstract, and tightly organized language comes by accident into the mind of every four-year-old child. If there were not an innate restriction on the form of grammar, then the child could employ innumerable theories to account for his linguistic experience, and no one system, or even small class of systems, would be found exclusively acceptable or even preferable. The child could not possibly acquire knowledge of a language. This restriction on the form of grammar is a precondition for linguistic experience, and it is surely the critical factor in determining the course and result of language learning. The child cannot know at birth which language he is going to learn. But he must "know" that its grammar must be of a predetermined form that excludes many imaginable languages.

The child's task is to select the appropriate hypothesis from this restricted class. Having selected it, he can confirm his choice with the evidence further available to him. But neither the evidence nor any process of induction (in any well-defined sense) could in themselves have led to this choice. Once the hypothesis is sufficiently well-confirmed, the child knows the language defined by this hypothesis; consequently, his knowledge extends vastly beyond his linguistic experience, and he can reject much of this experience as imperfect, as resulting from the interaction of many factors, only one of which is the ideal grammar that determines a sound-meaning connection for an infinite class of linguistic expressions. Along such lines as these one might outline a theory to explain the acquisition of language.

As has been pointed out, both the form and meaning of a sentence are determined by syntactic structures that are not represented directly in the signal and that are related to the signal only at a distance, through a long sequence of interpretive rules. This property of abstractness in grammatical structure is of primary importance, and it is on this property that our inferences about mental processes are based. Let us examine this abstractness a little more closely.

Not many years ago, the process of sentence interpretation might have been described approximately along the following lines. A speech signal is received and segmented into successive units (overlapping at the borders). These units are analyzed in terms of their invariant phonetic properties and assigned to "phonemes." The sequence of phonemes, so constructed, is then segmented into minimal grammatically functioning units (morphemes and words). These are again categorized. Successive operations of segmentation and classification will lead to what I have called "surface structure"—an analysis of a sentence into phrases, which can be represented as a proper bracketing of the sentence, with the bracketed units assigned to various categories, as in Figure 3. Each segment—phonetic, syntactic, or semantic—would be identified in terms of certain invariant properties. This would be an exhaustive analysis of the structure of a sentence.

With such a conception of language structure, it made good sense to look forward hopefully to certain engineering applications of linguistics—for example, to voice-operated typewriters capable of segmenting an expression into its successive phonetic units and identifying

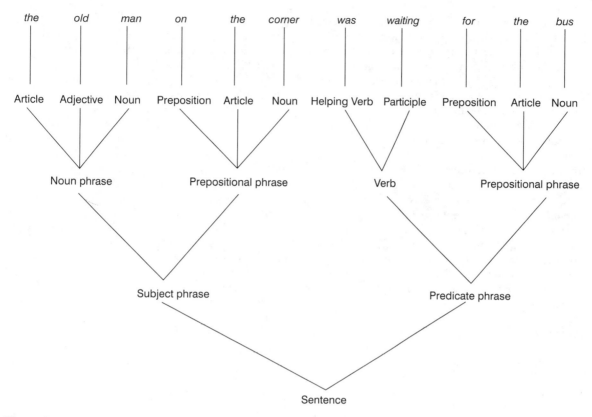

Figure 3
A type of sentence analysis now abandoned as inadequate at every level is this labeled bracketing which analyzes the sentence by successive division into larger units with each unit assigned to its own category.

these, so that speech could be converted to some form of phonetic writing in a mechanical way; to mechanical analysis of sentence structure by fairly straightforward and well-understood computational techniques; and perhaps even beyond to such projects as machine translation. But these hopes have by now been largely abandoned with the realization that this conception of grammatical structure is inadequate at every level, semantic, phonetic, and syntactic. Most important, at the level of syntactic organization, the surface structure indicates semantically significant relations only in extremely simple cases. In general, the deeper aspects of syntactic organization are representable by labeled bracketing, but of a very different sort from that seen in surface structure.

There is evidence of various sorts, both from phonetics and from experimental psychology, that labeled bracketing is an adequate representation of surface structure. It would go beyond the bounds of this paper to survey the phonetic evidence.

Deep structures are related to surface structures by a sequence of certain formal operations, operations now generally called "grammatical transformations." At the levels of sound, meaning, and syntax, the significant structural features of sentences are highly abstract. For this reason they cannot be recovered by elementary data-processing techniques. This fact lies behind the search for central processes in speech perception and the search for intrinsic, innate structure as the basis for language learning.

How can we represent deep structure? To answer this question we must consider the grammatical transformations that link surface structure to the underlying deep structure that is not always apparent.

Consider, for example, the operations of passivization and interrogation. In the sentences (1) John was examined by the doctor, and (2) did the doctor examine John, both have a deep structure similar to paraphrase of Sentence 1, (3) the doctor examined John. The same network of grammatical relations determines the semantic interpretation in each case. Thus two of the grammatical transformations of English must be the operations of passivization and interrogation that form such surface structures as Sentences (1) and (2) from a deeper structure which in its essentials also underlies Sentence (3). Since the transformations ultimately produce surface structures, they must produce labeled bracketings (see Figure 3). But notice that these operations can apply in sequence: we can form the passive question "was John examined by the doctor" by passivization followed by interrogation. Since the result of passivization is a labeled bracketing, it follows that the interrogative transformation operates on a labeled bracketing and forms a new labeled bracketing. Thus a transformation such as interrogation maps a labeled bracketing into a labeled bracketing.

By similar argument, we can show that all grammatical transformations are structure-dependent mappings of this sort and that the deep structures which underlie all sentences must themselves be labeled bracketings. Of course, the labeled bracketing that constitutes deep structure will in general be quite different from that representing the surface structure of a sentence. Our argument is somewhat oversimplified, but it is roughly correct. When made precise and fully accurate it strongly supports the view that deep structures, like surface structures, are formally to be taken as labeled bracketings, and that grammatical transformations are mappings of such structures onto other similar structures.

In speaking of mental processes we have returned to our original problem. We can now see why it is reasonable to maintain that the linguistic evidence supports an "active" theory of acquisition of knowledge. The study of sentences and of speech perception, it seems to me, leads to a perceptual theory of a classical rationalist sort. Representative of this school, among others, were the seventeenth-century Cambridge Platonists, who developed the idea that our perception is guided by notions that originate from the mind and that provide the framework for the interpretation of sensory stimuli. It is not sufficient to suggest that this framework is a store of "neural models" or "schemata" which are in some man-

ner applied to perception (as is postulated in some current theories of perception). We must go well beyond this assumption and return to the view of Wilhelm von Humboldt, who attributed to the mind a system of rules that generates such models and schemata under the stimulation of the senses. The system of rules itself determines the content of the percept that is formed.

We can offer more than this vague and metaphoric account. A generative grammar and an associated theory of speech perception provide a concrete example of the rules that operate and of the mental objects that they construct and manipulate. Physiology cannot yet explain the physical mechanisms that affect these abstract functions. But neither physiology nor psychology provides evidence that calls this account into question or that suggests an alternative. As mentioned earlier, the most exciting current work in the physiology of perception shows that even the peripheral systems analyze stimuli into the complex properties of objects, and that central processes may significantly affect the information transmitted by the receptor organs.

The study of language, it seems to me, offers strong empirical evidence that empiricist theories of learning are quite inadequate. Serious efforts have been made in recent years to develop principles of induction, generalization, and data analysis that would account for knowledge of a language. These efforts have been a total failure. The methods and principles fail not for any superficial reason such as lack of time or data. They fail because they are intrinsically incapable of giving rise to the system of rules that underlies the normal use of language. What evidence is now available supports the view that all human languages share deep-seated properties of organization and structure. These properties—these linguistic universals—can be plausibly assumed to be an innate mental endowment rather than the result of learning. If this is true, then the study of language sheds light on certain long-standing issues in the theory of knowledge. Once again I see little reason to doubt that what is true of language is true of other forms of human knowledge as well.

There is one further question that might be raised at this point. How does the human mind come to have the innate properties that underlie acquisition of knowledge? Here linguistic evidence obviously provides no information at all. The process by which the human mind has achieved its present state of complexity and its particular form of innate organization are a complete mystery, as much of a mystery as the analogous questions that can be asked about the processes leading to the physical and mental organization of any other complex organism. It is perfectly safe to attribute this to evolution, so long as we bear in mind that there is no substance to this assertion—it amounts to nothing more than the belief that there is surely some naturalistic explanation for these phenomena.

There are, however, important aspects of the problem of language and mind that can be studied sensibly within the limitations of present understanding and technique. I think that, for the moment, the most productive investigations are those dealing with the nature of particular grammars and with the universal conditions met by all human languages. I have tried to suggest how one can move, in successive steps of increasing abstractness, from the study of percepts to the study of grammar and perceptual mechanisms, and from the study of grammar to the study of universal grammar and the mechanisms of learning.

In this area of convergence of linguistics, psychology, and philosophy, we can look forward to much exciting work in coming years.

Encounter at Royaumont: The Debate Between Jean Piaget and Noam Chomsky

HOWARD GARDNER

Editor's introduction

Noam Chomsky's "nativist" position of language acquisition challenged Piaget's views that human linguistic capacities are part of intellectual development that is "constructed." In his writing and speaking, Chomsky began to comment quite critically on Piaget's works. At Piaget's urging, Jacques Monod, the president of the Center for the Study of Man, arranged a symposium entitled "On Language and Learning." In the following essay, Howard Gardner summarizes the arguments that were presented at the historic Piaget-Chomsky debate, highlighting the similarities and the key differences in these two influential leaders' work.

In October 1975 a confrontation of considerable importance to the temper of future intellectual discourse took place at a chateau in the Parisian suburb of Royaumont. The principal participants in this debate were Jean Piaget, the renowned Swiss psychologist and epistemologist, and Noam Chomsky, the noted American linguist and political activist. Their subject was no less than the nature of the human mind itself.

For a number of years, Piaget had hoped that such a meeting could be arranged. Sensitive to currents in contemporary social science, he had known about the threat to his position represented by the work of Chomsky and his collaborators. Chomsky had also been reading Piaget's works and had commented upon them critically. While less eager than Piaget for a personal encounter, he accepted the invitation proffered by the late Nobel laureate Jacques Monod, president of the Center for the Study of Man, to join together in a symposium dubbed (and later published as) "On Language and Learning."

The encounter at the Abbaye de Royaumont was historically important for several reasons. To begin

with, Chomsky and Piaget were recognized leaders of two of the most influential (possibly the most influential) schools of contemporary cognitive studies. Taken seriously by all scientists in their respective fields of linguistics and developmental psychology, they had achieved international reputations that far transcended their areas of specialization. Accompanied by colleagues who were associated in varying degrees with their own programs of research, Piaget and Chomsky presented their ideas to an illustrious gathering of scholars: Nobel laureates in biology, leading figures in philosophy and mathematics, and several of the most prominent behavioral scientists in the world today. Those in attendance listened critically to the arguments and joined vigorously in the ensuing discussion, seldom hesitating to make pronouncements and take

Source: Chapter 2, pages 16–26 from *Art, Mind, and Brain: A Cognitive Approach to Creativity* by Howard Gardner. Copyright (c) by Howard Gardner. Reprinted by permission of BasicBooks, a division of HarperCollins Publishers, Inc.

sides. It was almost as if two of the great figures of the seventeenth century—Descartes and Locke, say—could have defied time and space to engage in discussion at a joint meeting of the Royal Society and the Académie Française.

The Royaumont meeting may well have had additional significance. Possibly for the first time figures at the forefront of such relatively "tender-minded" disciplines as psychology and linguistics succeeded in involving a broad and distinguished collection of "tough-minded" scholars in debates formulated by the behavioral scientists themselves—with scarcely a hint of condescension by the representatives of such firmly entrenched disciplines as biology and mathematics. Equally noteworthy, the protagonists represented the cognitive sciences—a field hardly known (and not even christened) two decades ago, and one far less familiar to both the general public and the scholarly community than many other pockets of the behavioral sciences.

The stakes in the exchange were also considerable, for the outcome of the Royaumont meeting might very well influence the future awarding of research funds; the interests of the brightest young scholars; and, indeed, the course of subsequent investigations of human cognition—arguably the most important line of inquiry in the social sciences today. Would the next generation of scholars be more attracted to pursuing the method of Piaget, observing children as they slowly construct knowledge of the physical world, or, inspired by Chomsky, would they find more challenge in formulating abstract characterizations of the presumably innate knowledge that a child has in such rule-governed domains as language, music, or mathematics? The Royaumont meeting brought together two men who not only represent different approaches but who were also dissimilar in background and style. On the one hand there was Noam Chomsky, the intense, urban intellectual, forty-six years old, employed for many years in the highly technical study of linguistics, and long engaged in political commentary and disputation about United States foreign policy. Chomsky had, with his devastating critiques, almost singlehandedly discredited two dominant schools of social science—behavioral psychology and traditional structural linguistics. And on the other hand there was Jean Piaget, thirty-two years Chomsky's senior, a European savant in the grand tradition, involved for half a century in widely known studies of the growth of children's thought. While equally proud, Piaget, a relatively non-

political citizen of that most neutral of all countries, had always avoided drawing hard battle lines between himself and other investigators. Indeed, to use one of his own terms, he had filled the role of "perpetual assimilator," eager to make contact with those of apparently opposing points of view and to assimilate their ideas to his own or, if necessary, accommodate his to theirs.

If the two men's styles and backgrounds were different, their ideas seemed, at least from a distance, remarkably akin. Both had vigorously opposed those who believed in a science built up of elements, those who mistrusted theoretical constructs, and those who felt that overt behavior was all that should be studied. Both were firmly in the rationalist tradition, worthy successors to René Descartes and Immanuel Kant. Believers in the organized human mind as an appropriate subject for study, Chomsky and Piaget were eager to discover universal principles of thought, convinced of the severe constraints built into human cognition, and relatively uninterested in social and cultural influences and in differences among individuals. Both believed in the importance of a biological perspective, but both were equally attracted to the formulation of logical models of the human mind.

Indeed, their deepest similarity lay in a belief (shared with Freud) that the important aspects of the mind lie beneath the surface. One could never solve the mysteries of thought by simply describing overt words or behaviors. One must, instead, search for the underlying structures of the mind: in Chomsky's view, the laws of universal grammar; in Piaget's, the mental operations of which the human intellect is capable.

Why, then, given this common enterprise (at least Piaget saw it that way), was there need for a debate? And why was there such a heated dispute at Royaumont about the proper future course for the sciences of the intellect? The answer is that there were important differences in the basic assumptions and methods by which the two men arrived at their respective models of human thought.

It is instructive that neither Piaget nor Chomsky was a psychologist by training, nor would either have answered readily to the label of cognitive scientist. Originally trained as a biologist, Piaget long stressed the continuity of the evolution of the species and the development of human intellect. As an adolescent he was intrigued by alterations in the shape of mollusks placed into lakes of differing climates and turbulences;

he observed the same adaptiveness at work in the young infant gradually exploring the physical objects of the world. Moreover, Piaget realized that adaptation is never a simple reaction to the environment; rather, it is an active constructive process, in which problem-solving proceeds at first through the exercise of one's sensory systems and motor capacities, but eventually evolves to the height of cognition through logical operations "in the head."

All individuals pass through the same stages of intellectual development, Piaget proposed, not because we are "programmed" to do so but rather because, given the interaction of our inborn predispositions with the structure of the world in which we live, we are inevitably going to form certain hypotheses about the world, try them out, and then modify them in light of the feedback we receive. The image of thought that motivated Piaget was that of an active, exploring child systematically seeking solutions to a puzzle until he ultimately hits upon the right one, and then moves on to a yet more challenging puzzle. The "nativist" notion that all intellect is present at birth, waiting only to unfold, was anathema to Piaget, as was the rival empiricist view that all knowledge already exists in the world, just waiting to be etched into the blank infant mind.

And that was where the issue was joined with Noam Chomsky. A linguist from his earliest student days, ever committed to rigorous philosophical analysis and formal logical-mathematical methods, Chomsky's lifelong pursuit has been to understand the core of human language—the syntax that undergirds our verbal output. Chomsky views human language as marvelous and self-contained; he sees it, in fact, as a separate region of the mind. The phenomena that have intrigued Chomsky are the deep differences between superficially similar sentences: how we know instantly that "John is easy to please" functions differently from "John is eager to please"; how we recognize at once the underlying affinities between superficially different sentences, such as "The girl hit the boy," and "The boy was hit by the girl"; how we turn a statement effortlessly into a question or a question into a command.

But how did Chomsky move from these highly particularistic observations to a theory of mind? His route involved a demonstration that linguistic understanding requires mental work of a highly abstract sort. One must somehow be able to represent in one's mind the content of sentences at a level far removed from the surface properties of an utterance. Indeed, convinced early on of the inadequacy of previous attempts to explain language, Chomsky introduced into linguistics a set of wholly novel concerns. In fact he reformulated an agenda for scientific linguistics: to find a (and preferably *the*) set of grammatical rules that would generate syntactic descriptions of all of the permissible and none of the impermissible sentences in any given language. Such a grammar would constitute a valid description of the knowledge that a language user must employ when producing and understanding the sentences of his language.

Chomsky put forth a set of specific proposals concerning the formal nature of a grammatical system that could fulfill these goals. Because it is so difficult to determine how a child, exposed only to the surface structure of language, could ever "construct" these abstract representations, Chomsky arrived at a strong but highly controversial conclusion: knowledge of certain facets of language (and, by extension, of other intellectual "faculties") must be an inborn property of mind. Such knowledge requires, to be sure, a triggering environment (exposure to speech). But there is no need for active construction by the child or for more specific social or cultural input—the plan is all there. Nor are there separate stages of development based on changes in the child's mental capacities and on interaction with the environment: language unfolds in us in as natural a manner as the visual system or the circulatory system. The model lurking behind Chomsky's position, then, is that of a totally preprogrammed computer, one that needs merely to be plugged into the appropriate outlet.

And so we encounter the heart of the dispute between the two redoubtable thinkers. Whereas Piaget saw the child's efforts as engaging the full range of inventive powers as he stalks ahead from one stage to the next, Chomsky viewed the child as equipped with requisite knowledge from the beginning, only needing time to let that knowledge unfold.

At the conference both men made statements that were true to form in their examples, style of argument, and vision of science. Piaget characteristically focused on the arresting behavioral phenomena of children that he and his collaborators had discovered—the understanding of the permanence of objects, which does not occur until the end of infancy; the general capacity to symbolize, which is said to underlie both linguistic and pretend-play activities; the ability to appreciate the conservation of matter, which arises only during the early school years. Although Piaget criticized his old nemeses, the behaviorists and the nativists, for the most part he remained eager to convert others to his general picture of universal human development—a portrait attractive and convincing in its overall outlines but difficult to formulate in terms sufficiently precise for ready confirmation or disconfirmation.

Chomsky also offered a number of intriguing specific examples to support his point of view, but his overall approach was markedly different. Unlike Piaget's, his examples were not of dramatic behavioral phenomena; rather he pointed to abstract internal rules that seem necessary to account for certain regularities of linguistic output. For instance, he returned a number of times to the following illustration. When we transform the sentence "The man who is here is tall" into a question, we unfailingly produce the query "Is the man who is here tall?" rather than: "Is the man who here is tall?" Somehow we know that the relative phrase "the man who is here" must be treated as a single unit rather than broken up in the course of changing the order of the words.

Such rules are discovered by examining the features of correct linguistic utterances and of certain incorrect but "possible" syntactic constructions that seem never to appear. Once pointed out, such regularities are evident, and further experimentation to demonstrate their validity seems superfluous. Accordingly, Chomsky relied heavily on such examples to discount alternative rules and rival points of view. Disenchanted with accounts that had even a tinge of empiricism, he displayed little patience with the version of genetic-environmental contact that stands at the core of Piaget's interactionism. What impelled Chomsky's stance was a vivid image of what scientific practice should be like: metaphoric or impressionistic accounts must be avoided in favor of more precise statements phrased in a sufficiently formal manner to allow clear testing and decisive disconfirmation.

A number of other crucial differences emerged in the course of the debate. Perhaps the most dominant issue at Royaumont was one that took its original formulation from the pages of Shakespeare and has constituted a continuing source of contention between philosophers on opposite sides of the English Channel: whether (as Chomsky held) knowledge is largely inborn, part of the individual's birthright, a form of innate ideas existing in the realm of "nature"; whether

(as traditional empiricists like Skinner have contended) knowledge is better conceived of as a product of living in an environment, a series of messages of "nurture" transmitted by other individuals and one's surrounding culture, which become etched onto a *tabula rasa;* or whether (as Piaget insisted) knowledge can be constructed only through interaction between certain inborn modes of processing available to the young child and the actual characteristics of physical objects and events. This issue of genetic versus cultural contributions to the mind was pointedly phrased by the convener of the conference, Jacques Monod: "In asking myself the vast question, 'What makes man man?' it is clear that it is partially his genome and partially his culture. But what are the genetic limits of culture? What is its genetic component?"

Whether by design or happenstance, considerable time was spent discussing Chomskian nativism versus Piagetian "interactionism," a conflict that at Royaumont centered particularly on questions pertaining to the origins of language. At issue was whether human linguistic capacities can in any interesting sense be considered a product of general "constructed" intellectual development (as Piaget contended), or whether they are a highly specialized part of human genetic inheritance, largely separate from other human faculties and more plausibly viewed as a kind of innate knowledge that has only to unfold (as Chomsky insisted).

To be sure, whether language is interestingly dependent on certain nonlinguistic capacities is crucial, and this question was discussed at a sophisticated level during the conference. Yet the specific debate between nativism and interactionism strikes many observers, including me, as unnecessary and sterile. Within the biological sciences many feel it is no longer fruitful to attempt to sort out hereditary from environmental influences, and within the behavioral sciences even those seduced by this question often have difficulty agreeing on just what counts as evidence in favor of one side or the other. That Chomsky and Piaget could draw such different conclusions from equally pertinent bodies of data about early cognitive and linguistic milestones and that they occasionally shifted positions on what might count as evidence for their positions indicates to me that the reason this issue was so extensively reworked was that the two spokesmen had strong views on it, rather than that either of them was likely to convince the other or skeptical "others."

Topics more susceptible to solution were also addressed at Royaumont. In particular, three related and recurring issues are worth citing, for they underline pivotal differences between the two protagonists and, unlike the nature/nurture miasma, may well be resolved in the coming years. A first argument centers on the Rousseauan dilemma of the relationships between child and adult thought: whereas Piaget and his followers believed in the utility of stages, with children as they become older attaining qualitatively different (and increasingly more powerful) modes of reasoning, Chomsky and his colleague Jerry Fodor argued strongly that such an account of stages of thought is logically indefensible. In fact, according to Fodor, it is in principle impossible to generate more powerful forms of thought from less powerful ones; essentially, all forms of reasoning that an individual will eventually be capable of are specified at birth and emerge via a maturational process during development.

A second discussion concerned the nature of the mental representations by which we conceive of our experiences, including the objects and persons of the world. In the Piagetian view, the ability to represent knowledge to oneself and to others is a constructive process that presupposes a lengthy series of actions upon the environment. Mental representation awaits the completion of sensorimotor development at age two; its emergence makes possible symbolic play, dreams, mental images, language—in fact the whole gamut of symbolic capacities. Chomsky and his colleagues, on the other hand, expressed doubts about the legitimacy of grouping together a family of representations, and of referring to a symbolic function that is supposed to emerge at a certain point in development. In their view, language as a symbol system should be radically dissociated from other symbolic forms.

The final issue, intimately related to the first two, involved the generality of thought and of thought processes. According to Piaget, thought is an extremely broad set of capacities: identical mental operations underlie one's encounters with a wide range of cognitive materials and topics (space, time, morality, causality), and the roots of later forms of thought (for example, reasoning in language) can be located in earlier forms (such as sensorimotor problem-solving by the one-year-old). From Chomsky's radically different point of view, language is divorced from other (and earlier) forms of thinking. Moreover, each intellectual faculty is *sui generis*—a separate

domain of mentation, possibly located in a discrete region of the brain, exhibiting many of its own processes and maturing at its own rate. Indeed, Chomsky repeatedly invoked the striking, if somewhat bizarre, metaphor of the mind as a collection of organs, rather like the liver or the heart. We do not speak of the heart as learning to beat but rather as maturing according to its genetic timetable. So, too, we should conceive of language (and other "organs of the mind" such as those that account for the structure of mathematics or music) as mental entities that are programmed to unfold over time. Just as the physiologist dissects the heart in order to unravel its anatomy and its mechanisms, the linguist must perform analogous surgery on the human faculty of language.

The positions taken by the protagonists on these issues conveyed their general intellectual styles and substance, facets of their intellectual bequest that came across with increasing clarity and finality as the discussions progressed. Although both Piaget and Chomsky paid homage to models provided by biology and logic, they were fundamentally interested in quite different kinds of examples and explanations. Piaget was fascinated by the behaviors children emitted—and, more specifically, the errors they made—when solving the challenging puzzles he posed. He had developed an elaborate technical vocabulary, rooted in biology, to describe these phenomena—a rich description of the stages through which children pass in each of these realms of achievement. He also developed his own logical formalism to describe the affinities underlying structurally related behaviors and the differences that obtain across discrete mental stages. The phenomena he discerned offer a convincing series of snapshots of how development proceeds, but the specific terms he devised and the models he formulated have fared less well in the face of rigorous criticism. At most, Piaget's adventures into technical vocabulary and formal models offer a convenient way of synthesizing the enormous amount of data he accumulated. In the end, it is his overall *vision* of how capacities relate and of how knowledge in its varied forms develops that inspires workers in the field.

Though similar in certain respects, Chomsky's achievement is of a fundamentally different order. Rather than being struck by behavioral phenomena that he feels compelled to describe, Chomsky is driven by a powerful vision of how linguistic science should be pursued and by a belief in the way this analytic approach should be extended across the human sciences. In his view, the student of linguistics should construct models of human linguistic competence and thereby specify the "universals" of language. Stating the rules, steps, and principles with utmost (mathematical) precision becomes a prerequisite for work in this area. And so, even as Chomsky has high regard for models stated in such a way that they can be definitively tested, he dismisses more general and more allusive "positions," "schemas," and "strategies." Those domains of thought that are susceptible to study must be investigated in the way that a linguist studies language: the analyst must propose a formal system of rules that will either generate just the acceptable behaviors in that domain or will be shown in principle to fail (because, for example, they generate too many, too few, or the wrong behaviors), and he must strive to discover just those rules that the human mind actually follows.

Given those different approaches and philosophies of science, it is not surprising that, when the two scholars faced each other, there was serious and continuing disagreement. At the beginning of the discussion, each man paid homage to the other: Piaget noted "all the essential points in this about which I think I agree with Chomsky." And Chomsky acknowledged "Piaget's interesting remarks." As the discussion proceeded and became increasingly heated, the tone became distinctly less friendly. Piaget criticized the nativist position as "weak" and "useless," even as Chomsky described certain Piagetian assertions as "false," "inconceivable," and (in a mathematical sense) "trivial." Not surprisingly, neither of the scholars conceded that he might be wrong, even as each of their "seconds" rallied strongly to their positions. My reading of the interchanges suggests that most of the disinterested natural scientists were more swayed by Chomsky's presentation, but it is difficult to determine whether they were persuaded by Chomsky's rigor or were simply "turned off" by Piaget's old-fashioned, Lamarckian views on biological evolution. The social scientists in attendance at Royaumont seem to have been divided equally between the two camps.

It is too early to say which of these competing perspectives will carry the day in the burgeoning discipline of human cognition. While the issues at Royaumont are being widely discussed, the energies of future scholars have yet to be fully marshaled in either man's behalf. My own guess is that the kind of rigorous formal treatment espoused by the Chomsky circle will be increasingly embraced, but that it will be applied to the kinds of data, and addressed to the sorts of problems, that concerned Piaget and his colleagues. The academic journals of 1990 may well be filled with Chomsky-style grammars representing the child's knowledge at different stages of development. In other words, some kind of illuminating synthesis of the two men's theories may well be possible in the future.

In reading the transcript, I was struck by the grandeur of each perspective. No finer minds in our time have confronted the problem of the nature of thought: each exemplifies the power of his views both in formal presentations and informal exchanges.

At the same time, however, I was disturbed by a paradox. Piaget insisted throughout on the active exploratory nature of human intelligence; yet he offered a description of intellect that applies equivalently to all individuals and takes no account whatsoever of the heights of creative thought—the kind of inventiveness epitomized by his own work. For his part, Chomsky gave ample illustration of the creative genius of human language—the ways in which all of us are able to produce and understand sentences that have never before been uttered. Yet, at the same time, his assertion that we "know it all" in the beginning seems to leave remarkably little room for the flowering of genuinely new ideas—like those of Chomsky himself. As with many theorists, the works—and the lives—of the two men belie their own efforts to produce an overarching account of their field of inquiry.

In fact, to my mind the keynote for the conference at Royaumont was set by the biologist Guy Céllerier. After hearing the two presentations, Céllerier proposed a metaphor that he felt described the growth of intellect: he compared the development of the mind to climbing a hill. Extending that metaphor, we can assume that the broad steps of the journey are preordained but that the steps that one will actually take—the footholds gained, the heights one will ultimately reach, one's perspective at the end of the journey—cannot be anticipated.

Yet in their heroic effort to explain all of human thought, Piaget and Chomsky seem to have underestimated the extent to which such an exploration is open, impossible to predict, reducible neither to one's birthright nor to an inevitable sequence of stages. Perhaps the most apt metaphor for the colloquy on the regal mountain is the Sisyphean task—which each human is destined to repeat in his own turn and his own way—of striving to attain the summits of knowledge.

Relevant Models of Language

M. A. K. HALLIDAY

Editor's introduction

M. A. K. Halliday's contribution to language study is primarily in defining the functions of language. By concentrating on the meanings and purposes children ascribe to languages as they learn, Halliday developed a scheme for classifying different types of utterances. This article briefly presents Halliday's categories for the functions of language, categories that continue to inform many literacy programs in schools today.

The teacher of English who, when seeking an adequate definition of language to guide him in his work, meets with a cautious "well, it depends on how you look at it," is likely to share the natural impatience felt by anyone who finds himself unable to elicit "a straight answer to a straight question." But the very frequency of this complaint may suggest that, perhaps, questions are seldom as straight as they seem. The question "what is language?," in whatever guise it appears, is as diffuse and, at times, disingenuous as other formulations of its kind, for example "what is literature?" Such questions, which are wisely excluded from examinations, demand the privilege of a qualified and perhaps circuitous answer.

In a sense the only satisfactory response is "why do you want to know?," since unless we know what lies beneath the question we cannot hope to answer it in a way which will suit the questioner. Is he interested in language planning in multilingual communities? Or in aphasia and language disorders? Or in words and their histories? Or in dialects and those who speak them? Or in how one language differs from another? Or in the formal properties of language as a system? Or in the functions of language and the demands that we make on it? Or in language as an art medium? Or in the information and redundancy of writing systems?

Each one of these and other such questions is a possible context for a definition of language. In each case language "is" something different.

The criterion is one of relevance; we want to understand, and to highlight, those facets of language which bear on the investigation or the task in hand.

It is not necessary to sacrifice a generation of children, or even one classroomful, in order to demonstrate that particular preconceptions of language are inadequate or irrelevant. In place of a negative and somewhat hit-and-miss approach, a more fruitful procedure is to seek to establish certain general, positive criteria of relevance. These will relate, ultimately, to the demands that we make of language in the course of our lives. We need therefore to have some idea of the nature of these demands, and we shall try to consider them here from the point of view of the child. We shall ask, in effect, about the child's image of language: what is the "model" of language that he internalizes as a result of his own experience? This will help us to decide what is relevant to the teacher, since the

Source: Abridged from "Relevant Models of Language" by M. A. K. Halliday, 1969, *Educational Review, 22*, 26–37. Copyright 1969 by Carfax. Reprinted by permission of publisher.

(handwritten margin notes: ① instrumental ② regulatory ③ interactional ④ personal ⑤ heuristic)

teacher's own view of language must at the very least encompass all that the child knows language to be.

The child knows what language is because he knows what language does. The determining elements in the young child's experience are the successful demands on language that he himself has made, the particular needs that have been satisfied by language for him. He has used language in many ways—for the satisfaction of material and intellectual needs, for the mediation of personal relationships, the expression of feelings, and so on. Language in all these uses has come within his own direct experience, and because of this he is subconsciously aware that language has many functions that affect him personally. Language is, for the child, a rich and adaptable instrument for the realization of his intentions; there is hardly any limit to what he can do with it.

As a result, the child's internal "model" of language is a highly complex one, and most adult notions of language fail to match up to it. The adult's ideas about language may be externalized and consciously formulated, but they are nearly always much too simple. In fact it may be more helpful, in this connection, to speak of the child's "models" of language, in the plural, in order to emphasize the many-sidedness of his linguistic experience. We shall try to identify the models of language with which the normal child is endowed by the time he comes to school at the age of 5, the assumption being that if the teacher's own "received" conception of language is in some ways less rich or less diversified it will be irrelevant to the educational task.

We tend to underestimate both the total extent and the functional diversity of the part played by language in the life of the child. His interaction with others, which begins at birth, is gradually given form by language, through the process whereby at a very early age language already begins to mediate in every aspect of his experience. It is not only as the child comes to act on and to learn about his environment that language comes in; it is there from the start in his achievement of intimacy and in the expression of his individuality. The rhythmic recitation of nursery rhymes and jingles is still language, as we can see from the fact that children's spells and chants differ from one language to another: English nonsense is quite distinct from French nonsense, because the one is English and the other French. All these contribute to the child's total picture of language "at work."

Through such experiences, the child builds up a very positive impression—one that cannot be verbalized, but is nonetheless real for that—of what language is and what it is for. Much of his difficulty with language in school arises because he is required to accept a stereotype of language that is contrary to the insights he has gained from his own experience. The traditional first "reading and writing" tasks are a case in point, since they fail to coincide with his own convictions about the nature and uses of language.

Perhaps the simplest of the child's models of language, and one of the first to be evolved, is what we may call the INSTRUMENTAL model. The child becomes aware that language is used as a means of getting things done. About a generation ago, zoologists were finding out about the highly developed mental powers of chimpanzees, and one of the observations described was of the animal that constructed a long stick out of three short ones and used it to dislodge a bunch of bananas from the roof of its cage. The human child, faced with the same problem, constructs a sentence. He says "I want a banana," and the effect is the more impressive because it does not depend on the immediate presence of the bananas. Language is brought in to serve the function of "I want," the satisfaction of material needs. Success in this use of language does not in any way depend on the production of well-formed adult sentences; a carefully contextualized yell may have substantially the same effect, and although this may not be language there is no very clear dividing line between, say, a noise made in a commanding tone and a full-dress imperative clause.

The old *See Spot run. Run, Spot, run!* type of first reader bore no relation whatsoever to this instrumental function of language. This by itself does not condemn it, since language has many other functions beside that of manipulating and controlling the environment. But it bore little apparent relation to any use of language, at least to any with which the young child is familiar. It is not recognizable as language in terms of the child's own intentions, of the meanings that he has reason to express and to understand. Children have a very broad concept of the meaningfulness of language, in addition to their immense tolerance of inexplicable tasks; but they are not accustomed to being faced with language which, in their own functional terms, has no meaning at all, and the old-style reader was not seen by them as language. It made no connection with language in use.

(handwritten margin note at bottom: concept of family life)

Language as an instrument of control has another side to it, since the child is well aware that language is also a means whereby others exercise control over him. Closely related to the instrumental model, therefore, is the REGULATORY model of language. This refers to the use of language to regulate the behavior of others. Bernstein (1970) and his colleagues have studied different types of regulatory behavior by parents in relation to the process of socialization of the child, and their work provides important clues concerning what the child may be expected to derive from this experience in constructing his own model of language. To adapt one of Bernstein's examples, the mother who finds that her small child has carried out of the supermarket, unnoticed by herself or by the cashier, some object that was not paid for, may exploit the power of language in various ways, each of which will leave a slightly different trace or afterimage of this role of language in the mind of the child. For example, she may say *you mustn't take things that don't belong to you* (control through conditional prohibition based on a categorization of objects in terms of a particular social institution, that of ownership), *that was very naughty* (control through categorization of behavior in terms of opposition approved/disapproved), *if you do that again I'll smack you* (control through threat of reprisal linked to repetition of behavior), *you'll make Mummy very unhappy if you do that* (control through emotional blackmail), *that's not allowed* (control through categorization of behavior as governed by rule), and so on. A single incident of this type by itself has little significance, but such general types of regulatory behavior, through repetition and reinforcement, determine the child's specific awareness of language as a means of behavioral control.

The child applies this awareness in his own attempts to control his peers and siblings, and this in turn provides the basis for an essential component in his range of linguistic skills, the language of rules and instructions. Whereas at first he can make only simple unstructured demands, he learns as time goes on to give ordered sequences of instructions, and then progresses to the further stage where he can convert sets of instructions into rules, including conditional rules, as in explaining the principles of a game. Thus his regulatory model of language continues to be elaborated, and his experience of the potentialities of language in this use further increases the value of the model.

Closely related to the regulatory function of language is its function in social interaction, and the third of the models that we may postulate as forming part of the child's image of language is the INTERACTIONAL model. This refers to the use of language in the interaction between the self and others. Even the closest of the child's personal relationships, that with his mother, is partly and, in time, largely mediated through language; his interaction with other people, adults and children, is very obviously maintained linguistically. (Those who come nearest to achieving a personal relationship that is not linguistically mediated, apparently, are twins.)

Aside, however, from his experience of language in the maintenance of permanent relationships, the neighborhood and the activities of the peer group provide the context for complex and rapidly changing interactional patterns which make extensive and subtle demands on the individual's linguistic resources. Language is used to define and consolidate the group, to include and to exclude, showing who is "one of us" and who is not, to impose status, and to contest status that is imposed, and humor, ridicule, deception, persuasion, all the forensic and theatrical arts of language are brought into play. Moreover, the young child, still primarily a learner, can do what very few adults can do in such situations: he can be internalizing language while listening and talking. He can be, effectively, both a participant and an observer at the same time, so that his own critical involvement in this complex interaction does not prevent him from profiting linguistically from it.

Again there is a natural link here with another use of language, from which the child derives what we may call the PERSONAL model. This refers to his awareness of language as a form of his own individuality. In the process whereby the child becomes aware of himself, and in particular in the higher stages of that process, the development of his personality, language plays an essential role. We are not talking here merely of "expressive" language—language used for the direct expression of feelings and attitudes—but also of the personal element in the interactional function of language, since the shaping of the self through interaction with others is very much a language-mediated process. The child is enabled to offer to someone else that which is unique to himself, to make public his own individuality, and this in turn reinforces and creates this individuality. With the normal child, his awareness of himself is closely bound up with speech: both with hearing himself speak, and with having at his disposal the range of behavioral options that constitute language. Within the concept of the self as an actor, having discretion, or freedom of choice, the "self as a speaker" is an important component.

Thus for the child, language is very much a part of himself, and the "personal" model is his intuitive awareness of this, and of the way in which his individuality is identified and realized through language. The other side of the coin, in this process, is the child's growing understanding of his environment, since the environment is, first of all, the "nonself," that which is separated out in the course of establishing where he himself begins and ends. So, the child has a HEURISTIC model of language, derived from his knowledge of how language has enabled him to explore his environment.

The heuristic model refers to language as a means of investigating reality, a way of learning about things. This scarcely needs comment, since every child makes it quite obvious that this is what language is for by his habit of constantly asking questions. When he is questioning, he is seeking not merely facts but explanations of facts, the generalizations about reality that language makes it possible to explore. Again, Bernstein has shown the importance of the question-and-answer routine in the total setting of parent-child communication and the significance of the latter, in turn, in relation to the child's success in formal education: his research has demonstrated a significant correlation between the mother's linguistic attention to the child and the teacher's assessment of the child's success in the first year of school.

The young child is very well aware of how to use language to learn, and may be quite conscious of this aspect of language before he reaches school; many children already control a metalanguage for the heuristic function of language, in that they know what a "question" is, what an "answer" is, what "knowing" and "understanding" mean, and they can talk about these things without difficulty. Mackay and Thompson (1968) have shown the importance of helping the child who is learning to read and write to build up a language for talking about language, and it is the heuristic function which provides one of the foundations for this, since the child can readily conceptualize and verbalize the basic categories of the heuristic model. To put this more concretely, the normal 5 year old either already uses words such as *question, answer* in their correct meanings or, if he does not, is capable of learning to do so.

The other foundation for the child's "language about language" is to be found in the imaginative func-

tion. This also relates the child to his environment, but in a rather different way. Here, the child is using language to create his own environment, not to learn about how things are but to make them as he feels inclined. From his ability to create, through language, a world of his own making he derives the IMAGINATIVE model of language, and this provides some further elements of the metalanguage, with words like *story, make up,* and *pretend.*

Language in its imaginative function is not necessarily "about" anything at all: the child's linguistically created environment does not have to be a make-believe copy of the world of experience, occupied by people and things and events. It may be a world of pure sound, made up of rhythmic sequences of rhyming and chiming syllables, or an edifice of words in which semantics has no part, like a house built of playing cards in which face values are irrelevant. Poems, rhymes, riddles, and much of the child's own linguistic play reinforce this model of language, and here too the meaning of what is said is not primarily a matter of content. In stories and dramatic games, the imaginative function is, to a large extent, based on content, but the ability to express such content is still, for the child, only one of the interesting facets of language, one which for many purposes is no more than an optional extra.

So we come finally to the REPRESENTATIONAL model. Language is, in addition to all its other guises, a means of communicating about something, of expressing propositions. The child is aware that he can convey a message in language, a message which has specific reference to the processes, persons, objects, abstractions, qualities, states, and relations of the real world around him.

This is the only model of language that many adults have; and a very inadequate model it is, from the point of view of the child. There is no need to go so far as to suggest that the transmission of content is, for the child, the least important function of language; we have no way of evaluating the various functions relatively to one another. It is certainly not, however, one of the earliest to come into prominence, and it does not become a dominant function until a much later stage in the development toward maturity. Perhaps it never becomes in any real sense the dominant function, but it does, in later years, tend to become the dominant *model.* It is very easy for the adult, when he attempts to formulate his ideas about the nature of language, to be simply unaware of most of what language means to the child; this is not because he no longer uses language in the same variety of different functions (one or two may have atrophied, but not all), but because only one of these functions, in general, is the subject of conscious attention, so that the corresponding model is the only one to be externalized. But this presents what is, for the child, a quite unrealistic picture of language, since it accounts for only a small fragment of his total awareness of what language is about.

The representational model at least does not conflict with the child's experience. It relates to one significant part of it, rather a small part, at first, but nevertheless real. In this it contrasts sharply with another view of language which we have not mentioned because it plays no part in the child's experience at all, but which might be called the "ritual" model of language. This is the image of language internalized by those for whom language is a means of showing how well one was brought up; it downgrades language to the level of table manners. The ritual element in the use of language is probably derived from the interactional, since language in its ritual function also serves to define and delimit a social group, but it has none of the positive aspects of linguistic interaction, those which impinge on the child, and is thus very partial and one sided. The view of language as manners is a needless complication, in the present context, since this function of language has no counterpart in the child's experience.

Our conception of language, if it is to be adequate for meeting the needs of the child, will need to be exhaustive. It must incorporate all the child's own "models," to take account of the varied demands on language that he himself makes. The child's understanding of what language is is derived from his own experience of language in situations of use. It thus embodies all of the images we have described: the instrumental, the regulatory, the interactional, the personal, the heuristic, the imaginative, and the representational. Each of these is his interpretation of a function of language with which he is familiar.

Let us summarize the models in terms of the child's intentions, since different uses of language may be seen as realizing different intentions. In its instrumental function, language is used for the satisfaction of material needs; this is the "I want" function. The regulatory is the "do as I tell you" function, language

in the control of behavior. The interactional function is that of getting along with others, the "me and him" function (including "me and my mummy"). The personal is related to this: it is the expression of identity, of the self, which develops largely *through* linguistic interaction; the "here I come" function, perhaps. The heuristic is the use of language to learn, to explore reality: the function of "tell me why." The imaginative is that of "let's pretend," whereby the reality is created, and what is being explored is the child's own mind, including language itself. The representational is the "I've got something to tell you" function, that of the communication of content.

What we have called "models" are the images that we have of language arising out of these functions. Language is "defined" for the child by its uses; it is something that serves this set of needs. These are not models of language acquisition; they are not procedures whereby the child learns his language, nor do they define the part played by different types of linguistic activity in the learning process. Hence no mention has been made of the chanting and repeating and rehearsing by which the child practices his language. The techniques of mastering language do not constitute a "use," nor do they enter into the making of the image of language; a child, at least, does not learn for the luxury of being a learner. For the child, all language is doing something: in other words, it has meaning. It has meaning in a very broad sense, including here a range of functions which the adult does not normally think of as meaningful, such as the personal and the interactional and probably most of those listed above—all except the last, in fact. But it is precisely in relation to the child's conception of language that it is most vital for us to redefine our notion of meaning, not restricting it to the narrow limits of representational meaning (that is, "content") but including within it all the functions that language has as purposive, nonrandom, contextualized activity.

We are still very ignorant of many aspects of the part language plays in our lives. But it is clear that language serves a wide range of human needs, and the richness and variety of its functions are reflected in the nature of language itself, in its organization as a system: within the grammatical structure of a language, certain areas are primarily associated with the heuristic and representational functions, others with the personal and interactional functions. Different bits of the system, as it were, do different jobs, and this in turn helps us to interpret and make more precise the notion of uses of language. What is common to every use of language is that it is meaningful, contextualized, and in the broadest sense social; this is brought home very clearly to the child, in the course of his day-to-day experience. The child is surrounded by language, but not in the form of grammars and dictionaries, or of randomly chosen words and sentences, or of undirected monologue. What he encounters is "text," or language in use: sequences of language articulated each within itself and with the situation in which it occurs. Such sequences are purposive—though very varied in purpose—and have an evident social significance. The child's awareness of language cannot be isolated from his awareness of language function, and this conceptual unity offers a useful vantage point from which language may be seen in a perspective that is educationally relevant.

REFERENCES

Bernstein, B. 1970. "A Critique of the Concept of 'Compensatory Education.'" In S. Williams (Ed.), *Language and Poverty: Perspectives on a Theme*. Madison, WI: University of Wisconsin Press.

Mackay, D., and Thompson, B. 1968. *The Initial Teaching of Reading and Writing*. Programme in Linguistics and English Teaching. Paper 3. London: Longmans' Linguistic Library.

(MITCH)

Ian Caught in Infancy

RUSSELL MARTIN

· ·

Editor's introduction

Russell Martin's acclaimed book *Out of Silence: A Journey into Language* is a case study of one boy's struggle with autism and his parents' struggle to make sense of his needs. In this excerpt, Martin considers many of the theories of language development highlighted in the earlier articles. They come to life through the case of Ian, a boy who doesn't develop language in normal ways.

· · · · · · · · · · · ·

Infancy, a word we tend to associate only with the first few weeks and months of a child's life—life's brief beginning, a time, almost solely it seems, of suckling and untroubled sleep—comes to use from Anglo-French by way of Middle English, and it is most distantly rooted in the Latin word *infantia*, which means "without speech." Curiously, whether we are eight months or eighty years old—too young to have taken up words or old enough that stroke and disease insidiously have begun to take them from us—those of us who cannot speak are caught in the clutch of infancy. At ages two and three and then at four, the growing boy named Ian Drummond remained a troubled infant—absent speech, bereft of the kinds of language skills other children take command of in those years, Ian somehow lacking the cerebral apparatus with which this most *human* of his talents otherwise would have emerged.

Only three weeks following conception, the human embryo, three millimeters in length, has formed two paired structures at one end of its simple neural tube—bulging, symmetrical pieces of tissue that soon will become a brain. By the twelfth week of gestation, the brain's cerebrum and cerebellum have taken shape; at four months, the several forebrain structures are intact and the cerebrum has begun to form the lateral fissures that distinguish its temporal lobes; and at eight months, the fully developed brain is tightly packed inside the bony box of the cranium. By birth, an infant's head is almost half its body length; its brain weighs a quarter of its adult weight, and every one of its *billions* of neurons already is intact. Except for the intricate coating of long nerve fibers with insulating myelin and what in two years' time will be a doubling in its weight, the brain at birth is entirely ready to function, to begin to form the dazzling interconnections between its neurons that will allow it to engage with the world, to recognize, remember, and learn, someday even to speak.

Whether the phenomenon can be accounted for by the presence in the brain of a Chomskian language organ or whether it is simply the product of decidedly less mysterious natural selection, every human newborn with normal hearing quickly begins to focus on the sounds of speech. Tests performed in experimental

---

Source: From *Out of Silence: A Journey into Language*, by Russell Martin. Copyright (c) 1994 by Russell Martin. Reprinted by permission of Henry Holt & Co., Inc.

settings have shown that six-month-olds can distinguish between "ah" and "ee" sounds made by their mothers and that they likewise can discern the differences in those sounds when made by voices they have never heard. And just as infants spend the first six months of life listening to the sounds of speech, they devote the subsequent half year to trying them out for themselves. Babies begin to babble four to six months before their first word emerges, making speechlike sounds in a manner that is unmistakably playful, pleasurable; and intriguingly, they tend to begin to make the same sounds at roughly the same times and in the same sequences regardless of the language they have become accustomed to and are about to learn to speak—Arabic, English, or Chinese.

First words, the first fledgling elements of speech, are little more than labels, a means of identifying those people and objects the youngster considers most important—*cow, cookie, Mama, me*—the child's initial sense of self taking shape in the simple context of naming names. Then, subject-only utterances give way to subject and verb: an eager "me, me!" is soon supplanted by the more communicative "me juice," and not long later the phrase "give juice me" introduces a grammatical object well before a child gains command of the particularities of syntax and grammar. Finally, and now from a certified speaker—language alive in his or her brain—a sentence like "please give me some apple juice" emerges as if by some sleight of mind, a true linguistic accomplishment. And perhaps even more remarkably, toddlers at fourteen months and even tykes of four or five years are capable of learning two very different languages simultaneously, as effortlessly as one alone is acquired, and although their limits seldom are truly tested, they likely are capable of learning many more. Those first few years of a child's life appear, in point of fact, to be *for* learning language, for discovering ten thousand things through imitation and endless hours of play, for playing foremost with language.

Although Ian's first forms of autistic play were limited to his silent and solitary imitations of action in his movies, by the time he was three he did begin to entertain himself—to explore and exercise and even have a bit of irrefutable fun—in several other ways, normally alone but occasionally even in the company of others. He loved, for instance, to tug and push his mother, father, and sister Sarah into precise positions in their long, sunlit living room, where they could serve as sentient sorts of fence posts whom he could run beside;

and it seemed sure that it would have become one of his favorite recreations—combining the joys of running, repetition, and a real if rather peculiar way of interacting with his family—had it not become quickly obvious to the other three that they simply could not allow themselves to become prisoners to that particular pastime, stuck in place perhaps for hours as Ian brushed beside them, racing back and forth across the carpet.

But his other entertainments tended to be far easier to sanction—less disruptive of some semblance of regular family life, if often equally unusual: It was during the year he was three that Ian seemed to discover trees—the ponderosas, Douglas firs, and aspens that he lived among—and he would spend long stretches of time outdoors licking trees as if to determine what their taste could teach him, similarly pressing his cheeks against their trunks, craning his neck to peer into their upper branches, running past them in lieu of posts or people. And then he discovered water to similar delight, splashing in puddles and fearlessly jumping into shallow pools. Bathtime too became an occasion he eagerly sought out, several times a day if his parents would acquiesce—the tub's warm and soapy water a realm he comfortably could enter with his prized plastic figurines, Pooh and Tigger and ten others joining him for his nightly soak, an environment where you could watch him subtly unwind, physically and somehow even emotionally, where the water seemed to hug him or caress him, or at least to offer some support, where he was free simply to splash and kick and play. Ian also became an intrepid climber, as fearless clinging to the upper rungs of the ladder that led to a loft in his bedroom as he was in the water, regularly scrambling up the metal slide outside the house with what appeared to be a kind of cool disinterest, scrambling too to the tops of the granite knobs as big as barns that lay scattered across the rolling steppe.

In his isolation—his bedroom door often shut to shield out some noise, some simple commotion he couldn't stand—Ian would spend hours burrowed under blankets pulled from his bed and mounded on the floor, sleeping bags and clothes dumped from drawers offering similar subterranean pleasures, the boy becoming a mole. And on those days when it seemed safe to venture into the larger world of the living room, he would pull the cushions from the couch and try as well to bury himself beneath them, or angle them to the floor to turn them into a makeshift, spongy slide.

But for the longest time, Ian didn't play with vocal sounds in any way. Unlike other children, he didn't babble as if engaged in some splendid experiment, he didn't try to imitate words he heard. He seemed instead to be deaf, hearing nothing—neither his mother's patient and tender pledges nor the songs his father sang, neither his sister's carefully scripted fantasies nor his own continuing shrieks. He seemed as mute as those rocks and trees were, incapable of speaking polished words, incapable of their practice, unable to make himself understood, as other children could, with nascent sounds that sprang from his mouth.

Theoretical explanations of how normal children somehow utter their first words and then rapidly acquire language tend to be composed of opposing and contradictory perspectives. It isn't surprising, nor is it news, that one of them is championed—quite persuasively, for many people—by Noam Chomsky. Yet it is curious that many of Chomsky's ideas about the specific ways in which language comes to life in almost all children first emerged not in the context of his own primary writing but rather in his 1959 review of Harvard psychologist B. F. Skinner's 1957 book *Verbal Behavior*, a widely influential account of how language is acquired, then used throughout a lifetime.

Skinner's ideas dominated psychology back in that era, particularly his contention that all of human behavior is best explained by what he called operant conditioning. In the context of the theory that has become known as behaviorism, an "operant" is any action that achieves a specific outcome. If the outcome is favorable, the probability increases that the action will occur again, and the action is "reinforced"—positively reinforced if it produces some sort of pleasant or attractive outcome, negatively reinforced if the operant is followed by the end or removal of something painful or unpleasant. If, on the other hand, the outcome of an operant is unfavorable, the probability *decreases* that it will occur again, and rather than being reinforced, that operant is "punished."

In terms of the acquisition of language, Skinner theorized, all linguistic stimuli are external—morphemes, word, sentences—and an individual child develops the ability to respond to those stimuli via the principles of operant conditioning, the spoken word "juice" tending to result in the offering of juice, for instance, while "juice please" is even more likely to produce the desired result. But a specific operant can be generalized to apply to a variety of related behaviors as well, and can also be associated with a wide range of unrelated behaviors. "Cookie please" is readily "learned" by generalization, in other words, and "teddy bear please" is acquired with similar ease by means of association. In Skinner's view, a child learns to talk, just as he or she learns to walk, because talking tends to produce so many favorable outcomes.

But Chomsky was unpersuaded by a theory based entirely on response to external stimuli. Although he could imagine, for instance, that the rules of operant conditioning might comprehensively account for the way in which an infant shakes a rattle, then shakes it again repeatedly because he or she delights in the sounds it makes—or the way in which a child learns to walk because certain operants, certain physical actions, result in the positive reinforcement of reaching a parent's outstretched arms—Chomsky simply dismissed Skinner's attempt to treat language analogously. Neither Skinner nor anyone else could make the case, he argued, that language acquisition was solely the product of external conditions, in part because its "stimuli" inherently were so difficult, if not impossible, to identify and quantify. And how could Skinner account for one of language's most elemental attributes, its creativity? If language was acquired solely from external sources, were the concepts of generalization and association enough to explain the ways in which children begin to link words they have never heard linked before?

In Chomsky's opposing view, language acquisition cannot be imagined to be set in motion by external forces, by stimuli that lead to specific linguistic responses. Instead, he proposed the existence of a "language organ" in every child that receives external input in the form of so-called primary linguistic data—parents' words, phrases, pauses, and inflections. The acquisition device then somehow cooks that data down into the stew of syntax—the linguistic rules and regulations that the parents' words adhere to—finally allowing the output of a grammatically acceptable version of the very language from which the original data have been drawn. What emerges is a facility with that language that is capable of enormous creativity, of course, because it is not mimicry, nor is it a specific operant response. Rather, it is language built on an innate apprehension of those rules and on a similar ability to employ them, on what Chomsky labeled a "universal grammar," which he has defined more recently as "a characterization of the genetically determined language faculty. One may think of this faculty as a 'language acquisition device,' an innate component of the human mind that yields a particular language through interaction with presented experience." The average six-year-old, in other words, becomes expert at speech production and comprehension because he or she is born with its rules already in hand, or, if you will, somewhere within the neural walls of that acquisition device.

Chomsky's assessment of the way in which children acquire language seems clearly wrongheaded to a linguist like Philip Lieberman, who remains far more charitable toward the ideas of Skinner and his fellow behaviorists than does Chomsky and who argues for the primacy of evolution, rather than syntax, when it comes to the question of language's rules and regulations. The fundamental flaw in the universal grammar theory, as far as Lieberman is concerned, is that it assumes that all humans are born with an identical "plan," a genetically coded set of interlocked principles, components, and conventions that allows a child to turn the aural data of spoken speech into creative language—a system in which every component plays a specific and crucial role, and in which every component therefore is always present in everyone who learns to talk. But that assumption, he argues, flies in the face of the formidable verity of genetic variation: No two individuals (save identical twins) are genetically alike, and those genes at the specific chromosomal locations that account for each particular aspect of who we are vary between us and our parents about ten percent of the time. It is an evolutionary certainty, Lieberman contends, that if a universal grammar were genetically transmitted, all its components could not always be present in every individual. If a genetically coded "language faculty" is absolutely necessary to acquire language, he writes in *Uniquely Human,*

[t]hen it would follow that some children would lack one or more of the genetically coded components of the language faculty. Some "general principle" or some component of the "markedness system" would necessarily be absent in some children because it is genetically transmitted. This is the case for all genetically coded aspects of the morphology of human beings or any other living organisms. . . . A biologically plausible universal grammar cannot have rules and parameters that are so tightly interlocked that the absence of any single bit of

putative innate knowledge makes it impossible for the child to acquire a particular language. In other words, we cannot claim that a single set of innate principles concerning language exists that is (a) absolutely necessary for the acquisition of language and (b) uniform for all human beings.

Yes, Lieberman acknowledges—anticipating the responses of Chomsky and fellow "nativists" who view language as genetically innate—all people do have lungs, hearts, brains, and it may be that all of us also possess universal grammars, but if so, and as is the case with those other organs, they necessarily would vary from person to person, and in some people, they necessarily would be faulty—faulty far more often than could be accounted for by children like Ian who do not learn to speak. Instead, suggests Lieberman, children learn how to speak simply because they know how to play.

Lieberman does not argue with the notion that the input of parents' (particularly mothers') spoken speech is a crucial and catalytic component of language acquisition; without it, the acquiring process could not get under way. But as far as he is concerned, "there is nothing very mysterious about syntax," particularly with regard to its supposed innate role in turning complex, sometimes contradictory, often garbled input into grammatical output. What happens instead, he posits rather more concretely, is that children begin to respond to the language sounds they hear simply by imitating them. Studies have shown that newborns at just a day or two of age are capable of imitating adult facial expressions, and by age six months children can imitate the sounds their mothers make; by nine months, they are able to imitate expressions, sounds, and activities they discerned the day before; by fourteen months, they can replay by imitation what they saw or heard a week ago. Are these children dutifully and determinedly going about the business of learning language as they do so? No, says Lieberman, they are *playing,* a highly evolved form of behavior that allows us to learn a multitude of things, languages among them, without having to knuckle down or even to sit still—learning by association, generalization, analogy, and the kinds of trial and error that are the nuts-and-bolts business of Skinner's behaviorism.

There is no argument among these linguistic partisans that children learning language are confronted with what would seem to be a daunting task. Although it takes them years of schooling to master geometry or algebra, they quickly come to grips—in the most casual of look-Ma-no-hands fashion—with a system of communication and representation that scientists cannot completely or even adequately describe. It isn't surprising therefore that one attractive explanation for children's cheery facility with language's complexity is that knowledge of its rules, or perhaps the rules themselves, are innate, somehow built into every baby. But that perspective digs too deeply and with far too blunt a shovel, Lieberman believes, when a much more plausible possibility can be observed readily in almost every household. Children learn language so effortlessly, he contends, because they inherently are so playful, so curious, because they can pay rapt attention without knowing they do so, and because their brains are utterly impelled to learn.

Children—and former children as well—daily employ a diverse and varied number of so-called cognitive strategies in order to learn, one of the most important and fundamental of which is known as "concept formation," or rule learning. And in the context of learning the rules of language, children make use of concept formation to acquire the foundations of syntactic structure; syntax isn't so complex that it must be innate, Lieberman says, but rather it is so simple that it's discernible just from listening.

All humans are adept at generalizing—forming categories, patterns, and rules from separate cases or incidents—and children begin to generalize very early on. Their interest in naming objects, for instance, is part of an obsession with creating categories—all four-legged animals likely included in a category called "dog" at first, then soon divided into subcategories called "dog" and "horse" and "cat." Similarly, and surely unaware, children generalize from the language that they hear, noting—among many other things—that utterances tend to come in bursts separated by breaths, that key words receive intonational stress, that those words are made up of specific sounds, and that words, once recognized, tend to be grouped in repeated and dependable patterns. As children then begin to imitate what they hear, their first words, not surprisingly, tend to be those key words, words their parents have spoken a thousand times and each time have given a vocal stress. Later, as they begin to link words grammatically, their grammars simply reflect those orderings, those rule-governed arrangements that they have heard most often. If they hear "I goed

to town" more often than "I went to town," then *I goed* becomes grammatical; if "I went to town" is commonplace and "Town went I to" is odd, then the latter is discarded. Rather than depending on an innate rule-dispensing system, they depend instead on their abilities to generalize from observation—learning by listening, and then by imitating those curious articulations that they most often hear.

In making this behavioral kind of case, however, Lieberman does not quarrel with the proposition that the acquisition of language involves specialized brain mechanisms or some set of highly evolved neural capabilities. The brain's adaptability and its task-specific prowess, in fact, have allowed us to achieve all manner of miracles in the millennia since we lumbered to our feet. But there simply is no need, he argues by analogy, to postulate a special-purpose innate fork-using mechanism to account for the way that children learn to use forks, or universal clothes or cars grammars to account for the way that people rush to outfit themselves in the latest style in clothes or cars. Imitation and a desire to "be like the others" clearly can account for most of the short-term changes in human culture, and perhaps for many of its major achievements.

Of all our human acquisitions and accomplishments, only language is utterly dependent on being acquired at an early age, during the "critical period," from twelve months of age to six or seven years, perhaps to the onset of puberty, during which time language proficiency must be won, if it ever will be. By the time we become adolescents our language-acquisition device seems somehow to have atrophied, or perhaps to have moved on to another neural occupation. Have the folds and creases of our cortices by then become so definitively formed that we cannot reshape them and effectively teach ourselves new tricks? Do we forget after only a short expanse of years how to pay wide-eyed attention and to play?

From the cows he first was fascinated by to the elephants and monkeys in his movies, from the squirrels and rabbits he encountered in the nearby forests to a wily character called Tigger he certainly seemed to cherish, Ian, like most children, took great interest in animals, particularly if they were at an imaginary or spatial remove from him. He would utterly ignore long-suffering Sheila, the collie who had come west with the family from Illinois, when she would wander into his room, and the cat Sarah lived for during that time surely seemed invisible to him. Yet books like *The Smiley Lion* and *Franny Bunny* at last began to intrigue him—*books!* to his parents' pure pleasure and excitement—Ian sitting still and seeming briefly comfortable beside them as they read, Ian sometimes pointing with the help of their wrist prompts to the colorful drawings of these creatures, sometimes even pointing to the words his parents read. He still loved to—still demanded to—make the daily drive to call on the cows, and despite his fears and anxieties about most exotic settings, he once responded with his own sort of enthusiasm to an experimental trip to the zoo. In subsequent visits to zoos both in Denver and in Colorado Springs, Ian would demonstrate—by means of those places where he chose to run ritually back and forth—the animals he liked best: snakes of all shapes and sizes, as well as the apes, who would stare inscrutably back at him.

They did then and still do intrigue me—these two choices he made without anyone's direction or influence. Wasn't it curious that a boy who was terribly afraid of so much that seemed innocuous was, nonetheless, drawn to those slithering reptiles that so many of the rest of us are innately fearful of? And what did he see in the faces of the gorillas, orangutans, and chimpanzees that made him tarry near their cages? Did their silence make them seem kindred to him? Did the cages themselves seem to be something he knew well by analogy?

Much experimentation has been done during the second half of the twentieth century in an effort to determine whether our close cousins the apes are capable of acquiring true language, and several impressive results indeed have been obtained—from the young gorilla named Koko in California who built a working vocabulary of four hundred signed words to the sardonically named Nim Chimpsky, a chimpanzee in New York city who once spontaneously produced a string of sixteen words in American Sign Language (ASL): *Give orange me give eat orange me eat orange give me eat orange give me you;* a lot of words for a rather simple request.

This series of separate studies began in the 1960s with a chimpanzee named Vicki who was trained literally to speak, but her vocabulary was limited to four words—*mama, papa, cup,* and *up*—each produced only with real effort and pronounced in a kind of whisper. Then early in the 1970s, a chimp named Sarah made news when she mastered rudimentary elements of a visual-symbol language, reaching a level at which she could begin to communicate creatively, generalizing from a phrase like *Randy give apple Sarah* to *Randy give banana Sarah,* a very subtle but nonetheless significant step. Subsequently, two chimps called Sherman and Austin, who were trained simultaneously to use a similar visual language called Yerkish, were sometimes observed using it to communicate privately with each other after class sessions had ended and trainers had gone away for the day.

But surely the star of these whiz chimps was Washoe, a chimpanzee who was brought at eleven months of age to live with Allen and Beatrix Gardner and their family in Nevada, each of whom had learned ASL prior to her arrival. In Washoe's presence, the Gardners communicated only in ASL, and soon she began to sign herself. By the time she was five, her vocabulary included at least 132 signs. Her exaggerated, expansive style of signing was similar to that of human children learning ASL, and she could employ the signing equivalent of intonation to give her words emphasis; but she seldom offered more than a two-word utterance, and she was far more repetitive than human children normally are, whether signing or speaking. Yet Washoe had become quite creative: After she had acquired the sign for *flower,* she began to use it in the context of a variety of smells, but as soon as she learned the actual sign for *smell,* her use of *flower* reverted solely to its proper usage. Impressively, a nightcap she had never seen before she called a *hat;* a Brazil nut seemed to her to be a *rock berry;* and the first time she saw a duck, she labeled it a *water bird.*

In the intervening years, no other pongid has significantly surpassed the achievements of Washoe and her fellow captives. The most precocious of them have been capable of reaching a language level roughly comparable to that of a two-and-a-half-year-old child, and they have learned—normally, and perhaps significantly, only with the aid of the rigorously controlled techniques of operant conditioning—how to use complex symbolic systems to communicate. Yet they have been unable to progress beyond those plateaus they reached, and that, as well as the virtual absence of a grasp of syntax, combine to make most researchers unwilling to call their communication "language." But if these chimps and gorillas aren't employing language, then what is this marvel of which they've become capable?

If Nim Chimpsky isn't using language when he signs *Me sorry hug me*, what else can we possibly call it?

Derek Bickerton, the University of Hawaii linguist who, like Chomsky, views an inherent sense of syntax as key to language's emergence in our species as well as to its acquisition by each of us individually, posits intriguing answers to those questions in *Language and Species*. There are at least two allied but fundamentally distinct *types* of language, Bickerton contends—both having come to us evolutionally in ways Philip Lieberman wouldn't argue with—what Bickerton calls "language" and "protolanguage," and the case he makes for them depends as much on rare examples of so-called wild children who have grown up in worlds without language as it does on eloquent and pioneering pongids like precocious Nim and Washoe.

It was in the autumn of 1970 that a tiny thirteen-year-old-girl—just four feet six inches tall and weighing fifty-nine pounds—appeared with her cataract-blinded mother at a social services office in suburban Los Angeles, the two of them seeking help, seeking asylum from the father and husband who long had made their lives nightmarish beyond belief. Inside the father's autocratic and horrific household, the girl—who became known by the pseudonym "Genie"—had been harnessed naked to a potty chair since infancy, able to move only her fingers and hands, her feet and toes, the room where she was kept empty except for the potty chair and a wire-covered crib where she sometimes was placed at night, her only glimpse of the world two slivers of sky she could see above the curtains that covered the windows.

Genie was incontinent when she first was examined by doctors. She could not chew solid food, her vision was very poor, she could not stand erect or fully extend her limbs, and she virtually was mute. She understood the words *red, blue, green, brown, Mother, walk,* and *go;* she could utter only what sounded like "stop it" and "no more." Genie was admitted to Children's Hospital of Los Angeles for initial treatment of severe malnutrition, and as she slowly began to gain strength and then quickly to acquire new skills, she also became the subject of an enormous amount of curiosity on the part of social scientists from several disciplines. By the time a battery of tests determined that Genie was not retarded—although, as hospital psychologist James Kent put it, she was "the most profoundly damaged child I've ever seen . . . [her] life was a wasteland"—a number of researchers in linguistics had become fascinated by her, by what, in particular, she might now be able to acquire in the way of speech and language skills. Yet although Genie did make enormous progress, although she could say "I want Curtiss play piano," "Think about Mama love Genie," and could utter hundreds of similar simple phrases by 1977, seven years after her liberation, her language skills seemed stuck at that rather primitive level.

According to Susan Curtiss, the UCLA linguist who had worked most intensively with Genie during those years and whose doctoral dissertation had been published under the title *Genie: A Psycholinguistic Study of a Modern-Day "Wild Child,"* Genie quickly had developed an impressive vocabulary, but, in large part because she had aged beyond the critical acquiring period by the time she began to learn language,

she never mastered the rules of grammar, never could use the little pieces—the word endings, for instance. She had a clear semantic ability but could not learn syntax. There was a tremendous unevenness, or scatter, in what she was able to do. . . . One of the interesting findings is that Genie's linguistic system did not develop all of a piece. So grammar could be seen as distinct from the non-grammatical aspects of language, and also from other mental faculties. . . . She demonstrated that after puberty one could not learn language simply by being exposed to it.

Yet as Russ Rymer would note in his *New Yorker* series based on Genie's story and the research she engendered, her linguistic development also posed a substantial theoretical conundrum:

Though it appeared to affirm Chomsky, it could also be read as refuting him. If some parts of language were innate and others were provided by the environment, why would Genie's childhood hell have deprived her of only the innate parts? How could a child who lacked language because she had been shut away from her mother be proof that our mothers don't teach us language? Why should she be unable to gain precisely the syntax that Chomsky said she was born with? . . . [I]f syntax is "innate" why must it be "acquired" at all?

Derek Bickerton's sharply drawn distinction between language and protolanguage considers those questions by forging a linguistic—actually, a *proto*linguistic—link between adolescents and adults like Genie, who have been deprived of language, normal children who are acquiring their initial speech, and the speaking apes, connections that at first perhaps appear implausible. Bickerton is convinced that the kinds of language the three groups produce have much in common: they are comprised solely of lexical (vocabulary) items and they lack discernible grammatical structure—the same observation Susan Curtiss makes regarding Genie's speech—and Bickerton goes to some length in making his case for their commonality.

Yet if all are virtually the same sort of speech, why does only one of the three transform itself into fully flowered language? Bickerton's response is that no satisfactory or even passable explanation is possible so long as it depends on the assumption that mature language evolves or derives from its primitive counterpart, so long as language acquisition is seen as a single continuous process. But on the other hand, he writes,

[i]f we assume that there exists some primitive type of language—some protolanguage, as we might call it, that is just as much a part of our biological endowment as language is, but that lacks most of the distinguishing formal properties of language—then all three . . . can be readily explained. Genie acquired protolanguage because protolanguage is more robust than language (having formed part of the hominid endowment for much longer) and it does not have a critical period. . . . Genie's acquisition ceased because the faculties of protolanguage and of language are disjoint, and acquisition of the one in no way entails acquisition of the other.

This is the core of Bickerton's contention: Hominids and pongids alike can pick up protolan-

guage, whether at thirteen months or thirteen years or thirty. And it is this rough and spotty kind of speech that is acquired through the application of normal cognitive processes to the input of experience, in much the same way that Philip Lieberman describes. Yet the other sort of language—the one almost all of us acquire when we are small as if by some strange metaphysical frolic, the one that depends on syntax for its clarity and nuance and a kind of fluid grace—clearly must be latched onto very early in our lives; and we alone among the primates, among *all* animals so far as we know now, are capable of achieving it. It is a curious thought to consider: It isn't our ability to communicate that makes us unique; neither is it our register of words that we can count into the many thousands. What sets us truly apart, it seems, is that while we are young—and somehow *only* then—we discover how wonderfully to weave those words.

But Rymer's queries still echo here: If Chomsky is correct in claiming that this stuff called syntax with which we create true language is genetically handed down to us, then why does it disappear? Or if, in contrast, Lieberman's outlook is the clearer one, then why is it that we can acquire words at any age, but grammar only in the years soon after we are infants?

REFERENCES

Bickerton, D. 1990. *Language and Species*. Chicago: University of Chicago.

Lieberman, P. 1991. *Uniquely Human: The Evolution of Speech, Thought, and Selfless Behavior*. Cambridge, MA: Harvard University Press.

Skinner, B. F. 1957. *Verbal Behavior*. New York: Appleton-Century-Croft.

The Study of Nonstandard English

WILLIAM LABOV

Editor's introduction

William Labov is a New York City researcher whose work has affected teachers in two ways. He was one of the first language researchers to explain how dialects are rule-governed. Labov also emphasized the importance of teachers understanding speech patterns in the dialects of their students who speak nonstandard English. In this article, he explains the rules governing different aspects of Black English and the implications of those rules for classroom language practice.

Since language learning does take place outside of the classroom, and the six-year-old child does have great capacity for learning new language forms as he is exposed to them, it may be asked why it should be necessary for the teacher to understand more about the child's own vernacular. First, we can observe that automatic adjustment does *not* take place in all cases. Even the successful middle-class student does not always master the teacher's grammatical forms; and in the urban ghettos we find very little adjustment to school forms. Students continue to write *I have live* after ten or twelve years in school; we will describe below failures in reading the *-ed* suffix which show no advance with years in school. Second, knowledge of the underlying structure of the nonstandard vernacular will allow the most efficient teaching. If the teacher knows the general difference between standard negative attraction and nonstandard negative concord, he can teach a hundred different standard forms with the simple instruction: *The negative is attracted only to the first indefinite.* Thus by this one rule we can make many corrections.

He don't know nothing   → He doesn't know anything
Nobody don't like him   → Nobody likes him
Nobody hardly goes there → Hardly anybody goes there
Can't nobody do it   → Nobody can do it

Third, the vernacular must be understood because ignorance of it leads to serious conflict between student and teacher. Teachers in ghetto schools who continually insist that *i* and *e* sound different in *pin* and *pen* will only antagonize a great number of their students. The knowledge that *i* and *e* actually sound the same before *m* and *n* for most of their students (and "should" sound the same if they are normal speakers) will help avoid this destructive conflict. Teachers who insist that a child meant to say *He is tired* when he said *He tired* will achieve only bewilderment in the long run. Knowledge that *He tired* is the vernacular equivalent of the contracted form *He's tired* will save teacher and student from this frustration.

Granted that the teacher wishes to learn about the student's language, what methods are available for him to do so? Today, a great many linguists study English through their own intuitions; they operate "out of their own heads" in the sense that they believe they

---

Source: *The Study of Nonstandard English* (pp. 10–17) by W. Labov, 1970, Urbana, IL: National Council of Teachers of English and the Center for Applied Linguistics.

can ask and answer all the relevant questions themselves. But even if a teacher comes from the same background as his students, he will find that his grammar has changed, that he no longer has firm intuitions about whether he can say *Nobody don't know nothing about it* instead of *Nobody knows nothing about it.* He can of course sit down with a student and ask him all kinds of direct questions about his language, and there are linguists who do this. But one cannot draw directly upon the intuitions of the two major groups we are interested in, children and nonstandard speakers. Both are in contact with a superordinate or dominant dialect, and both will provide answers which reflect their awareness of this dialect as much as of their own. One can of course engage in long and indirect conversations with students, hoping that all of the forms of interest will sooner or later occur, and there are linguists who have attempted to study nonstandard dialects in this way. But these conversations usually teach the subject more of the investigator's language than the other way around. In general, one can say that whenever a speaker of a nonstandard dialect is in a subordinate position to a speaker of a standard dialect, the rules of his grammar will shift in an unpredictable manner towards the standard. The longer the contact, the stronger and more lasting is the shift. Thus adolescent speakers of a vernacular make very unreliable informants when they are questioned in a formal framework. The investigator must show considerable sociolinguistic sophistication to cope with such a situation, and indeed the teacher will also need to know a great deal about the social forces which affect linguistic behavior if he is to interpret his students' language.

NONSTANDARD DIALECTS AS "SELF-CONTAINED" SYSTEMS

The traditional view of nonstandard speech as a set of isolated deviations from standard English is often countered by the opposite view: that nonstandard dialect should be studied as an isolated system in its own right, without any reference to standard English. It is argued that the system of grammatical forms of a dialect can only be understood through their internal relations. For example, nonstandard Negro English has one distinc-

tion which standard English does not have: there is an invariant form *be* in *He always be foolin' around* which marks habitual, general conditions, as opposed to the unmarked *is, am, are,* etc., which do not have any such special sense. It can be argued that the existence of this distinction changes the value of all other members of the grammatical system and that the entire paradigm of this dialect is therefore different from that of standard English. It is indeed important to find such relations within the meaningful set of grammatical distinctions, if they exist, because we can then *explain* rather than merely describe behavior. There are many cooccurrence rules which are purely descriptive—the particular dialect just happens to have X' *and* Y' where another has X and Y. We would like to know if a special nonstandard form X' *requires* an equally nonstandard Y' because of the way in which the nonstandard form cuts up the entire field of meaning. This would be a tremendous help in teaching, since we would be able to show what sets of standard rules have to be taught together to avoid confusing the student with a mixed, incoherent grammatical system.

The difficulty here is that linguistics has not made very much progress in the analysis of semantic systems. There is no method or procedure which leads to reliable or reproducible results—not even among those who agree on certain principles of grammatical theory. No one has yet written a complete grammar of a language—or even come close to accounting for all the morphological and syntactic rules of a language. And the situation is much more primitive in semantics; for example, the verbal system of standard English has been studied now for many centuries, yet there is no agreement at all on the meaning of the auxiliaries *have . . . ed* and *be . . . ing.* The meaning of *I have lived here,* as opposed to *I lived here,* has been explained as (a) relevant to the present, (b) past *in* the present, (c) perfective, (d) indefinite, (e) causative, and so on. It is not only that there are many views; it is that in any given discussion no linguist has really found a method by which he can reasonably hope to persuade others that he is right. If this situation prevails where most of the investigators have complete access to the data, since they are native speakers of standard English, we must be more than cautious in claiming to understand the meaning of *I be here* as opposed to *I am here* in nonstandard Negro English, and even more cautious in claiming that the meaning of nonstandard *I'm here* therefore differs from standard *I'm here* because of the existence of the other form. Most teachers have learned to be cautious in accepting a grammarian's statement about the meaning of their own native forms, but they have no way of judging statements made about a dialect which they do not speak, and they are naturally prone to accept such statements on the authority of the writer.

There is, however, much that we can do to show the internal relations in the nonstandard dialect as a system. There are a great many forms which seem different on the surface but can be explained as expressions of a single rule, or the absence of a single rule. We observe that in nonstandard Negro English it is common to say *a apple* rather than *an apple*. This is a grammatical fault from the point of view of standard speakers, and the school must teach *an apple* as the written, standard form. There is also a rather low-level, unimportant feature of pronunciation which is common to southern dialects: in *the apple*, the word *the* has the same pronunciation as in *the book* and does not rhyme with *be*. Finally, we can note that, in the South, educated white speakers keep the vocalic schwa which represents *r* in *four*, but nonstandard speakers tend to drop it (registered in dialect writing as *fo' o'clock*). When all these facts are put together, we can begin to explain the nonstandard *a apple* as part of a much broader pattern. There is a general rule of English which states that we do not pronounce two (phonetic) vowels in succession. Some kind of semiconsonantal glide or consonant comes in between: an *n* as in *an apple*, a *"y"* as in *the apple*, an *r* as in *four apples*. In each of these cases, this rule is not followed for nonstandard Negro English. A teacher may have more success in getting students to write *an apple* if he presents this general rule and connects up all of these things into a single rational pattern, even if some are not important in themselves. It will "make sense" to Negro speakers, since they do not drop *l* before a vowel, and many rules of their sound system show the effect of a following vowel.

There are many ways in which an understanding of the fundamental rules of the dialect will help to explain the surface facts. Some of the rules cited above are also important in explaining why nonstandard Negro speakers sometimes delete *is*, in *He is ready*, but almost always delete *are*, in *You are ready*; or why they say *they book* and *you book* but not *we book*. It does not always follow, though, that a grammatical explanation reveals the best method for teaching standard English.

Systematic analysis may also be helpful in connecting up the nonstandard form with the corresponding standard form and in this sense understanding the meaning of the nonstandard form. For example, nonstandard speakers say *Ain't nobody see it*. What is the nearest standard equivalent? We can connect this up with the standard negative "foregrounding" of *Scarcely did anybody see it* or, even more clearly, the literary expression *Nor did anybody see it*. This foregrounding fits in with the general colloquial southern pattern with indefinite subjects: *Didn't anybody see it*, nonstandard *Didn't nobody see it*. In these cases, the auxiliary *didn't* is brought to the front of the sentence, like the *ain't* in the nonstandard sentence. But there is another possibility. We could connect up *Ain't nobody see it* with the sentence *It ain't nobody see it*, that is, "There isn't anybody who sees it"; the dummy *it* of nonstandard Negro English corresponds to standard *there*, and, like *there*, it can be dropped in casual speech. Such an explanation is the only one possible in the case of such nonstandard sentences as *Ain't nothin' went down*. This could not be derived from *Nothin' ain't went down*, a sentence type which never occurs. If someone uses one of these forms, it is important for the teacher to know what was intended, so that he can supply the standard equivalent. To do so, one must know a great deal about many underlying rules of the nonstandard dialect, and also a great deal about the rules of English in general.

NONSTANDARD ENGLISH AS A CLOSE RELATIVE OF STANDARD ENGLISH

Differences between standard and nonstandard English are not as sharp as our first impressions would lead us to think. Consider, for example, the socially stratified marker of "pronominal apposition"—the use of a dependent pronoun in such sentences as

My oldest sister she worked at the bank.

Though most of us recognize this as a nonstandard pattern, it is not always realized that the "nonstandard" aspect is merely a slight difference in intonation. A standard speaker frequently says the same thing, with a slight break after the subject: *My oldest sister— she works at the bank, and she finds it very profitable.*

There are many ways in which a greater awareness of the standard colloquial forms would help teachers interpret the nonstandard forms. Not only do standard speakers use pronominal apposition with the break noted above, but in casual speech they can also bring object noun phrases to the front, "foregrounding" them. For example, one can say

My oldest sister—she worked at the Citizens Bank in Passaic last year.

The Citizens Bank, in Passaic—my oldest sister worked there last year.

Passaic—my oldest sister worked at the Citizens Bank there last year.

Note that if the foregrounded noun phrase represents a locative—the "place where"—then its position is held by *there*, just as the persons are represented by pronouns. If we are dealing with a time element, it can be foregrounded without replacement in any dialect: *Last year, my oldest sister worked at the Citizens Bank in Passaic.*

It is most important for the teacher to understand the relation between standard and nonstandard and to recognize that nonstandard English is a system of rules, different from the standard but not necessarily inferior as a means of communication. All of the teacher's social instincts, past training, and even faith in his own education lead him to believe that other dialects of English are merely "mistakes" without any rhyme or rationale.

In this connection, it will be helpful to examine some of the most general grammatical differences between English dialects spoken in the United States. One could list a very large number of "mistakes," but when they are examined systematically the great majority appear to be examples of a small number of differences in the rules. The clearest analysis of these differences has been made by Edward Klima (1964). He considers first the dialect in which people say sentences like

Who could she see?

Who did he speak with?

He knew who he spoke with.

The leader who I saw left.

The leader who he spoke with left.

What is the difference between this dialect and standard English? The usual schoolbook answer is to say that these are well-known mistakes in the use of *who* for *whom*. But such a general statement does not add any clarity to the situation; nor does it help the student to learn standard English. The student often leaves the classroom with no more than an uneasy feeling that *who* is incorrect and *whom* is correct. This is the state of half-knowledge that leads to hypercorrect forms such as *Whom did you say is calling?* In the more extreme cases, *whom* is seen as the only acceptable, polite form of the pronoun. Thus a certain receptionist at a hospital switchboard regularly answers the telephone: "Whom?"

The nonstandard dialect we see here varies from standard English by one simple difference in the order of rules. The standard language marks the objective case—the difference between *who* and *whom*—in a sentence form which preserves the original subject-object relation:

Q—She could see WH-someone.

The WH-symbol marks the point to be questioned in this sentence. When cases are marked in this sentence, the pronoun before the verb receives the unmarked subjective case and the pronoun after the verb the marked objective case.

Q—She (subjective case)—could—see—WH-someone (objective case).

The combination of WH, indefinite pronoun, and objective case is to be realized later as *whom*. At a later point, a rule of WH-*attraction* is applied which brings the WH-word to the beginning of the sentence:

Q—Whom—she—could—see.

and finally the Q-marker effects a reversal of the pronoun and auxiliary, yielding the final result:

Whom could she see?

Here the objective case of the pronoun refers to the underlying position of the questioned pronoun as object of the verb.

The nonstandard dialect also marks cases: *I, he, she, they* are subjective forms, and *me, him, her, them* are objective. But the case marking is done after, rather than before, the WH-attraction rule applies. We begin with the same meaningful structure, Q—*She could see* WH-*someone*, but the first rule to consider is Wh-*attraction:*

Q—*WH-someone—she—could—see.*

Now the rule of case marking applies. Since both pronouns are before the verb, they are both unmarked:

Q—*WH-someone (unmarked)—she (unmarked)—could see.*

Finally, the question flip-flop applies, and we have

Who could she see?

The same mechanism applies to all of the nonstandard forms given above.

We can briefly consider another nonstandard grammatical rule, that which yields *It's me* rather than *It's I.* The difference here lies again in the rule of case marking. As noted above, this rule marks pronouns which occur after verbs; but the copula is not included. The nonstandard grammar which gives us *It's me* differs from standard English in only one simple detail—the case-marking rule includes the verb *to be* as well as other verbs. It is certainly not true that this nonstandard grammar neglects the case-marking rule; on the contrary, it applies the rule more generally than standard English here. But the order of the rules is the same as that for the nonstandard grammar just discussed: we get *Who is he?* rather than *Whom is he?* Like the other verbs, the copula marks the pronoun only after WH-attraction has been applied.

In all of the examples just given, we can observe a general tendency towards simplification in the nonstandard grammars. There is a strong tendency to simplify the surface subjects—that is, the words which come before the verb. This is most obvious in pronominal apposition. The foregrounded part identifies the person talked about, *my oldest sister;* this person is then "given," and the "new" predication is made with a pronoun subject: *she worked at the Citizens Bank.*

A parallel tendency is seen in the nonstandard grammars which confine the objective marker to positions after the verb. But this tendency to simplify subjects is not confined to standard colloquial English. Sentences such as the following are perfectly grammatical but are seldom if ever found in ordinary speech:

For him to have broken his word so often was a shame.

Most often we find that the rule of "extraposition" has applied, moving the complex subject to the end of the sentence:

It was a shame for him to have broken his word so often.

In general, we find that nonstandard English dialects are not radically different systems from standard English but are instead closely related to it. These dialects show slightly different versions of the same rules, extending and modifying the grammatical processes which are common to all dialects of English.

Any analysis of the nonstandard dialect which pretends to ignore other dialects and the general rules of English will fail (1) because the nonstandard dialect is *not* an isolated system but a part of the sociolinguistic structure of English, and (2) because of the writer's knowledge of standard English. But it would be unrealistic to think that we can write anything but a superficial account of the dialect if we confine our thinking to this one subsystem and ignore whatever progress has been made in the understanding of [standard] English grammar.

REFERENCES

Klima, E. 1964. "Relatedness Between Grammatical Systems," *Language,* 40, 1–30.

A Lot of Talk About Nothing

SHIRLEY BRICE HEATH

Editor's introduction

Shirley Brice Heath's work builds upon the studies of researchers like Labov, emphasizing the logic governing language styles of different social, economic, and cultural groups. But her work was also groundbreaking in the ways she clearly articulated how schools are biased toward certain language patterns, ignoring the language strengths of students who aren't from mainstream cultures. This article presents findings from her landmark study *Ways with Words*. In the interview that follows, she talks further about the influence of this work on teachers and her own later studies of language and culture.

Inside a third-grade classroom described by the principal as a class of "low achievers," several pairs of children are working over tape recorders in dialogues with each other. One small group of children is dressed in costumes performing "Curious George" scenes for a few kindergartners who are visiting. Yet another group is preparing illustrations for a story told by one of their classmates and now being heard on tape as they talk about why their drawings illustrate the words they hear. A lot of talk about nothing? Why are these children who presumably lack basic skills in language arts not spending their time with obvious instruction from the teacher in reading, writing and listening?

These are students in the classroom of a teacher-researcher who has adapted information about the oral and written language experiences of these children at home into a new language arts curriculum for school. She has developed for her children a program in which they spend as much of the day as possible talking—to each other and the teacher, and to fifth- and sixth-graders who come into the class one-half hour each day to read to small groups. This teacher has 30 children and no aides; she enlisted the help of fifth- and sixth-grade teachers who were willing to have some of their students write stories for the younger children and read to them several days of each week. The kindergarten teacher helps out by sending a few of her children for the third-graders to read to each week.

Talk in the classroom is about personal experiences, stories, expository textbook materials and, perhaps most important, about their own and others' talk. Their teacher gives no reading or writing task which is not surrounded by talk about the content knowledge behind the task and the kinds of language skills—oral and written—needed to tackle the task.

Since the beginning of the year, the teacher has asked visitors from the community into her class to talk about their ways of talking and to explain what they read and write at home and at work. The chil-

Source: "A Lot of Talk About Nothing" by S. B. Heath, 1983, *Language Arts, 60* (8), pp. 39–48. Copyright 1983 by the National Council of Teachers of English. Reprinted with permission.

dren have come to think of themselves as language "detectives," listening and learning to describe the talk of others. Grocery clerks have to use many politeness terms, and the questions they ask most often of customers require only a yes or no answer. On the other hand, guides at the local nature museum talk in "long paragraphs," describing what is around them and usually asking questions only at the end of one of their descriptions. The children have also learned to analyze their talk at home, beginning early in the year with a simple record of the types of questions they hear asked at home, and moving later in the year to interviews with their parents about the kinds of talking, reading and writing they do at their jobs.

The teacher in this classroom comments on her own talk and the language of textbooks, of older students, and of the third-graders themselves during each day. "Show and tell" time, usually reserved for only first-graders, occurs each day in this class, under the supervision of a committee of students who decide each week whether those who participate in this special time of the day will: (1) narrate about an experience they or someone else has had, (2) describe an event or object without including themselves or another animate being, or (3) read from their diary or journal for a particular day. The children use terms such as *narrative, exposition,* and *diary* or *journal* with ease by the end of the year. Increasingly during the year, the children use "show and tell" time to talk, not about their own direct experiences, but about content areas of their classroom. Also by the end of the year, the children are using this special time of the day for presenting skits about a social studies or science unit. They have found that the fifth- and sixth-graders can offer assistance on these topics, and planning such a presentation guarantees the attention of the upper classmen. By the end of the year, most of these children score above grade level on reading tests, and they are able to write stories, as well as paragraphs of exposition on content areas with which they feel comfortable in their knowledge. This is clearly no longer a class of "low achievers."

TEACHERS AS RESEARCHERS

All of these ideas sound like pedagogical practices that many good teachers bring intuitively to their instruction. What was different about the motivations of this third-grade teacher for approaching language arts in these ways? The teacher described here was one of a group of teacher-researchers who cooperated with me for several years during the 1970s. I worked as an ethnographer, a daily participant and observer in homes and communities similar to those of the children in their classrooms, studying the ways in which the children learned to use oral and written language. As I studied the children at home, the teachers focused on their own language uses at home and in the classroom. We brought our knowledge together for comparison and as the baseline data from which to consider new methods and approaches in language arts.

We do not need educational research to tell us that different types of attention spans, parental support systems, and peer pressures can create vast differences among children in the same classroom, school, or community. But what of more subtle features of background differences, such as the amount and kind of talk addressed by adults to children and solicited from children? How can teachers and researchers work together to learn more about children's language experiences at home? And what can this knowledge mean for classroom practice?

For nearly a decade, living and working in three communities located within a few miles of each other in the southeastern part of the United States, I collected information on ways in which the children of these communities learned to use language: (1) Roadville is a white working-class community, (2) Trackton is a black working-class community in which many of the older members have only recently left work as sharecroppers on nearby farms, (3) the townspeople, black and white residents of a cluster of mainstream, school-oriented neighborhoods, are school teachers, local business owners, and executives of the textile mills.

Children from the three groups respond differently to school experiences. Roadville children are successful in the first years of the primary grades. Most Trackton children are not successful during this period, and only a few begin in the higher primary grades to move with adequate success through their classes. Most of the mainstream children of the townspeople, black and white, are successful in school and obtain a high school diploma with plans to go on to higher education. Children from backgrounds similar to those of these three groups make up the majority of the students in many regions of the southeastern United States. They bring to their classrooms different patterns of learning and using oral and written language, and their patterns of academic achievement vary greatly.

Intuitively, most teachers are aware of the different language background experiences children bring to school, but few means exist for providing teachers with information about these differences and their implications for classroom practice. Recent development of the notion of "teacher-as-researcher" has begun to help bridge the long-standing gap between researcher and teacher. This approach pairs the roles of teacher and researcher in a cooperative search for answers to questions raised by the teacher about what is happening in the classroom and why. Answering *why* questions more often than not calls for knowledge about the background experiences of both children and teachers. Thus, researcher working with teacher can help bridge yet another gap—that between the classroom and the homes of students.

Throughout most of the decade of the 1970s, I worked in the Piedmont Carolinas with teachers in several districts as research partners. Together, we addressed the questions teachers raised during the sometimes tumultuous early years of desegregation and ensuing shifts of curricular and testing policies. These teachers accepted the fact that language was fundamental to academic achievement, and their primary concerns related to how they could help children learn to use oral and written language in ways that would bring successful classroom experiences. They asked hard questions of language research. Why were some children seemingly unable to answer straightforward questions? Why were some students able to give elaborate directions and tell fantastic stories on the playground, but unable to respond to assignments calling for similar responses about lesson materials? Why did some children who had achieved adequate success in their first two or three years of school begin to fail in the upper primary grades?

In the 1960s, social scientists had described the language habits of groups of youngsters who were consistently failing to achieve academic excellence. The teachers with whom I worked were familiar with these studies, which had been carried out primarily in black urban areas. Most accepted the fact that children who spoke a nonstandard variety of English had learned a rule-governed language system and, moreover, that these students reflected learned patterns of "logic," considerable facility in handling complicated forms of oral discourse, and adeptness in shifting styles. But knowing this information about language learned at home did not answer the kinds of questions

noted above about classroom performance. Neither did it provide for development of improved classroom materials and practices.

ETHNOGRAPHY OF COMMUNICATION

Late in the 1970s, as some language researchers tried to describe the contexts in which children of different cultures learned to use language, they turned to ethnographic methods. Participating and observing over many months and even years in the daily lives of the group being studied, these researchers, who were often anthropologists, focused on oral and written language uses. My work in Roadville, Trackton, and among the townspeople centered on the children of these groups as they learned the ways of acting, believing and valuing around them in their homes and communities. Following the suggestions of anthropologist Dell Hymes, who first proposed in 1964 that ethnographers focus on communication, I lived and worked within these three groups to describe where, when, to whom, how, and with what results children were socialized as talkers, readers and writers. The three communities—located only a few miles apart—had radically different ways of using language and of seeing themselves in communication with their children.

Roadville parents believe they have to teach their children to talk, and they begin their task by talking with infants, responding to their initial sounds as words. They respond with full sentences, varying their tone of voice and emphasis, and affectionately urging infants to turn their heads in the direction of the speaker. As they talk to their infants and young children, they label items in the environment, and as children begin to talk, adults ask many teaching questions: "Where's your nose?" "Can you find Daddy's shoes?" Adults fictionalize their youngsters in talk about them: "He's a little cowboy; see those boots? See that cowboy strut?" Parents read to their children and ask them to name items in books, answer questions about the book's contents and, as they get older, to sit quietly listening to stories read to them. Parents buy coloring and follow-the-number books for their children and tutor them in staying within the lines and coloring items appropriately. All of these habits relate to school practices, and they are transferred to the early years of reading and writing in school. Yet, by the fourth grade many of these children seem to find the talking, reading and writing tasks in school foreign, and their academic achievement begins to decline.

In nearby Trackton, adults immerse their children in an ongoing stream of talk from extended family members and a wide circle of friends and neighbors. Children become the responsibility of all members of the community, and from birth they are kept in the center of most adult activities, including eating, sleeping, or playing. Adults talk about infants and young children, and as they do so, they fictionalize them and often exaggerate their behaviors and physical features. They nickname children and play teasing games with them. They ask young children for specific information which is not known to adults: "Where'd that come from?" "You want what?" By the time they are toddlers, these children begin to tell stories, recounting events or describing objects they have seen. Adults stop and listen to their stories occasionally, but such stories are most often addressed to other children who challenge, extend, tease, or build from the youngster's tales. By about 2, children begin to enter ongoing conversations by actively attracting adults' attention with some physical gesture and then making a request, registering a complaint, or reporting an event. Very quickly, these children are accepted as communicating members of the group, and adults respond directly to them as conversational partners.

Most of these children first go to school with enthusiasm, but by the end of the first half of the first grade, many are coming home with reports that their teacher scolds them for talking too much and working too little. By the third grade, many Trackton children have established a record of failures which often they do not break in the rest of their school careers.

After hearing from me how children of these communities learned to use language, some of their teachers agreed to work with me to study either their own uses of language with their preschoolers at home or those of their mainstream friends. They found that when talking to very young infants, they asked questions, simplified their sentences, used special words and changed their tone of voice. Moreover, since most of these mainstream mothers did not work outside the home while their children were very young, they spent long hours each day alone with their pre-schoolers as their primary conversational partners. They arranged many outings, usually with other mothers through voluntary associations, such as their church groups or local social memberships.

These teachers' findings about mainstreamers' uses of language with their pre-schoolers indicated that they and the Roadville parents had many language socialization habits in common. Parents in both communities talked to their children and focused their youngsters' attention at an early age on labels, pictures in books, and educational toys. Both groups played with their children and participated in planned outings and family recreation with them. Yet mainstream children and Roadville children fared very differently in their progress through the middle primary grades.

A close look at the home habits of these two groups indicated that a major difference lay in the amount of running narrative or ongoing commentary in which mainstream parents immersed their young children. As these youngsters pass their first birthday, mothers and other adults who are part of their daily network begin to provide a running commentary on events and items surrounding the child. In these commentaries, adults tell the child what is happening: "Mummy's going to get her purse, and then we're going to take a ride. Mummy's got to go to the post office." As soon as the child begins to talk, adults solicit these kinds of running commentaries: they ask children what they are doing with their toys, what they did when they were at someone else's house, and what they had to eat on a trip to the grocery store. These requests for running descriptions and cumulative accounts of past actions provide children in these families with endless hours of practice of all the sentence-level features necessary to produce successful narratives or recounts of experiences.

In using their own experiences as data, children begin their developmental progression of story conventions and narrative structures which they will be asked to replay in school from the first day of school through their college courses. They learn either to use an existing animate being or to create a fantastic one as the central actor in their stories; they take these actors through events in which they may meet obstacles on their way to a goal. The scripts of the stories that the children have heard read to them and the narratives that have surrounded them and storied their own and others' experiences are replayed with different actors and slightly different settings. Gradually, children learn to open and close stories, to give them a setting and movement of time, and occasionally, even to sum up the meaning of the story in a moralistic pronouncement ("He shouldn't have gone without his mother"). Some children move from linking a collection of events related to one another only by their immediacy of experience for the child to tying a story together by incorporating a central point, a constant goal or direction, and a point of view which may not be that of the child as experiencer and narrator.

When children are very young toddlers, parents talk of and ask children about events of the here-and-now: the immediate tasks of eating, getting dressed, and playing with a particular toy or person. Of older toddlers, adults increasingly ask questions about events that occurred in the past—tasks, settings, and events that the child is expected to recount from memory. These recountings are, however, then interpreted by adults or older siblings in a future frame: "Do you want to go again?" "Do you think Billy's mother will be able to fix the broken car?" Questioners ask children to express their views about future events and to link past occurrences with what will come in the future.

In many ways, all of this is "talk about nothing," and adults and older siblings in these mainstream households model and elicit these kinds of narratives without being highly conscious of their having a didactic purpose or a heavily positive transfer value to school activities. Yet when teacher-researchers examined closely the instructional situations of the classrooms into which these children usually go, they found that, from first-grade reading circles to upper-primary social studies group work, the major activity is producing some sort of commentary on events or objects. In the early primary years, teachers usually request commentary in the form of labels or names of attributes of items or events ("What did the boy in our story find on his walk?"). Later, the requests are for descriptive commentary ("Who are some community helpers? What kinds of jobs do they do for us?"). Gradually the requests are mixed and students have to learn when it is appropriate to respond with labels or features (brief names or attributes of events or objects), fantastic stories, straightforward descriptions, or interpretations in which they comment on the outcome of events, the relative merits of objects, or the internal states of characters.

A CLOSER LOOK

On the surface, these summaries of the early language socialization of the children from these three communities support a commonly held idea about links between language at home and at school: the more parents talk to their children, the more likely children are to succeed in school. Yet the details of the differences and similarities across these three communities suggest that this correlation is too simple. Trackton children hear and take part in far more talk around them than the children of either Roadville or the townspeople. Yet, for them, more talk does not have a positive transfer value to the current, primary-level practices of the school. Roadville children have less talk addressed to them than the townspeople's children. Yet, from an early age, they are helped to focus on labels and features of items and events. They are given books and they are read to by parents who buy educational toys for their children and spend many hours playing with their toddlers. As the children grow older, these parents involve their children in handicrafts, home building projects, and family recreational activities such as camping and fishing. Both Trackton and Roadville parents have strong faith in schooling as a positive value for their children, and they believe success in school will help their children get jobs better than those they have held as adults. Yet, neither Roadville nor Trackton children manage to achieve the same patterns of sustained academic success children of townspeople achieve with relatively little apparent effort. Why?

A primary difference seems to be the amount of "talk about nothing" with which the townspeople surround their children and into which they socialize their young. Through their running narratives, which begin almost at the birth of the child, they seemingly focus the attention of their young on objects and events while they point out verbally the labels and features of those that the child should perceive and later talk about. It is as though, in the drama of life, these parents freeze scenes and parts of scenes repeatedly throughout each day. Within the frame of a single scene, they focus the child's attention, sort out labels to name, and give the child ordered turns for sharing talk about these labels and the properties of the objects or events to which they refer; adult and child thus jointly narrate descriptions of scenes. Through this consistent focus, adults pull out some of the stimuli in the array surrounding the child and make these stand still for cooperative examination and narration between parent and child. Later occurrences of the same event or object are identified by adults who call the child's attention to similarities and differences. Thus, townspeople's children are not left on their own to see these relations between two events or to explore ways of integrating something in a new context to its old context. These children learn to attend to items both in real life and in books, both in and out of their usual locations, as they practice throughout their pre-school years running narratives with adults.

In much of their talk, mainstream adults ask: "What do you call that?" "Do you remember how to say the name of that?" Thus, children are alerted to attend to the particulars to talk about talk: names, ways of retelling information, and ways of linking what one has told with something that has gone before. Thus, mainstreamers' children hear a lot of talk about talk and are forced to focus on not only the features and names of the world around them, but also on their ways of communicating about that world. From the earliest days of their infancy, these habits are modeled repeatedly for them, and as soon as they learn to talk, they are called upon to practice similar verbal habits. Day in and day out during their pre-school years, they hear and practice the kinds of talk in which they will display successful learning in school.

The teacher in the third-grade classroom described at the beginning of this essay recognized that her students needed intense and frequent occasions to learn and practice those language uses they had not acquired at home. She therefore created a classroom that focused on talk—all kinds of talk. The children labeled, learned to name the features of everyday items and events, told stories, described their own and others' experiences, and narrated skits, puppet shows, and slide exhibits.

Many classrooms include such activities for portions of the day or week; others provide some of these activities for some children. A critical difference in the case given here, however, and one driven by a perspective gained from being part of a research team, was the amount of talk about talk in this classroom. School-age children are capable of—and can be quite proficient at—stepping back from and commenting upon their own and others' activities, *if* the necessary skills are modeled and explicated. In this classroom, and in others which drew from ethnographic data on the home life of their students, teachers and visitors to the classroom called attention to the ways they used language: how they asked questions, showed politeness, got what they wanted, settled arguments, and told funny stories. With early and intensive classroom opportunities to surround learning with many different kinds of talk and much talk about talk, children from homes and communities whose uses of language do not match those of the school *can* achieve academic success. A frequently heard comment, "Talk is cheap," is, in these days of bankrupt school districts and economic cutbacks, perhaps worth a closer examination—for more reasons than one.

Crawling on the Bones of What We Know: An Interview with Shirley Brice Heath

●●

by Brenda Miller Power

In talking with Shirley Brice Heath, you realize that Heath accomplishes more in a day than most of us manage in a week. A faculty member at Stanford University since 1980, Heath's study *Ways with Words: Language, Life and Work in Communities and Classrooms* is recognized as one of the most important language research projects of all time. A 10-year qualitative longitudinal study of differences in language among lower-income whites, middle-income blacks and whites, and lower-income blacks in the Piedmont range, *Ways with Words* (Cambridge University Press, 1983) demolished some long-held axioms about language norms. The study was awarded the David Russell Research Award from the National Council of Teachers of English in 1984. Heath has received many other awards and accolades for her research, including the prestigious MacArthur Fellowship in 1984.

On the day we chatted, it was 8 p.m. Heath's time. Heath had just finished emotional goodbyes with her freshman English students after the last class of the quarter. Earlier in the day, she had read through all the applications for an English department position on her faculty. Heath had also found time that day to send out some ethics guidelines for youth reporting to hundreds of newspaper editors across the country. Loose ends from her just-completed research trip to a rare-book library in Boston were tied up, and plans for a conference and museum display in England she is coordinating were developed. What you realize in talking to Heath is that she not only uses the full 24 hours in her workday, she has more fun in the process than most of us manage in a month of Sundays!

What this interview also reveals is Heath's heartfelt commitment to teaching. While most researchers of her stature have long since given up most of the daily practice of teaching, Heath finds herself in the classroom 4 days a week, working with the youngest students on the Stanford campus. After more than 30 years in the field, Heath still provides fresh insights into all of the possibilities for language research in schools and communities. And she sees these possibilities through a teacher's eyes.

Brenda Power: Can you tell me what led you into language research?

Shirley Brice Heath: I think what got me most interested in language was both the gentle gift and curse of where and how I grew up. My parents weren't around very much, so I lived with foster families and a grandmother in a mostly black area for much of my early life. I grew up around children who were speaking varieties of English, so I grew up speaking these varieties. I think southern African-American vernacular was my first dialect. My grandmother would also shift across these dialects. So, I had an intrinsic interest in language, but no education whatsoever. I grew up in southwestern Virginia in a corner of the tobacco growing area of the state. The nearest town was about 60 miles away. There wasn't anyone around with a sophistication about language; people just knew how to communicate.

Then I began teaching when I was in college. The natural thing for me to do was to begin to teach about aspects of language. So that's what I began doing, teaching English as a second language to so-called "mentally retarded" kids in California. They weren't mentally retarded, they were Spanish-speaking! I have continued these interests in English as a second language and dialect work all my life.

BP: I was just rereading the first section of Ways with Words *where you talk about your research process. It was interesting thinking of you as a beginning language researcher. I couldn't help but connect your work with the process of teachers doing language research in their classrooms. It seems so natural the way you merged your life with your research interests.*

SH: It's been quite curious to me that no one ever looks at *Ways with Words* as an illustration of teacher research. From my point of view, those teachers that I learned from were some of the best researchers I ever worked with. They're not seen as teacher researchers in the way we typically use that term today. I think that for me, as it was for many women before the present generation, a lot of learning to teach was learning by intuition. We were always working in new situations, and those were the situations that for the most part didn't come up in the textbook cases. We had learned our Thorndike, and we learned our William S. Gray, and all the things you could teach in textbook cases. But a lot of what you did in the classroom was based on intuition. As we know now, many women went into teaching because they were highly creative, highly professional, and highly committed to getting something new for themselves, as well as doing something for their students.

This is a very delicate balance that I believe in many cases we've lost these days. Teachers always need to get something for themselves out of teaching. We spend a lot of time talking about what teachers could be doing and should be doing for their students. I suspect if you talked to most of us over 40, we would say we got into teaching because it was a way of learning. It was a way of pushing ourselves. I grew up in a three-room school, where I was always teaching someone else or learning on my own while waiting to be taught by the teacher. That was what started me in this interest of watching how people learn and teaching others to learn about the most effective ways of getting them to learn. Teacher research is an important concept now, but teacher research comes out of a spirit that many of us had carried on for many years. Any time you're teaching, you have to be getting an awful lot in terms of what you're learning about learning.

BP: The delicate balance is between your own learning and what it is you're doing for others?

SH: Right. That is still true now for me. I never teach the same course twice. It may have the same title. But I tell students, "if you talk to someone who has taken this course before, it will not be the same course they took." I cannot teach the same class twice—I would become so bored. That doesn't mean I won't teach some of the same strategies or principles, but I have to teach it through a different medium. You can never step into the same river twice. I have to be coming to new knowledge or new ways all the time. I hope it's a way of getting students to think that there is this incredible adventure or romance (or whatever you want to call it that doesn't trivialize it) out there in learning. There is so much to learn. Every little venture into that path is just that—an adventure. Part of the adventure is finding our learning self.

BP: Let's switch gears just a bit. In terms of finding your learning self, in Ways with Words *we get these glimpses of you with your daughter going to baby-sit, or standing at an ironing board. When or how did you start turning the tape recorder on? How did you get into the process of detailed analysis of language?*

SH: I've always been interested in the grains of sand. I'm not so interested in the dunes on the beach. Once I can understand the grains, I can lift my head and see the dunes. I was always listening and watching for the grains of sand. I was looking at the way a head was held when some laughter came around the table. I was always observing the responses to a joke by males or females. That enabled me to have something of a photographic memory of scenes.

In terms of tape recorders, I was determined not to bring things in that weren't indigenous to the community and tape recorders were not as common as they are now. Once I could write things down, because I had paid such attention to the grains, I could recreate a scene almost nod by nod. That happens to be a talent that has stuck with me all my life. I can walk into a situation, and if I'm in my observing mode (which I usually am), I can recreate that incident or situation almost down to the minute detail within a few hours after the event.

BP: Maybe we're missing the boat by emphasizing tape recording in language research so much. You seem to be talking about the teacher or researcher as the instrument, and developing yourself as the instrument. It's a whole lot more involved than turning on the tape recorder and doing some transcribing. It's about living in the moment— that moment-to-moment awareness of those nuances.

SH: Absolutely. It's one thing I try so hard to do in training my students. I try to get them to think of themselves always as the research instrument. Your questionnaire, your survey, your interview or think-aloud protocol are nothing more than additional instruments. Certainly now I use tape recordings because they help. They allow you to retrieve the data in ways that other people can look at it as well. But *you* are the key instrument, and you must keep that instrument on all the time.

For myself, this is what's most important in long-term anthropological work. It is both a great advantage and a great disadvantage. Once you get habituated to close observation, it's very difficult to cut it off. You're on at the dinner table, you're on at the family holiday party. It's not a particularly healthy state in which to handle human relations!

BP: I've experienced that inability to turn it off myself at times.

SH: My friends say to me that I'm always living on the edge. I'm always putting myself in these new positions where I have to pick up every new cue in order to survive.

BP: One of the challenges that will face readers of this book is the many ways language can be analyzed. If someone is just beginning, what advice do you have for them?

SH: I think the first advice I have is to listen generically. Then you need to ask yourself, what are you hearing as the major kinds of differences? Are you hearing differences between the playground and classroom? Where would you demarcate time and space and language differences? I think time and space are neutral. If I said, "How would you demarcate the cultural differences in your classroom?" all kinds of things come roaring into the air. I have people look at spatial and time differences, and then begin to tease apart other differences. What language do children use when they are creating the rules for a game on the playground, as opposed to monitoring a game? These are the patterns we need to observe and then track how these vary with surrounding situations. Cultural or ethnic differences are always situated.

I often talk with my students in my freshman classes about how I talk to them. I talk early in the term more formally than I do the last month of class. By the last four weeks of class, I know them so well that I am teasing them. I know them by nicknames, I'm giving them my own nickname. I ask them to notice the changes in language, and then think about why my language has changed. What is the knowledge base? What are my presuppositions that cause these changes? The first few weeks of class, students think I'm the meanest woman on campus. But by the end, they see I'm a firm but warm person. I ask about how much sleep they got the night before, I give them teasing directions about how to get to my house for dinner.

BP: My language pattern with students is similar. It's an issue of student power for me. I think it does give students more power early in the semester if the boundaries are firm and fair. I've been embarrassed more than once early in the term when a student calls as they're being wheeled into the emergency room, or from a funeral home, to explain an absence. They know how strict I am about attendance and checking in. But those clear boundaries are critical for all of us. They know the rules, and there is safety in that.

SH: That's exactly the way I feel about it. I say, "I would love to have you stay if you want to work within the rules. Make no mistake—these are my rules. But they are rules for your safety, because you always know where you stand."

In the recent work I've done with inner-city kids, it's clear that they yearn for people who will give them strict guidelines. They want to know where they stand. I was with a high school teacher last week in Boston who was grading her end-of-term papers. She read from one of them to me. It was from a high school senior who was doing drugs and staying out all night and running around with her boyfriend. The student used this wonderful expression, "I'm constantly daring my parents to show me they care." What a wonderful expression! I *dare* you to care. I think a lot of times we're afraid to show we care by setting down very strict rules. I want students to observe and feel those safety nets.

BP: *I think this does circle back to teachers' language. Teachers wonder what their role is in a whole language classroom or writer's workshop, when they read so much about students being in control. Teachers read that children should set the curriculum, and the teacher is just an equal participant. I think to believe this you'd have to ignore the social structures in your classroom. There is never complete equality among students. The language patterns are important—between peers and with the teacher. If you do want to understand issues of control, you have to look closely at your language and that of your students.*

SH: That's so true. I will also often say to students, "Reflect on how your own language has changed." As you know from *Ways with Words*, I learned that from Mrs. Gardiner who would have her second graders talk about the way their language changed. These kids were also noticing the way the principal talked on the intercom differed from the way he talked to them when he said hello in the hall.

I had a student in my freshman English class this term who used this incredibly convoluted language. His high school teacher had taught him that when in doubt, use the word with the greatest number of syllables. Of course, when he came into my class, I said, when in doubt, use the quickest and fastest Anglo-Saxon word you can find. And *don't ever* write "utilize" in my class! "Use" will do fine, thank you. By the end of the term, he said, "I know I'm changing some of my habits finally, but they die hard. I was so attuned to that SAT mentality. I thought if I had the vocabulary, I had to use it." I told him, "Most of us can read those words, but we don't *speak* them. We don't create sentences just to put five-syllable words in them." He reflected on how he changed, how it was changing his language in other classes. That's the point—to crawl on the bones of what you know, instead of flying above it.

One of the things we do is have "grandma" talks in class. After my freshmen have done their research studies, I have them talk about the research in class as if they were explaining it to their grandmother. I tell them, "If you haven't done work that you can talk about in words that others can understand, you haven't done anything that's good for you." I want my students to leave class knowing how to have a good, intelligent conversation.

BP: *What are you working on now?*

SH: I'm working on several different things, which is my usual bent. I've been doing research into 16th century manuscripts from Bolivia and Peru, working on the history of the Aymara in the highlands of Latin America. Though I'm giving up my Latin American work, I haven't given up my interest in social history.

What I'm working on now is the manuscript library of a woman who was a vicar's wife in Lincolnshire, England in the early 18th century. She created the only manuscript library for children that we now have in existence. It's over 400 different pieces in over 20 sets of reading materials for young children. She had three children of her own. I have worked with the manuscripts in rare book libraries over five years. I'm preparing for an opening to a conference that will be held in Cambridge, England in April on her work. It's called "Scrapbooks and Chapbooks: Visions of Domestic Literacy In the 18th Century." I've also been looking at all the ladies' magazines and novels published at this time to figure out what this mother might have been reading, what might have influenced her in creating this marvelous set of materials for her children. I've arranged an exhibition that I'll be setting up and artistically designing for the Fitzwilliam Museum in Cambridge, England. That's going to be great fun. It's called "Hand-Made Readings."

I'm also continuing to do the work on the lives of inner-city youth. That work is with Milbrey McLaughlin in youth organizations. We have just this year finished the first year of our work with youth in rural and midsized towns. We're looking at issues related to causes of violence and how kids spend their time. Knowing that kids spend 78% of their time *not* in classrooms, how do they spend their discretionary time? What are they doing? What's available for kids? How are they using oral and written language and other symbol systems in that space of time?

As always, I have practical things going, too. I have just come back from a meeting with the American Society for Newspaper Editors. The issue of representation of youth in American newspapers was what I talked about. I'm trying to get them to establish a code of ethics and principles of operation with respect to the presentation of youth. I just today arranged for a report on young people's reading of newspapers to be reproduced for all the members of the society. I hope I can influence some people to think more positively about young people and the ways we represent them.

BP: It's interesting to me in terms of youths that you've talked a lot about teaching freshmen. I think academics reading this interview might be surprised that you're not working solely with graduate students. With your research agenda, they might even be surprised that you're still teaching.

SH: People are always very surprised. In fact, I'm working with a number of research networks across the country where it suddenly hit me like a great dash of cold water between the eyes that most other members of these teams were teaching only graduate students, or they weren't teaching at all.

I'm usually teaching four days a week. I've had a conversation with people about this over the last few months. An anthropologist can't spend a lot of her time going to class meetings because you have to be in field sites. You can't simply pull up your database on the computer. Your database exists in the boys' and girls' clubs in a city that's 1,500 miles away. I've had to rethink the frenetic pace of my life, particularly as this manuscript work is coming to a head with the conference and a book.

One of the things that is amusing to me is that people are surprised at how rarely I teach graduate students. I don't teach graduate courses more than once a year. Most of my classes are undergraduate, and my favorite classes are with first-quarter freshmen. I *love* getting them early, because I can really exert some influence over them at that point. I can make them think seriously about what their intellectual life might be like at Stanford. Everyone else is telling them to take advantage of all there is to do at Stanford and in the Bay Area. I'm saying that this is the only time you'll have four years of an intellectual life. Live it to the fullest. I'm not saying don't have any fun, but an intellectual life can be fun as well.

BP: What would you call yourself—teacher, researcher, ethnographer?

SH: When I'm asked by strangers, the first thing I say is that I'm an anthropologist. And then I say that I'm an anthropologist who studies the way that people use language and culture in all sorts of settings, from the hillsides of New Guinea to freshmen English courses in America.

Secondly, I see myself as a social historian. These two are encased in the notion that I'm ever the teacher-researcher. I don't know how to be one without the other.

BP: It only makes sense that you'd like to work with first-year students. From an anthropological perspective, they are the most interesting culture on campus.

SH: Exactly. They bring so much that they haven't sorted out. They have to sort it out at the same time that they are living in a totally new culture. A lot of my students come to me after the first few weeks and ask for help with something they are having a hard time figuring out. You can see quite literally how they are working their way through this new culture.

I am first and foremost an anthropologist. Studying the uses of language and culture in all sorts of different settings includes dealing with the reading of literature, the learning of reading, the reading of children's literature, why people read certain kinds of literature, why is the reading of children's literature in the western world so different than it is in other cultures. . . . When you say that you're an anthropologist and the province of your study is language and culture, you realize you're either incredibly arrogant, or naive, or both. There isn't much that's left out of that province. As my friend Milbrey says, living life with these kinds of questions means a life with no seams.

BP: One of the things that impresses me is that you really have broken all the rules. You were doing ethnography when few people were, especially within the place you were living. You don't have a clear, systematic profile to your research. Your research is all over the place. This is not the way you're supposed to build a professional life, according to. . . .

SH: According to all the rules. What's interesting is that I'm on a search committee in our English department here, and I read all the candidate files today. It's clear that the top four or five candidates are very much all over the map already. Whatever they've done, they've done well. But they are not confined to a narrow set of questions. They also borrowed from many different disciplines. It's no accident that those folks rose to the top of the pile for us. This is what interdisciplinary means—you're able to bring to your region of interest a multitude of interests, and you can apply them in a very disciplined and theory-based way. It's something that it took me a long time to learn. I look at these new young candidates. I think, "Oh my gosh, you're so young! How did you learn to do that so quickly?" It is extremely impressive when young people can pull it off so well. I feel I'm continually learning how to do it better.

In my case, it had nothing to do with thinking that this was the way to do it, or that I was smart or theoretically advanced. It had to do with what is characteristic of the way I've run my life. I've never been able to figure out what I am going to be when I grow up. That meant that I found it necessary to explore lots and lots of things. Someone once said to me, "If I asked you for a recipe for apple pie, you'd take me all the way back to the story of Adam and Eve. You never know where to stop." It's irritating for people, but it has to do with my sense that I'm not sure I know something well enough yet. I have to go off into this other little branch or that new direction.

That was certainly the case in my first work in the 1960s on the history of Mexican language policy. I started with the arrival of Cortez. But then I said, "Gee. How come he had this woman at the border when he arrived on the shores of Mexico who could already speak Spanish? Hmm. This is very strange." So then I had to search back to her origins, to find out that she had been taken captive and had been in Cuba with earlier Conquistadors.

That's an example of how I get captivated by a question. It's those questions that keep teaching exciting. Those are the same kinds of questions you ask about every student in your class. "What is it about her that enables her to reach around these questions in this way? What is it about him that enables him to see only these dimensions, or to prefer this style of writing? How can I challenge him to move out into more conversational styles?" You're constantly pushing the boundaries.

BP: It's almost a passion for the ordinary. It's being engaged where you are right now, linked to what you talked about earlier in looking for the nuances, following back to the earliest threads.

SH: The passion for the ordinary is the passion for the grains of sand. Seeing in every grain of sand how it is that that grain goes to make up certain kinds of dunes, that respond in certain ways to the wild oats or to the wind, or give you a certain feel between the toes. It is definitely trying to get that understanding.

I talk to my freshmen students about it, in terms of this adventure story I'm working on about this 18th century woman. I try to imagine what it must have been like to sit around the hearth of her home in 1737. How much of Jane Austen's *Emma* is there? How much can I recreate? It means I've gotten back into the ballads of the time. I'm researching the nursery furniture. Given her level of income, what kind of furniture would she have been likely to have? I actually found the house that she and her husband built in the 1750s. It is a sense of trying to recreate it all.

A friend reading *Ways with Words* asked me, "Shirley, *why* did you have to tell us that the doily around the lamp was starched? What *difference* does it make?" I said, "Oh, it makes all the difference in the world! Don't you understand? It's an indication of the way the Roadville people lined and circled everything." That circle around the doily and the stiffness in it is emblematic of the furniture lined against the walls, of the kinds of stories they told of domestic labor by women. It's not that you expect consistency in a culture, but there are certain consistencies in the ways that these people used space to provide boundaries and to get a sense of place.

BP: That starched doily is the grain that can tell more than a dozen language transcripts.

SH: Especially when you see that and compare it with the way the middle-class people line up their furniture and trim their hedges and leave their tables bare with no starched doilies. I can still close my eyes and see the color of those shears, and when they first got electric shears. I can still see them on Saturday mornings with those shears and those crazy long extension cords. It's those grains, all piled together, that begin to give you a sense of the dunes.

BP: One last thing I wanted to ask. Every time I read your work or hear you speak it's something that's almost totally different than what I've heard before from you. Do you ever get bored with people asking you about Ways with Words, *because you have such a diverse agenda?*

SH: I don't get bored. I sometimes wish that people wouldn't stay with what they regard as the classics. I'm delighted that people like *Ways with Words*, and I'm delighted they've learned from it. But we need to move on beyond that. There are so many new interesting questions now. Not that they are more interesting than some of the questions raised there at that time. In a sense, I'm very gratified and honored, but I'm saddened that there isn't more opportunity, particularly for graduate students, to read more widely, to seek more widely, to expand their grasp of a whole range of things beyond what's already recognized.

Extension: Historical Perspectives and Landmark Studies

REAL LIFE'S REAL WORDS: LISTENING CLOSELY TO LANGUAGE

All classroom language communities are unique. "Normal" language development encompasses a wide range of cultures, styles, and standards. You can use your knowledge of language development—and build on it—through exploring in your own classroom the theories and practices in the articles from this section.

What types of communication exist in my classroom? How can I create the best learning opportunities for *all* the children I work with? These questions are at the heart of how teachers can strengthen their understanding of language development through research in their own classrooms. In the extension sections at the end of each part of this text, you will find many ways to do research. "Research" is an ominous word for many teachers, but it shouldn't be. Examining language theory through the lens of your own students and through self-examination can be enlightening, eminently practical, and even fun.

You probably already keep some form of anecdotal records, and this is a good start. But taping and transcribing audio- and videotapes will add a powerful tool to your repertoire, helping you to understand the language interactions in your classroom in new ways.

Kindergarten teacher and noted writer Vivian Gussin Paley describes turning on her tape recorder in the classroom as a turning point in her teaching. In a recent interview, she recounts how "the tape recorder, with its wondrous ability to replay," allowed her to really hear her children. Her transcripts show what she calls "high drama" in the kindergarten: "philosophical discussions about God, fairies, and robbers, as well as speculative discussions about whether stones melt when they are boiled" (*Classroom Crusaders* (p. 20), edited by R. Wolk and B. Rodman; 1994, San Francisco: Jossey-Bass.).

Paley also wanted to look at how she responded to children. She claims that pushing the record button changed her teaching—and her life. "Like a rabbi who spends a year pondering one line of the Torah, Paley would analyze the things she said to children" (Wolk & Rodman, 1994). Listening to the tapes helped her understand her own language and her children's, as well as the messages about communication that were a part of her classroom life.

We believe that, like Paley, you will find your understanding of language transformed by pushing the record button. Of course, it isn't feasible or necessary to add many hours onto your teaching day with taping and transcribing. You needn't record every exchange in the classroom. But if you are going to do any kind of analysis of talk in a classroom, you will need to purchase a tape recorder and think about how you will use it. Without some verbatim recordings, you risk losing much of your students' dialect, phrasing, pausing, and interruption patterns. This is certainly true in much published classroom research. Regardless of where the study was completed, the students' voices seem to rise from the page in a strange homogenized Midwestern radio-announcer style of speech. This often happens when researchers jot down children's speech without transcribing, inadvertently changing the dialect and speech patterns of the speaker.

One of the most important aspects of taping and transcribing classroom language is the gift it brings teachers—the gift of time. You have the leisure to listen carefully to interactions and hear things that you might miss if you only heard them once. And the tapes can help break down some of the solitude of teaching: you can share your transcripts with others and get new insights, talking through possibilities and courses of action.

To make the most of this tool, it helps to give careful thought to *how* you will incorporate it into your teaching life. It's easy to become overwhelmed at first. You will almost surely end up collecting more information than you can productively analyze when you record students at work. As you're collecting, label the tapes so you will have easy access to them as you need them.

We've seen researchers leave tape recorders running at all times in different parts of the room. It's also become common practice to leave a video camera running from one classroom corner. But an accumulation of raw tapes like these, with no thought or function to the taping, will lead to too much data, too little focus, and lots of frustration.

The quality of your recordings can facilitate transcription, too. Teacher researcher Lynne Young reflected on the unexpected interference on her early recordings:

> I placed tape recorders in our teachers' lounge [with teacher permission] in two different locations and all we got was static and conversations I could not decode. Then I decided to tape two groups of children in my classroom at opposite ends. Part of the two conversations overlap each other and on one of them, we got lots of coughing from one of the girls who had a bad cold. Not much else could be heard. . . .

Over time, Lynne adjusted the placement of the tape recorder. She narrowed the focus of the study and the number of audiotapes collected as she continued to collect data. It helps to try out different placements in your room for using your equipment. Fluorescent lights and aquarium motors are among the kinds of interferences that might affect your ability to hear the conversations you've recorded when you play them back.

EQUIPMENT[1]

Humans are equipped with phenomenally good audio processing systems. We have the ability to zero in selectively on conversations in noisy environments, screening out much of the background interference and focusing on what we really want to hear. Not so for the lowly tape recorder; it faithfully records everything. The trick— or the art—of making your recordings sound as good as what you are able to hear in the classroom is to practice with the equipment you will be using. It should not take much time to figure out what your recorder's electronic strengths and limitations are, and you can, in turn, make the necessary adjustments.

Your first step is to find a tape recorder. The ideal would be to purchase one that meets the needs of recording that will allow you to capture quality recordings with a minimum of effort. But first, we need to talk about how to get the best results from a wide variety of recording devices. We realize that many of you will be borrowing recorders from friends or using school equipment, and that finding the "perfect piece of recording equipment" does not head your list of priorities. However, we have included advice for those of you who find yourself in the enviable position of helping your school select new equipment, writing small grants for teacher research, or investing in your own equipment (see Table I-1).

GETTING STARTED

1. Find a recorder and thoroughly familiarize yourself with how it operates.

-   Does it still have an owner's manual? If so, read it carefully.
-   What is the power source? Batteries, electricity, or both? Are the batteries rechargeable? If so, your manual should say how long it takes to charge the batteries. The batteries themselves usually list the recharge time as well. How long can you record on a set of batteries? As the batteries in the recorder wear down, does the motor also begin to slow down during recording? This is very common occurrence in many recorders and you won't really know you have a problem until you plug in the recorder at a later date or play the tape back on another machine, only to hear your kids sounding like Alvin the Chipmunk. (If this does happen, don't panic. Many

[1]The authors wish to thank videographer James Whitney for the explanations and insights, as well as the purchasing and recording suggestions included in the technical sections of this reader.

Table I–1
New Equipment Selection: What to Look for

Good recording systems have three basic components: the recorder itself, microphones, and a way to hear clearly what is recorded.

The Recorder

Many models and brands of recorders are available, with many different specialty features or functions. Prices range from $40 to $500. You can buy a very good recorder for $200–$250. We recommend that you look for a recorder with the following features:

    a sensitive built-in microphone
    an external microphone jack
    automatic and manual record levels
    an external headphone jack
    a rechargeable battery
    two-way power (AC or DC)
    direct-connect telephone jack (to record phone interviews)
    and a good built-in speaker.

Microphones

Often, even with a good built-in microphone, you will not be able to position the recorder to pick up all of the conversation clearly. We therefore recommend purchasing an additional external microphone. There are as many different microphones as there are recorders, from shotgun to choir mikes. Check with local vendors to find out what type of microphone best meets your needs. We can tell you from past experience that the right external microphone can make an enormous difference in the quality of your recordings.

Playback

You need to be able to hear what you have recorded clearly in the field to make the necessary adjustments. A recorder with a good built-in speaker will be able to reproduce what you have recorded faithfully, but it may affect the flow of activity in the classroom, since everyone will hear what you are playing back. Headphones offer a better alternative. They will also allow you to hear the recording much more clearly in a busy classroom. They are relatively inexpensive—a good pair will cost $35–$45. A note of caution: make sure that the plug on the headphone matches the plug and stereo or mono playback capability of the recorder.

tape transcribers or recorders have a knob that varies the playback speed and will allow you to correct a slowly recorded tape.)

- Recording levels: Almost all recorders are equipped to automatically adjust the recording level. Your recorder may have both a manual and an automatic level setting. Locate the switch that controls the automatic/manual setting and set it to automatic. Manually setting the record level will give you a better recording, but like everything else, it takes quite a bit of practice—and a set of headphones.

- Sound pick-up (the microphone): Chances are, your tape recorder has a built-in microphone. Where is it on your recording device? Try a number of test recordings to determine the best position of the recorder for the clearest tapes. The general rule of thumb is to position the microphone as close as possible to your informants, within three to four feet at most. It also helps to place the recorder on a piece of foam rubber if you find you're picking up a lot of surface noise from the table.

2.   Use name-brand, high quality tapes. Many of the generic brands *will not* withstand the rigors of many fast forward/rewind functions that are part of the transcription process. Also, avoid using anything longer than a 90-minute cassette (45 minutes per side).

3.   Before you go out and record:

- Are your batteries charged? Do you have spare batteries?
- If your power source is electricity, do you have a cord?
- Do you have spare tapes and material to mark them?

4.   On site set-up and test: Go to the area where you will be making the recording. Set the recorder up and conduct a test recording. Talk into the recorder in a normal tone of voice, stating the date and any other pertinent marking information. Rewind and play back the tape. If possible, conduct a short test to make sure that the microphone is positioned to pick up all of the participants' voices.

TRANSCRIPTION MARKERS

The goal of adding transcription markers to your texts should be to enhance understanding of the language used (see Table I–2). Most teachers we've worked with prefer to use these conventions sparingly. Depending on what you are researching, it can be very useful to be aware of pauses, overlapping sentences, or even volume. You may even find that you need to create a marker for the particular needs of your study. But using *all* the possible transcription conventions can actually hinder a reader's sense of language in the classroom. Because of this, most classroom researchers choose only a few when they transcribe.

Figure I–1 shows how Martha Pojasek used transcription markers selectively in her work. If you do use markers, you should always begin your text by defining these markers, as Martha does. Most teachers find three markers the most useful: the period, the bracket, and the # or /?/ symbols.

The period, denoting pauses in speech, helps readers gain a sense of the rhythm and pace of conversation. As teachers, we're often curious about wait time and pace of instruction, and these transcription marks convey a sense of time and pace.

Another transcription marker frequently used by teacher researchers is the bracket (see Table I–2), a marker denoting overlapping conversation. This mark shows when a child is interrupted, frequently leading to a change in topic.

Table I-2
Key to Transcription Conventions

Source: The Art of Classroom Inquiry: A Handbook for Teacher-Researchers (p. 44) by R. S. Hubbard and B. M. Power, 1993, Portsmouth, NH: Heinemann.

. . noticeable pause or break in rhythm (less than 0.5 second)

 . . . half-second pause, as measured by stop watch

an extra dot is added for each half-second of pause, hence,

 . . . . full second pause

 . . . . . second-and-a-half pause, and so on

<u>underline</u> marks emphatic stress

CAPS mark very emphatic stress

musical notation is used for amplitude and appears under the line:

> *p* piano (spoken softly)
> *pp* pianissimo (spoken very softly)
> *f* forte (spoken loudly)
> *ff* fortissimo (spoken very loudly)
> *acc* spoken quickly
> *dec* spoken slowly

The above notations continue until punctuation, unless otherwise noted

/?/ indicates transcription impossible

/words/ within slashes indicate uncertain transcription

[brackets] are used for comments on quality of speech and context

⌈ Brackets between lines indicate overlapping speech
⌊ Two people talking at the same time

Brackets on two lines ⌉
              ⌊ indicate second utterance
latched onto first, without perceptible pause

The # or /?/ denotes words that are indecipherable on tape. These markers help readers know that some of the speech is missing. They don't indicate if the words are missing because the person mumbled, the recorder didn't pick up the words, or a toilet flushed in the background, but it reminds the researcher, and any reader of the transcripts, that something important may be missing.

One of the purposes of the transcription markers is to add more dimension to classroom communication. The more you can record a sense of the context surrounding conversations in your classroom, the better you will be able to understand the interactions on the tape. You may want to consider setting the tape transcriptions from your classroom in a broader frame. Marilyn Cochran Smith does this in her study of *The Making of a Reader*, an analysis of literacy in a nursery school setting. An excerpt is included in Part II. Smith's chart of interactions at the nursery rug during "reading time" helps her and her readers gain a clear picture of talk about books in the context of the classroom.

TOPIC ANALYSIS

Topic analysis is a transcription technique that is less time-consuming than a detailed rendering of every word spoken. It is used for some research questions that don't

Transcription Key

-	false starts
. . .	pauses
____ (underline)	emphatic stress
CAPS	very emphatic stress
/?/	unintelligible word
[ ]	comments

Kara and Harry
Tracing pictures from *Eyewitness Book of Birds*

1. K: This is an interest - interesting book. Look at these big bones from birds Harry . . . .

2. H: I see.

3. K: You didn't see it . . . . These <u>are</u> bones.

4. H: I know, I know, I know, I know.

5. K: Eeew!

6. H: What!

7. K: [makes noise of disgust with tongue]

8. H: UGH!

9. K: These are GROSS! Let's see what's at the end.

10. H: Well?

11. K: This is the end.

12. H: WOW!

13. K: /?/ OH!

14. H: What?

15. K: This is how they start out, yech! [Looking at a series of pictures on chicks' development inside the egg]

16. K: This is how they start out, yech!

Figure I–1
Martha Pojasek's tape transcription with markers.

require verbatim transcription of each conversation. You may be looking instead at who controls the topics, or an analysis of when a student or particular group of students enter into conversations.

In topic analysis, you note who is speaking when and who controls when the topic changes. Teacher-researcher Karen Achorn found it most helpful to note who controlled topic change in her transcription analysis. As the transcript in Figure I–2 shows, Ronnie is clearly in control of introducing topics that relate to discussions of his goals.

You'll come to understand these tools as you try them. If you are planning to attempt some language research, it will also help you to read some of the examples of classroom language research from the next section of the book before you begin. But it's never too early to try to find the equipment you need and to test it out with students in your classroom. Like Lynne Young, you may find you need to experiment with placement and times of day before you get clear recordings.

Digital Counter	Topic	Participants	How it came up
001	Goals	All	R: I want to be a toxicologist
020	Decision to become a toxicologist	All	R: mentions Tim Landry and "Auntie's" influence
040	Dinosaurs	All	R: Most third graders "don't know it yet"
060	How to prepare to reach goal in Gr. 3	All	R: "teach others"
080	Experiments	All	R: talks of mixes
100	Rotten wood experiment	All	R: "magnifying, chlorophyll"
120	Other goals	All	R: interested in writing, would write all the bad things about Mike 0
140	Brother	All	R: hits, kicks "really not a good kid," must be something about being seven
160	Self-esteem	All	R: dissected then ate a sunfish to improve himself
180	Taking Chances	All	R: risk is good, "I'm a lucky guy!"
	Most Exciting Event in Life	All	R: I climbed Mt. Katahdin

Figure I–2
Achorn's topic analysis: Flow of topics in discussion of Ronnie's goals.
Source: The Art of Classroom Inquiry: A Handbook for Teacher-Researchers (p. 70) by R. S. Hubbard and B. M. Power, Portsmouth, NH: Heinemann.

Talk in Schools

Language Development: Issues, Insights, and Implementation

KENNETH S. GOODMAN

Editor's introduction

Kenneth Goodman's work in literacy has had an enormous impact in schools over the past three decades. His research on miscue analysis, begun in the 1960s, changed the way researchers and teachers viewed children's development as readers. As both a developer and proponent of the whole language philosophy and method of teaching, Goodman has been an advocate for making classrooms more student-centered. In this essay, he explores some of the links between theories of language learning and how these theories should influence classroom instruction.

To be born human is to be born with a potential for thinking, for knowing, for understanding, for interaction, for communicating, and for developing language. Human infants immediately begin to realize this potential by forming a schema for assimilating and accommodating the experiences they have with the world. With a universal human ability to think symbolically—that is, to let something symbolically represent something else—and a universal need to communicate, human societies and human infants universally develop language.

Only humans are capable of the level of interaction we achieve because only humans have language, and language is necessary for the full sharing of feelings, needs, wants, experiences, and insights. Language becomes the medium through which thoughts are shared, but it is also the medium of thinking and of learning. Through language, people may link their minds, pool their experiences, and form a social base for a shared life view. Language is both the product of a culture and the principal means by which the culture is created. According to Halliday (1969), as children develop language they learn how to "mean" as the society around them does.

Language is social as well as personal; it is learned in the process of its social use. Thus parents, caregivers, siblings, peers, and others with whom the developing infant interacts play vital roles in the infant's linguistic development. They are less teachers than essential communicative partners, less role models than respondents, less to be imitated than to be understanding and understood.

NATURE, NURTURE, AND SOCIAL-PERSONAL INVENTION

While all that I've said so far is not novel, it represents a necessary major shift in focus from behavioral views in which language is seen as something outside the child, somehow taught to the child, or learned through conditioning.

Source: "Language Development: Issues, Insights, and Implementation" by K. S. Goodman, 1989. In *Teachers and Research: Language Learning in the Classroom* (pp. 130–139), G. S. Pinnell and M. L. Matlin, Eds., Newark, DE: International Reading Association.

It also is a shift from an old view, recently revived, that language is not learned at all but is innate. In this view, language in some underlying and universal form is preprogrammed into the human brain, needing only exposure to some real human language to be realized. Such a view stems from two sources.

The first is the amazing feat of language learning itself. Scholars are astounded by how quickly, how early, and with what ease language develops. It's too complicated to be learned by such young minds so easily and so well.

The second source stems from the rejection of the alternative behavioral explanations as totally inadequate to explain language learning. Developmental research and linguistic theory have demonstrated the complexity of human language learning and particularly of the development of implicit rules by which novel language can be created by the learner. Some scholars, in rejecting the behavioral language learning theory, could find no alternative so they assumed language to be innate.

But the innate view of language development is at best unproductive. It causes scholars to treat development as uninteresting. Why study something if it is innate and happens universally anyway? At worst the innate view leads to the neglect of the social and personal functions, circumstances, and contexts within which human language develops. If language is innate, the most that social and physical environmental factors can do is inhibit the innate development.

Language learning in the past has been reduced to nature (nativistic) or nurture (behavioral) views, neither of which can explain how or why language develops. The how and why of language development are inseparable in attempting to understand both oral and written language development.

While progress on understanding oral language development has surmounted the obstacles of these inadequate theories, understanding written language development has been considerably retarded by them until recently. Partly, this difference stems from the obvious, spontaneous, and universal development of oral language, evidence of which was too overt to be ignored, whether oral language was treated as behaviorally conditioned or natively endowed.

Written language development is more subtle and becomes fully evident at a later point, usually after children enter school. So behaviorists could argue that written language development required explicit, controlled exposure to be a carefully sequenced hierarchy of skills and subskills for its development. They could further argue that those who have more difficulty in learning literacy need even more highly structured skill instructions; the inability to learn to read and write through the skill instruction is used to argue for even more tightly controlled and sequenced instruction.

And nativists could argue that it is oral language for which humans are preprogrammed. To them, written language is a secondary and abstract representation of oral language. It is thus not learned like language but requires "metalinguistic awareness"—that is, explicit knowledge of how language works—for its development. Their view is that oral language develops so easily because it is not learned but innate; written language is more difficult to develop because it is learned. To some nativists it is not surprising that written language is hard to learn; in fact, it is surprising that it isn't harder.

An old issue in philosophy and psychology is the difference between knowledge *of* something and knowledge *for* something. Confusion between these kinds of knowledge has troubled both research and instruction. There is a strong tendency to judge what people know or how well they've learned by what they can discuss explicitly and abstractly. We have tended to judge the language knowledge of children by what they can say about it rather than by what they can do with it. Sometimes we go so far as to think of the knowledge of language as prerequisite to its effective use. Linguistic awareness or metalingustic awareness are terms used variably, as Dybdahl (1980) points out. But to some they are used to cover abstract ability to discuss how language works.

Sometimes schools are encouraged to "put learners in touch" with what they know about language, that is, to help them reach a point where they can analyze what they do when they use language. While children may find this interesting, it's hard to find a justification for it as an aid to learning either oral or written language. At best, encouraging pupils to think about what they're doing while they speak, write, read, or listen makes them self-conscious and distracts them from the meaning being communicated.

Perhaps we are misled by the fact that children ask questions and make comments about language as they are gaining control over it. Furthermore, the more proficient children are in the use of language, the more they tend to be able to talk about it, since they can draw on their own intuitive knowledge to support their conclusions. Neither of these obvious facts establishes that metalinguistic awareness is a cause for or prerequisite to language development. In fact, it is more likely that metalinguistic awareness is a by-product of language development.

Of course, those who regard written language as an abstract school task to be mastered will see knowledge of language as a logical prerequisite to its use. In doing so, however, they are falling into an old trap of believing that children must be taught the symbols, structure, and rules of written language before they can read and write. The only argument in that case will be over which is the true knowledge to teach. Yet all that we have learned about language development indicates the fallacy of the assumption that knowledge of form must precede use.

A personal-social invention view cannot support these distinctions between how oral and written language develop or the relative ease of their development. If language develops to meet universal personal and social needs, then written language development is simply an extension of that process. It comes when oral language is insufficient to meet the communicative needs of the individual and the society. Furthermore, children growing up in a literate society in which written language performs vital functions will begin at early ages to internalize these functions, to experiment with the use of written language to meet their own functional needs, and to gain control over the forms of written language. In short, they will begin to develop as readers and writers before they reach school age and without instruction.

The differences in pace and degree of oral and written language development are not so much in how and why each develops but between the functions, purposes, and contexts in which they are used.

APPLICATION OF NEW KNOWLEDGE AND NEW THEORETICAL INSIGHTS

New research evidence and theories have given us insight into language and language development to use in developing new criteria for building sound, effective instructional programs. Viewing language as social-personal invention puts the teaching and learning of literacy in a new light. It can now be seen as a natural extension of language learning. That makes it possible to think in terms of building on what children already know, working with them rather than at cross pur-

poses to them. Literacy is neither something to be taught a piece at a time nor something hard and abstract, but simply another language form to use in the functional context of its use.

Perhaps the most important new insight on language development is the personal-social perspective itself. That enables us to put language development, receptive and productive, in social and situational context. It enables us to see what is happening in speech acts as a series of transactions between speaker and listener within a social-cultural context. We then can focus on the speaker, listener, discourse or text, and context, but only in relationship to all of the other components. This same view can apply to written language, except that the reader and writer are seldom in one another's presence, and the situational context is less complete.

In this new perspective, we have been able to gain new insights into language by looking at its functions—what it does and what it is used for, and then relating both linguistic form and language development to those functions. Here's an illustration of how useful that has been.

For some time, teachers have noticed the overwhelming tendency of school beginners to write using capital letters. It's been commonly assumed that this is the result of parents teaching children to write with capitals. But there is little evidence that parents do much overt teaching of writing, and the writing that parents produce and children observe is generally cursive.

How then do children learn to write using capitals? The answer is all around us. One important use of print is in the signs that label our stores and buildings, call attention to commercial messages and offerings, and guide and control us. Street signs and traffic signs are examples of the latter. Overwhelmingly, these signs are printed in capital letters. So children who use capital letters in their writing must be learning to do so through their interactions with print in their environment.

Environmental print is not the only written language children experience as they grow up in a literate society. They see books, newspapers, magazines, and print on television, and handwritten lists, notes, and letters. But environmental print is pervasive and serves an easily inferable function.

This example illustrates how we frequently must put aside what we thought we knew about language when we look at language in the context of its use. We've all learned the rules for capitalization in writing texts. These rules are verified in the wide range of texts we read: letters, newspapers, books, and stories. But the rules do not apply in the range of other uses of print, particularly the print that children most frequently encounter on packages, television, street corners, and billboards. In fact, the print that is most attractive and situationally made meaningful is likely to be in capital letters. That doesn't make the rules wrong. But it means that they do not apply to all written language contexts and functions.

The example also illustrates some important insights about children's written language development. Print is part of the social and physical world in which children in a literate society are growing up. Piaget (1969) demonstrated that children engage in transactions with their world, interpreting what they see, feel, hear, and otherwise experience. They form hypotheses about what things are for and how they work. They develop schemata for their interpretations and modify these schemata as they gain further insights.

Drawing on Piagetian concepts, Ferreiro and Teberosky (1979) demonstrated that children in a wide range of cultures and socioeconomic circumstances are treating print as a significant part of the physical world. They are generalizing about how print as a system works, what it's for, and which features are important.

Clay (1977), Goodman (1980), Harste, Burke, and Woodward (1984), and others have shown that most children have developed strong roots for literacy before they have any school experience. Goodman has found that children's awareness of the function of written language in representing meaning begins separately and at least as early as any knowledge of letter forms and names. Others have found uninstructed children using sophisticated rules for relating the spelling system to phonology, letter names, morphemic features, and orthographic features.

While these rules don't always work and don't always correspond to adult rules, they show the active minds of young language learners at work in developing written language, just as they are in developing oral language. They show children learning the form of language as they try to use it functionally.

The example of children's early use of capitals is, of course, relatively trivial compared with many things that our new perspectives have made it possible to understand and appreciate about children's oral and written language development. What's most important about these new insights is that there are virtually universal beginnings of reading and writing among children in literate societies. Written language is developmental, very much as oral language is. Children are well on their way to literacy before they enter school. What we do to help them expand and build on what they've begun becomes the crucial issue.

We are redefining, in the context of this developmental view of how children become literate, what effective teaching must be. We have come to see teaching as supporting the learning, not controlling or necessarily causing it.

Much past research on effective teaching was focused on whether Method A or Method B produced the most learning judged by pupils' gains in scores on achievement tests. Such research was virtually useless since it was not likely to be rooted in any theory of language development or coherent view of what the pupils were learning.

Other research dealt with ways of teaching specific skills, often under controlled laboratory conditions. Such research was even less useful since neither the skill learned nor the laboratory conditions could be easily or meaningfully related to what happens with real language users reading, writing, speaking, or listening in real classrooms.

Now techniques borrowed and adapted from ethnography are being applied to the classroom. Researchers, operating from a theoretical perspective, are carefully monitoring what teachers are doing in classrooms as they interact with pupils. Often the teachers are part of the research team, verifying the observations and their interpretations. Now we can see the interrelationships of teaching and learning at the points where they are happening.

The research of Goodman (Allen & Watson, 1976) and others analyzing the miscues of readers has provided insights into the reading process and how it develops. The work of Graves (1975) and others has provided similar insights into writing development. We can begin to relate these research-based theoretical perspectives of reading and writing to what we are learning about how teaching can support learning.

As important as they are, research and theory on language processes and language development do not translate directly into curriculum and instruction strategies and methodology. They provide foundational knowledge upon which educators—using their knowledge of children, learning, and curriculum—can build sound and effective practice. Educators must decide the value of knowledge to curriculum and methodology. New curricula must grow from the integration of new knowledge about processes and development with sound pedagogical theory.

We cannot afford to wait for all the returns to be in. There is a tendency for teachers, administrators, and curriculum specialists to throw up their hands at the unsettled and unsettling nature of the state of knowledge of language and language development. These are dynamic fields with conflicting schools of thought and new theories overturning old. It can be more comfortable for practitioners to sit on the sidelines and wait for the dust to settle. But too much is being learned to be ignored. We owe it to our pupils to utilize the best educational practice possible. If we wait for consensus, we will be staying with increasingly outmoded practice.

Furthermore, there must be two-way communication between the practitioners, who have knowledge of the realities of teaching and learning in real classroom circumstances, and the researchers and theoreticians. In fact, we need interdisciplinary teams composed of academic scholars, researchers, integrators, disseminators, and practitioners who can make new insights available to teachers and learners. Such cooperation depends on mutual respect, particularly respect of teachers by the others. Teachers have the reality-based insights that can turn new knowledge into effective practice. They can use the knowledge to monitor their pupils' progress, to plan instruction, and to evaluate and modify their own teaching.

THE BATTLE TO APPLY WHAT WE ARE LEARNING

The implications of our growing insights into oral and written language development for educational practice are already profound. We know so much about how and why children learn forms of language, about the conditions under which language develops most easily and best, and about how teaching can support this development. And the implications of what we have yet to learn are even more profound.

I foresee a time when our school practice will be conceived as an expansion of children's language development, when we will be working in harmony with their natural language learning. Then we will see the importance of all language experience in school being useful and relevant to the learner. At that time, we will appreciate the strength of children as language learners and know how to support and build on such strength.

There will come a time in our schools when we will no longer talk about readiness as a separate set of prerequisites to learning but understand that what is learned must be functional in its own right, although it also forms a foundation for further learning.

I can see a time when the entire curriculum will be centered on integrating development of language and thinking. Teachers then will be aware of their essential double agenda. They will monitor children's language development in the context of their cognitive development, and they will understand that pupils need to keep their focus on the meaning they are expressing and comprehending, and not on language forms.

Literacy will soon come to be accepted as a natural development for all learners, and we will have school programs that involve whole language right from the beginning. The classroom will become a literate environment in which children read and write in increasingly more effective and varied ways.

This is no Utopian dream I've conjured up; I believe it is easily possible to achieve it. All it takes is hardworking, dedicated professionals who believe in kids and in themselves and who are willing to fight to make it happen. We've had some aspects before; there was a flourishing child study movement in the 1930s. But education, like all human endeavors, is not a totally rational institution. It takes constant efforts by all those concerned—particularly teachers and other school professionals—to keep the gains that have been made on improving practice and keep things moving forward through progressive application of new knowledge and theories.

The fight is a professional fight. In contemporary conditions, it is also a political fight. Researchers, scholars, and parents must join the school professionals in waging this fight on behalf of learners. Knowledge is of no use if it is not applied. And there is much new knowledge to apply to the teaching and learning of oral and written language.

REFERENCES

Allen, P. D., & Watson, D. J. (1976). *Findings of research in miscue analysis: Classroom applications*. Urbana, IL: National Council of Teachers of English.

Clay, M. (1977). "Exploring with a pencil." *Theory into Practice 16* (5). 334–341.

Dybdahl, C. (1980). "Language about language." In M. Haussler, D. Strickland, and Y. Goodman (Eds.), *Oral and written language development research: Impact on the schools.* Urbana, IL: National Council of Teachers of English.

Ferreiro, E., & Teberosky, A. (1982). *Literacy before schooling.* (K. Goodman, Trans.) Portsmouth, NH: Heinemann.

Goodman, Y. M. (1980). "Roots of literacy." In Malcolm Douglass (Ed.), *Reading: A humanizing experience.* Claremont, CA: Claremont Graduate School.

Graves, D. (1975). "An examination of the writing processes of seven-year-old children." *Research in the Teaching of English, 9,* 227–241.

Harste, J., Woodward, V., & Burke, C. (1984). *Language stories and literacy lessons.* Portsmouth, NH: Heinemann.

Piaget, J. (1969). *The language and thought of the child.* New York: Meridian Books.

How Knowledge About Language Helps the Classroom Teacher—Or Does It? (A Personal Account)

COURTNEY CAZDEN

Editor's introduction

Courtney Cazden was already an internationally known researcher at Harvard in 1974 when she decided to return to elementary teaching for a year. This account of her year in the classroom explores how she struggled with applying her language theories to real situations and describes her many new insights into the role of language in the lives of children and teachers.

Two years ago, an exhibit of Native American children's art was shown around the country. Among the strikingly beautiful drawings and paintings, a few pieces of writing were also displayed. Two of those writings can speak for many children:

From a Navajo child in New Mexico:

Our teachers come to class,
And they talk and they talk,
Till their faces are like peaches.
We don't;
We just sit like cornstalks.

And from an Apache child in Arizona:

Have you ever hurt
    about baskets?
I have, seeing my grandmother weaving
    for a long time.
Have you ever hurt about work?
I have, because my father works too hard
    and he tells how he works.
Have you ever hurt about cattle?
I have, because my grandfather has been working
    on the cattle for a long time.

Have you ever hurt about school?
I have, because I learned a lot of words
    from school,
And they are not my words.

These are not new ideas; rather they are particularly effective expressions of ideas that are all too familiar. In a setting where we hope there can be important growth in children's use of language for learning and for life, teachers talk too much, and the words in the air are more ours than theirs.

When I took a leave from Harvard in the fall of 1974 to become, for one year, a fully certified and full-time public school teacher of young children, I was determined that my classroom would be different. After 13 years in a university, it was time to go back to children, to try to put into practice some of the ideas about child language and education that I had been teaching and writing about, and to rethink

Source: "How Knowledge About Language Helps the Classroom Teacher—Or Does It? A Personal Account" by C. B. Cazden (1992). In *Whole Language Plus: Essays on Literacy in the United States and New Zealand* (pp. 17–38), C. B. Cazden, Ed., New York: Teachers College Press.

questions for future research. In this personal account, I will try to explain some of the reasons why it turned out to be so hard, and why those Native American children are so often right.

WHY IT WAS SO HARD

I taught in a section of San Diego that is one of the lowest in the city in income and school achievement, a community that is now about evenly divided between black and Chicano families. I had 25 children in a combined first, second, and third grade. From the very beginning there were objective problems, as anyone who knows urban schools could have predicted.

From September until Christmas, there was construction on the school site, construction that would have been finished by September in any middle-class area. As a result, the school was on double sessions, and a fifth-grade class of nearly 40 entered our room at noon as we left. Our room had to be filled with desks, all in rows, and none of our materials could be left out overnight.

Actually, in the fall we didn't have materials. My room had been a library the year before and so was empty in September except for an oversupply of bulletin board decorations. The school's central storage area had been demolished during the summer, and so no surplus was available for me. Everything we eventually used had to be deliberately selected and then borrowed, bought, or made—in all ways very different from the well-stocked room of my last pre-Harvard teaching years.

After Christmas, the fifth grade could move out, and we were able to organize our own room. Then in the spring, construction started again, this time on a new lunchroom. We didn't go back on double sessions. But periodically it was too dangerous for children to go outside at all. Lunch was served in the classroom for the rest of the year. For a while, there was no recess and we all had to go to the outdoor bathrooms in lines and on schedule. In such conditions, interest in the quantity and quality of children's language seemed a luxury in the extreme.

Subjective impediments were added to the objective conditions. People ask whether children had changed in 13 years. I don't know; but I'm sure I have changed. My subjective impediments are less generalizable to all teachers, but I suspect not unique to me either. Any colleagues going back to the classroom may have some of these reactions.

First was my rustiness as a teacher of children. Rustiness means that a repertoire of ideas isn't available on the tip of one's tongue and one's fingers. Not only my room was poorly prepared; my mind was too.

Second, there are the contrasts between teaching in a university and teaching in a public school. I had thought physical stamina would be a problem. It wasn't. But whereas in the university every day is different, in schedule and place, in a public school there are six or seven hours every day within the same four walls. And nothing in the university is like the crowded living during most of those hours, where one can never tune out the visual and auditory stimuli, and the demands for attention of 25 children.

As Jane Torrey wrote me from Connecticut College last year, "the problem is to think abstractly in the face of all that concrete reality." I lived in LaJolla, 17 freeway miles from school, not so much because LaJolla was richer and prettier—which it is—but because it was where I could live a more familiar mental life for a few hours every afternoon. There, in an office at the University of California San Diego (UCSD), I could read and write and think different kinds of thoughts in the peace and quiet that became particularly blessed by contrast with the rest of the day.

Finally, there were my multiple, often conflicting ideas about the kind of teacher I wanted to be. Ideas from 13 years ago; from the classrooms I have visited since then in the United States and England; from more theoretical ideas about child language and multi-cultural education; from what I've read of national evaluations of Head Start and Follow Through; from prevailing practices heard or overheard in the teacher's lounge; and from my more immediate, less reflective responses to the level of children's voices and actions. I wanted to be firm and open, structured and authentic, and all the other good adjectives at the same time. I had been one kind of good teacher 13 years before. Having learned about alternative and not wholly compatible models, I seemed less able to be any one model really well.

Other people have described similar conflicts. David Reisman, talking last fall about experiments in college teaching, spoke of the "pedagogical despair" that results from too many incompatible goals (lecture, Harvard Graduate School of Education, September 18, 1975). And the philosopher and theologian Paul Tillich (1966) has the following paragraph at the beginning of his autobiographical book, On the Boundary.

In the Introduction to my *Religious Realization* I wrote—"The boundary is the best place for acquiring knowledge." When I was asked to give an account of the way my ideas have developed from my life, I thought that the concept of the boundary might be the fitting symbol for the whole of my personal and intellectual development. At almost every point, I have had to stand between alternative possibilities of existence, to be completely at home in neither and to take no definite stand against either. Since thinking presupposes receptiveness to new possibilities, this position is fruitful for thought; but it is difficult and dangerous in life, which again and again demands decisions and thus the exclusion of alternatives. (p. 13)

When William Sloan Coffin announced his resignation as Yale's chaplain, he said that "Growth demands a willingness to relinquish one's proficiencies" (*New York Times*, February 20, 1975). I know what he meant. I nearly gave up more than once, and probably would have without warm and strong support from many people. First, from the school staff. That support was partly due to the way my year was arranged. Because I was not paid by the San Diego school system, I did not count in official calculations of the number of teachers at school. Therefore, my presence meant that the other five primary teachers each had about five fewer children than usual. So I was a help where it counts. More personally, the teachers all have to take courses at local colleges for salary increments and advanced degrees, and rightfully resent being told what to do by professors who have never been in a classroom. Knowing exactly who I was and why I was there, they were genuinely glad to watch, and even participate in, the continuing education of a professor who came to live her working life again, even if for only one year.

Other people helped, too, such as LaDonna Coles, who became my co-teacher when funds were cut and my aide was transferred. And finally there were Hugh (Bud) Mehan, director of the Teacher Education Program at UCSD, and two of his students (Sue Fisher and Nick Maroules), who spent hours every week talking over what I had done and they had seen.

THE CHILDREN

To give you a flavor of the children, here are some notes on their language—their talking and reading and writing:

First, Their Attitudes Toward Spanish. In the beginning of the year, negative attitudes toward the Spanish language were very strong. The community had been largely black. With more and more Mexican-American families moving north from the border, the community is now balanced at about half-and-half and will probably become dominantly Chicano in future years. I am not bilingual, but my co-teacher LaDonna Coles is. In the fall, when she or the Chicano children talked Spanish, the black children literally put their hands over their ears.

To validate and enhance the status of Spanish in the classroom, we turned on *Villa Alegre*, as well as *The Electric Company*; made many bilingual word puzzles; and tore out all the illustrations with bilingual captions from my year's accumulation of *Sesame Street Magazine*. And I took every opportunity to have the Chicano children teach me Spanish. However limited the status of translation as a technique for second-language learning, all the children enjoyed these translation games. When two children arrived from Mexico after Christmas, translation became a necessity as well as a game. Rodolfo, one of those two, was very talkative and participated, in Spanish, in all discussions. Miguel, the third grader least motivated and least successful in reading and math, was by far the most capable translator in both directions—into Spanish and into English—and achieved positive recognition in the classroom for the first time.

The attitudes of the black children did change, dramatically so. Greg, for example, who in the fall always put his hands over his ears, began to assert himself by saying *Callete* to a noisy neighbor. He would ask Rudolfo to teach him to count in Spanish. And he eagerly attended a Spanish class for bilingual education teachers who needed children to practice on.

Second, Their Comments on Language. Everett, a tiny first grader whose excess energy sometimes erupted in cartwheels across the room, sits quietly and reflects on words in a husky whisper. "*Little* is a big word and *big* is a little word." Then seeing *on* written on the blackboard, he said, "You take the *n* off *on* and put it in front and it'd be *no*." Another time, while reading, he came to w-h-a-t and asked, "What's this word?" I told him *What* and he laughed—"When I asked you 'what's the word,' I said it myself!"

Third, Their Invented Spellings. Alberto, another first-grade boy, writing illustrated stories everyday on drawing paper at school or paper towels at home (Figures 3.1, 3.2, and 3.3), invented spelling to fit his Spanish accent:

> *An tis coner is drragn. (In this corner is dragon).*
>
> *I like to go to the scwl on the wek. (I like to go to the school in the week.)*
>
> *I like fruwt to et on th morning. (I like fruit to eat in the morning.)*
>
> *Tis is the syde. (This is the city.)*
>
> *At tree I see Popy. (At three I see Popeye.)*
>
> *I like to ryd a bwk wet the tehr. (I like to read a book with the teacher.)*

Fourth, Their Delight in Reading Nonsense Material.   Not just the easy-reading trade books by Dr. Seuss and others that have multiplied since I taught before; but also the new *Monster* books from Bowmar Press, the *Spidey* comics jointly published by The Electric Company and Marvel Comics, and the zany sentences with jazzy musical punctuation on the 90-second Sound-Out films in Houghton Mifflin's Interaction program. Such material, plus good multiethnic realism, seems the best combined answer to the problem of "relevance."

Fifth, Their Attitudes Toward Sex Roles.   One day, Alfredo projected his concept of male superiority onto an innocuous-looking Row-Peterson preprimer illustration of a boy and a girl in the water. Noticing that only the girl was on a rubber animal, Alfredo said, "The girl is scared of the water. Her got that. The boy no got that. He no scared."

Last, Their Sense of Humor.   When LaDonna, my co-teacher, was explaining to me that she was taking some of the children to her bilingual education class after school because "we need some real live children," Greg overheard her and quipped, "Ain't no one dead in here is there?" And at the end of another day, when I wished out loud during a spelling lesson for a key to turn Greg on and off, Wallace said, "Yeah, and you'd leave him off most of the time, wouldn't you!"

But such anecdotes, lively as they may be, don't depend on special knowledge. I've tried hard—at moments of encounter with the children last year, during more reflective times for planning ahead and remembering later, and this year back at Harvard thinking retrospectively about the classroom experi-ence—to consider how knowledge about language helps the classroom teacher.

In a more recent review of six new educational psychology texts in *The Educational Psychologist*, A. J. H. Gaite wrote:

> Educational psychologists or at least those who write textbooks have a love-hate or an approach-avoidance relationship with the topic of human development. Rarely can they leave it alone (or out) but rarely do they afford it anything like proper coverage. Further, many seem particularly blind to the importance of language development as a topic relevant to educational settings. (1975, p. 203)

I welcome Gaite's remarks. But as the title of this chapter suggests, I am less sure than I was two years ago about the points of relevance, and more aware of the limitations of what we now know. Admittedly, there probably were subtle but pervasive influences of knowledge on my teaching that I was not and still am not aware of. I can only recount the "aha" experiences, where an explicit connection was made between knowledge and classroom practice.

WHERE KNOWLEDGE HELPS

Three clear examples come to mind of children's language that I interpreted and responded to differently than I might otherwise have done. First, were the invented spellings exemplified so well by Alberto's captions for his pictures. I welcomed them as expressions of powerful and important cognitive activity and felt confident that they would gradually shift, as they did, toward conventional orthography without explicit correction.

Second, there was Black English, so omnipresent that I ceased to hear it and occasionally talked it myself. For instance, from Carolyn:

> *He on the wrong page.*
>
> *There go Leona's (about a painting on the wall).*

I knew that there was no evidence that sentences such as these are in any way cognitive liabilities for the children who speak or hear them. Carolyn's Black English features reflect cultural differences, not the developmental differences of invented spellings. But cognitively they belong in a single category: examples of powerful language-learning capacities at work, in chil-

Figure 3.1
Alberto's drawings.

dren's minds at particular stages of development, and with particular models of language to learn from.

These two examples suggest that one important function of knowledge about language for teachers is to put the language forms used by children back where they belong, out of focal awareness. Normally, in out-

of-school conversations, our focal attention as speakers and listeners is on the meaning, the intention, of what someone is trying to say. Language forms are themselves transparent; we hear through them to the meaning intended. But teachers, over the decades if not centuries, have somehow gotten into the habit of hear-

Figure 3.2
Alberto's drawings *(continued)*.

ing with different ears once they go through the class-room doors. Language forms assume an opaque quality. We cannot hear through them; we hear only the errors to be corrected. One value of knowledge about language—its development and its culturally different forms—is not to make the language of our children more salient to our attention. Quite the opposite. That knowledge reassures, and it lets language forms recede into the transparency that they deserve, enabling us to talk and listen in the classroom as outside, focusing full attention on the children's thoughts and feelings that these forms express.

Shuy (1973) has discussed how the study of Black English has been a factor in educational change. His is the only attempt I know of to document such change from research on language. I hope he is right that progress exists and that the change is not only in curriculum materials, but also in our ears.

A third example from my experience came in interpreting test-induced distortions in children's speech. In response to requests from early childhood coordinators in several California school districts, I tried out the CIRCUS battery of tests of oral language put out by Educational Testing Service to see if it might be useful in fulfilling the requirement for oral language evaluation now mandated by California's early childhood education program. One of the subtests asked the children to complete such statements as *Here is a child. Here are two* _____. Eight of these items asked for such irregular forms, and the

Figure 3.3
Alberto's drawings *(continued)*.

seven first- and second-graders in my class who were native speakers of English gave 35 overgeneralizations out of 56 possible responses—*childrens, feets, mines, morest, gooder,* etc.

Having spent months of my graduate student life coding transcripts of child speech for the presence of such overgeneralizations (Cazden, 1968), I felt sure I would have been sensitive to them if they had appeared with such relative frequency in the children's spontaneous conversation. I could not believe that the test responses reflected the children's more spontaneous speech. On the regular plural, possessive, and comparative items, the children got 74 out of 98 right. Something was strange about only the irregulars.

I could think of no way to obtain tokens of *mine, most, better* and *best* in a more casual and less contrived situation, but eliciting plurals seemed possible. From *Ebony* magazine (since all seven children were black), I cut pictures of a group of children and a group of men. For pictures of feet, I drew around my own. A few days later after completing the tests, I found a moment to ask the seven children individually and as casually as possible, "What's that a picture of?" The overgeneralized plurals dropped from 15 to 6. (See Cazden, 1975a, for more extended discussion.)

My experience with these eight items is not intended at all as a general criticism of CIRCUS. That is an important effort to test productive oral language of young children, and the Spanish version now in preparation will be even more welcome. The point here is not criticism of the test, but rather a demonstration of how knowledge about situational influences on child language can give the classroom teacher a basis for interpreting and questioning the language elicited in tests, and even in some cases a basis for obtaining more representative samples of speech as a check on test validity.

WHERE KNOWLEDGE IS LIMITED

All three of these examples of relevant knowledge—about development, cultural differences, and situational influences on children's language—concern language form, not content; structure, not function. Despite the many times that I and others have written (e.g., Cazden, John, & Hymes, 1972) that it is the way language is used in the classroom that is important in influencing educational achievement—and I still believe that is true—it was knowledge about language

structure that was in my head as I set out across the country from Harvard to San Diego.

In a symposium at which Follow Through sponsors discussed their work in progress on assessments of children's productive language (American Educational Research Association, San Francisco, April 20, 1976), Elizabeth Gilkeson of the Bank Street College of Education spoke of the significance of such assessments for staff development. In her words, what happens to teachers as they use particular evaluation instruments is "the internalization of an analysis system." I had internalized one such system that handles structural features of language very well. But it was too narrow for classroom relevance, as those Follow Through sponsors (Bank Street, EDC, Far West Laboratory, High/Scope, and Tucson) know so well.

This focus on structure separate from use, on linguistic means separate from social and cognitive purposes, is not only where I had been, but where the language development field as a whole has been. The field is changing. The communicative aspects of competence are beginning to be studied as rigorously as linguistic competence, more narrowly defined, has been. But these beginnings are understandably with the youngest children. It will be a while before these more functional developmental studies provide even suggestive extrapolations to children in the elementary school years. It will be even longer before we understand the relationship between the development of communicative competence and the development of cognition. In terms of academic disciplines, the fields of sociolinguistics and cognitive psychology have to converge in an analysis of language as it is used with others and to ourselves.

I'm not suggesting that teachers shouldn't listen more carefully to what children say. But I am suggesting that it's not obvious what the most productive focus for their attention should be. Further, I am suggesting that the best focus is probably not what existing research can say the most about.

Of course, research knowledge about language is not the only basis for improved action. I think it's fair to say that there is a general trans-Atlantic contrast at this point. Whereas Americans like me have worked "down," trying to derive implications for education from theories about language and its development, colleagues in England have worked "up" from instances of the best classroom practice. An excellent example of the English genre, perhaps the best there is, is *The Language of Primary School Children* by

Connie and Harold Rosen (1973). It is one outcome of a project of the Schools Council in England, designed to collect materials which would show the range of language actually used by children in the 5-to-11 range and also exemplify the best current practice in the schools. An assumption of the opening chapter on "Context," as James Britton points out in his Preface, is that "it is the particular kind of shared life created by all those who work together in a school which determines how language will be used by teachers and pupils (p. 12)." In the beginning of the chapter on "Talking," the Rosens together ask "Can we be more specific about both the kinds of experience of talking which a good school should offer and the most propitious conditions in which to offer it?" (p. 41). They answer that "we still lack the analytical tools for handling taped talk. . . . But we cannot afford to wait and must do what we can" (p. 42). At the end of the book are some 20 pages of "Notes" where links to theory and practice are explored. These notes speak optimistically about what we will be able to learn from sociolinguistics about a theory of context that "could perhaps lead teachers to decide more precisely what features of the situation they wish to alter and in what way so that children will speak more powerfully and act more effectively" (p. 260).

EXAMPLES OF POTENTIAL RESEARCH

It is not surprising that there should be a time lag between the development of a field, in this case sociolinguistics, and the application of its concepts and methodologies to a specific setting, the classroom. Work on this application is now in progress at four sites at least—the Center for Applied Linguistics (Roger Shuy and Peg Griffin), Rockefeller University (William Hall, Michael Cole, and Ray McDermott), UCSD (Hugh Mehan), and Harvard (with Frederick Erickson and Jeffrey Schultz). This work has two interrelated but separable foci: children's functional or communicative competence and socio-linguistic analyses of the language of teaching. I'll give an example of potential research in each category from my experiences last year [1974–1975].

Children's Functional Competence

Giving instructions is one important functional competence. In any classroom, children often help each other

with their academic work. Sometimes this is formalized by the teacher who specifically asks one child to help another. A multigrade classroom such as mine in San Diego was a particularly natural setting for this activity, and such tutoring very frequently took place.

Many reasons can be given why encouraging children to teach each other is a good thing: We all learn something best by having to teach it to another; self-confidence is built when a child can successfully fulfill such a leadership role; the community is strengthened when members understand that having particular knowledge or skill entails a responsibility to teach others who don't. But the value of peer teaching doesn't mean that it happens easily or always successfully. Surprisingly, in reports of children as tutors, only achievement gains are reported. Analyses of the actual teaching interaction are not given. (See Gumperz & Herasimchuk [1973] for one rare analysis.)

When a wireless microphone became available to the Cazden/Mehan teacher-researcher team, we planned what we called an "instructional chain" for part of the hour in which a particular child wore the microphone. Instructional chains are an example of what I have called "concentrated encounters": naturally occurring interactions that are more carefully planned for language assessment or research. They contrast with the less natural "contrived encounters" of most tests, including the CIRCUS example above. (See Cazden, 1975b, for further discussion.) I taught the focal child a task; the child rehearsed back to me what he or she was going to do and say, and then that child became the tutor for other children. Naturally occurring groups, as for reading and spelling, were used. Tasks were selected so that the knowledge and skills required were within the capabilities of the peer group, but so that some essential information had to be taught by the child teacher; the tasks could not be self-evident from the materials alone or the tutor would have no essential work to do. For example, in a puzzle from *The Electric Company Activity Book*, a coded message is deciphered by crossing out letters that spell the opposite of a given word. The original directions that explained about crossing out opposites were deleted so that part of the instruction could only be learned by the children from their child tutor.

In some cases, child tutors and tutees were selected to make code-switching from English to Spanish likely. For example, I taught a bilingual first-grade girl two spelling tasks in English and then asked her to teach them to a bilingual boy. The child's rehearsal of the instructions in English were halting, brief, and incomplete. To her tutee, she rephrased the instructions in fluent Spanish, combined with crisp, exaggerated pronunciation of the English words her tutee had to spell.

Mehan has analyzed two instructional chains in which two black girls, Carolyn and Leola, each taught a task to the same reading group of five second- and third-graders. He shows how my verbal instructions were partially transformed into less verbal but functionally equivalent demonstrations by both child tutors (personal communication, 1975). A large body of research on children's referential communication strategies comes immediately to mind (e.g., Heider, Cazden, & Brown, 1969; and review by Glucksberg, Kraus, & Higgins, 1975). But more than referential communication is required in any teaching act—by children and adults alike. And we know far less about how children accomplish other interactive requirements of the teaching role.

Although Carolyn and Leola were alike in substituting more ostensive demonstrations for my verbal description of the tasks, the two tutoring sessions were also very different. There was much more off-task behavior when Carolyn was teaching, even though Leola had to teach a harder task. Many questions about functional language competence can be examined in this one speech event. For example:

> How does the tutor try to get the attention of the tutees? Where does the tutor look while teaching, and how does she try to control the tutees' gaze? Can the tutor engage simultaneously in teaching and visual monitoring of her tutees? How does the tutor cope with questions? With interruptions? Can she avoid getting sidetracked and successfully keep herself and tutees on task?
>
> How do tutors cope with errors in the work, and with behavior problems during it?
>
> Does the tutor try in any way to achieve a status difference between herself and her usual peers? Does she engage in noninstructional peer talk or not? Does she laugh or remain solemn? While the tutor has been so designated by the teacher, she must maintain that status relationship by her own interactional work. (Even adult teachers soon learn that ascribed status is not sufficient!) In

some tapes of instructional chains being collected at the Center for Applied Linguistics, child tutors stand while the tutees sit, use a pen while tutees use pencils, and carefully guard a paper that the tutees can't see.

The Language of Teaching

Important influences on talk are the relationships of power and social and psychological distance that occur among the speakers. Questions about power and distance are admittedly of special interest to me because I felt them both acutely last year. But I don't believe they were idiosyncratic phenomena. I think I just lived a more extreme version of widespread aspects of teacher-pupil relationships.

I had problems with power—or discipline, as it's usually called—partly from my ambivalence (or more accurately, multi-valence) about models of teaching that I mentioned earlier. And in social distance, I was—or at least I started out—at the extreme, too. Not just that I'm Anglo and all my children were black and Chicano; that, I knew, would be the case before I entered the classroom. But I hadn't thought about other ways in which that distance would be so extreme. I was from Boston and I was teaching in San Diego. I didn't know southern California, and when children talked to me about their lives, I didn't even know the places they were talking about. I came not only from a different cultural world, but also from a different physical, visual, geographical world. Finally, when I was teaching in the 1950s, my own two daughters were about the age of the children I was teaching. They were in the elementary grades at the same time, so that I was more a part of a children's culture. At least I listened to some of their television programs, and I saw some of their movies. Thirteen years in a university, and my daughters have grown up. I am now totally out of that children's world. I rarely watch television; I don't know one sports team from another. In all ways, not just the obvious cultural ones, I was about as far from those children as anyone could have been.

But there I was. What could be done to change that situation, to lessen the distance, to come closer to shared life that nourishes talk in the ways Connie and Harold Rosen describe? Mehan and his students, who spent so many hours in my classroom, commented on how much I physically reached out to touch the children. I don't think that was true 13 years ago. I personally may have changed in the intervening years, and there is supposed to be generally more touching now than in the 1950s. But I think these general changes were accentuated in the classroom by an impulsive reaching out across the gap that seemed so enormous. Fortunately, we did more than touch.

In retrospect, attempts to decrease the distance fall into three categories. One was some overlapping of lives outside school. In the fall, especially during the time when there was double session and I had to stay on the school grounds a couple of hours after the children left but couldn't even get into my room, I took turns walking children home, seeing the important landmarks along the way—candy store or tavern, creek to cross or abandoned car to avoid, saying "hello" to their mothers if they wanted to come to the door. I sometimes carried a Polaroid camera with me and took a picture of the child and his or her bicycle, or of a clubhouse under the foundation of his or her house.

Then the children started asking me, "Where do *you* live?" Well, I lived 17 miles up the freeway across the street from the ocean in LaJolla. That's another kind of distance that is social as well as physical. Again, perhaps an extreme, as those who know LaJolla may think. But most teachers commute to the children's world from their own. And so we took the children to LaJolla, in small groups, in LaDonna's car and mine. Again, it was easier because of the double sessions in the fall. We had ice cream and cookies; they wandered around and marveled at the little two-room apartment I had all to myself. Then we walked across the street to swim and play on the beach. (I wasn't the only teacher in the school who took children to her home; at least one other had done it for years.)

A second way to build a shared life was the creation and use of memorable events within the classroom life itself. Visitors became important because there were a number of them. Some of them were visitors who came through the children. For one social studies unit we talked about where we and our families came from, and put this on a large map of North America: orange for us, green for parents, and so forth (an idea gleaned from David and Frances Hawkins's Mountain View Center in Boulder, Colorado, on my way west). As our map showed, I had come from a long way away; many of the Chicano children had come from Mexico; and the black children's parents had come from many different parts of the country (for reasons I still don't understand, an especially high

proportion came from Arkansas). Mothers came in to share their experiences in growing up in another kind of place and their reasons for moving to San Diego.

Some of the visits were from my friends; one was a woman from Santa Fe who is a bilingual folk singer and sang with the children in both Spanish and English. A teacher on vacation from Boston spent a week in the classroom and did science. Another teacher from Berkeley stopped in for a day and brought some beautiful Chicano legends his group had published. Almost accidentally at first, and then deliberately, we started taking Polaroid pictures of these visitors, tape-recording on cassettes their songs and stories. These pictures and cassettes became treasured by all the children. They would say "Do you remember when . . . " and tell other people who came into the classroom about these special events. They would listen to the cassettes again and again; and with the science teacher they started a correspondence that lasted the rest of the year.

A third way to lessen distance is to avoid activities that increase it. We didn't pledge allegiance to the flag all year. The decision to omit it was triggered the very first morning. Before school officially started, a mother appeared with her daughter who would be in our class. She explained firmly that she was a Jehovah's Witness and Jeanie could not pledge allegiance or do any holiday activities. Almost without thinking, I told her we wouldn't be pledging allegiance and I wasn't big on holidays either. This was post-Watergate United States, in a city where one is rarely out of sight of reminders of the Air Force, Navy, or Marines. I had no inclination to pledge allegiance to them. But more important than Jeanie's religion or my politics was my sense that pledging allegiance was not an activity these children and I could meaningfully share. Robert Coles's (1975) quote from a white school-teacher in Alabama confirmed my decision:

I had a girl once, she was quite fresh; she told me she didn't believe a word of that salute to the flag, and she didn't believe a word of what I read to them about our history. I sent her to the principal. I was ready to have her expelled, for good. The principal said she was going to be a civil rights type one day, but by then I'd simmered down. "To tell the truth," I said, "I don't believe most of the colored children think any different than her." The principal gave me a look and said, "Yes, I can see what you mean." A lot of times I skip the salute to the flag; the children start laughing, and they forget the words, and they become restless. It's not a good way to start the day. I'd have to threaten them, if I wanted them to behave while saluting. So, we go right into our arithmetic lesson. (pp. 13–14)

There are clear indications of these relationships of power and distance in the videotapes of my classroom. One way to deal with tensions about discipline is to talk. If silence seems potentially a dangerous vacuum, fill it; talk can maintain power as well as express it. People who have used various systems of classroom interaction analysis come up with a 66 percent rule. If you tally who talks by words, by lines in a transcript, or by moments of time, teachers talk about 66 percent of the time. Recently, some students in a Harvard seminar did such a tally on the discussion that I had with my children on Martin Luther King's birthday. It turned out that I talked 62 percent of the time, disastrously close to the 66 percent average. Those two Native American children, whose writing I quoted at the beginning of this paper, could have been writing about my classroom. (Mehan [1979] and Cazden [1988] give further analyses of talk in this classroom.)

Other people have written of power and distance in ways that suggest hypotheses for further research. Waller, in his fine book on *The Sociology of Teaching* (1961), discusses them both. From recent work in sociolinguistics, we know something about the effects of power and distance, and its opposite, intimacy or solidarity, on language use. One of the earliest and most elegant sociolinguistic analyses is Brown and Gilman's (1972) historical and cross-language study of the distribution of second person pronouns: intimate T as in French *tu* versus formal V as in the French *vous*. I realized only in rereading their work recently that Brown and Gilman report how the choice of T or V is not always inherent in people and their static relationships, but can also express shifts in feelings of solidarity accompanying changes in the context of their activities. In their words,

We have a favorite example . . . given us independently by several French informants. It seems that mountaineers above a certain critical altitude shift to the mutual T. (p. 262)

Not only forms of address change along dimensions of power and solidarity; other aspects of that change seem to affect educationally important aspects of interaction. There is accumulating evidence that power relationships exert a constraining effect on the language of the less powerful person. Labov's (1970) contrast between the one-word responses of a black child to a white interviewer and his fluent and complex talk to black peers is a familiar example. Mishler (1975) finds in his analyses of natural conversations in first-grade classrooms that children's responses to other children's questions are more complex than their responses to adult's questions and suggests that "questions from persons with more power (that is, adults) tend to constrain a child's response so that it is less complex than if the questioner is more equal in power (that is, another child)" (p. 2).

Goody (1978) has made an ethnographic study of question-asking in Gonja which is particularly rich in hypotheses that should be tested in the United States. She focuses on the contrast between the information and command functions of questions. "Where is my dinner?" for example, may be either a request for information or an implicit command that the dinner be brought. She finds that children freely ask information questions of each other, but never of adults. She suggests as an explanation that "people ask information questions most readily of those in a similar status" (p. 36), and conversely "that it is very difficult for those in high-status roles to ask a question that is perceived as being *just* about information" (p. 38).

Because these generalizations do not fit close kin relationships, Goody suggests,

a cross-cutting dimension which might be described as intimacy or privacy at one extreme with casual public relations at the other . . . [and which] seems to have a systematic effect of exaggerating or deemphasizing the command channel. Within the family familiarity appears to cushion the effects of status imbalance to some extent. (p. 38)

Power tempered with intimacy may partly explain why parents can be such superb teachers of the truly remarkable learnings that happen in the preschool years. In a rare study, Hess, Dickson, Price, and Leong (n.d.) compared the ways mothers and teachers talk to 4-year-old children from varied socioeconomic backgrounds in the San Francisco area. In two tasks, both sets of adults were asked to play a communication game with the children and to teach them to sort blocks in particular ways. Overall, the children learned as well from their mothers as from their teachers. More interestingly, the mothers used a more direct style.

Examples of mothers' direct requests:
Tell me how these blocks are alike.
Now match the O's. Match the letter there.
Tell me what it is as you do it.

Examples of teachers' indirect requests:
I wonder how these blocks are alike.
Where do you want to put that?
Can you show me where you would put that one?

Combined with these more direct requests, the mothers more often elicited elaborated answers from the children while teachers more often posed questions in a form that invited merely *yes* or *no*.

Personal intimacy seems to be replaceable, as a tempering influence on power, by strong cultural solidarity. To put it bluntly, discipline and order maintained by someone perceived as an insider to the community is psychologically very different from attempts at comparable discipline ("oppression") imposed from without. That contrast is probably the best way to distinguish "education" from "intervention," and may also explain at least part of the hoped for educational benefits of "community control." The combination of power and cultural solidarity occurs in some of the most effective schools we know of: the Jewish *heder* in Eastern Europe, Makarenko's residential youth community in post-revolutionary Soviet Union, Black Muslim schools in the United States, and classrooms in the People's Republic of China. According to McDermott (1977), the Amish schools in Pennsylvania fit this description also.

Given the problem of distance that many Anglo teachers like me have ("white liberals" in Piestrup's [1973] analysis), I suspect I am not alone in expressing an ambivalence about the exercise of power. It may be better for education, however, to retain that power firmly and consistently, as parents do, and temper it with whatever forms of solidarity or intimacy are individually available. I could never be a true insider to the children's community. But people like

me can become, if we work at it, familiar, trusted, and therefore educationally effective adults. Social distance is a fact of life like age and caste; psychological distance is not an inevitable result.

REFERENCES

Britton, J., Burgess, T., Martin, N., McLeod, A., & Rosen, H. (1975). *The development of writing abilities* (pp. 11–18). London: Macmillan.

Brown, R., & Gilman, A. (1972). "The pronouns of power and solidarity." In P. P. Giglioli (Ed.), *Language and social context* (pp. 252–282). Baltimore: Penguin.

Cazden, C. B. (1968). "The acquisition of noun and verb inflections." *Child Development, 39*, 433–448.

Cazden, C. B. (1972). *Child language and education.* New York: Holt, Rinehart, & Winston.

Cazden, C. B. (1975a). "Hypercorrection in test responses." *Theory into Practice, 14*, 343–346.

Cazden, C. B. (1975b). "Concentrated versus contrived encounters: Suggestions for language assessment in early childhood education." *The Urban Review, 8*, 28–34. [Longer version in A. Davies (Ed.), *Language and learning in early childhood* (pp. 40–54). London: Heinemann, 1977.]

Cazden, C. B. (1988). *Classroom discourse: The language of teaching and learning.* Portsmouth, NH: Heinemann.

Coffin, W. S. (1975, February 20). *New York Times.*

Coles, R. (1975, March 6). "The politics of middle-class children." *The New York Review*, pp. 13–16.

Gaite, A. J. H. (1975). "Review approaches to educational psychology—some recent textbooks." *Educational Psychologist, 11*, 197–204.

Gilkeson, E. (1976, April 20). Lecture at American Educational Research Association.

Glucksberg, S., Kraus, R., & Higgins, E. T. (1975). "The development of referential communication skills." In F. D. Horowitz (Ed.), *Review of child development research (Vol. 4)* (pp. 305–345). Chicago: University of Chicago Press.

Goody, E. N. (1978). *Questions and politeness: Strategies in social interaction.* Cambridge, UK: Cambridge University Press.

Gumperz, J. J., & Herasimchuk, E. (1973). *Sociolinguistics: Current trends and prospects.* Washington, DC: Georgetown University Press.

Heider, E. R., Cazden, C. B., & Brown, R. (1969). "Social class differences in the effectiveness and style of children's coding ability." *Project Literacy Reports, 9*, 1–9.

Hess, R. D., Dickson, W. P., Price, G. G., & Leong, D. J. (n.d.) "The different functions of parenting and child care: Some mother-teacher comparisons." Stanford University, mimeo.

Labov, W. (1970). "The logic of nonstandard English." In F. Williams (Ed.), *Language and poverty: Perspectives on a theme* (pp. 153–189). Chicago: Markham.

McDermott, R. P. (1977). "The ethnography of speaking and reading." in R. Shuy (Ed.), *Linguistic theory: What can it say about reading?* (pp. 153–185). Newark, DE: International Reading Association.

Mehan, H. (1979). *Learning lessons.* Cambridge, MA: Harvard University Press.

Mishler, E. G. (1975). "Studies in dialogue and discourse: III. Utterance structure and utterance function in interrogative sequences." Harvard Medical School, mimeo.

Piestrup, A. M. (1973). "Black dialect interference and accommodations of reading instruction in first grade."

(Monographs of the Language-Behavior Research Laboratory, No. 4). Berkeley: University of California.

Reisman, D. (1975, September 18). Lecture at Harvard Graduate School of Education.

Rosen, C., & Rosen, H. (1973). *The language of primary school children.* Baltimore: Penguin.

Shuy, R. W. (1973). "The study of vernacular Black English as a factor in educational change." *Research in the Teaching of English*, 297–311.

Tillich, P. (1966). *On the boundary: An autobiographical sketch.* New York: Scribner's.

Waller, W. (1961). *The sociology of teaching.* New York: Russell & Russell.

Testing the Fault Lines in Classroom Talk: A Conversation with Courtney Cazden

by Brenda Miller Power

Courtney Cazden's interest in language development is rooted in her experience as a classroom teacher. She has looked carefully and critically at children's language development for more than 40 years, a process that began with a rich ethnic mix of young students in the 1950s. Cazden has been a professor at Harvard University for many years. Among her many articles and books, *Classroom Discourse* (Heinemann, 1988) has probably been the most influential in helping scores of teachers consider patterns of talk in their classrooms. This classic text weaves Cazden's own studies with the findings of others, presenting a compelling portrait of ways learning is helped and hindered by the kinds of talk that occur in classrooms.

A newer work, *Whole Language Plus* (Teachers College Press, 1992), is having a similar impact on classrooms and teachers. Cazden supports yet challenges many current views of the teacher's role in effective classrooms, arguing for a redefinition of relationships among students and teachers in literacy programs.

This interview took place during a power outage, over the phone. I pecked responses into the computer in the dim light as Cazden spoke. I am thankful for battery packs and Courtney Cazden's gracious flexibility in allowing on-the-spot transcribing of her words. What jumps off the page is fresh energy and insight from someone who will probably redefine retirement in the next few years, in the same way as she has helped redefine patterns of talk in classrooms over the past four decades.

Brenda Power: Tell me a little bit about your personal history. What inspired your interest in language development?

Courtney Cazden: Before coming back to doctoral study at Harvard in 1961, I taught for seven years in the '50s in Stratford, CT. I was teaching in a working-class, stable community of low-income federal project housing. This was three- to four-story buildings, with grass, playgrounds, where parents had stable, good-paying jobs in factories nearby like Singer and General Electric. This was a time when these kinds of jobs and this kind of housing community still existed for African Americans and newly arriving Puerto Ricans.

It was at the time of the Sputnik and post-Sputnik interest in improving education. I can remember sitting in the Bridgeport Public Library, reading Jerome Bruner's *Process of Education* (1961, Cambridge: Harvard University Press) and getting so excited at the new ideas in education, particularly psychological aspects of language development. I went back to Harvard with questions about the role of language in children's development. I wanted to know what role it might play as part of a sad truth—the children in the school where I was teaching were always in the lower academic tracks once they reached high school. So I had questions about language very much in my mind. It was an exciting time to be interested in the psychology of language.

At that time, Eric Lenneberg taught the first course I took, and Roger Brown and Noam Chomsky were guest lecturers. I got hooked on language, though since then aspects and contexts of my interest in language have varied. The early '60s were a very exciting time to be in Cambridge. Roger Brown was there, the cognitive psychology revolution was just starting, and I became very involved in that work. I became Roger Brown's research assistant, and Jerome Bruner's teaching assistant. I also became fascinated with the work of the anthropologist Dell Hymes, though I met him only after getting my degree. His studies of the functions and context of language in the field he called the "ethnography of education" were a very important complement to the cognitive, individual perspective I was studying.

BP: It sounds like there was a great deal of breadth in your training.

CC: Yes. Part of this came from being in Cambridge at that time, and part of it I stumbled into because of my classroom experiences and interests. That classroom experience gave me questions. I find this is still true today. Our graduate students at all levels who have been working as teachers, either in formal schools or other contexts like tutoring, come to graduate study with more interesting questions.

BP: This collection has a strong emphasis on teacher research, especially teachers taping, transcribing, and analyzing language in their classrooms. What advice do you have for someone who is just beginning this research process?

CC: I need to say that the year in San Diego when I went back as a classroom teacher is not a year when I was a teacher researcher. I was a teacher, period. Hugh Mehan was in my classroom, and he was the researcher. So the essay from that year you include in this book is not teacher research. I had all I could do to be the teacher, and what's in this collection is an "after the fact" narrative.

The message that I would want to emphasize from my experience that year, and this comes through clearly in almost all teacher research I read, is the importance of having some kind of a group. You need a community to which you can bring your questions, and gain support and the further stimulation through collaborative discussion of each teacher's interests, problems, and efforts. The year I was in San Diego, researchers and I met every week over a pot luck supper. We could talk over what was going on in my classroom and why certain things were happening. We planned together the research that would be done, and the work we were going to do together. The teacher researcher efforts that I know of that have lasted, that haven't been just a part of a course, that have become a continuing part of regular professional life, have all been cases where the teachers in a community meet regularly and have this kind of forum for discussing their work.

BP: Teachers are most intrigued by patterns of teacher-student talk analyzed in your work. They become more aware of the way they speak with or at students. What good is this awareness? What do you want to see happen with teachers as they develop language awareness?

CC: I hope that they don't get stuck on IRE (Initiation—Response—Evaluation). I think that discourse pattern has almost taken center stage in analyses of classroom language patterns. I don't think it's as evil as some people think it is. Different patterns have different functions. I think the IRE pattern has a function at different times. It's a mistake if teachers judge any classroom talk by the presence or absence of IRE. I don't want teachers to think if their talk doesn't follow IRE patterns it's great, and if it does it needs to change. The more important questions for teachers are: What kind of thinking and talk do you want around this subject matter? Is there evidence of students having a chance to do this kind of talk? What's the distribution of participation? Who's getting a turn? Who's not? Who's silenced? Those are the questions that are more interesting. I hope teachers think about whose voices aren't there.

There is one other suggestion I would make. This isn't done often, but it can be very illuminating. Share these tape recordings with students. Get students looking at and thinking about what's going on. There's one report of a Philadelphia teacher, Sara Allen, in Dixie Goswami's book *Students Teaching and Teachers Learning* (Branscombe, A. N., Goswami, D., & Schwartz, J., 1992, Portsmouth, NH: Boynton/Cook-Heinemann) who had a teacher research grant. She did some taping with that grant, and then showed the tapes to her students and involved them in the conversation. They were thinking together about who was getting a turn, and who wasn't. They noticed the boys talking too much and girls not enough, which is one of the issues the teacher was interested in. This work is a very interesting example of involving students as co-researchers. With this kind of research, everyone can learn something about the patterns of classroom talk. They can keep some aspects of the patterns, and change others.

BP: There are many debates now around the issues of language standards and the place of different languages, cultures, and dialects in the classroom. What do you believe teachers need to know or do about these issues in their classrooms?

CC: I don't think my perspective on this issue has changed much over the years. In oral conversation, including classroom talk, I would not try to change anyone's way of speaking. But I think we would be doing kids a disservice if we didn't have expectations for standard English in some contexts. This might be through role playing or any other kind of simulation, or even better, through preparation for real world encounters. Through interviewing in the community, students learn that standards of appropriateness vary. And the same principles would apply in writing.

African American parents to my knowledge want their children to have those expectations held for them. But that doesn't mean that it's necessary to correct kids or expect them to carefully monitor their speech in the regular discourse in the classroom, where the focus should be on other things—learning, trying out new ideas, and listening carefully to other people for their meaning. I would never carry an expectation for standard English into the moment by moment discourse in classrooms. Children who speak other dialects understand the relationship of language to contexts, and they need some help or practice through interesting projects in speaking and writing standard English. And I use that phrase "standard English" consciously.

BP: That's a provocative statement. Can you say more?

CC: There is always debate about the value or even the existence of "standards." Historians can show the changing nature of standards over the years. For example, the distinction between "who/whom" is dropping out right now in standard English. But at any one time, there is a kind of language (syntax) that is spoken by people who have significant positions of authority in society.

BP: This reminds me of the debates we have in academia about defining literacy. They sometimes seem a bit precious to me. We talk about literacies, and how some people can be "highly literate" in certain contexts, even though they can't read or write. But ask people who don't read and write what it means to be literate, and they know darn well they are missing something important for mobility in society.

CC: That's right. The argument will always be: Whose standard? It is a power matter. But the people who argue against acknowledging any standard or any power invariably talk or write within the standards quite well.

I do think we need to recognize that learning to talk in a certain way does not in itself bring benefits. If there are no jobs for people of color, the fact that they can talk standard English is not going to help in and of itself. We can't oversell the future material benefits of oral and written language standards.

BP: What language researchers do you most admire? Which researchers have had the most influence on your work?

CC: I hate to mention any people, because it only means I will forget so many others who have been important. I've already mentioned a few, but I do want to say that Shirley Brice Heath has been important. Shirley influenced me not only through her written work, but especially her historical articles about English text forms were important to my thinking in a different way. She also involved me in a new way in English teaching. Through her, I first started teaching at Bread Loaf in 1986 and that's been a very important connection and stimulus for thinking for me over a number of summers. The other people who have been important to me have been researchers, not English teachers. Shirley really helped me put those initial influences that drove my early work back together, getting me back to questions of the curriculum and pedagogy around literacy.

BP: What's next in your research?

CC: You've caught me at a watershed time in my career. This is my last year at Harvard—I plan a June retirement. While I'm very committed to staying in this community, I wanted to get out of Cambridge for the first year of retirement. I didn't want to leave the first year as an empty space. I have made arrangements to live in Berkeley, CA. While I'm out there I'm going to spend time documenting what goes on in a special two-semester English program in community colleges there. This program is specially designed and has been successful in getting Hispanic students to finish community college, transfer to a four-year program, and graduate. It is called *Puente*, "bridge" in Spanish, and it's been going for more than 10 years now. The success rate has been well documented. But the teachers who have been teaching and mentoring in the program have been too busy to write up all that they do. I want to make sure it is adequately described. This will be a more intense immersion in the issues of English teaching for me, including issues of second language, second dialect, and which genres of writing are needed to meet the demands of college. This raises the same issues we've talked about in terms of standards—whose standards, and where and when are they applied? I was never afraid of retirement, and I'm really looking forward to this project.

BP: *Is there anything else you'd like to say to the teachers who will be reading this book?*

CC: I want to talk a little more about analyzing language; there are so many different ways to do this. The literature on this can raise a lot of questions. People make a lot of suggestions for things to look at, but after some taping that provides an initial sensitization to language, I think teachers singly or collectively have to decide what their priorities are. The one question I do think every teacher has to ask is: Whose voices are being heard? Teachers need to dare to look at the distribution of talk and what I call "the politics of participation" in their classrooms. The fault lines in society are likely to be fault lines in classroom participation in each individual classroom. So that's something that teachers should look at—not only who talks, but who responds to what parts of the curriculum.

In the end, I would hope teacher research would help teachers accomplish what Maxine Greene describes as the benefits of "teacher as stranger." I have a quote about this on page 38 of *Whole Language Plus*:

> To take a stranger's vantage point on everyday reality is to look inquiringly and wonderingly on the world in which one lives. . . . We do not ask that the teacher perceive his existence as absurd, nor do we demand that he estrange himself from his community. We simply suggest that he struggle against unthinking submergence in the social reality that prevails. . . .

Teacher research is the best means for avoiding that unthinking submergence. Social reality is so powerful in classrooms. It is such a densely populated social scene that it's easy to become submerged in just keeping it going. Teacher research really is the best means of avoiding that exclusive submergence, and getting the distance that enables reflection, and then going back into the reality with some new vision.

Do Teachers Communicate with Their Students As If They Were Dogs?

Lowell Madden

Editor's introduction

Lowell Madden challenges teachers to think about the way they use language with students. In this humorous and challenging essay, he compares the talk of many teachers with the language people use to train their pets. He ends with recommendations for how "teacher talk" might change to support students without promoting dependence.

PROLOGUE

Ambi, my three-month-old Golden Retriever puppy, and I strolled through a community park early one summer morning. As she walked beside me, I began to put her through the standard obedience-training procedures. "Heel, sit, stay, come, down!" were the commands to which she was learning to respond. Her rewards for following my orders were commendations from me, "Good doggy! What a nice puppy! You did such a good job!" She was my puppy, and I wanted her to behave in ways which pleased me. Ambi was trained to walk beside me, sit when I stopped, and lie down and stay when I lowered my hand. This was all accomplished by using the language of praise. Through the use of positive, verbal reinforcers, I shaped her behavior to meet my expectations. Through the language of praise I was dedicated not only to the goal of turning her into a well-trained pet but also to helping her become a happy and well-adjusted dog.

DO TEACHERS TREAT THEIR STUDENTS LIKE DOGS?

As Ambi's behavior continued to be shaped during our many walks, it gradually became apparent to me that well-meaning teachers, including myself, try to affect the behavior of human students in like manner. By also using the language of praise with such statements as "You did a great job!" or "You are an excellent student!" the desired behavior of students is "engineered." Although the use of the language of praise is well intentioned, it is also judgmental and manipulative. Teachers also tend to use the language of praise to affect their students' self-perceptions. Beane and Lipka (1984) state that self-perception has two dimensions. One is self-concept which is defined as the way a person views himself or herself; the other is self-esteem which is the degree to which one values or is satisfied with the self-concept.

Although developing positive self-perceptions in students is a commendable objective and although Purkey (1970) relates that there is a positive relationship between how students feel about themselves and academic achievement, the use of the language of praise to accomplish this goal may put students in the same learning circumstance as trainers place dogs.

Source: "Do Teachers Communicate with Their Students As If They Were Dogs?" by L. Madden, 1988, *Language Arts*, 65 (2), pp. 142–146. Copyright 1988 by the National Council of Teachers of English. Reprinted with permission.

When their behavior pleases their teachers, they are rewarded with statements of praise and they view themselves as having worth; if they displease them, their worth becomes questionable. Their feelings about themselves become contingent on teachers' judgments of their performances. They become dependent on these judgments rather than on their own feelings of satisfaction of personal growth and contribution. Unfortunately these students become adults who continuously look for approval from significant others in their lives.

WHAT HAPPENS WHEN STUDENTS TRY TO PLEASE TEACHERS?

It probably is safe to say that most students want to please their teachers. However, in their attempts to please they distribute themselves across a "teacher pleasing continuum." Those who are unable to meet their teachers' expectations tend to gravitate toward one side of the continuum and ultimately decide to give up trying. They become discouraged and tend to act out their disappointment by misbehaving. According to Walton and Powers (1978), the misbehavior of students can be described as attempts to gain the goals of attention, power, revenge, or to exhibit inadequacy. The following self-messages illustrate what is happening within students who elect misbehavior to reach such goals:

Attention	I'm not outstanding, but at least I will not be overlooked if I can obtain special attention, fuss, or service.
Power	I may not be a winner, but at least I can show people that they cannot defeat me, or stop me from doing what I want, or make me do what they want.
Revenge	People do not care for me, but at least I can do things to strike back when I am hurt.
Inadequacy	I will not be able to measure up, but at least if I do nothing people may let me alone. (p. 6)

On the other hand, those who are quite capable of meeting teacher expectations gather toward the opposite side of the continuum. These students are the ones who receive positive reinforcers for jobs well done. They perform so well that in time they tend to become trapped by rewards and see their worth as contingent on teacher-pleasing performance.

Of the two situations described, perhaps students who avidly please may experience more difficulty gaining control of their lives than those who withdraw and find validation in other ways. Although very capable students are able to function at high levels of performance, their abilities to achieve may far exceed their ability to manage emotionally the pressures and consequences of their own successes. They may find themselves laden with well-deserved awards, but the price they pay may be emotional upheaval and the lost control of managing their academic progress as well as their own lives. Their worth remains contingent on teachers' opinions or judgments.

Teachers tend to use beginning sentence patterns such as the following to impact their student's behaviors:

> My expectations for you are . . .
> You should . . .
> You shouldn't . . .
> I'm proud of you for . . .
> You please me by . . .
> I'm disappointed in you for . . .

Although these messages are intended to be positive insertions into the lives of their students and are very effective in managing behavior they, in effect, may keep students from taking control of their own progress and development. This condition has potential for the long-range effect of keeping students from becoming independent and self-reliant adults.

It is obvious that canine pets can never be independent and are merely loved property of their owners, but students are not possessions. They are unique individuals who have the right to self-determination and the joy of personal worth and dignity based on the undisputed value of their personhood.

UPON WHAT SHOULD SELF-PERCEPTION BE BASED?

It certainly is prudent to manage dogs in such a way that they are well-disciplined and adjusted, but should there be a difference between the way they are controlled and the way in which students are educated?

Even though there is a positive relationship between academic achievement and self-perception, shouldn't teachers be careful in the type of communication that they use in elevating students' feelings of worth? Should students' feelings of self be based on pleasing teachers or should their feelings about self be based on the unrefutable fact that they have unquestionable value, because they exist? To state it in another way, should students' self-perceptions be based on their performance or their personhood? The poster which depicts the young boy saying, "I know I'm somebody, because God don't make no junk!" exemplifies the difference. He does not need to behave at a desirable level of performance to be worthy, because he is already good enough, as is, because he exists.

Marquees of flower shops often give prices for frequently purchased flowers, such as "roses one dollar each" and "carnations three for a dollar." It may be simple advertising, but it also asserts that some flowers are worth more than others. Perhaps this situation is analogous to what sometimes happens in classrooms. Through the use of reward systems, such as the language of praise, students receive the message that some of them are valued more than others due to their performance level. Being considered number one in academic achievement makes them more valuable than being rated as number twenty-five. Rarely are students made to feel valuable for being just plain and ordinary and certainly not for below-average achievement in anything. Students certainly do not have equal talents, but all students have equal worth. The way that teachers communicate with them may affect their understanding of that truth. If students are praised for their performance, they may erroneously infer that their worth is based on behavior or achievement. This misunderstanding may greatly impact their self-perceptions.

WHY SHOULD STUDENTS DEVELOP GOOD SELF-PERCEPTION?

What is the bottom line for helping students attain healthy self-perceptions? Should they be aided to grow up thinking that the major purpose in their lives is themselves? If students continue to receive messages of praise, they risk growing up with a personal orientation of "I and Me, I and Me, I and Me." Should students develop positive self-perceptions only to enhance

themselves? Or should students with good self-perceptions make substantial contributions for the welfare of others? Which is a more important outcome?

What can be done to develop their "We and Us" orientations? Perhaps teachers might wish to change the way in which they communicate with students. Rather than use the language of praise, they might wish to consider employing the *language of encouragement*. What is the difference? According to Dinkmeyer and Losoncy (1980) the language of praise is judgmental and usually tells students how great they are or how great their works are. Praise is based on achievement; it communicates to students that they will be valued if they please their teachers. Although it holds great potential for bringing out adult-pleasing behavior, it also may cause students to be anxious, dependent, and very competitive.

Dreikurs and Cassel (1972) state that the language of encouragement recognizes the growth and contributions that students make and promotes within them self-reliance, self-direction, and cooperation. The use of the language of encouragement implies that students are good enough as they are, rather than as teachers wish them to be. This does not mean that students may not wish to please their teachers, because they may truly wish to do so because they admire and respect them. It does mean that their feelings of self-worth should not be based on their successful attempts to please. Rather, their feelings of self-worth should be based on the fact that they exist.

Through the language of encouragement students' specific actions are recognized and are appreciated for the growth or contributions that are made. Comments such as "Thank you! That was very helpful! You are obviously learning a lot about . . . !" are examples of the language of encouragement. Ginott (1972) states that encouragement consists of two parts: What is said to the students and what the students say to themselves. He offers the following example:

> Marcia helped the teacher rearrange the books in the class library. The teacher avoided personal praise (You did a good job. You are a hard worker. You are a good librarian.) Instead she described what Marcia accomplished. The books are all in order now. It'll be easy for the children to find any book they want. It was a difficult job. But you did it. Thank you. (pp. 126–127)

The teacher's words of recognition allowed Marcia to make her own inference. "My teacher likes the job I did. I am a good worker." Statements of praise can be changed to statements of encouragement by recognizing the contribution or growth of the behaviors of students and refraining from making judgments about the students as a result of their behavior. For instance, the following praise judgments have been changed to encouragement declarations: "You are an excellent student" to "You really enjoy learning. Your skills are growing. All of your hard work is paying off."; "You are terrific for helping me" to "Thank you for helping me. It will make our work go much easier."; and "You wrote the best essay in the class" to "It is obvious that you are working hard on your writing techniques."

Through the use of encouragement students can develop good feelings about self without becoming dependent upon teachers' judgments. They may learn that making a contribution for the welfare of those around them is appreciated and they develop a "We and Us" spirit of cooperation. They can learn to gain control of their own lives without becoming super competitive and self-centered.

All of us as teachers have a choice to make regarding how we will educate our students. We can control them through the use of behavioral engineering as dogs are trained and consequently make them dependent upon us, or we can nurture and encourage them to become who they can be. Ultimately the bottom line is found through the thoughtful answers to the questions, what is the purpose of education and what should students become?

EPILOGUE

Two years after the initial walk in the park, Ambi died of epilepsy. Although her life span was brief, perhaps it was a fruitful one, because it led to this manuscript. Thank you, Ambi. Your contribution is highly valued. Perhaps we as teachers, because of you, will learn a new way to communicate with our students and in so doing avoid treating them like dogs!

REFERENCES

Beane, J., & Lipka, R. (1984). *Self-concept, self-esteem and the curriculum.* Boston: Allyn and Bacon.

Dinkmeyer, D., & Losoncy, L. (1980). *The encouragement book.* Englewood Cliffs: Prentice-Hall.

Dreikurs, R., & Cassel, P. (1972). *Discipline without tears.* New York: Hawthorne.

Ginott, H. (1972). *Teacher and child.* New York: Macmillan.

Purkey, W. (1970). *Self-concept and school achievement.* Englewood Cliffs: Prentice-Hall.

Walton, F. & Powers, R. (1978). *Winning children over.* Chicago: Practical Psychology Associates.

Faces in the Crowd: Developing Profiles of Language Users

ANNE HAAS DYSON

Editor's introduction

Anne Haas Dyson's qualitative work in socio-cultural analysis of talk in classrooms has been widely published. In 1994, she received the prestigious David H. Russell Award from the National Council of Teachers of English for her research. In this article, she writes about the ways simplistic labels for children's language abilities can inhibit a teacher's ability to see clearly the strengths and needs of each student. She advocates an alternative approach to language assessment, one that considers the purposes, processes, and unique development of each student.

On the first day of school, we greet our class—a small crowd of new faces. We guide this new group of students through the classroom day, helping them get a feel for the new room and the new teacher, as we get a feel for them. As language arts teachers, we are attuned to the sounds as well as the actions of our new group, and over time, the faces in the crowd become more clearly visible to us. Consistent with Eleanor Gibson's (1969) theory of perceptual learning, our initial perception of a mass (of children) differentiates as we notice individuals with distinctive characteristics and patterns of behavior. And so our "class" becomes Nathaniel, Mary, Joanne, Ruthy, David. At the same time, however, we cannot ignore the existence of the "crowd" and its classroom setting, for children, like all living things, influence and are influenced by the contexts of people and things in which they live.

In the following pages, I discuss the process of forming clearer visions of children and the contexts within which they grow, stressing the value of observation for assessing children's oral and written language use. Since perception is influenced by understanding, I suggest key concepts about language, language learning, and children that guide our observing. To illustrate these concepts, I

will draw on my own observations of a lively young language user, Jake, and a few of his friends.[1]

KEY CONCEPTS IN THE ONGOING ASSESSMENT OF YOUNG LANGUAGE USERS

As teachers, we aim to foster children's development as communicatively competent people who can use

---

[1]The samples of children's behavior discussed in this chapter are drawn from a larger study of young children's composing development. Support for that study was provided in part by a seed grant from the Spencer Foundation, distributed by the School of Education, University of California at Berkeley, and by the Office of Educational Research and Improvement/Department of Education (OERI/ED) through the Center for the Study of Writing. However, the opinions expressed herein do not necessarily reflect the position or policy of the OERI/ED, and no official endorsement by the OERI/ED should be inferred. Details of data collection and analysis are available in Dyson 1989.

Source: "Faces in the Crowd: Developing Profiles of Language Users" by A. H. Dyson, 1991. In *Context-Responsive Approaches to Assessing Children's Language* (pp. 20–31), J. Roderick, Ed., Columbus: National Conference on Research in English.

language to reflect upon and participate in the world. Through assessment, we aim to more clearly see— understand—the child as a language user and, thus, make more informed decisions about how to nurture continued language growth (Genishi and Dyson 1984). Assessment of a child's language use cannot be made by observing children's performance in any one action or on any one day; rather it is through daily encounters that new questions emerge, revealing a tentative, sharpened, and then blurred vision of each child. Central to this ongoing process of assessment are the related concepts of *purpose, situation, orchestration, support sources*, and *development*.

PURPOSE AND SITUATION: BROADENING OUR VISION

"Language assessment" often initially calls to mind teachers' judgments about children's vocabulary and sentence structure and, in written language, about their decoding and encoding skills as well (e.g., spelling). The concepts of purpose and situation suggest that, to understand children's language use, we must take a broader view. For the way language is used—the way we speak, read, write, and even how carefully we attend— varies with the purposes that motivate us and the situations within which we act; these situations include the people involved, the materials used, the communication channels employed (e.g., speech or writing), even the physical time and setting (Hymes 1974). Thus, our developing profiles of individual children must be dynamic ones, which couch observations of how a child "reads," "writes," "listens," or "speaks" within descriptions of particular purposes and situations.

To illustrate, children are often labeled as "good" or "average" or "poor" readers. Such labels tend to cloud rather than to clarify our vision, masking the rich variability of language behavior. For how children read, including their use of varied strategies for discovering meaning, is dependent upon their purpose for reading (pleasure, information, performance), the kind of reading material (their own writing, a favorite trade book, a "linguistic" reader), their interest in and knowledge about the content and style of that material, and the audience for the reading (self, a friend, a teacher) (Bussis, Chittenden, Amarel, and Klausner 1985).

Similarly, in speaking and in writing, purpose and situation influence the words children use, the ways

they arrange those words in sentences and larger discourse structures (e.g., stories)—even the way they pronounce or spell them. So assessing children's language inevitably entails observing how individual children use language for a range of purposes across a range of situations. Such observation allows teachers to identify situations that tap "the leading edge of the child's meaning potential," in Halliday's (1980) words, that is, situations that bring forth behaviors teachers aim to foster and build upon. At the same time, the influence of purpose and situation means that we must make judgments about the classroom as well as about the individual child. What purposes for using language are available in the child's classroom? What situations for language use are created? With what materials? With what people (teachers? peers? which peers?)? When? Where?

JAKE'S CLASSROOM

To illustrate these concepts of purpose and situation, imagine Jake's first/second-grade classroom. Here, the children had ample opportunities for talking, reading, and writing. The classroom, a part of an urban magnet school, brought together children from diverse social and ethnic backgrounds; but, through their shared activities, and with the support of a skilled and sensitive teacher, the children became a community of talkers, readers, and writers.

The children's talk accompanied a range of school activities, including writing in their journals, completing social studies or science projects, constructing with building blocks, or dramatizing in the "home center." As they worked, the children offered each other criticism and advice, imagined together possible worlds, and argued about the nature of the "real" world.

They also spoke more formally as they told stories about recent experiences during "class news" time, gave others explanations and instructions (how to make a paper airplane, do an exercise from "Mom's gym class"), and addressed questions or comments to guests, who were often parents who had come to share an experience or a skill.

Children's talk flowed around and often undergirded print, for written language was in ample use. The children read trade books, their own and each other's writing, basal readers, and the myriad labels and captions on the children's artwork that adorned the school walls. They wrote in their journals, producing imaginary and real narratives and commentaries on school and family life. They reported information in group-composed books about field trips and described favorite books or completed projects using paper specially designed for those purposes.

RECORDING OBSERVATIONS

Within this language-filled classroom, we will bring one class member, Jake, into clearer focus. To distinguish Jake from his peers, I present examples of his behavior, pulled out from the flow of classroom activity.

There are many procedures for documenting—preserving and organizing—child behaviors so that they may serve as a basis for assessment, for coming to understand individual children. Such procedures may be open-ended, for example, saving data samples of children's written work in file folders, recording handwritten anecdotes on index cards, perhaps supplementing such anecdotes with audiotapes of child talk. And procedures may be as structured as observation forms and checklists. For numerous examples of such records for a range of language behaviors, see Genishi and Dyson 1984. Consistent with the point of view of this chapter, all forms of documentation should note both child behavior and classroom situation, including the nature of the activity, the participants' names, and time and place. The observations shared in this chapter will be presented as anecdotes, supplemented with samples of written work and audiotaped comments.

Jake

Jake was a lively member of the classroom community, in part because of his facile and confident use of language. One sample of Jake's language could not reveal his strengths as a language user, since his flexibility was evident only across situations. Even an aspect of language considered a single "skill," like "narrating a story," could not be revealed in one situation. For example, consider the following representative sample of Jake's written stories in the first grade. What judgments do you initially make about his ability to narrate a story? About fine-grain aspects of his language, like his vocabulary or his sentence structure?

> I saw a jet flying over the desert. And the little jet almost got away. But the little jet is trying to get away. [text descriptive of accompanying picture]

Your initial judgment might be that Jake's vocabulary was simple, his sentence structure unelaborated, his knowledge about the structure of stories limited. But a child's "vocabulary," "sentence structure," and "story knowledge" are not static but variable phenomena. In other situations, Jake used and displayed language quite differently.

When he drew his journal entries, Jake narrated dramatic stories and displayed his love of invented or unusual words and phrases like "flying earthling" and "demonstration earthling holder" and sophisticated words like "conclusion," "doing research," and "hovering teacher." Further, when Jake recited for a friend his planned "jet" story (before actually writing the version included above), the piece he recited contained more narrative movement, having a clear beginning, middle, and end, and it flowed easily through complicated phrases and clauses:

> One day I saw a tiger jet going over the desert, and it bombed—it bombed the, the, the desert, and the desert made a volcano and the volcano erupted and the, all of the people that lived on the . . . um . . . desert were dead from the volcano.

Jake's vocabulary, then, was not always simple, nor was his sentence structure necessarily unelaborated. Further, his story knowledge was not limited; it included information about appropriate beginnings ("One day"), tension-building actions, and dramatic endings.

To more clearly envision Jake, we can compare him to his classmate Ruben. Like Jake, Ruben often wrote journal entries that were descriptive of his pictures, for example:

> The elephant was sitting down and the boy was riding A horse and the boy was looking out the window is The End

Unlike Jake, however, Ruben did not produce imaginary stories in other school contexts. For example, he did not tell imaginary stories while drawing, nor did he orally compose them in response to a wordless picture book. On the other hand, he often spontaneously narrated stories about his daily experiences for his friends, and, in addition, he could interactively create dramas with his friends in the home center.

Jake and Ruben illustrate that even a seemingly straightforward use of language, like narrating a story, can be variously revealed in different situations or contexts. They illustrate as well how a certain language situation can make particular language behaviors visible—and thus available for teachers to build upon. The imaginary narratives Jake created while drawing and those Ruben participated in during dramatic play brought forth their most sustained imaginary language. So, teachers may discover contexts that easily bring forth words and meanings from individual children as they observe children across a range of situations calling for a range of language purposes (narrating personal and imaginary stories, reporting information and offering explanations, persuading, dramatizing, questioning, and so on). Awareness of these contexts (these purposes and situations) can make it possible for teachers to help children transform such experiences into other channels or forms for other audiences. Vivian Paley (1981; 1988) illustrates beautifully how an observant teacher interacts with children to both tap child experiences and encourage their transformation into written stories and drama.

ORCHESTRATION: FOCUSING ON PROCESS

The concept of orchestration brings us closer to individual children for a more sustained, considered focus on children's language behaviors—the language processes they engage in. Of all aspects of language assessment, documenting children's progress in the written language arts—the processes of writing and reading—often receives the most attention in the early grades. Parents, administrators, and others understandably concerned about children's growth may envision that progress linearly, asking, "Are the children progressing in their mastery of literacy skills?" Reading and writing, though, seem better envisioned as holistic processes that children more skillfully orchestrate or manage, rather than as activities that improve through children's mastery of linearly ordered skills.

Orchestration is critical because reading and writing are complexes of varied subprocesses. In reading, the child works to fluently uncover a message and, at the same time, to be accountable in some way to the printed graphics. Similarly, in writing, the child works to formulate a message and to get that message into print.

To aid in this orchestration, children draw upon a range of kinds of knowledge: knowledge of text content and function, of grammatical structure, of literary style, and of the relationship between letters and letter sequences, on the one hand, and sounds and sound units (word parts) on the other (Bussis, Chittenden, Amarel, and Clausner 1985). Children engage in reading and writing by using whatever knowledge they have and, through use, gain new knowledge. But, as Jake illustrated, children may know certain things (e.g., how stories are structured) without drawing upon that knowledge when they actually read or write. When learning a complex process, children, like most learners, cannot handle all aspects of the process at once. So, they concentrate more on some aspects than others.

Individuals differ in what they hang on to and what they let go of as they work to control complex activities. For example, Bussis and her colleagues (1985) illustrate that some young readers may focus more on keeping the message flowing smoothly, while others may be relatively more concerned about the accurate decoding of words. Of course many, if not most, children may fall between the extremes or vacillate between styles, depending upon the situation. In time, children will attend in an integrated way to both demands.

So, in assessing young children's reading and writing, we cannot have a rigid conception of what constitutes "good" reading and writing, but rather need a conception of the complexity of these processes, of the variable ways children might initially manage them, and of the increasingly skilled orchestration that marks progress.

Jake

Again we turn to Jake, here for an illustration of this concept of orchestration. During daily journal time, Jake, like his classmates, was to compose a story; that is, he was to formulate a message and encode it so that it could be shared with others. As described above, Jake's message evolved as he spun imaginative entries while drawing, an activity that initially preceded his writing. But, as also noted, his written text entries were primarily descriptions of his pictures. During the physical activity of writing, Jake focused on encoding, not on message content. He spelled words himself, asked his peers and available adults for help, and looked words up in his personal dictionary. To hang on to his message through this demanding encoding process, Jake leaned on his drawing. As he said, "I copy offa the picture." And so, although he usually enacted a story with narrative movement—and sometimes even planned a written story with narrative movement—his dependence on the pictures, which were stuck in time, seemed to lead to stories that were stuck in time. In his struggle with encoding, he lost the elaborate language and extended plots.

Jake's way of initially orchestrating composing was very different from his peer Manuel's. When Manuel drew, unlike Jake, he did not tell a verbal story at all. He focused on the visual image he was creating, its lines, colors, and shapes. So, after drawing, when Manuel was supposed to begin writing his story, he had no story to write. Manuel might simply have written a description of his pictures, but as he said, "I don't write about my pictures. I just write stories." He spent a great deal of time during writing carefully planning, considering possible content, and choosing words for his story. Thus, Manuel was a slower writer than Jake, and he also paid much less attention to spelling. Both Manuel and Jake, however, evidenced more integrated approaches to composing, attending to planning content and encoding that content, in the second grade.

SUPPORT SOURCES: LINKING PURPOSE, SITUATION, AND PROCESS

Children's language processes are energized and sustained by meaningful (purposeful) use of language in varied situations. Sensible activities, and the people and things entailed in those activities, provide support for children's language learning. So, as teachers, we are interested in the support sources available to children in classrooms and in how individual children make use of those support sources.

To elaborate, in the home, young children's talking is supported by the daily rhythms of their lives. In the course of meaningful activities—eating, bathing, getting dressed—young children hear and soon map the sounds of language onto meanings (Bruner 1983; Nelson 1985). Written language too is couched within familiar activities that young children observe and join in on—letter writing, sign reading, list making, book reading, name signing.

In school, language is also couched within activities. If the goals or rules of those activities are not sensible to individual children, they may not be able to participate effectively in them (Au & Kawakami 1985; Dyson 1984; Heath 1978, 1983; Philips 1983). For example, certain children may have had more experience engaging in learning activities with peers than with adults; therefore they may function more comfortably in small groups of peers than in teacher-led lessons. Thus, their teachers may want to incorporate small-group activities into the daily classroom routine. Similarly, if a child appears to have not been read to extensively in the home, the teacher will certainly want to help the child find pleasure in such an experience; at the same time, though, the teacher may want to find familiar print-filled activities, like making lists of names or reading signs, in order to tap and build on the child's sense of him- or herself as a literate person.

Two aspects of school activities deserve particular emphasis for the support they can potentially offer young children. To begin, activities may involve the use of varied *symbolic media* or tools. Young children often use movement, drawing, and speech to respond to and organize their perceptions of their experiences. For example, the meaning a child finds in a book may be reflected in drawing or dramatic play rather than in explicit statements (Hickman 1984). And when trying to capture meaning in words alone, as in writing, a child may initially lean on these other forms of symbolizing. As Jake and Manuel illustrated in the previous section, differences in ways of using other media can influence the nature of young children's writing.

Support sources include not only varied symbolic media but also *varied people*. Since young schoolchildren are interested in each other and, in fact, have more opportunity to talk with each other than with their teacher, relationships among individual children can influence language use. Children who are not able, for whatever reason, to turn to a friend for help or for a playful engagement with language are denied a powerful source of both emotional and academic support.

Jake

For Jake, peers were an important source of writing support. As illustrated above, not only his drawing but his talk with his friends helped him create his stories. In time, he began to dramatize his stories with his friends during writing, rather than only during drawing. Eventually he incorporated his friends directly into his texts, as he began to write narratives in which he, Manuel, and, at times, other peers had adventures with "bad guys."

Jake's sensitivity to language and to his peers did not only lead to written language change. These characteristics may have accounted for Jake's use of street talk with his peers in the second grade. To elaborate, while Jake was not the only child in his classroom from what he called "the middle, the crazy part" of the city, he was the only second-grade child to make extensive use of the words like "busted," "ripped off," "straight deal," and so on. While not everyone would applaud his new facility with language, Jake may find his new "competency" helpful outside of school, and inside of school he was careful to direct such language to peers, never to teachers.

Jake can be contrasted with Jesse, a child for whom peers seemed temporarily less helpful for written language growth, although they may have been critical for another area of learning. During the previous kindergarten year, Jesse had enjoyed working in his journal. He drew and acted out adventurous narratives, much like Jake's, and dictated summaries of those adventures to his teacher. However, Jesse had a quick temper in the kindergarten, and, when upset, he would cry loudly, sometimes crumpling up rag-doll fashion on the floor.

When Jesse moved from the kindergarten into the first/second-grade room, his behavior changed notably, perhaps because Jesse greatly admired Manuel and, even more so, Jake, both of them self-assured, slow-to-anger second graders. Jesse visibly worked to maintain his composure when upset. Jesse, then, made progress during his first-grade year as he worked to become a more sociable, self-controlled member of the peer group. On the other hand, his writing seemed to suffer. He copied the story themes and the artwork of both Jake and Manuel, losing his own strong dramatic style. In a situation such as this, then, the teacher cannot understand what is happening academically with a child unless the teacher also sees what is happening socially. Once one "sees," there are no easy solutions, just a careful consideration of the possible consequences of possible moves (e.g., manipulating whom the children sit with during writing time, structuring certain kinds of interaction between children, such as a peer conference in which an admired peer talks with a child about that child's own work).

DEVELOPMENT

And, finally, we focus on the concept of development. Taking a developmental view of language behavior means, first, acknowledging that language growth is con-

tinuous and cumulative. It is difficult to identify a "point" at which a child becomes a "talker," a "reader," a "writer," for, from infancy on, children communicate using whatever knowledge or know-how they have, relying on the support of varied tools (movement, sound) and varied people. Thus, we must hear the baby's cries and coos and see the toddler's lines and swirls as both authentic communication in the present and the seeds of more skillful communication in the future.

Second, taking a developmental view means recognizing that language growth is complex. Development, as scholars like Piaget and Vygotsky demonstrated, implies some kind of internal reorganization of a child's understandings or ways of functioning. Since the change is internal, development is not directly observable; we have to look for indicators in behavior. And, since development involves successive reorganizations, it may lead to behavior changes that are not immediately recognizable as progress. Thus, assessment through observation is not a simple task, but a thoughtful and thought-provoking activity requiring both broad knowledge about language and learning and particular knowledge about individual children.

For example, an observer would not appreciate the intelligence of Jake's written word *an'*, unless that observer knew that Jake had previously been able to spell *and*, that he had recently discovered contractions, and that he had thus reorganized his sense of the possibilities of written language encoding to include the option of eliminating letters. ("You know," he explained to me, "'cause you're leaving a letter out.")

FACES IN THE CROWD

Throughout this chapter, I have given glimpses of Jake as a language user, often highlighting Jake's behavior by contrasting it with that of a peer. Through Jake and his classmates, I have hoped to illustrate concepts about language use that may guide assessment and to suggest the sorts of changes in language behavior teachers work toward. These changes include an increased flexibility in the use of language for differing purposes in differing situations and an increased ability to orchestrate varied aspects of reading and writing.

At the same time, I have aimed to illustrate that these changes happen as children make use of the opportunities and instructional support offered in the classroom environment. These opportunities and support sources include the activities that are both structured by and structure language, the networking of peers that can energize and sustain language use, and the availability of other symbolic media to help children express and organize their feelings and perceptions about their worlds.

And so I end this chapter where I began—talking about faces in the crowd. Jake became sensible to me and, I hope, to you as readers, as his distinctiveness from others became apparent and as the support system nurturing his growth as a language user was clarified. These sorts of understandings do not emerge through tests we give children on a Wednesday morning. They emerge slowly, as we live and learn with our children. We thus come to see our young students as separate individuals who join together to enjoy and nurture each other as vital parts of the classroom crowd.

REFERENCES

Au, K. H., & Kawakami, A. J. (1985). Research currents: Responding to children. *Language Arts, 62*, 270–276.

Bruner, J. (1983). *Child's talk: Learning to use language.* New York: Norton and Company.

Bussis, A. M., Chittenden, E. A., Amarel, M., & Klausner, E. (1985). *Inquiry into meaning: An investigation of learning to read.* Hillsdale, NJ: Erlbaum.

Dyson, A. H. (1987). Individual differences in beginning composing: An orchestral vision of learning to write. *Written Communication, 4*, 411–442.

Dyson, A. H. (1984). Learning to write/learning to do school: Emergent writers' interpretations of school literacy tasks. *Research in the Teaching of English, 18*, 233–264.

Dyson, A. H. (1989). *Multiple worlds of child writers: Friends learning to write.* New York: Teachers College Press.

Genishi, C., & Dyson, A. H. (1984). *Language assessment in the early years.* Norwood, NJ: Ablex.

Gibson, E. J. (1969). *Principles of perceptual learning and development.* New York: Appleton-Century-Crofts.

Halliday, M. A. K. (1980). Three aspects of children's language: Learning language, learning through language, learning about language. In Y. M. Goodman, M. M. Haussler, & D. S. Strickland (Eds.), *Oral and written language development research: Impact on the schools* (pp. 7–20). Urbana, IL: National Council of Teachers of English and the International Reading Association.

Heath, S. B. (1978). *Teacher talk: Language in the classroom.* Arlington, VA: Center for Applied Linguistics.

Heath, S. B. (1983). *Ways with words: Language, life, and work in communities and classrooms.* New York: Cambridge University Press.

Hickman, I. (1984). Research currents: Researching children's response to literature. *Language Arts, 61*, 278–284.

Hymes, D. (1974). *Foundations of sociolinguistics: An ethnographic approach.* Philadelphia: University of Pennsylvania Press.

Nelson, K. (1985). *Making sense: The acquisition of shared meaning.* Orlando, FL: Academic Press.

Paley, V. G. (1988). *Bad guys don't have birthdays: Fantasy play at four.* Chicago, IL: University of Chicago Press.

Paley, V. G. (1981). *Wally's stories.* Cambridge, MA: Harvard University Press.

Philips, S. U. (1983). *The invisible culture: Communication in classroom and community on the Warm Springs Indian Reservation.* New York: Longman.

Rug-Time, Framework for Storyreading: Sitting, Listening, and Learning New Things

Marilyn Cochran Smith

Editor's introduction

The Making of a Reader explores how children are socialized in subtle and not-so-subtle ways into literate behaviors during oral share sessions. Marilyn Cochran-Smith's findings came from a year-long qualitative study in a nursery school. In this excerpt, "Rug Time," Smith considers the emergence of specific behaviors and social codes during oral discussion periods and looks at how the teachers fostered these behaviors and codes.

RUG-TIME AS A SPEECH EVENT

Rug-time was a nursery-school activity during which children and adults gathered at a rug- and pillow-covered corner of the room surrounded on three sides by bookshelves, cabinets, and a piano; this area was known spatially as "rug." At rug-time sessions, the teacher (and occasionally individual children) sat on a wooden bench facing the children with back against a bookshelf while the children sat, knelt, or lay down on pillows and rug facing the teacher. Other adults present sat with the group, holding their own or other children on their laps.

Although many activities occurred within the actual rug area at various times of the day, only specific activities occurred when the event was framed as rug-time: individual children showed items brought from home; the teacher discussed and verbally shared art, craft or story projects made at the nursery school; she led discussions of past or future nursery-school events, showed sound-filmstrips, or read stories aloud to the children. Verbal sharing, discussions, and other activities varied from day to day; storyreadings, however, always occurred and served as the major rug-

time activity. In fact, storyreading was often the only activity during daily rug-time sessions. Many of the rug-time activities that were not storyreadings were directly based on or related to storyreadings, such as a filmstrip based on a picture-book already familiar to the children, or a discussion of a real wolfskin pelt in comparison to the pictures of wolves in "Little Red Ridinghood."

Interactional and Interpretive Norms

Rug-time was pivotal to the organization of nursery-school days. Like free play outdoors and snack-time, rug-time was never omitted from the nursery-school day; some nursery-school sessions even included two rug-time events. Although clock time was never mentioned, rug-time occurred consistently between 10:00 and 11:00 a.m., usually following indoor activities and preceding either outdoor play or snacktime. It served as an important temporal and sequential marker for

Source: The Making of a Reader (pp. 102–124) by M. Cochran-Smith, 1984, Norwood, NJ: Ablex.

other nursery-school activities and events. "Rug-time," a phrase consistently used by nursery-school adults and children alike, was perceived by participants as a discrete event within the nursery-school day. It was initiated ritually by the teacher, who played a few introductory piano chords and then sang the "rug-time song." Together, the ritual of the rug-time song, the physical location of activities on the rug, and the temporal location of rug-time after a period of child-initiated project work and indoor play signalled the beginning of the speech event known as rug-time. When these three features did not occur together, participants were sometimes confused.

In Narrative Segment 29, for instance, we see that a child was uncertain about what was going on because rug-time was already in progress when she arrived at school a few minutes after 9:00 a.m. Rug-time rarely occurred prior to indoor play, and although the space, the activity, and the physical configuration of participants told her it was rug-time, the child had not heard the rug-time song and the temporal cue was misleading.

Narrative Segment 29 at Rug-time.   Rug-time is early today because Dori's father has come to play his guitar for the children. Children and adults are all seated on the rug. The teacher has just finished showing the children a wolfskin pelt and comparing it to the illustrations in two different versions of "Red Riding Hood" read earlier in the week. The children are now resettling in their places for "Jingle Bells" and then a Christmas storybook.

Susie arrives and sits down on the rug next to me. She shows me two carrots that she has brought from home; they have grown together, completely twisted around one another.

Marilyn (Researcher): Do you want to show them to the other children?
Susie: Yes, but I want to do it on rug-time.
Marilyn: That's what this is.
Susie: Yeah, but I wanna do it later.

Susie's confusion about the status of rug-time was clearly related to the lack of the usual temporal indicator. Her desire to show the carrots at rug-time and not any other time also indicated that she was aware that rug-time was uniquely appropriate for showing and verbally discussing concrete items with the group. During rug-time, all nursery-school participants gathered together, and one person (almost always the teacher, but occasionally a child) had the floor. The children were expected and encouraged to attend visually to the item being shown and to direct relevant comments to the person who had the floor.

In this way and in several other ways, rug-time was unlike other nursery-school activities: all children were required to participate; verbal rather than nonverbal interaction was expected; the children were physically passive rather than active; they were expected to be present throughout rug-time and were not free to come and go as they wished; and rug-time was teacher-initiated, teacher-controlled, and teacher-dominated. The oral language rules and strategies of rug-time further set it apart from all other nursery-school activities. During rug-time, all the children were to listen to one person, and they were discouraged from having individual conversations with other children. Rug-time was the only activity that required this sort of attention and selective verbalization. During this time the children were, in one sense, learning to be a class, to listen and respond within the framework of whole-group activity. Even more important, during rug-time they were learning to be "readers" and were being instructed in behaviors that accompanied and supported the activity of reading.

Verbal Sharing

Verbal sharing occurred during rug-time when children brought items from home to show their peers, or when the teacher called on individual children to show projects made at the nursery school. Sharing occurred rather casually, and often spontaneously, when the teacher learned during the larger rug-time episode that children had things to share. Sharing Segments 1 and 2 illustrate the range of formality among verbal sharings. Sharing Segment 1, which continued from Narrative Segment 29, illustrates an informal verbal sharing. The group had sung "Jingle Bells", and the teacher had just finished reading a picture book. Susie was then convinced that it was indeed rug-time and had crawled up to sit next to the teacher.

The verbal sharing in Sharing Segment 2 was more formally organized than the previous sharing example. In Sharing Segment 2, the teacher had just finished reading a book to the children. The children began to disperse when Davey told the teacher he had brought

Focal Points	Readers		Listeners	
	Verbal	Nonverbal	Verbal	Nonverbal
	Amy: AND IT'S CALLED "FATHER CHRISTMAS!"	holds up cover of book		Susie on knees, leans against teacher, taps teacher
	ALL RIGHT, NOW . . . OH! (very interested)	puts book in lap	Susie: Amy! Look, what!	holds up two carrots twisted together
	THAT IS THE MOST . . . DID YOU BUY A BAG OF CARROTS AND IN IT CAME THAT?	holding carrots with Susie		Susie nods, giggles
	WOW! OH ME! (impressed) LET'S HOLD 'EM UP.	holds carrots up so all can see		
	DID EVERYBODY SEE THIS?		Nat: I did! Alice: It's a carrot!	
	A CARROT ALL WOUND AROUND (delighted) . . .	traces path of carrots with finger		several laugh
	LOOK! WHERE DOES IT START, AND WHERE DOES IT END?	points to top, bottom of carrot . . .	Ris: (Egyptian girl, does not speak English): Ga-zar! Ga-zar! Ga-zar!	pointing to carrot, calling out, excitedly
			Anna: I know what makes carrots! (excited, playful)	
	WHAT?		Anna: (pause) Pigs! (playful, laughing)	
	PIGS! (mock astonishment)	laughs	[Alice: Hey Amy, guess what? [Anna: I know what makes ham.	

Sharing Segment 1: carrots and pigs.

Focal Points	Readers		Listeners	
	Verbal	Nonverbal	Verbal	Nonverbal
			⌈ Alice: Hey Amy, guess what?	
			⌊ Anna: I know what makes ham. (louder)	
	What?		Anna: Pigs! (gruff voice, playful)	
			Alice: Hey, Amy, guess what?	
			⌈ Anna: I know what makes milk, I know what makes milk! (fast repetition, silly voice)	rises to knees
			⌊ Alice: Amy, Amy, Hey Amy, guess what?	taps Amy
	WHAT?		⌈ Anna: Co-ow-ows! (very gruff, silly voice)	
	YES?		⌊ Alice: Amy, guess what?	
	WHAT?		Alice: Amy, guess what?	
			Alice: I have ate carrots before, and they're good	
	YES, AND THEY'RE DELICIOUS.		(several children talking to each other)	
	ALL RIGHT, WE HAVE A SPECIAL TREAT TODAY. DORI'S DAD CAME AND HE'S GONNA PLAY WITH US. (leads into singing of Christmas carols and other songs with guitar) ⋯			

Sharing Segment 1 *continued*.

from home a little musical instrument. The teacher played a few notes of the rug-time song to call the children back to the rug. In the informal sharing of Segment 1, Susie showed the carrot with no preamble except for "Look, what!"; based on the teacher's expressions of interest, a brief interaction followed. Part of this interaction was playful, and although the interaction ended with a remark about carrots, it also included a riddle-like sequence initiated by Anna and having nothing to do with the topic. In contrast, Sharing Segment 2 was more formal. The teacher played a very active role in the sharing process by modeling sharing behavior and structuring Davey's oral sharing by asking specific questions about the harp.

The type of sharing represented by Sharing Segment 2 resembles the "topic-centered" discourse required of primary-school children during "sharing circle" or "show-and-tell" activities in many schools (Michaels, 1981). Both informal sharings and more formal ones were common during rug-time. When nursery-school newcomers brought items to show the group, they were encouraged by the teacher to wait until rug-time. The older, more experienced nursery-school children had already learned that rug-time was the appropriate setting for this sort of activity, and—as Susie did above—usually saved their sharing items for this time. However, verbal sharing at Maple Nursery School was not a discrete event to which the children

Focal Points	Readers		Listeners	
	Verbal	Nonverbal	Verbal	Nonverbal
	Amy: TAKE YOUR SEAT AGAIN, CLAY!			many children moving around on the rug
	DEARIE, COME SIT WITH ME	motions to Clay that he can sit beside her		Jeffrey plunking on piano
	OKAY … DAVEY HAS SOMETHING HE'D LIKE TO SHOW YOU.			Davey comes and stands by Amy at bench
	YOU KNOW WHAT THIS IS? ANYBODY KNOW WHAT THIS IS THAT DAVEY BROUGHT?			Davey holds up little harp-like instrument
			Lyn: (helping mother): Oh boy! A harp. ?: Harp	several children yelling, fussing with toys
		…	Davey: Amy, Amy, I need this because my uncl—	Ris pulling on harp: Davey doesn't let go

Sharing Segment 2: Something to show.

Focal Points	Readers		Listeners	
	Verbal	Nonverbal	Verbal	Nonverbal
	OKAY, GIVE IT TO DAVEY, GIVE IT TO DAVEY.	mimics action for Ris		
				Ris lets go
	WHAT IS IT CALLED, HONEY?		Davey: A harp.	
	IS IT?	puts arm around Davey		Mark runs back in and yells loudly: tries to get others to come with him
	AND WHERE DO YOU GET IT?		Davey: Um, um, my next door neighbor got it.	
				Davey nods
	AND GAVE IT TO YOU?		Lyn: That's really nice, Davey.	
				Dan runs out to join Mark
	YOU'RE VERY LUCKY. YOU'RE LUCKY TO HAVE THAT	pats Davey		
		picks up book from lap		
				Davey sits on rug

Sharing Segment 2 *continued*.

were consistently exposed as part of their literacy orientation. Rather, verbal sharings occurred as more or less spontaneous fillers between major rug-time events, which were almost always literacy or literacy-based or related events.

RUG-TIME AS PREPARATION FOR READING

Although there were ostensibly no rules for storyreading that were separate from rules for rug-time as a whole, the rules of rug-time were most often explicitly introduced and restated when the teacher was preparing for or attempting to read aloud to the children. Furthermore, when the rug-time rules broke down, as they frequently did, they were most often repaired when storyreading was in preparation or in progress, but often not repaired during other rug-time activities.

The rug-time framework, in other words, was generally synonymous with preparation for reading. It provided guidelines for the nonverbal behavior that was to accompany bookreading and helped to structure for the children the experience of reading. Storyreading Segment 1 is composed of chronological excerpts from one storyreading event. In it you will see many examples of the storyreader's reminders of the norms of storyreading behavior, including rules for: appropriate seating arrangements, listening and behaving attentively, paying exclusive attention to the book being read, and not interfering with the attending habits of others. Interactions during storyreadings that centered on the norms of storyreading behavior are what I have called Type I "Readiness interactions."

STORYREADING SEGMENT 1: CHRISTOPHER COLUMBUS (MCGOVERN)

The teacher has played the rug-time song and has begun to gather the children on the rug. Mark asks what book they will hear, and the teacher holds up a biography of Columbus. Several children, however, are still not settled on the rug.

Interactional and Interpretive Norms for Reading

As this storyreading Segment indicates, appropriate reading behavior for Maple Nursery School children demanded more than the use of specific language strategies. It also involved specific nonverbal behavioral norms for seating arrangements, posture, visual attention, and listening patterns. Negotiation of seating arrangements was quite elaborate at times. Children were to sit on the rug in such a way that they did not block the view of others. Although sitting up was preferred, standing and kneeling were permitted at the back of the rug, and lying down was allowed when only a few children were present. The children were not supposed to play with toys, look at other books, or play with one another during storyreadings. The large plastic barrels that sat in the corners of the rug area could be climbed on and into at any time of the day except during rug-time; large wheeled toys (e.g., riding-horse, doll carriage, train) could be brought from the dollroom into the general-purpose room except during rug-time. Children were supposed to be quiet during rug-time and listen to the storyreader.

The actions of the storyreader were highly predictable during rug-time storyreadings, and there is little doubt that the children knew both what to expect of the storyreader and what was expected of them. Key illustrations of the predictability of storyreading behavior were those occasions when children themselves took over all or part of the storyreader's role. (Three such instances occurred in my data, and two others were reported to me.) The following instance is unique in that it was completely unelicited. The teacher did not plan ahead for the child to share her book, nor did the child's parent practice with the child, as was true of three of the other four instances. Instead, sharing the book in storyreading Segment 2 was completely spontaneous. Pay particular attention in this sharing to the little girl's knowledge of the proper orientation for bookreading—how to hold the book, how listeners ought to be attending to the book, how to relate pictures to the discussion around them, and how to pace turning of the pages. Behaviors that indicate knowledge of a bookreading orientation are marked with arrows.

STORYREADING SEGMENT 2: THE LITTLE GOLDEN BOOK OF DOGS (JONES)

The teacher has played several rug-time song chords on the piano, and the children have gathered on the rug. At one child's insistence, the group plays a boisterous charades-type game, following which the teacher replays the rug-time song to call the group back to order. Voluntarily, Anna perches on the storyreader's bench. As she does so, she draws a stuffed Babar the Elephant toy from her bag. The teacher sits on the piano stool and interviews Anna about the toy as Anna pretends to be the toy in her answers. (Note: The listener named Lyn is an adult, the helping mother of the day; she is sitting with the children on the rug. The listener, Amy, is the nursery-school teacher who sits on the piano bench throughout the storyreading. The reader, Anna, is a child.)

In storyreading Segment 2, no one actually read, or decoded, the text; rather, the teacher and, to some extent, the helping mother talked with the children about each picture. Anna took on many of the storyreader's duties, and in doing so, indicated her knowledge of what was involved in storyreading. She sat in the teacher's spot on the bench and held the book at shoulder height, facing the children. She turned each page individually and held the picture on the page being discussed in a more prominent position than its opposite page. She moved the book slowly from side to side in a kind of arc so that children on all parts of the rug could see the pictures. Anna pointed to the dog pictured on a particular page at precisely the time when the breed of the dog was being discussed and identified.

Focal Points	Readers		Listeners	
	Verbal	Nonverbal	Verbal	Nonverbal

→	Amy:
	ALL RIGHT DAN?
	(two second pause)
	DAN? DAN, COME ON,
	  DEARIE. I WANT YOU
	  TO SIT NEXT TO ME
	  WHILE WE READ.
		goes toward
		  workroom
			(many children are get-
			  ting settled on the rug,
			  talking, playing)
				Dan and Jeffrey
				  racing from rug
				  to workroom

	HERE, DEARIE. DAN?
	DAN, COME ON OVER,
	DAN. COME ON OVER
	SO YOU CAN BE MY
	HELPER.
		motions for
		  Dan to
		  come
		points to seat
		  on bench
		  for Dan
				Dan looks over,
				  keeps running

→	COME ON, DEARIE. I
	  WANT YOU TO BE THE
	  LEADER.
		walks toward
		  Dan
			(many children talking to
			  each other, looking at
			  books, toys)
				Jody comes to
				  Amy, wants to
				  be cuddled,
				  to sit on
				  Amy's lap

				Dan starts toward rug

→	(to Jody) SIT DOWN,
	  SWEETIE. I'LL HUG YA
	  LATER. ALL RIGHT,
	  WE'RE NOT GONNA
	  HAVE MUCH TIME.			

→	COME ON OVER HERE.			Jody sits beside
				  Amy on one
				  side of bench

→	HERE, DAN, ROUND
	  THIS SIDE. SIT RIGHT
	  OVER HERE.
		guides Dan to
		  spot beside
		  her on
		  other side
		  of bench		

				Jeffrey runs in,
				  has been rac-
				  ing around in
				  workroom

→	OKAY, JEFFREY, WHERE
	  WOULD YOU LIKE TO
	  BE?
	THE NEXT HELPER?
		looks around
		  for a spot
			Dori: I wanna be . . . there	points to gen-
				  eral area in
				  front of bench

Storyreading Segment 1.

124

Focal Points	Readers		Listeners	
	Verbal	Nonverbal	Verbal	Nonverbal
→	OKAY, WOULD YOU LIKE TO BE THE NEXT HELPER?		Dori: Can I be there?	
				Dori nods yes
→	OKAY, YOU SIT RIGHT THERE	points to spot		Dori sits on rug directly in front of Sally
		turns to shelf, starts to get book		
	WE GOTTA . . . WE GOTTA HAMMER THAT NAIL PRETTY SOON (murmurs more to me than to the children)	taps nail sticking out of bookshelf		
		looks up at children, stands		
→	OKAY, I'D LIKE TO HAVE ALL THE BOOKS. I'LL PUT THESE ONES AWAY AND YOU GUYS CAN HAVE THEM LATER.	holds up hand, gathers up books children have been looking at; puts books on shelf; holds out hand for Mark's book	?: Amy, can I . . .	Jeff gets up, starts to run toward doll-room again
→	MARK? HAND ME OVER YOUR WHALE BOOk. WOULD YOU LIKE TO LEARN MORE ABOUT WHALES ONE TIME SOON?			
	YOU KNOW WHAT'S THE BIGGEST OF ALL?		Mark: Blue!	Mark nods, gives Amy his book
	THE GREAT BLUE WHALE? THE GREAT BLUE WHALE'S IN THIS BOOK MMMMM-	patting book		

Storyreading Segment 1 *continued*.

Focal Points	Readers		Listeners	
	Verbal	Nonverbal	Verbal	Nonverbal
→	MMM, HMMMMM, HE'S IN THERE TOO. OKAY . . . JEFF! JEFFREY, COME ON, DEARIE, WE'RE WAITING FOR YOU.	turns toward dollroom sits on bench stands, quietly takes toys from children	several children talking, looking at small toys on rug	Ris runs into dollroom
			Mark: Amy, call Brad (referring to fact that Brad is sitting way at back of rug)	
→	BRAD, COME ON OVER! (inviting) CAN YOU HEAR FROM THERE, HONEY? CAN YOU HEAR VERY WELL?	sits on bench gets up, goes over to Jeff	Brad: Yes, I can	Jeff comes back from dollroom riding horse; Ris comes pushing doll carriage
→	WAIT A MINUTE, RIS. RIS, ALL RIGHT. LOOK, JEFF, JEFF (calling to him)	goes over to Jeff		Jeff starts to ride away
→	JEFF, WHEN WE HAVE RUG-TIME, THESE THINGS GO IN THE DOLLROOM.	takes carriage and horse, puts in dollroom		
→	COME ON, JEFF, JEFF, WE'RE GOING TO PUT THESE THINGS IN THE DOLLROOM 'CAUSE WE CAN'T HEAR.	at door of dollroom		Jeff follows her into dollroom to retrieve horse
→	YOU MUST LEAVE IT IN HERE. COME ON, HONEY.	***	children playing and talking on rug while waiting	Jeff gets horse

Storyreading Segment 1 *continued*.

Except for the first page of the book where she was prompted, Anna, unprompted, turned to each new page of the text after allowing a period of time for discussion. She had clearly internalized a reading orientation—she knew that attention should be focused on the book, that pictures should be studied in relation to the discussion about them, that participants had to be able to see the appropriate pages, and that ample time had to be given for processing each page. From her many experiences as a listener in group storyreadings, she had extracted the patterns of behavior that accompanied reading. Her actions are good evidence for an image of the child as active learner, working to sort out the rules for approaching and interpreting print.

Focal Points	Reader		Listeners	
	Verbal	Nonverbal	Verbal	Nonverbal
→		Anna pulls dog book out of her bag, holds it up	Lyn: Dogs! Wow! Amy: Dogs! This is good! (excited) We needed that	
→		Anna holds up the book to show all the children	book because we needed to show the kids about all the different kinds of dogs.	
→		Anna turns to first page and shows picture		
→	[PIC: cocker spaniel]	Anna points to picture	?: I know! (calling out)	
			⌈ Amy: What's that? That's . . . a cocker spaniel. What kind of dog is that? ⌊ (Lyn is explaining something about dogs to several other children—indiscernible) Nat: Cocker spaniel! (in loud, silly voice)	
	Anna: (looks pointedly at Nat): YES!		⌈ Amy: A cocker . . . ⌊ Several children: Amy! Amy! (yelling) ⌊ Amy: . . . spaniel! Amy: See, there's a black cocker spaniel. (several children yelling)	points to PIC Mark climbs into barrel in the corner, calling out to others

Storyreading Segment 2.

Rug-time rules for storyreading were frequently in need of repair. As Storyreading Segment 1 indicated, some children consistently did not sit quietly and listen. Rules were by no means rigidly enforced; the teacher's treatment of disruptions varied according to the situation and according to the needs of the disrupting child.

Behavior that was in keeping with rug-time rules was more consistently demanded of five-year-olds than of three-year-olds. When the rules broke down, the teacher usually initiated interactions that reminded the children of rug-time rules. Sometimes, she also physically managed children by seating them next to her, interrupted

Focal Points	Reader		Listeners	
	Verbal	Nonverbal	Verbal	Nonverbal
→		Anna turns page, holds LP out to children	Amy: Okay . . . tur-ur-urn. (to Anna in drawn-out voice)	
	[LP: girl hugging collie] [RP: boy telling Scottie dog to sit up]			
→		Anna holds out the LP, emphasizes it, points to it	Amy: What kind of dog is that? You saw that one on television. What kind is that?	nods toward picture of collie
			?: I don't know	
			Davey: Amy, Amy (calling out), can you . . . (breathless)	is at other barrel in corner, wants to get in
			Amy: What kind is Lassie?	
			Amy: What kind is Lassie?	
			Lyn: Ahh! (breathless) Lassie's a collie! My favorite.	
→	[LP: Irish setter] [RP: Saint Bernard]	Anna turns page and holds out LP, (skips RP on previous page)	Lyn: Uh oh, and there . . . is an Irish setter, that red one.	points to LP
→		Anna points to LP	Amy: And what is that? That red one?	looks up at book

Storyreading Segment 2 *continued.*

rug-time to put away distracting toys or games, or required that some children leave the rug-time group. At other times, she ignored behavior that deviated from rug-time rules or tried to distract disrupters by drawing them into the story being read: she would call on specific children to answer a question, label a pictured item, or imagine themselves in the place of storybook charac-ters. The use of any of these techniques depended upon the situation, the needs and abilities of particular children, and the needs of the group as a whole.

Most children, however, did follow rug-time rules and did conform to expectations of appropriate reading behavior. In preparation for storyreadings and during storyreadings, the children were expected to:

Focal Points	Reader		Listeners	
	Verbal	Nonverbal	Verbal	Nonverbal
			Lyn: An Irish setter.	
			Amy: An Irish setter?	
→		Anna points to RP	Amy: How 'bout this kind? This great big one that can pull sleds if you want?	
			(several children talking to one another in loud voices—indiscernible)	
		***		
→		Anna closes book and holds it in her lap		
			Amy: Let's clap for Anna, very nice!	starts to clap
			Lyn: Very nice, thank you, Anna.	several children clap
			Amy: (to Lyn and to me, [the researcher]): Very nice pacing, I think.	
→		Anna leaves bench, takes place on the rug		Lyn and I nod

Storyreading Segment 2 *continued*.

1. Sit on the rug facing the storyreader.

2. Visually attend to the book being read, and look carefully at the pictures.

3. Listen to the words being read.

4. Pay attention to relationships between words and pictures.

5. Listen to the words and look at the pictures for *every* page (not giving intermittent attention).

6. Remain quiet and avoid distracting others by talking or making noise. (Certain kinds of talk *were* allowed and very much encouraged during storyreadings; these are discussed in later chapters.)

7. Attend to the nonverbal actions of the reader. Notice especially the pictured items that the reader pointed to or emphasized. Watch the reader pantomime actions, make gestures, or change facial expressions.

8. Attend to the verbal actions of the reader. Listen carefully when the reader reads softly or loudly. Notice inflectional or intonational variations.

9. Attend to the world created symbolically in the book and not to the immediate real situation of the children or objects nearby.

10. Concentrate only on the book being read. Avoid extraneous matters that could distract.

11. Avoid interfering with other listeners' abilities to follow these rules.

By teaching them a reading orientation, this set of behavioral norms framed for the children the experience of getting information from decontextualized print. The experience was different from other nursery-school activities and also from reading and writing events that occurred during activities off-the-rug. In off-the-rug reading and writing, the children were generally encouraged to interpret print in relation to the context in which it occurred. They were exposed to the idea that part of the information about the meaning of print was in its environment and purpose. In on-the-rug storyreading, on the other hand, the children were encouraged to attend only to the book itself. The rug-time activity within which storyreading occurred was an important interpretive cue only insofar as it signalled the listening and looking bookreading orientation. Likewise, the physical environment of the print

(a paper and cardboard object) was not helpful in interpretation. Rather, all of the information for interpretation had to come from the book itself. The children were oriented in this direction by following the rug-time rules.

Consistency of Interpretive and Interactional Norms

Many rug-time rule-messages underlay the teacher's actions and responses to the behavior of the children. In addition to the rules that were implicit in her responses, the teacher also explicitly stated norms for rug-time in interactions during or before storyreading. The following summary of rug-time is pieced together from several different storyreading events; all of the words, however, are verbatim quotations from the teacher:

> This is rug-time, a quiet time. . . . This is a place for sitting. . . . It's a time for sitting and looking and listening. . . . When it's rug-time you need to keep your voice quiet so you can hear. . . . It's not a time for playing with other things. When Amy (the teacher) is reading to you at rug-time, that's a time for you to leave all other things alone. Otherwise you miss the story, and then you'll come back and say, "Amy, I didn't hear that part," or, like Susie, "Wait a minute, I missed that page" because you were busy doing something else. . . . This is rug-time, a quiet time, a time for learning new things.

Preschoolers entered Maple Nursery School with many experiences in listening to and getting information from storybooks and other printed materials. The consistent rug-time framework of the nursery school seemed to further contribute to the children's literary socialization by teaching them a set of behaviors for group attention to textual materials. The only other group bookreading experience that these preschoolers had was at storyhours provided periodically for the nursery-school group at local public libraries.

Library Storyreading: A Contrast

The children's experiences with library storyhours were quite different from their nursery-school storyreading experiences. At the libraries, rules were precisely stated and uniformly and strictly enforced; no allowances were made for the special needs of particular children. Even more significant were differences in the nature of storyreading interaction. Nursery-school storyreadings were interactive reader-listener negotiations based on the sense-making of the audience. Library storyreadings, on the other hand, were one-sided performances of set texts within which the children's participation was not encouraged and, in most cases, not permitted. In library storyhours there was little or no negotiation of text and little mediation between text and listeners. Despite these differences, which made for two strikingly contrasting kinds of storyreading experiences, the nonverbal behavior required of the listeners in preparation for and during storyreadings was essentially consistent at both nursery school and libraries. The following example illustrates this consistency:

Narrative Segment 30 at the Library.   The nursery-school group arrives at the public library a few minutes after their scheduled time. The librarian quickly herds them into a straight line and takes them to the reading room. Carpet-square mats are already laid out in a triple semi-circle on the floor. The librarian directs each child to sit on a mat on the floor; she sits on a chair facing them. She instructs the children that they are to sit with legs crossed "Indian style"; everyone is to behave in the same way and remain quiet throughout the storyreading time. This way, they are told, they will listen better, hear the story better, and see the pictures better. During the storyreadings, when individual children rise to their knees or begin to lounge down on their mats, the librarian immediately asks them to sit up "like everyone else."

Interspersed with the stories that the librarian reads aloud to the children are little rhymes and finger plays intended to "get all the wiggles out of you, so you'll be ready to be quiet." When children call out responses or comments during the readings, the librarian puts her finger to her lips and sharply reminds, "Sh!"

As can be seen, the rules of library storyreadings were much more uniformly and strictly enforced than they were for nursery-school readings. Nevertheless, the messages in both settings were consistent: first, children had to sit in proper upright posture, direct visual, aural and mental attention at the book held up by the storyreader, and remain silent; then they could have a bookreading experience.

The children's behavior during nursery-school and library bookreading sessions indicates that in at least these two settings, the children were expected to, and for the most part did, adopt a specific set of nonverbal behaviors in preparation for and during bookreadings. Despite frequent disruptions and breakdowns of bookreading behavioral norms, the majority of storyreading events were strikingly uniform in terms of the children's behavioral patterns. Thus, group bookreading was consistently associated with this particular set of expectations for behavior.

Although we have evidence that the nursery school children were internalizing a particular set of rules for group storyreading, we can only speculate on the extent to which they might have internalized and applied this bookreading orientation to other group reading situations. It seems worthy of speculation, however, to consider the possible implications of such a preschool bookreading orientation for school reading instruction, which is almost exclusively located within teacher-dominated reading groups of one kind or another.

Educators have long claimed that preschool experiences with books are correlated with early school success. It may be that an important part of what preschool children who have had group reading experiences bring to their school reading groups is a knowledge of the nonverbal behavior that many teachers expect to accompany reading. Such nonverbal behavior may indicate to teachers that children are prepared for and attentive during reading lessons. Maple Nursery School children, for example, might appear to exhibit certain reading and prereading skills by sitting up properly, looking at reading materials, listening carefully to teachers' words, associating words and pictures, and concentrating only on textual materials rather than on extraneous factors in the environment. None of these nonverbal behavior patterns have directly or necessarily to do with strategies for interpreting (decoding, making sense of, and using) written language. They may, however, help to provide for children a significant frame within which bookreading occurs and, to similarly-orientated adults, signals that "appropriate" reading behavior is occurring.

REFERENCES

Michaels, S. (1981). "'Sharing time': Children's narrative styles and differential access to literacy." *Language in Society 10*(3), 423–442.

Telling Stories

Tom Newkirk and Patricia McLure

• •

Editor's introduction

In *Listening In: Children Talk about Books (and Other Things)*, the authors examine the kinds of talk that occur during the small literature discussion groups in McLure's first- and second-grade classroom. This excerpt, "Telling Stories," shows how these groups are a powerful tool for teachers and students in understanding student culture.

• • • • • • • • • • •

Near the end of *The Catcher in the Rye* (Salinger, 1951), Holden Caulfield reflects on an oral expression class he took at one of the several prep schools he had attended. In the class, students were coached to yell "Digression!" at any speaker who strayed from his topic. The "digression business" got on Holden's nerves because he liked it when someone digressed, it was "more *interesting* and all." He recalls a boy in the class who didn't stick to the point.

> There was this one boy, Richard Kinsella. He didn't stick to the point too much, and they were always yelling "Digression!" at him. . . . He made this speech about this farm his father bought in Vermont. They kept yelling "Digression" at him the whole time he was making it, and the teacher, Mr. Vinson, gave him an *F* on it because he hadn't told what kind of animals and vegetables and stuff grew on the farm and all. What he did was, Richard Kinsella, he'd *start* telling you all about that stuff— then all of a sudden he'd start telling you about this letter his mother got from his uncle, and how his uncle got polio and all when he was forty-two years old, and how he wouldn't let anyone come to see him in the hospital because he didn't want anyone to see him with a brace on. It didn't have much to

do with the farm—I admit it—but it was *nice*. (Salinger, 1951, 183–84)

Holden, unlike his former teacher, Mr. Vinson, views talk as organic, evolving, unpredictable. For him, it has the power to illuminate experience when it deviates from a preset agenda. He insists on the openness of talk, and, despite the urging of a battery of advisors that he reduce his life to a plan, he is unwilling to eliminate the role of chance in his life.

> A lot of people, especially this one psychoanalyst guy they have here, keeps asking me if I'm going to apply myself when I go back to school next September. It's a stupid question, in my opinion. I mean how do you know what you're going to do till you *do* it? The answer is, you don't. I *think* I am, but how do I know? I swear it's a stupid question. (213)

Vinson's class is a parody of normal classroom talk, but it doesn't miss the reality by much. Courtney Caz-

Source: Listening In: Children Talk about Books (and Other Things) (pp. 80–94) by T. Newkirk and P. McLure, 1992, Portsmouth, NH: Heinemann.

den (1988) argues that teacherly expectations for relevance and conciseness are often dramatically at odds with the storytelling patterns of students. She offers the following example in which a teacher seeks to narrow and focus a child's account of an outing. In her own way, the teacher is yelling "Digression!"

Nancy: I went to Old Ironsides at the ocean. [*Led by a series of teacher questions, Nancy explains that Old Ironsides is a boat and that it's old. The teacher offers the real name, the* Constitution. *Then Nancy tries to shift her story.*]

Nancy: We also spent our dollars and we went to another big shop.

T: Mm. 'N what did you learn about Old Ironsides? [*Led by teacher questions, Nancy supplies more information about the furnishings inside and the costumes of the guides, and then tries to shift focus again.*]

Nancy: And I had a hamburger, french fries, lettuce, and a—

T: OK. All right, what's—Arthur's been waiting and then Paula, OK? (16)

In a way, we can sympathize with the teacher's reluctance to allow the story to move to Nancy's lunch (and the rest of her outing). Arthur and Paula are waiting. But Cazden warns that "while there may be situational reasons for pressing children to speak relevantly and to the point, there are developmental and cultural reasons why it may be difficult for children to meet such expectations" (193).

Underlying this reluctance to allow stories and conversations to evolve is a concept of topicality or task-centeredness. Few distinctions in education are as uncritically invoked as those of on-task/off-task behavior or on-topic/off-topic talk. Most of the research I have read treats these binary distinctions as significant and self-evident. And if we think of the turn-of-the-century factory as the model for the classroom, it is easy to see why. Workers in these factories were typically involved in acting upon raw material in a preset way; they were not allowed to make decisions. Talk among themselves was considered a distraction, so breaks were instituted to segregate socializing from on-task work.

In reading, the student is the worker, the text the raw material, and understanding of the text is the uni-

form product the teachers (bosses) want manufactured. The primary action of the worker, aside from actually reading the text, is to answer questions about the text posed by the teacher or the collateral materials created by the reading system. Answering a question about the text is "on topic"; telling a story related to the text is "off topic." If a child tells a story, he or she is no longer working on the raw material of text to manufacture comprehension. The child has strayed from the assembly line.

According to this mechanical view of classroom talk, each text sets clear and firm boundaries for discussion—just as Richard Kinsella's topic, the farm, set boundaries for him. Yet one of the features of conversation is the shifting of topics: each turn shifts the topic to some degree; each speaker bridges to something new. Few social skills are as important as the capacity to handle what Irving Goffman has called "the etiquette of reach" (1976, 291). We admire the speaker who listens carefully and moves the discussion gracefully forward; we are put off by those who abandon topics that are still warm and cause the talk to lurch unpredictably. And I believe that we resist situations in which we cannot digress at all; we find it unpleasant to talk to people who must immediately get down to business, who resist any deviation, who always talk as if they are double-parked.

Goffman's term "etiquette of reach" is useful for looking at the storytelling that goes on in Pat McLure's first- and second-grade classroom. The word "etiquette" suggests that "topicality," being on topic, is socially defined instead of being a self-evident function of the texts under discussion. If we consider six- and seven-year-olds to constitute a culture, as I have argued, it becomes clear that the etiquettes of their social group may be quite different from those of adults (and even adult conversations, when they work, are less rigidly on topic than so-called discussions led by a teacher).

I became aware of these conventions several years ago when I was recording class discussions for a chapter in *More than Stories* (1989). It was chick season, and Joshua shared his three-page information book on chicks.

The eggs have to be turned twenty-two times and the last three days you do not turn them.
You must keep the incubator moist.
We put letters on one side, numbers on the other.

Imagine the questions you would ask regarding this text: Why do you keep the incubator moist? Why do you put letters on the side? The discussion turned out to be on copying machines. Pat asked how Joshua got the information on chicks.

Joshua: Well, we went to the library and we asked the librarian how we could get a copy of this paper and she said the copy machine and my mother said, "How does it work?" and somebody said, "I'll do it," and then they came over and they put the book like this [*demonstrates in pantomime*]. This was a heavy book. It had the picture like this and you put it like this and it goes "shhhhhhhh" and then it spits out.

Aaron asked how long it took to learn the information, and Joshua answered, "One night." Then we were back to the copying machine.

Aaron: Did you mean when the copy machine spit out the paper did it go "vroo, vroo?"
Joshua: It just went "shhhhhh." The lady said it would spit out at you, but it didn't.

There were a couple of comments about Joshua's illustrations—and then back to copying machines.

Carin: Once when I went with Mrs.____ we had to use the copy machine and she laid the book flat on the thing, whatever you call it. . . .
Joshua: They buckle it in, the book in. And it goes "shhhhhh" and then it comes out.
Carin: We just used Mrs. ____'s and we just put it flat down and then it just went "rrrrrr" like that and then she had to get it off and put another page on it until it was done.

As the discussion continued, several other students told their copying stories, each adding a new element, a new piece to the puzzle. John told about putting a cover over the book. Jimmy described a copier from his old school that was smaller and slower than the one Joshua used. Ginger told about working the copier at her dad's office and feeling the warmth of the copy as it came out.

In general, the members of Pat's class treated the text being shared, whether by a student or by a professional author, as a first long turn in a conversation. But a turn does not permanently fix in place the topic (or

even the general theme) to be discussed. In the share group on Joshua's book on chicks, the ostensible topic of chicks was dropped once he told the more interesting narrative about using the copy machine. It was that narrative that set the theme for the discussion. According to the "etiquette of reach," this shift from chicks to copying machines was perfectly acceptable.

If the published text is treated as a turn in a conversation, it is no longer the inescapable focus of attention. It does not set fixed boundaries (patrolled by the teacher). Instead, it becomes one story among many. Ezra Jack Keats (1974) has his *Snowy Day*, and, as I watch the snow pile up on the frozen Oyster River, so do I. Keats takes his turn, and I take mine. His story evokes mine, enables me to see mine. The initiating text may become a focus for talk or, as in the case of Joshua's chick story, it may give way to a different kind of narrative, which in turn sets off a chain of stories. Ultimately, the stories go on forever. Ellen Blackburn Karelitz, who has described how this chain of narratives works in her own classroom, quotes one of her students, Brian: "You know, Mrs. Blackburn, when you said that numbers never end. Well, I just noticed something. Stories never end either" (1985, 13).

THE ETIQUETTE OF REACH

According to Goffman, the etiquette of reach defines the kinds of bridges we can properly construct when taking a conversational turn. The speaker can "respond to something smaller or larger than the [previous] speaker's statement, or to one aspect of it, or even to the non-linguistic elements of the situation" (1976, 291). In the case of Joshua's sharing session, members of the class were not constrained to respond to the text being shared; they could pick up on a piece of contextual information—using the copying machine—and then, as a group, make that the central topic. This freedom to shift subjects, to take an element from a previous turn and bridge to a new topic, was the defining characteristic of their etiquette of reach. Sometimes the shifts were so abrupt that Pat and I were left in the dust—along with some of the second graders who played by more conventional rules. In cases like these, Pat would not try to rein them in; she would ask, "How is that connected? How did we get here?"

The purest example of this freedom to shift topics came in a discussion of *The Night Before Christmas*, which Jennifer, a first grader, shared. The experience of listening to this discussion was a little like holding on to a runaway toboggan. Up to this point, the group had talked about three Christmas shows, summarizing the plots; they had noted the double-page illustrations in Jennifer's book; and Pat had complimented Jennifer on her fluent reading. Then the toboggan took off. As you read it, try to follow the bridges that participants make to new topics. The ride begins with Jennifer remembering other Christmas stories.

Jennifer: And that reminds me I got one that's about a reindeer.

Pat: Oh, another Christmas story.

Jennifer: And I got Christmas carols and my sister got Christmas carols too. Kristy got *Santa's Runaway Elves* and Christmas stories.

Pat: Um, you got lots of books.

Sandy: Well, I got *The Bear That Slept Through Christmas*—

Michelle: Me too.

Sandy: —and I got a pop-up book and a tape.

Jennifer: That reminds me. Last year I got Tic-Tacs. I don't remember what else I got but I know I got some potatoes and oranges. I didn't eat my oranges at all. It was all sort of plastic. So it wasn't—

Sandy: What color Tic-Tacs did you get? Orange?

Jennifer: Light green.

Sandy: Light green? I like the orange.

Jennifer: So do I. I like the colored. Once my sister went to the emergency room to get stitches. My mom was working and we had to call my mom. Our neighbor is a nurse so she really needed to get stitches. She got seven stitches, two on top and five on bottom.

Michelle: I had four stitches all on my forehead.

Sandy: I've never had stitches.

Corrine: I've had stitches.

Michelle: They don't hurt at all. [*Overlapping talk about whether they hurt.*]

Pat [to Jennifer]: What made you remember that right now?

Jennifer: When she had green stitches.

Pat: Oh, she had green stitches and the green reminded you of Tic-Tacs.

Corrine: I had white stitches.

Michelle: When I first had my stitches it didn't hurt at all on my forehead.

Sandy: When you said stitches it reminded me of the day when . . . I think it was a wedding . . . and we went too and my aunts and my cousin and he was playing with the cat's toy and they had a glass table up there and it fell on the floor and he was on the couch on his knees and tried picking it up but he fell down and hit the glass and he had fifteen stitches.

Jennifer: That reminds me . . . that reminds me, my cousin's friend got a hundred stitches.

Corrine: Sandy reminds me of when I was a flower girl—

Sandy: I was too.

Corrine: My cousin, he was the person that carries the rings and he was looking over the balcony and he was at the hotel and he was looking over the balcony—and he didn't have the ring.

Pat [laughs]: You mean he lost the ring?

Corrine: But my aunt, she had one.

The conversation goes on for a couple more turns and concludes with Sandy saying to Pat, "Boy, that was a lot of talking." It surely was. Even Pat, with her considerable tolerance for digression, admitted that the discussion went "far afield" and wondered in the margins of the transcript whether she shouldn't have stepped in earlier. In four minutes, the conversation had shifted from *The Night Before Christmas* to Christmas books to Tic-Tacs to stitches to weddings.

Yet if we view the participants in this group as members of a six- and seven-year-old culture that has its own conversational rules, it is not as easy to dismiss such talks as off-topic and educationally insignificant. For one thing, members of the group easily found their way into the discussion, even Corrine, who was consistently reticent at other times. This ease of participation was created by the minimal bridge requirement. To take a turn, according to this requirement, a speaker must simply connect with any element in the previous turn, as when the greenness of Tic-Tacs led to a story featuring green stitches. The child may announce the connection with "that reminds me" but does not have to make the connection explicit.

This simple bridge requirement is less constraining than is the etiquette of other, more adult types of talk. One more stringent type of connection is the story-type bridge that we saw in the discussion of the copying machine. According to that constraint, a turn must connect to major thematic elements of the previous turn. For example, if someone tells a lost tooth story, the following speakers will also tell lost tooth stories (or stories that keep to major themes of that story type, such as pain, loss, or fear) until the topic becomes cold, at which point it is time for a more substantial shift.

An even more stringent rule might be called the text-based bridge. It is based on the presupposition that one text has priority in the discussion and that no bridge can take the speaker away from commentary on the text that has been given priority. Many conventional book discussions (and the report of Richard Kinsella) are expected to work within this more stringent set of constraints. Therapeutic and counseling discussions similarly focus on the principal narrative of the person seeking help.

From the standpoint of the six- and seven-year-old culture, however, the less stringent bridges seem the most congenial and allow for a wider range of participation. To exclude these less stringent bridges is to turn a deaf ear (literally) to this culture.

STORIES AND COMMUNITY

Theories of reading comprehension have acknowledged the value of personal narratives, particularly *before* students read a text. By exploring and telling their prior knowledge, by activating frames of experience, readers put in place lenses that will help them comprehend a story. Rather than passively processing a story, they actively use this prior knowledge to anticipate what will happen. The storytelling, according to this view, is subordinate to the act of comprehension, an oral means to a literate end.

In many of the book discussions in Pat's class, the priorities were reversed. The text activated schemas, suggested story types that enabled the children to tell their own stories. This is not to say there was no traditional comprehension work (for example, in the summaries). But it does mean that telling stories was not viewed simply as a means to comprehension. Pat does not continually nag students to get back to the text because the stories themselves are central to the way these groups work—just as they are central to all communities.

Collectively, the stories told by the group members celebrated life in rural New Hampshire. A great many concerned animals, wild and domesticated. Abby was the class expert on cats and had a seemingly inexhaustible set of stories about them. In one session, Jennifer asked Abby how her sister had named her cat. Abby responded:

I don't know. Because her first name was Tiger Eyes because when her eyes closed up they looked like tiger eyes. And then she said, "Mom, I wish I could name her Jessica Fisher just like me" [*laughs*]. And my mom goes, "Go ahead, if you want to." And then she changed her name to Jessica Tiger Eyes Fisher. Probably by next year her name will be a different name.

Billy, as we have seen, loved tooth stories, but he also told dog stories.

Once I saw this dog going past our house and then I saw three people running right after it. And then just when I opened the door to get out the dog came in our house and we had to get it out of the house. And then it went and people asked, "Did you see a dog coming into your house?" and we said, "Yes, it's over there." And they had to run all the way around and finally they caught it.

There was also a type of "gross" story that the boys told. The electricity scene in *Two Bad Ants* (Van Allsburg, 1988) reminded Martin of a dream.

Last night I had a dream about this lady. She picked up the phone and then electricity started coming out and into her ear and she went "Ahhhhh." And the phone was being sucked into her ear and she kept on screaming and her body got all wrinkled and she fell down dead.

More typically, the gross stories involved the mutilation of insects like spiders:

Rob: My brother thinks that daddy longlegs have long legs so they take off and put them to make a web [*calls on Martin*].
Martin: That reminds me when we went to Scott's party, remember the part when we took the daddy longlegs spider and he picked off the legs and he saw the legs still moving.
Rob: Yeah.
Martin: That was neat.

Or flies:

Jake: Have you ever seen a black fly stick out his tongue?

Pat [laughs]: I don't think I've seen one.

Jake: That's what [the space creatures] look like. I've seen one. Really. They have this pink thing goes [*pantomimes it sticking out from his head*]. Because one day we were eating fish. We were camping and my dad caught some fish and we were eating it and all these flies came over and we had this fire and we started burning them up, all the flies. We would trap them and then *sssssss* [*sound of flies sizzling*].

While the mutilation stories were told only by boys, both sexes shared accounts of dealing with raccoons and skunks.

Susan: I think we had a raccoon in our house because our trash can was tipped over and there were four holes inside the trash can.

Sandy: That reminds me at my grandmother's house, one night. They're watching TV and then they heard a big bang out in the front and they went and they saw this mother raccoon and a baby raccoon. They knocked over the rubbish and they ran off.

Vicky: In "The Great Outdoors at Night" these raccoons get in a trash can and so in the morning the father has to clean up all the trash and the mother gets to cook.

Tommy: Just like a cat does.

Sandy: That reminds me once at my young Dad's friend's, well, a raccoon kept getting into the trash so he had to put these rocks on and one night they took a picture of a raccoon in someone else's chimney.

Each participant in the discussion added a new element to the general raccoon narrative (just as in the copier discussion). In Susan's, there was evidence of the raccoons' presence (teeth marks); in Sandy's first story, the raccoons are discovered, and the rubbish overturned; in Vicky's, the raccoons make a major mess; and, in Sandy's second story, the raccoon is photographed.

Many of these digressions during talk about animals could be justified fairly easily because they extended the children's knowledge of the natural world—reading time turned into science time. But the TV/video-game culture was also a major part of these children's experience, and it, too, made its way into the talk about books. For example, in the discussions of the *Stupids* books that I have quoted, the talk moved to TV shows and video games. The picture of the dog, Kitty, driving the car reminded Rob of a scene in "America's Funniest Home Videos."

Don [pretending to be Kitty driving the car]: RRRRRRRRRRR. There goes one door. RRRRRRRR. Konk. [*He makes an explosion sound to indicate a crash.*]

Jed: There goes everything.

Rob: On "The World's Funniest Home Videos" there was this person—

Jed: Oh, yeah.

Rob: He was in a car. There was only the front of it. But the back was broken off so there was only front wheels so he was like this [*demonstrates*] and driving the car.

Jed: Yeah, he was like this. The guy said, "Hey, Mom, do you like my new car?" And he was driving with the back off. And it worked good.

At another point in the discussion, the boys in the group made a fairly extensive inventory of video games. The picture of King Stupid the Fourteenth reminded Jed of the video game *King Friday the Thirteenth*, and they were off:

Jed: Have you ever played *King Friday the Thirteenth*?

Rob: King Friday the Thirteenth. Yeah.

Jed: It is fun.

Rob: Mm-hm.

Scott: How do you do it?

Jed: I don't know.

Don: It is a Nintendo game?

Jed: Yeah.

Scott: What do you do with it?

Jed: I don't know.

Don is reminded of the movie *Friday the Thirteenth*.

Don: I do not want to look at the cover of the movie *Friday the Thirteenth* one bit.

Pat [laughing]: No, I don't like it either.

Don: It's like URRRRRRRRR and it's like this gigantic thing bigger than the universe coming up and smashing the whole world into two thousand pieces.

Then the conversation goes back to how to play *King Friday the Thirteenth* and on to the games that Rob has rented—*Mario, Batman, Sesame Street*, and *Jeopardy*. Jed asks Rob how to play *Sesame Street*, and Rob starts a fairly complicated description of "Ernie's Magic Skates."

As I was transcribing this section of the tape, I inserted a question: "I would bet many teachers would try to get back to the book at this point. Why do you let them go on?" Pat's answer, I feel, was one of the most revealing comments she made concerning these groups.

> I'm not sure—I see this as a very interesting social situation for these boys. I feel almost like I'm eavesdropping on some "free play." It's like they're not really aware that we're there.

In reading and thinking about her answer, I realized that I was still thinking in binary terms—wondering when she would get back on task. But Pat does not view talk in on/off terms. She is interested in what children say and saw this talk about Nintendo games as important for the social functioning of this group. She didn't split the talk into social and academic, on task (what counts) and off task (what diverts). Her position is closer to one taken by Anne Dyson:

> Talk about academic tasks is often contrasted with social talk: individuals achieve because of the time they spend "on task." My observations suggest that the "academic" and the "social" are not so simply—or so profitably—separated. The social laughing, teasing, correcting, and chatting that accompany children's academic work are byproducts of the need to link with others and be recognized by them. But they can also be catalysts for intellectual growth. (1987, 417)

The share groups that failed were the ones that lacked social interaction and energy; they stuck to questions and answers (usually formulaic) about the book. They seemed to lack digressionary possibility. They never moved.

When Pat invites the children in her class to share their culture in reading groups, she subtly influences which parts of the culture they bring in. As I reread the video-game discussion, I was surprised to see that it really wasn't that long, not nearly as long as some lost-tooth discussions. I suspect that it seemed long because it was not the type of story—not the type of

digression—that usually occurred. More typically, the stories featured animals, brothers and sisters, other books, topics that did not center on secondhand video experiences and on acquisitions.

A colleague of mine, Brenda Miller Power, who had spent considerable time in Pat's class once made the distinction between holiday time (measured by special days when children receive candy and presents) and seasonal time (ordered by natural growth and change). When Pat brings the brood hens into class, for example, she is announcing a preference for natural time. In this classroom, it is turning eggs, counting days, and then watching chicks hatch that mark the coming of spring. Likewise, stories of lost teeth and of younger brothers and sisters enable these students to measure their own growth.

Literature has the power to evoke these stories. It offers a way into memory. It opens up our own experiences and enables us to talk about them. Sometimes, when I see children tied to preset questions about a text, I imagine tiny lilliputian creatures dwarfed by the giant book that they are crawling over. The book is dominant and imposing; those attending to it are antlike to the point of insignificance. A more companionable image is of the author seated at a table—or better, with others around a campfire—ready to take the first turn in a conversation, to begin a chain of stories that cannot be predicted ahead of time. It's a position, I believe, that many authors would like to take.

REFERENCES

Cazden, C. (1988). *Classroom discourse*. Portsmouth, NH: Heinemann.

Dyson, A. H. (1987). "Individual differences in beginning composing: An orchestral vision of learning to write." *Written Communication 4*, 411–442.

Goffman, I. (1976). "Replies and responses." *Language in Society 5* (December). pp. 257–313.

Karelitz, E. B. (1985). "Common ground: Developing relationships between reading and writing." *Language Arts 61* (April). pp. 10–17.

Keats, E. J. (1974). *The snowy day*. New York: Viking Press.

Newkirk, T. (1989). *More than stories: The range of children's writing*. Portsmouth, NH: Heinemann.

Salinger, J. D. (1951). *Catcher in the rye*. Boston, MA: Little, Brown.

Van Allsberg, C. (1988). *Two bad ants*. Boston, MA: Houghton Mifflin.

A Love of Words

RALPH FLETCHER

. . . .

Editor's introduction

Ralph Fletcher is a writer who has spent many years working with children in public schools. His book, *What a Writer Needs*, draws on his own experience as a writer and teacher to look at the essential support writers of any age need. In this excerpt, Fletcher looks at how his love of language emerged, and how schools can foster a similar love.

. . . .

Language permits us to see. Without the word, we are all blind.

Carlos Fuentes, *The Old Gringo*, 1985

STRANGE OCCURRENCES. In November I took a group of kids to the Bronx Zoo. We reached the buffaloes and stopped to admire the immense bulk, the shaggy shredding coats.

"Buffaloes!" a little boy said, and I felt a stab of pure emotion, sharp, bittersweet.

"C'mon, let's go," another kid said. But I couldn't move. Buffaloes. The word reverberated oddly inside my head. I was dazed, rooted to the spot. I was actually on the brink of tears. Yet I couldn't quite bring it to the surface, that deep memory fragment. I shook it off and all but forgot it. But on the way home from the zoo the kids started singing "Home on the Range," and when they got to the part "where the buffaloes roam" there it was again—pungent emotion, pure and sad and sweet, surging up inside me.

Months passed. One day I was hanging up JoAnn's white bathrobe and just like that the memory came flooding back. Dad's bathrobe. When I was little, for some reason (the shaggy bulk?) we always called Dad's bathrobe his "buffalo." He traveled a lot during those years, selling books all over New England. The first thing he did when he came home on Friday night was to don slippers and that big white terrycloth bathrobe. We would snuggle hard against that buffalo while he read stories to us before bed.

Some nights during the week while Dad was away we would start pestering my mother. Couldn't we take Dad's buffalo out of his closet? Just for a little while? If she agreed, we'd race upstairs to the closet in his bedroom. The buffalo always hung on a particular hook; we would jostle each other to be first to pull it down. The buffalo got dragged downstairs to the living room where we would wrap it around us while we watched tv. It was so big that two or even three kids could nestle within its white bulk. Beyond its warmth and softness, the most wonderful thing about the robe was how it had soaked up Dad's essence, his *smell*. We would sit there, wrapped in the warmth and comfort-

Source: What a Writer Needs (pp. 31–41) by R. Fletcher. Reprinted by permission of Ralph Fletcher: WHAT A WRITER NEEDS (Heinemann, A division of Reed Elsevier Inc., Portsmouth, NH, 1993).

139

ing scent of the father we missed so much. I discovered that if I closed my eyes it was nearly possible to believe that he really was there himself, holding us in his strong arms.

Today the word *buffalo* sounds to me like power commingled with regret: the mighty beasts that were all but wiped out as white America moved west. But also a deeper and more personal regret tangled up with missing my father.

Artists develop a love for the feel of their tools, the smell and texture of clay, wood, or paint. My brother Jim has imported ebony all the way from Nigeria for some of his most memorable sculptures. The lithographer Tanya Grosman searched the world to find paper of astonishing beauty and rarity to lure artists such as Jasper Johns, Larry Rivers, Buckminster Fuller, and Robert Rauschenburg to her Universal Limited Art Editions studio in West Islip, New York.

Writers are no different. Writers love words. And while some writers get excited over a particular pen or a more powerful word processing program, words remain the most important tool the writer has to work with.

"If you want to write and you're not in love with your language, you shouldn't be writing," Jane Yolen says bluntly. "Words are the writer's tools."

"When I write," Cynthia Rylant says, "my mind's not filled with visual imagery. It's filled with language. Words. I seek words, I chase after them. When I write I'm trying to put the most beautiful words in the world down on paper."

Not all writers work like Rylant; some writers do begin with images, others with emotion. Either way the writer must use words to communicate the story/image/emotion. Writers obsess over words, their origins, their sounds. Writers have pet words, favorite and worst words, words imbued with other associations and personal meanings. In *One Writer's Beginnings*, Eudora Welty (1984) describes the sensual awareness she developed of particular words such as moon: "The word 'moon' comes into my mouth as though fed to me out of a silver spoon. Held in my mouth the moon became a word. It had the roundness of a Concord grape Grandpa took off his vine and gave me to suck out of its skin and swallow whole, in Ohio."

Writers love their language, but the language they love may not be a conventional tongue. Mark Twain's many books captured the colorful vernacular of the Mississippi region. Eloise Greenfield is one of many African-American writers to use Black English for her

sparkling book of poems, *Honey, I Love* (1978). And Darrell H. Y. Lum, a Hawaiian writer, uses a rich and musical pidgin English in a short story like "The Moili-ili Bag Man" (1992). The language used by a writer may be powerful or lyrically beautiful even while it does not conform to conventional grammar.

The writer's fascination with words has roots in the child's natural play with language. In late May of 1989, my friend Jenifer Hall took a trip up north with her daughter, Emma. Jenifer explained that they were going to see Ralph and JoAnn get married in Ludlow, Vermont. Emma, who was about twenty months old at the time, fell instantly in love with that word: Ludlow. For two solid hours she sang and chanted and played with its sounds: "Lud-low, lud-low . . . lud-lud-lud and low-low-low . . . LUD-low LUD-low, LUD-low-low-low-low . . . luddy-luddy-luddy-lud . . . luddy-luddy-luddy-low . . . "

"Read like a wolf eats," Gary Paulsen says to young readers, and as a boy I did that. I was a ravenous reader, and it didn't take long to figure out that each new word brought you into a whole new room, with new views and distinct intellectual furniture. The Boy Scout Oath's lofty aims ("trustworthy, loyal, helpful, friendly, courteous, kind, obedient, cheerful, thrifty, brave, clean, and reverent") were counterbalanced by less pure descriptors such as *voluptuous*, and *callipygean*—exotic and barely understood words I first encountered in books, words that took on sultry new nuances as I moved into adolescence.

One sweltering summer day, while my young father struggled to mow the lawn with a hand mower, I was sitting with my best friend on the porch. He confided to me the worst swear in the world. Only nine years old, I watched from a safe distance my father mop sweat off his forehead while my friend whispered the muggy monosyllabic word, softly, so my father would not hear. It seemed monstrous that such a word could co-exist juxtaposed (another of my favorite words) against the image of my saintly, toiling father. Swears amazed me. "Duck" was perfectly all right, but if your mother heard you rhyme that word with another word only two letters after the "D" you could get your mouth washed out with soap.

Another amazing thing: Words could mean different things at different times. The spoken word "see" might also mean "sea"—or even the letter "C." Many words contained delightful shades of ambiguity. When I was five I loved to play with homonyms: "bear" and "bare," "red" and "read." This early language play would later blossom in a poem like "Waves" (from *Water Planet*):

Waves on the ocean,
Ripples on the sand,
My father calling me
With a wave of his hand.
The wavy grain of wood,
The wave in my hair,
Waves of fiery autumn leaves
Tumbling through the air.
A wave of sadness
When I think of the way
My best friend Vinnie
Moved far far away.

I grew up in Brant Rock, Massachusetts, where there was a fabulous candy store: Buds. Once a week, if we were lucky, my mother would walk us down to Buds, where the bins and counters were crammed with chocolate cigarettes and bubblegum cigars, red wax lips and black wax mustaches, dots and red hots, jaw-breakers and ju-ju beads . . . Many of the candies were priced two or even three for a penny; if you shopped wisely you could end up with a whole bag of sweets for a nickel or a dime.

At that time *bamboozled* and *flabbergasted* were my favorite words. I loved the feel of those words in my mouth, and still cannot conjure them up except in terms of taste. *Bamboozled* has a fizzly Sweet Tart taste that begins in a rush of sweetness but always ends with a tingly, tickly feeling at the top of the mouth. *Flabbergasted*, on the other hand, tastes and sounds as nutty as a Heath Bar.

I kept a mental list of my favorite words, some of which I loved for the odd pictures they made in my mind, others merely for their exotic sounds: *babushka, cockatoo, pumpernickel,* and *periwinkle.* Later I would keep actual lists of words and trade them with similarly inclined friends. (We were not necessarily the most popular kids in the school.) Each word carried its own peculiar kind of melody. While words like *umber, mellow, sonorous,* and *quiescent* sounded smoothing, words like *obstreperous, truculent, vituperative,* and *obdurate* seemed to jut their very chins out at the world.

The Fletcher family was a den of rabid Boston Bruin hockey fans. Back then the Bruins had a few future Hall of Fame players, like Phil Esposito and Bobby Orr. Otherwise, the team consisted primarily of players who hustled, checked hard, and enjoyed fighting, or appeared to, at least. The Bruins were forever getting into brawls. I was an avid reader of the *Boston Globe* sports section, and it was great fun trying to envision the sports writers thumbing through their thesauruses in search of new words for these nightly altercations. My siblings and I roared over the words they came up with: *imbroglio, fisticuffs, slugfest, donnybrook,* and (my favorite) *brouhaha.*

In high school, while other kids admired teachers with the best looks, biggest muscles, or fastest cars, I admired those teachers with the most remarkable vocabularies. Mr. Thompson and Mr. Plumer were able to take words like *perspicacious, numinous,* or even *contemporaneous* and weave them seamlessly into their lectures. I would copy down the words and race home to look them up.

Fancy words like *perspicacious* were one thing. But sometimes, I discovered two ordinary words placed next to each other could wake up and create an effect that went far beyond the capabilities of either one. This is exactly what led to my deciding to title my first book *Walking Trees* (1991), taken from a conversation I had with a first-grade girl. Put together, these two words try to pull each other in opposite directions. The phrase *walking trees* embodies a concept almost impossible to put in words: paradox, when two opposing ideas can both be true at the same time.

In the early 1960s, my siblings and I roamed through the thick pine woods around our house in Marshfield, Massachusetts. My brother Jim was a born naturalist, with vacuum eyes that sucked up incredible treasures during his long solitary treks through the woods. Every single day he would bring home some unusual insect, snake, or turtle he had found.

One day, after a bad windstorm, Jim and I were walking through a swampy part of the woods. A tree had fallen in the storm; a shallow pool had formed in the crater left by the huge mass of uplifted roots. At the edge of the water we saw something lurch into the water, a kind of lizard we had never seen before. We got just the briefest glimpse of red before the creature disappeared.

"Didya see that?"

"It looked some kind of newt," I said. "A salamander."

"That was no salamander," Jim said. "Didn't you see the red on its gills?"

Jim went home and proceeded to pull out several volumes of the World Book Encyclopedia. For two hours he sat poring through volumes A (amphibians), L (lizard), and R (reptiles).

"I found it," he said, showing me a picture. "A mud puppy. That's definitely it. We saw a mud puppy. They're common around here, found in the swamps, rivers, and lakes of northeastern America. Their external gills are bright red."

Mud puppy! I fell in love with the odd name, the internal rhyme, the funny image it forced into my head. The name clicked. By the end of that week all the kids in the neighborhood were calling the swampy area near that uprooted tree Mud Puppy Place.

Journal entry, January 30, 1991. JoAnn is studying for the GREs. Three hundred core words for the vocabulary section. Stacks of vocabulary cards in the bathroom. Big, cocky, multisyllabic words. Abstemious, convivial, concatenation. These words strut around the house, loud and arrogant. Worse, they have actually shouldered their way into our spoken sentences.

"Don't you think the war is *reprehensible?*"

"Don't *prevaricate*. The point is that when it comes to contributions, some of our allies certainly haven't been very *munificent*."

These words are obnoxious, but we cater to them. At least for now, we need them far more than they need us.

Words are the writer's primal tools. But anyone who tries to write English—child or adult—immediately gets caught in a kind of linguistic stranglehold that makes it difficult to use those tools. Our English language contains about 490,000 words, along with another 300,000 technical terms. No one, of course, not even the great writers, can utilize so much richness. It has been said that Shakespeare had a working vocabulary of around 33,000 words. In 1945, the average American student between the ages of six and fourteen had a written vocabulary of 25,000 words. Today, that vocabulary has shrunk to about 10,000 words.

The mass media has helped to further tighten this noose. Popular print media draw from a small group of words; television, of course, draws from the smallest word pool of all. The implications for this stranglehold go far beyond the dangers of falling SAT scores.

It seems to me that the first step toward breaking this linguistic stranglehold is for teachers to model our own curiosity with words. Recently I decided to bring a bag of words into the schools where I work as a writing consul-

tant. I wanted to let kids know how crucial words are to me as a writer. But how to proceed? I was surer about what I *didn't* want to do. I knew I didn't want to turn it into a vocabulary lesson, carefully disguised instruction on roots or suffixes, or an exercise in using the dictionary.

I walked into a fifth-grade classroom and began by writing some of my favorite words on the blackboard. Some were funny sounding words: *persnickety*, *oxymoron*, and *troglodyte* (which the students especially liked for its usefulness in insulting people). I had chosen several small words for their sheer potency: *triage*, *quisling*, *quietus*.

Kids started scrambling for the dictionaries. It turned out, however, that the school-use dictionaries in the classroom didn't house most of the words I had brought in with me. I sent a student down to the library. A few minutes later he returned, grunting under the weight of Webster's monstrous 2,347-page 320,000-word *New Universal Unabridged Dictionary*. We were in business.

Mnemonic. Touchstone. Onomatopoeia. The kids were delighted to learn that *fontanel* is the word for the soft spot at the top of a baby's head. Next, I scribbled on the board several truly bizarre words:

> *jirble*—a craving for unnatural food, such as dust
> *geniophobia*—fear of chins
> *xenoglossy*—understanding a language one has never learned

"Probably the longest word in the English language is *pneumonoultramicroscopicsilicovolcanoconiosis*," I told the students. "Forty-five letters. It's a kind of lung disease miners can get."

The kids howled, impressed that I knew what it meant and could actually pronounce it. They asked me to say it several more times, and insisted I write it on the board.

"How about you?" I asked. "Do you have any favorite words?"

"I've always liked *plummet*," one boy said. "I like the way it sounds."

"I like *tintinnabulation*," one girl said, pronouncing the word perfectly. "It means the ringing of the bells."

I wrote down their words: *déjà vu, exposé, deciduous*.

"I like the word *mistress*," one very tall girl said. "I mean, I don't like what it means but I like how it sounds." She paused and looked at me with narrowed eyes. "What *does* it mean?"

I glanced at the fifth-grade teacher. The teacher answered quickly, casually, as if she had been expecting the question.

"Mistress is one of those words with more than one meaning," she explained. "Mistress can be a proper title for a woman. And it can also be the word for a woman who goes out with a married man."

"Oh," the girl said.

Jane Yolen (1973) describes three different vocabularies: a reading vocabulary, a writing vocabulary, and a speaking vocabulary. "There are some words that are wonderful but they're reading words only, or writing words—not speaking words," Yolen says. "And those of us who are writers also have a secret vocabulary."

My secret vocabulary includes words I often save for a long time, several years, until I can actually use them in a piece of writing. I hoarded *postprandial* (an adjective meaning "after dinner," as in "postprandial coffee") for no less than five years and was thrilled to actually be able to use the word in my first book. Another secret word of mine is *gegenschein*—a faint, glowing spot in the sky exactly opposite the position of the sun; also called "counterglow." I have kept this word for a long, long time; I'm not at all sure I shall ever find a legitimate place to use it in a sentence. Still, it's good to have such a word around in case the need arises.

A rich vocabulary allows a writer to get a richness of thought onto the paper. However, the writer's real pleasure comes not from using an exotic word but from using the *right* word in a sentence. Not long ago, while writing an article, I labored over this sentence: "Many school districts are finding it difficult to _____ a whole-language approach with existing reading programs, which rely heavily on basals."

I could not think of the missing word. But I knew it was out there—the single word that would make the sentence click, make its meaning snap into instant focus. It had something to do with paradox, with linking two things that don't quite go together. *Juxtapose* was close, but it wasn't the right word. I kept plugging other, less precise words into the sentence and rereading to see how it sounded. Link? No. Equate? No. Compare? Bridge? Nope. Finally, I gave up and moved to another part of the article.

That night, in bed, I suddenly opened my eyes. Sat bolt upright.

"RECONCILE!" I said to JoAnn.

"Huh?"

"Reconcile!" I grinned at her. "The word I've been looking for. 'School districts are finding it difficult to *reconcile* a whole-language approach with existing reading programs, which rely heavily on basals.' Eureka!"

As teachers, we can share with students the pleasure in finding the precise word to communicate a nuance of thought. We can encourage students to play naturally with language. And we can celebrate their language breakthroughs wherever and whenever they occur. After reading *Charlotte's Web* (White, 1952), Donna, a third grader, told her teacher: "I think I want to use the word *perish* in my story instead of *die*."

Is *perish* a better word than *die*? Not necessarily. Not always. Often a simple word is better than the fancy word. But in this case Donna took a big risk: She moved a word from her reading vocabulary to her writing vocabulary, a word she had never before used in a piece of writing. That's what I mean by a language breakthrough.

In the Bronx, Denton, a first grader, wrote the story shown in Figure 3–1.

Where had Denton come upon *beloved*, an old-fashioned word that intermingles love, respect, and a kind of religious reverence? I told Denton: "It's a wonderful piece of writing. That word *beloved* makes it even more special to read."

I hoard yet one more vocabulary. This one has less to do with exotic words than with words saturated in strong memories. Words and phrases like *buffalo* and *mud puppy* contain potent medicine; their music conjures up an entire era of my life. I think of them as "trapdoor" words. For some words, the conventional meaning hides a secret trapdoor that leads down to an unexpected or previously forgotten layer of memory underneath. The mere mention of such a word is enough to bring it all back in a flood.

Take the word *sheriff*. This serious word has been altered forever by the association I have with Valerie Sheriff, a girl on whom I had a hopeless crush (the perfect word!) during eleventh and twelfth grades. She was stunning, and she was in the classes with all the smartest kids, which only intensified the awe in which I held her. Today I cannot watch a western with outlaws and sheriffs without immediately thinking of Valerie Sheriff, her straight blond hair and flawless features, the cool California air about her, the impossibly long legs beneath her cheerleader miniskirt, the energetic splits she did on the sidelines during football games that always left me feeling weak.

Figure 3–1

Or take *elegant*. My grandmother, Annie Collins, came from Arlington, Massachusetts, each year to spend Christmas with our family in New York. At our Christmas Eve dinner, Grandma Annie, Aunt Mary, my parents, and all seven or eight or nine kids would be sitting around the big table with the best plates and silverware, the food heaped high, a glass of red wine for the grownups, even a thimbleful for the kids. After the food was served, and grace said, everyone paused. We kids had to wait, drooling over our drumsticks, mouths watering over mounds of butternut squash with molten craters of butter on top. It was traditional that before the rest of us could dig in, Grandma Annie had to be the first one to take a mouthful of turkey.

"Oh, Jean, this is *elegant*," she would say. That set everything into motion. Now Mom could blush her thanks, everyone else could laugh, and we could all start eating. But we knew. Young as we were, we understood some of the significance of that word spoken here in New York by our Bostonian grandmother, a word that seemed to rhyme with "delicate," a word that carried its nostalgic ring of old Boston, maybe more civilized times, legends of Ted Williams and Jack Kennedy, the times she marched on the Boston Commons as a suffragette, and the night she danced with "Honey" Fitz at an office party in Filene's Bargain Basement, where she worked.

Grandma Annie died in 1979, at the age of ninety-two. Today, in my family, the word "elegant" still gets spoken around the holidays, and always with a great deal of reverence.

REFERENCES

Fletcher, R. (1991). *Walking trees*. Portsmouth, NH: Heinemann.

Fuentes, C. (1985). *The old gringo*. New York: Farrer Straus Giroux.

Greenfield, E. (1978). *Honey, I love and other love poems*. New York: Crowell.

Lum, D. (1992). "The Moiliili Bagman" in Watanabe, S. (Ed.), *Talking to the dead and other stories*. New York: Doubleday.

Welty, E. (1984). *One writer's beginnings*. Cambridge, MA: Harvard University Press.

White, E. B. (1952). *Charlotte's web*. New York: Harper and Row.

Yolen, J. (1973). *Writing books for children*. Boston, MA: The Writer, Inc.

Ways to Look at the Functions of Children's Language

Gay Su Pinnell

Editor's introduction

Gay Su Pinnell is a national leader in Reading Recovery. In her work, she is a strong voice for teachers developing skills as close observers of students. In this article, she applies Halliday's categories for the functions of language to the talk of students in one classroom. Her work is a fine example of how language theories can inform and extend the work of teacher researchers.

Six year old Andrew has just been to a concert given by a harpist at his school. He is now drawing a harp and talking to himself: "Harperoo. Harperoo. Harperdy dart, harperdy dart, parperdy dart, arp arp, arpity, dart, dart, arpity dart, arpity, dart, arpity, dart, dart, arp, arp, parpity, dart. . . . OK, this was a fine assembly . . . but I can tell you something. That harp was about six feet tall! And if you don't believe me, ask the woman that was playing it. Whew! Boy!"

"New, new, new" declares a catalog designed to persuade teachers to purchase the latest materials to help children develop skills in language. Some of the catchy titles include "growth in grammar," "phonics in context," "word attack and comprehension," "spelling for beginners." These materials may indeed help youngsters look at various forms of language and perhaps to perform well on worksheets and tests designed to measure the lessons the materials teach. But most are usually based on assumptions about what children do not know about language while ignoring their competence—what they do know. Such materials fail to recognize and respond to the natural and enthusiastic language play we observe in Andrew's example above. And they are not "new." Most important, they are inconsistent with language research of the past decade which urges us to focus less on the form of language and more on its social function and meaning.

This article will concentrate, therefore, on what teachers can learn about children's language—their ability to communicate and to engage in conversation—through observation and on ways to extend their language for a range of uses in real life situations.

DEVELOPING A FUNCTIONAL VIEW OF LANGUAGE

A functional view of language means focusing on how people use language in their everyday lives to communicate, to present themselves, to find out about things, to give information, to negotiate and interact. What is important about language is what we can do with it— how it functions in a world of people. What we can *do* with language is worth assessing and teaching.

Source: "Ways to Look at the Functions of Children's Language" by G. S. Pinnell, 1985. In *Observing the Language Learner* (pp. 57–72), A. Jaggar and M. T. Smith-Burke, Eds., Newark, DE: International Reading Association.

Children live in a rich social world of language. They hear language, reorganize it and use it to express their own meanings. As they interact with others, they gradually learn how to share their meanings and, as they do so, construct a set of beliefs and expectations about language. They learn that language can be used to meet their needs, to learn and to communicate with others. The more they use language the more they learn about the forms of language—the words and patterns—that will help them to accomplish their purposes. When we think about children learning language, we can apply the simple principle: form follows function.

As Harold and Connie Rosen (1973) have pointed out, "language is for living with," and we might add, "learning with" (p. 21). Research for at least the past decade supports the idea that function and meaning are the most important, and probably the most neglected, concerns of parents, researchers, teachers, and others who must make decisions about the assessment and development of young children's language (Cazden, John, & Hymes, 1972).

A productive way to monitor language development—and one which will also help teachers to evaluate their own effectiveness in fostering language use—is to observe children in a systematic way to determine the range of language functions used in the classroom. There are several established systems for observing and categorizing functions of language. These systems are useful for assessment and also for devising strategies to extend children's use of language for a variety of social purposes.

One simple and useful category system has already been developed by M.A.K. Halliday (1973, 1975), who maintains that the linguistic system is a "range of possible meanings, together with the means whereby these meanings are realized or expressed" (1975, p. 8). He identifies seven categories for functions of language and stresses the importance of children experiencing the whole range in their homes, communities, and schools. The categories based on Halliday's framework are listed below. The definitions were formulated by Pinnell for use in a study (1975) of language in the classroom.

Function Categories

Instrumental Language.   Instrumental language is what we use to get what we want, to satisfy needs or desires. At the early stages it may be to satisfy simple needs or wants; at later stages of sophistication, it may take the form of polite requests or persuasion. Appropriate and effective use of instrumental language in conversation, on the telephone, and in writing is important for the skillful language user. Little intervention is needed to elicit instrumental language. Children use it all the time. As they grow more independent, instrumental language should, in fact, decrease and become more complex, taking on forms of persuasion and argument.

Regulatory Language.   The regulatory function means using language to control the behavior of others, or getting them to do what we want them to do. Regulatory language may include giving orders or at more subtle levels, manipulating and controlling others. This kind of language is often used in competitive game situations in which there is a rule-governed "right" answer. Positive regulatory language is one of the "life skills" that every parent, shop owner, foreman, or administrator must know. The student who leads a committee or serves on Student Council will practice regulatory language every day.

Interactional Language.   Interactional language is used to establish and define social relationships. It may include negotiation, encouragement, expressions of friendships, and the kind of "maintenance" language all of us use in group situations. The "setting, joking and small talk" adults do before a meeting begins is also an example. Because those who are effective in building informal relationships are likely to succeed, children need to develop a comfortable awareness of their ability to use language to establish relationships with other people, to work cooperatively with them, and to enjoy their companionship.

Personal Language.   Personal language is used to express individuality and personality. Strong feelings and opinions are part of personal language. Personal language is often neglected in classrooms and thought inappropriate. Yet, it is through personal language that children relate their own lives to the subject matter being taught, establish their own identities, build self esteem and confidence.

Imaginative Language.   Imaginative language is used to create a world of one's own, to express fantasy through dramatic play, drama, poetry or stories. This use of language flourishes in the kindergarten with its house corner, big blocks and toys. Unless it is fostered, it will rapidly disappear in later years. Its importance cannot be underestimated, especially when we consider how difficult some teachers find it to get students to write with imagination. Poetry, stories, drama—all are the result of active use of the imaginative function.

Heuristic Language.   Heuristic language is used to explore the environment, to investigate, to acquire knowledge and understanding. Heuristic language is for investigation, for wondering, for figuring things out. It is the language of inquiry and is one of the most important functions.

Informative Language.   Informative language is used to communicate information, to report facts or conclusions from facts. It is the language of school. Teachers most frequently use it themselves and require it of children, but informative language is not only recall of facts. Helping children synthesize material and draw inferences and conclusions is also important.

In this article, Halliday's framework will be used to look at children's use of language. But it is not the only system. Tough (1977), Smith (1977), Wood (1977) and others provide different frameworks for looking at the functions of language. Teachers can easily develop their own by thinking about all the ways they use language; these are the functions the child must eventually develop.

Whatever the system, sensitive observation, using a simple category system for language functions, can help a teacher determine children's competence in using language that relates to real life situations. Teachers need ways of assessing language that will help them to monitor the child's growing ability to use language skillfully in the social milieu. Test scores may be part of the assessment, but teachers' judgments of language ability are still the most trusted and reliable assessment. Studies (Black, 1979; Tough, 1977) show that observing and recording children's language behavior is a viable way to look at what they *can* do, thus giving an effective starting point for instruction.

The important thing is that teachers need to think carefully about the social interaction going on in the classroom, perhaps asking themselves questions such as:

1. Does each child use language for a variety of purposes? How is the function of language linked with what the child is doing and who he/she is talking to?

2. What range of language functions do we hear in the classroom? What situations promote different uses for language?

3. How can I extend children's use of language as I work with them?

In order to answer these questions teachers must pay attention to the context in which language is used, in this case, the school and the classroom.

Children learn how to use language within a social context and as they do so, they learn the needed forms of expression. The language context, the environment, and the climate of the classroom and school are important factors that influence how children will use language. Context includes the other people in the situation, the expectations and background knowledge of speakers and listeners alike, as well as the physical surroundings in which the language takes place. As Clark and Clark (1977) have pointed out, the "function of language is intimately bound up with the speakers' and listeners' mental activities during communication, in particular with the speakers' intentions, the ideas speakers want to convey and the listeners' current knowledge" (p. 25).

WHAT CAN WE LEARN FROM WATCHING AND LISTENING?

As the following examples will demonstrate, a great deal can be learned by careful watching and listening. In the example below, Anne and Amy, two first graders, are painting clay ash trays they have made.

Anne: Yeah, 'cause my mom really does need a ash tray. She only got three or four ash trays and she smokes a lot. And we always have to clean the ash trays out for. . . . I use the, uh, stuff that you dust the tables with but in the ashtrays and they turn out real clean. Don't you, Amy?

Amy: Mm, hm.

Anne: You're my sister but you had to get adopted by somebody cause mommy didn't like you. You were mean! (She giggles.)

Amy: She liked me, but she didn't wanta have that much children and . . .

Anne: Why? 'Cause she already got five kids now. 'Member, she gave away sister, and brother. We had two brothers until she had to give you and then two. We did have eight kids. Wasn't it? Yea, it was eight kids. (Pause) 'Cause five plus three equal eight.

Amy: I'm done with the inside now. Where's that pretty blue?

Monica: I know.

Amy: Here's that pretty blue on there. See the pretty blue on there, Sue Anne?

Anne: Yeah. (Laughs) Gosh, your ash tray is little. How come you just put it on a straw?

Amy: I'm gonna put some string around it.

Anne: It has tape underneath. I just made a big one because my mom smokes a lot. You know mommy's been smokin' more than she usually does since you've been gone. And she has to sleep with me at night. She thinks I'm you. 'Cause she likes to sleep with you. 'Member, she always did? But you never did wanta clean. I always did.

What do we know about Amy and Anne now that we have listened to them? Using Halliday's categories as a guide, we can identify many skillful uses of language in the girls' conversation. They can readily switch from interactional language (talking about work arrangements, etc.) to regulatory language (giving orders) to imaginative language (playing a role, such as "sisters"). When they switch to imaginative language, there is no verbal signal such as "let's pretend." They simply follow each others' cues. There is a system of subtle signals between the girls which helps them to make these switches smoothly and maintain their conversation. We also notice that they report and utilize knowledge gained from other situations; for example, "five plus three equal eight." They certainly weave some personal language, opinions, sharing of feelings and thoughts, etc., into the conversation. They seem relaxed and comfortable with each other. The work continues productively. Each girl is accomplishing her task while engaged in purposeful talk. The clay/painting situation was a fruitful context for developing both work skills and language skills.

A little later on in the same scene, Anne is still painting her ash tray; Monica is painting at the easel; Amy has been wondering what to do.

Anne: Why don't you paint your ash tray? It might be dry. Mine was dry and now I'm gonna paint it.

Amy: Ok, ok, ok.

Anne: I just said, "Why DON'T you." I didn't say "PAINT your ash tray," Amy. I just said "Why DON'T you paint your ash tray."

Amy: (inaudible)

Anne: Well, how come you have to say it when you go "ok"? (She imitates Amy's earlier intonation.)

Monica: I'm going to make mine green!

Anne: I'm doin' . . . on the outside of mine I'm doin' it dark green but I ain't painting the bottom, girl, 'cause when you set it on a piece of paper to let the paint dry then it, the paint'll get stuck on that and then the paper'll come up with your ash tray and you won't get to take it home. You'll have to spend all your time takin' off that paper. That's why I won't put the, uh, I got to set this thing down. I can't paint with it like that.

What more do we know? Further observation of Anne and Amy shows that Anne can use language to describe, to report prior knowledge, and to project into the future. We also notice Anne and Amy are capable of using language to talk *about* language. Anne, in fact, makes a very fine distinction between an order, "Paint your ashtray," and a suggestion, "Why don't you paint your ashtray?" They are examining language and its meaning as they talk with each other.

During a more formal classroom activity, two first graders, Matt and Brett, are talking as they complete an assigned task, writing numerals. Their talk is casual, but they are using language to describe the work they are doing.

Matt: Ten hundred! That's far isn't it? Ten hundred's far isn't it?

Brett: Nine hundred's farther than ten hundred.

Matt: No, it's not.

Brett: Yes, it is.

Matt: Ten hundred is.

Matt: Oh, I messed up! (He has made a mistake on the paper.) How do you make a ten like, oh, I know how to make a ten.

Brett: You make a one, then you make a zero.

We might be tempted to direct a "shhh . . . " to the boys above. Yet, looking at it another way, the conversation is actually adding to the learning experience. They are learning to write numerals and learning to talk about math at the same time. Brett and Matt are helping each other understand complicated ideas through language. They are wondering aloud, asking questions and instructing each other. In Halliday's terms, they are using informative, interactive, heuristic, and personal language in a complex interaction while concentrating on the task at hand.

While the teacher's intervention is necessary to expand children's language, peer language is a rich social context in which to try out new language uses and receive feedback. Although teachers often think they must be everywhere doing everything and providing all the instruction, observation of children reassures us that children do encourage, instruct, and help each other effectively. And, in so doing, they develop communicative competence in using language. . . .

The above samples were of conversations between young children in the first year of school, but it is equally important to be aware of and foster a range of language functions with older children. The following group of Canadian fifth graders discussed a problem of national interest.

Graham: If Quebec separates from Canada, the Maritime Provinces will probably go to the United States. The Grand Banks fishing area is important and the U.S. could use it.

Doug: I kinda do hope they separate, 'cept in one way—the Maritimes would be poor! But, I would be glad in another way because they cause so much trouble.

Jeremy: Doug, I don't think they cause all that many problems. They just want to speak their own language there. . . .

Graham: Doug, you have to remember that the French came over and did a lot of exploring as well as the English so it just wasn't the English people who have a right to Canada!

Jeremy: (nodding) I think the Canadians are being selfish to want just one language. There is no reason why we can't speak many languages and live together.

Bob: Yeah, we should be able to speak many languages but the French only want to speak French, Jeremy. They have to be willing to give a little, too!

Doug: Bob's right, they don't have the right to cause so much trouble! Even the labels on the cans have to be written in French. That's why we can't get half the stuff from the states!

Caroline: I think we should have only one main language. The labels cost a lot for the rest of us.

Martine: I would say the same as Caroline.[1]

The children in this example had had much experience in using language in a variety of ways and were accustomed to participating in discussion groups. Here they are using informative and personal language to deal with complex ideas, to make inferences, and to argue skillfully. The students were expressing opinions and backing them up with information. It is in genuine argument that one must muster his or her best command of language in order to be persuasive enough to get the point across. Youngsters need many opportunities to try themselves out in arguments and discussions with peers, older students, and even with adults—teachers, principals, and others in the community. The demands of group interaction are seldom assessed in classroom situations; yet, they are critical language skills and deserve careful attention.

In a study of first graders, Pinnell (1975) found that at least two elements are usually present when children are actively engaged in using language functionally: 1) students are encountering real problems to which they want to find the solutions, and 2) two or more students are working and talking together about the problems. The interactions in the examples above took place in classrooms with these characteristics. The activities were interesting and challenging so that children had something to talk about, a chance to guess, argue, make predictions and check them out, and a chance to use their imaginations. Rather than seeing talk as distracting, their teachers saw it as valuable. They structured activities and the environment to take maximum advantage of the way children learn. That is, they gave children a great many opportunities to talk. The key is a teacher who is aware of the importance of fostering a wide range of language use and who is a good observer.

OBSERVING LANGUAGE USE

By observing language use in the classroom, we can make two kinds of assessment:

1. We can assess an individual child's competence by looking at the extent to which he/she uses the various functions of language and how effectively.

2. We can assess the language environment by determining which functions occur and where, and which are being neglected.

---

[1]Example from Mary Louise Skinner, Deep Cove Elementary School, Sidney, British Columbia.

For the first kind of assessment, the teacher should observe the same child in several different settings in the classroom and in formal and informal activities in other areas of the school. Observations may be brief (three to five minutes), but they should be recorded and reported periodically so that progress can be noted. For the second kind of assessment, a teacher may observe the entire class or small groups in different areas of the classroom or at different times of the day. The teacher can also combine data from observations of individual students to form a group composite. For both kinds of assessment, simple forms and checklists connected to the teachers' own goals and classroom activities could be used.

Since Halliday's categories are relatively easy to use, a teacher might start with them. Become familiar with the categories and then observe students in several different settings. A simple approach would be to make a list of the seven functions, or use a form like the one in Figure 1, and jot down examples of each type of language. Statements may seem to fulfill several functions at once. That is not surprising since language is complex and the categories are not discrete. What we are looking for is a profile that describes the variety of functions used. While it seems impossible to note all the language that is taking place, teachers will be surprised how much they can record in a short time. And, observations over a period of time provide a good picture of students' language.

This simple system provides a guide for observing language in the classroom and for monitoring student progress. It also provides a framework for teachers—

Name: _____
           (individual, small group, large group observed)
Time: _____
           (time of day)
Setting: _____
           (physical setting and what happened prior to observation)
Activity: _____
           (activity, including topic/subject area)

LANGUAGE FUNCTION	EXAMPLES
Instrumental	
Regulatory	
Interactional	
Personal	
Imaginative	
Heuristic	
Informative	

Note: Check each time a language function is heard and/or record examples.

Figure 1
Functions of language observation form.

individuals, teams or the whole staff— to use in designing instructional activities that encourage students to use language for a variety of purposes. By examining observational records, the teacher can determine which functions are being used and which are not and plan accordingly. For example, if no personal language is noted over several observations of a child, the teacher may want to make some time for an informal one-to-one conversation or for a home visit to establish a more productive relationship with the child. If little or no heuristic language is used by the children, the teacher might need to introduce materials or plan problem situations that stimulate curiosity and question asking. If most of the talk in the classroom falls into only a few categories, the teacher may want to reexamine the whole environment and reorganize learning activities so that the use of a greater variety of functions is encouraged.

Listed below are a few instructional strategies for each language function. Teachers can add others to the list. Try them and observe the results.

Instructional Strategies to Promote Language Functions

Instrumental Language—The teacher can:

1. Be accessible and responsive to children's requests, but teach independence by having children state their requests effectively.
2. Encourage the use of instrumental language with other children, helping them to expand their own language through providing help and direction to peers.
3. Analyze advertising, propaganda, etc., to help children become aware of how language can be used by people to get what they want.

Regulatory Language—The teacher can:

1. Create situations that let children be "in charge" of small and large groups.
2. Find instances in which regulatory language is used inappropriately to teach appropriate regulatory language or the alternative, instrumental language.
3. Attempt to use less regulatory language as a teacher.

Interactional Language—The teacher can:

1. Create situations that require children to share work areas or materials and talk about how they are to do it.
2. Find ways of having small group (especially pairs or trios) discussions in a variety of subject areas. Through these discussions, students not only learn the subject matter more thoroughly, they practice communication.
3. Let students work together to plan field trips, social events, and classroom and school projects.
4. Whenever possible, mix children of different ages, sexes, races in work groups or discussion groups.
5. Have informal social times and, as a teacher, engage in some talk that is not "all business."

Personal Language—The teacher can:

1. Use personal language to give permission to children to share personal thoughts and opinions.
2. Be willing to listen and talk personally during transition times; for example, when children are coming in in the morning. Converse with children while on cafeteria or playground duty.
3. Provide some comfortable, attractive areas in the classroom where students can talk quietly.
4. Encourage parents and family members to visit and participate in classrooms.
5. Read stories or books that prompt a very personal response from students.

Imaginative Language—The teacher can:

1. Create situations that naturally elicit spontaneous dramatic play; for example, house corner, dress up, blocks for younger children, and drama and roleplaying for older children.
2. Read stories and books which feed the imagination and which are a stimulus for art, drama, and discussion.
3. Provide time for children to talk in groups and/or with partners before they begin their writing or imaginative topics.

4. Encourage "play" with language—the sounds of words and the images they convey.

Heuristic Language—The teacher can:

1. Structure classroom experiences so that interest and curiosity are aroused.

2. Create real problems for children to solve.

3. Put children in pairs or work groups for problem-solving activities.

4. Use heuristic language to stimulate such language in children. Saying "I wonder why" often promotes children to do the same. (This should, however, not be contrived; it should be an honest problem.)

5. Try projects which require study on the part of the entire class, including the teacher. Find some questions that no one knows the answer to.

Informative Language—The teacher can:

1. Plan activities which require children to observe carefully and objectively and then to summarize and draw conclusions from their observations (field trips are a good opportunity).

2. Require children to keep records of events over periods of time and then to look back at their records and draw conclusions; for example, keeping records on classroom pets.

3. Use questioning techniques to elicit more complex forms of information giving.

4. Instead of having tedious classroom reports, have children give their reports to small groups and encourage feedback and discussion of those reports.

Once teachers have increased their sensitivity to the range of language functions used in their classrooms and in the school, several things happen:

1. They have good information on children that can be used to support and defend instructional strategies to develop language.

2. They can talk more specifically and persuasively to parents and others about each child.

3. They are more aware of language functions so they can informally and constantly perform assessment without using the checklists and only occasionally making records.

4. They can more effectively plan educational experiences.

GETTING STARTED: SUGGESTIONS FOR TWO FACULTY MEETINGS

Studying language development in your own classroom is often difficult. Observing, recording, and teaching at the same time can be tricky. And sometimes questions come up—how to categorize a particular statement, how to interpret a puzzling remark, how to help a certain child use regulatory language more effectively. It is much more exciting and much easier when there are others to hear your ideas and to make suggestions. The following guide could be used by a school staff or student teachers to get started in assessing and fostering the uses of language.

Meeting #1

1. Ask the group to "brainstorm" all of the uses of language they can think of. (In brainstorming, every idea is accepted and written down on the chalkboard or chart paper so everyone can see). You will come up with a long list, including joking, gossip, lecturing, giving directions, etc.

2. With their own list before them, have the group examine the categories established by Halliday. Provide an introduction to the idea of functions of language.

3. In small groups or as a whole group, ask participants to generate examples from their own experiences for each of Halliday's categories. For each example, try to specify elements of context: where the language occurred, the topic, who was speaking, who the speaker was addressing, what the people were doing at the time.

4. The group should then develop a plan for observing in the school. They can observe classrooms—their own or each others'—and someone should observe on grounds, in the library, in the cafeteria, and in the hallways. They should specify times of day so that a variety of observations can be collected.

5. Each person leaves the meeting committed to observing for a designated period or periods of

time during the next week and recording examples, with full contextual information, on the observation form.

Meeting #2

1. Staff members work in small groups or (if there are not too many) in the large group. They share and compile their observations from the previous week. They note the range of language observed and try to relate context to kinds of language. They come up with some summary statements about the language environment.

2. Using a checklist of the functions of language, the group discusses and generates a list of strategies for extending children's language.

3. Each group selects one or two language functions that they particularly want to observe for and foster during the next week. For each function they make a list of strategies to try. They specify the action plan they will follow.

4. Each person leaves the meeting committed to an action plan for extending children's language. They are to report on their success at the next meeting.

Meetings need not be as formally structured as the ones described above. The central goal is for school staff members to explore children's language together and to help each other become more aware. The greater a teacher's sensitivity to language, the less formal assessment tools will be needed.

REFERENCES

Black, J. "There's more to language than meets the ear: Implications for evaluation," *Language Arts*, 56 (May 1979), 526–533.

Cazden, C. B., John, V. P., & Hymes, D. (Eds.). (1972). *Functions of language in the classroom.* New York: Teachers College Press.

Clark, H., & Clark, E. (1977). *Psychology and language: An introduction to psycholinguistics.* New York: Harcourt Brace Jovanovich.

Halliday, M. A. K. (1973). "The functional basis of language," in B. Bernstein (Ed.), *Class, codes, and control, Volume 2. Applied studies toward a sociology of language.* London and Boston: Routledge & Kegan Paul.

Halliday, M. A. K. (1975). *Learning how to mean: Explorations in the development of language.* London: Edward Arnold Ltd.

The Literate Potential of Collaborative Talk

GORDON WELLS AND GEN CHANG-WELLS

B. S.

Editor's introduction

Gordon Wells' 10-year longitudinal studies of children moving from home to school in urban England settings in the 1970s is still one of the most influential works in socio-cultural analysis of home-school links. In this article, coauthored with his colleague Gen Chang-Wells, he considers the ways that teachers can implement and research environments that encourage collaborative work among children.

It is just after recess on a Thursday in February. The place is a combined grade three and four classroom in an inner-city school in Toronto. Outside, although the sun is shining in a cloudless sky, the temperature is minus fifteen degrees Celsius. Inside, too, it is the arctic climate that is the focus of attention as the children engage in the exploration of self-chosen topics arising from the schoolwide theme of "The Enchantment of Winter."

The project had started for these children with a reading of Robert Service's poem "The Cremation of Sam McGee." Now, three days later, almost all of them have chosen their projects, most of them arising from the brainstorming session that followed the reading of the poem. After the initial macabre fascination with Sam's mode of cremation, it is the Yukon itself—its vast size and harsh climate that has captured the children's imaginations and most of the projects have a natural history flavor. Susan and three friends, for example, are making a study of polar bears; one of them, Siew Tin, is making a stuffed model of a bear. Seth and two other boys are finding out about wolves. Brian and Kim, two Chinese-Canadian boys, have started with an interest in maps and travel, an interest which finally bore fruit in the form of a large map of

Canada and, with the help of another Asian boy, Luke, three board games involving questions about Canadian geography. Paolo is working alone on astronomy—an interest sparked by an initial question about the Yukon climate.

João and Eric started by deciding to study the terrain and, after reading in a book about three-dimensional mapping techniques, they have decided to make a model of Dawson City and its surroundings, using a photograph as a starting point. In the following extract, they are sitting on the floor with some of the necessary materials around them, preparing to begin the construction. [Note: See "Conventions of transcription" for an explanation of the transcription conventions used in this reading.]

Conventions of transcription

Layout — Each new utterance starts on a new line and, if more than one line is required to complete the utterance,

Source: "The Literate Potential of Collaborative Talk" by G. L. Chang and G. Wells (1988). In *Oracy Matters* (pp. 95–109), M. MacLure, T. Phillips, and A. Wilkinson, Eds., Buckingham, UK: Open University Press.

	continuation lines are indented. Utterances are numbered sequentially from the beginning of the episode for easy reference.
—	Incomplete utterances or false starts are shown with a dash, e.g., "Well — er —"
.	Pauses are indicated with a period. In the case of long pauses, the number of periods corresponds to the number of seconds of pause, e.g., "Yes. . I do."
?!	These punctuation marks are used to mark utterances judged to have an interrogative or exclamatory intention.
CAPS	Capitals are used for words spoken with emphasis, e.g., "I really LOVE painting."
<>	Angle brackets are used to enclose words or phrases about which the transcriber felt uncertain.
*	Passages that are impossible to transcribe are shown with asterisks, one for each word judged to have been spoken e.g., "I'll go ***."
__	When two speakers speak at once, the overlapping portions of their utterances are underlined.
(Gloss)	Where it is judged necessary, an interpretation of what was said or of the way in which it was said is given in parentheses.

J: Eric, look!
See, here is going to be the small mountain.
We're going to build it up how it is in the book.
Where's the book? (he picks it up to show it to Eric)
You know, building it up and everything.
E: Yes.
J: Here it is, see. It says "Building it up."
E: No, it doesn't mean—
J: So the small one then the big one (referring to the already cut pieces of cardboard).
We can make a little river and the town on the edge too.
E: Yes, that's what I mean.
J: Yeh, OK.
E: That's what we were talking about.
J: Yes, we're starting.
E: And we can do little boats because of the little trees.

J: Yes, OK. So we have to glue this (the cardboard).
E: And these are the *****
J: Yes. No, we're not going to put a church.
E: I know I know.
J: No, we're not going to do any of that, OK?
We are going to plan it how we planned it in the paper.
E: Yes.
J: OK, let's go.

João and Eric have already decided on their goal: to build a model of a particular location in the Yukon. What they still have to determine is the specific form their model is going to take and the means for achieving it. This extract forms part of the process of reaching shared understanding, which is essential if they are to engage in joint action. So, despite its limitations, it is an example of the sort of talk that we wish to concentrate on in this chapter. We shall call it *collaborative talk*. However, before going on to discuss this and other similar extracts from the recordings that we made in this classroom, we wish to explain our reasons for singling collaborative talk out for special attention from all the other kinds of talk that occur in a typical classroom.

THE ROLE OF TALK IN ACTIVE LEARNING

Let us start by stating our assumptions about learning and the role that interaction plays in learning. To do so, we must first make a distinction between the learning that is involved in coming to be able to recall relatively isolated items of information, and the learning that is involved in the acquisition and development of more complex conceptual structures and cognitive procedures. It is primarily with the latter type of learning that we shall be concerned, since it seems to us that to understand and make provision for this is likely to bear productively on the former, but not vice versa (Anderson 1982; Pascual-Leone 1980).

The learning that is essential to cognitive development, we want to argue, is most likely to occur from engaging in activities in which it is necessary to recognize and solve problems of increasing levels of difficulty. In order to tackle a problem—particularly one that has not been encountered before—it is necessary to be able to represent it to oneself in such a way that one is able to generate and choose between alternative means to its solution and then to carry out the procedures that one has judged likely to be effective.

It is important to recognize that this is not a simple, linear procedure, however, since at any stage feedback on success so far or information not originally available or seen to be relevant may call for revision of some aspect or, indeed, of the whole procedure. In our own field, this recursive nature of problem solving has been most fully explored in relation to writing (e.g., Flower and Hayes 1981; de Beaugrande 1984), but there are good reasons to believe that essentially the same principles apply in any kind of problem solving and thus they are of very general applicability in thinking about the provision of opportunities for the type of learning with which we are concerned.

Not everybody will be happy with this emphasis on learning as occurring in the course of conscious and deliberate problem solving. On the one hand, in early childhood, there must be some doubt as to how far mental activity is amenable to conscious control; indeed one of the major objectives of early education is to help children to develop reflective awareness of their own mental processes (Donaldson 1978). And on the other hand, the learning that takes place as a result of listening to a story, for example, may hardly seem to involve either problem or solution. However, insofar as reading or listening involve an active construing and interpreting of the text, it does not seem entirely inappropriate to assimilate them to a problem-solving model, which is clearly appropriate for the vast majority of activities in which children engage both in and out of school.

For learning of the desired kind to occur, however, it is not sufficient simply to organize a program of activities in which problems may be encountered. First, the learner must play an active role in selecting and defining the activities, which must be both challenging and motivating; second, there must be appropriate support. Let us consider these two requirements in turn.

The first requirement is that the activities chosen should make demands that are in certain respects at or just beyond the limits of the learner's current capabilities; the demands should also be such that the learner is willing to engage with them. Where individuals perform tasks of another's devising, carrying out procedures according to someone else's instructions (for example, writing a project report for which the structure and major section headings are provided by the teacher), there is little need for the application of critical intelligence in defining and planning the task or in executing it effectively. The more challenging aspects of the task have already been taken care of by the expert, and so the opportunity for the learner to develop that expertise is denied by the organization of the task itself. However efficient it is in ensuring the production of acceptable outcomes, therefore, the distribution of responsibility for task performance that vests control in the teacher is not well adapted to the development of knowledge and control by the learner.

Recognition that the construction of knowledge is an active process that each individual learner must carry out for him or herself (Wittrock 1974), on the other hand, has led to a greater emphasis being placed on what has been called "ownership" of the activities through which learning is intended to take place. This requires that learners be given a share in the responsibility for selecting the tasks in which they engage, for deciding on the means to be employed in carrying them out, and for evaluating the outcomes. Only in this way, it is argued (Barnes 1976), can they gain an active understanding of the principles involved and of the procedures that may be effective in achieving the desired outcome. A further, not unimportant, reason for encouraging the learner to take ownership of the task is that it increases his or her motivation to find and carry out a means of completing it successfully.

It nevertheless remains true that in many cases the learner will not be able successfully to carry out the whole task unaided. The second requirement, therefore, is for appropriate support. This means support that is related to the particular difficulty experienced and that is made available at the time when it is needed. The organizational difficulties that this requirement may seem likely to present are typically circumvented in the teacher-directed curriculum by breaking the activities in question into small steps and providing clear instructions on how each is to be carried out. In this way, the occurrence of difficulties is reduced to a minimum. However, as has already been argued, the consequence of such an approach is that the opportunities for active learning are also drastically reduced.

However, rather than seeing difficulties as something to be avoided, we should look at them as providing ideal opportunities for facilitative intervention. This, as we understand it, is what Vygotsky (1978) meant when he argued for engaging with the child in "the zone of proximal development." In contrast to Piaget (at least in his early work), Vygotsky saw the development of higher cognitive functions as originating in interpersonal interaction, through which the learner appropriates the knowledge and expertise that is made available in the support provided. In the words of his best-known formulation, "What the child can do today with help, tomorrow he will be able to do alone."

What Vygotsky meant by this rather cryptic remark is spelt out in more detail by Wertsch:

> When children come to a point in an activity that proves too difficult for them, they turn to an adult for help. The activity is then carried out on the interpsychological plane. The future development of the child with regard to this activity consists of gradual transference of links in the activity's functional system from the interpsychological to the intrapsychological (i.e. from the *social* to the *individual*) plane. The activity then becomes an intrapsychological function, since the child is capable of directing his/her own attention to the elements in the environment that are necessary for carrying out the task (1981, p. 30).

This, of course, is not a complete explanation. Exactly how the "transference" takes place still has to be spelled out in detail and, as Bereiter (1985) points out, we are still very far from having a satisfactory account. Nevertheless, while we may not be able to explain *how* learning takes place, there is little doubt that the availability of relevant models at the moment when they are needed has an important part to play. Equally important is the help that a collaborative partner can provide in enabling the learner to marshall and exploit resources he or she already has available, but over which he or she does not yet have explicit and conscious control (Karmiloff-Smith 1979).

The major role of interaction in learning, therefore, is that it provides the chief means through which the teacher can enable students to learn from engaging in activities that pose problems to be solved. We shall now go on to argue that, in this context, collaborative talk optimally meets the requirements just discussed.

ENABLING AND EMPOWERING LEARNING

So what is collaborative talk? Conceived quite generally, collaborative talk is talk that *enables* one or more of the participants to achieve a goal as effectively as possible. This may, as in the opening example, be a goal involving action, such as making a model or buying the right number of rolls of wallpaper to paper a room. On the other hand, the goal may be much more abstract, such as understanding a scientific principle or planning a piece of research. Or it may involve the interplay between thought and language that occurs in writing as, for example, in the compilation of a set of instructions or in the composition of a paper to be delivered at a conference. The occasions for collaborative talk may thus be very diverse. But what they all have in common is that, at some level of specificity, one of the participants has a goal that he or she wishes to achieve and the other participant engages in talk that helps the first to achieve that goal.

In most cases, the participants in collaborative talk are of approximately equal status, each able to take either of the roles of principal actor or facilitator and to benefit accordingly. Typically, too, the purposes of the collaboration are achieved when the task is completed or, at least, when the principal actor is able to continue with the next step. The talk has then served its instrumental purpose and, in the light of the effectiveness of this outcome, can be judged to have been more or less successful. This was the case in the extract from the two boys' discussion quoted above, just as it was in the collaborative talk that preceded and accompanied the preparation of this chapter. And the potential value of such enabling peer collaboration should not be underestimated.

However, the benefits of collaborative talk need not be limited to the function of facilitating achievement of the task. Where one of the participants has greater expertise than the other, he or she can engage in interaction with the learner about the task with the deliberate intention of enabling the learner to acquire some procedure, knowledge, or skill that will be useful in other situations beyond that in which he or she is currently engaged. In these cases, collaborative talk not only facilitates the task, it also *empowers* the learner. Indeed, we do not think it would be too strong a claim to say that, under ideal conditions, it has the potential for promoting learning that exceeds that of almost any other type of talk. It is the ideal mode for the transaction of the learning-teaching relationship.

For collaborative talk to have this empowering effect, however, it must meet two essential conditions. The first of these has already been addressed: it must be based on the assumption that the learner has ownership of the task and the teacher must strive to ensure that this ownership is respected. In practice, of course, ownership is a matter of degree, for the learner may not yet have sufficient confidence to take full responsibility for every aspect of the task or the necessary executive procedures for planning and carrying it out. A major objective of such talk will, therefore, be to help the learner to develop conscious and deliberate control over his or her mental processes, not only in order to complete the task in hand, but also so that he or she becomes progressively more able to take responsibility for his or her own learning more generally (Bereiter and Scardamalia 1989).

The second essential condition arises from the first: the expert's contributions to the dialogue should be "contingently responsive" to the needs of the learner (Wells 1986), as these needs are understood in the light of the immediate situation as well as of the longer term goals of education. To date, there has been little mention of this important characteristic of interaction in discussions of teacher-student talk, although its importance is clearly recognized in studies of much younger children. Schaffer (1977), for example, considers the contingent responsiveness of a caretaker's interactive behavior to be essential for the infant's earliest social and intellectual development. In studies of language acquisition, too, the same quality has been found to characterize the conversational style of parents whose children are accelerated language learners (Cross 1978; Wells 1985a). The content of adult-child conversation changes, of course, as the child increases in competence and experience. However, the learning process is continuous, as are the conditions that facilitate it. At every stage, the same conversations that provide the basis for the child's acquisition of the language system also simultaneously provide evidence about the way in which the community makes sense of experience and about how the resources of language can be used for thinking and communicating. Therefore, since there is no reason to believe that there is any radical change at the age of school entry in the basic strategies that the child uses to learn from the evidence provided in such conversations, there is equally no reason to believe that contingent responsiveness ceases to be the feature of adult contributions that best facilitates the learning process.

Thus, whether in incidental learning situations in the home or in the more deliberate situations that teachers arrange in the classroom, the principles that should guide the adult's participation in collaborative talk are essentially the same. Adapted from Wells (1986), they can be stated as follows:

- Take the child's attempt seriously and treat it as evidence of his or her best effort to solve the problem unaided.

- Listen carefully to the child's account and request amplification and clarification as necessary to ensure that you have correctly understood.

- In making your response, take the child's account as a starting point and extend or develop it or encourage the child to do so him- or herself.

- Select and formulate your contribution in the light of the child's current manifested ability as well as of your pedagogical intentions, and modify it, as necessary, in the light of feedback provided by the child.

Put much more succinctly, these principles can be summed up in the injunction to "lead from behind." What is important is that it is an understanding of the learner's conception of his or her task and of the way in which he or she plans to set about it that provides the basis for the teacher's decision as to how best to help the child to progress from where he or she is now towards the more mature understanding and control that the adult already possesses.

When the requirement for contingent responsiveness is met, collaborative talk can fulfill its empowering function. Not only the learner is empowered, however; so also is the teacher. For it is precisely through frequently engaging in collaborative talk that the teacher is able to increase his or her understanding of children's thinking in general (Duckworth 1987), and it is *only* by engaging in such talk with a particular learner while he or she is engaged on a specific task that the teacher can become knowledgeable about that learner's purposes and current state of understanding, and thus be able to make his or her contributions contingently responsive to the learner's needs.

THE CHARACTERISTICS OF COLLABORATIVE TALK

So far we have looked at collaborative talk in very general terms, considering the context in which it is likely to flourish and the conditions that must be met if it is to empower learning. Now we wish to examine the nature of collaborative talk more closely in order to identify those characteristics that promote the sort of reflective and systematic thinking on which such learning depends.

In order to achieve the benefits of having two minds focusing collaboratively on a problem, the participants must achieve intersubjectivity in their representation of the task in hand and of their proposals for dealing with it. Each needs to know the other's understanding and intentions, and both must take the appropriate steps to ensure that mutual understanding is maintained. There is a need, therefore, to be explicit. Thus, in order to explain the matter in hand sufficiently clearly for the other participant to make an informed response, each is forced to construct a more coherent and detailed verbal formulation than would be necessary if he or she were working on the problem alone. In the process, gaps and inconsistencies become apparent and can be repaired, with the result that the problem is seen with greater clarity.

However, it is not only the adequacy or inadequacy of the offered information that is revealed in these circumstances, but also the connections that are made between the parts. In developing the account, the role of cause-and-effect relationships, of inferences, generalizations, extrapolations, and so on, is also made apparent, as are failures to make such connections. In sum, the need for mutual understanding in collaborative talk requires each participant to make his or her meaning clear to the other, and hence also to him- or herself, with the result that thinking is made explicit and, thus, available for inspection, and, if necessary, for extension, modification, or correction.

Then, having achieved a shared understanding of the task, participants can now, from their different perspectives, offer opinions and alternative suggestions. Once again, there is a need for explicitness. But more importantly, opinions and suggestions need to be justified and supported by relevant arguments, and reasons need to be given why one alternative is more appropriate than another, if decisions are to have a principled basis. As a result, participants in collaborative talk cannot only learn from each other's differing knowledge bases, they can also learn the need for disciplined thinking and develop some of the strategies for achieving it.

Depending on the stage reached by the principal actor in the execution of his or her task, the collaborative talk may focus on any one or more of the following components: specifying the goal more precisely,

planning the means for achieving it, generating and choosing between alternatives, reviewing achievement to date, or modifying what has been done.

CHOICES AND CONNECTIONS: COLLABORATIVE TALK IN ONE CLASSROOM

In the first part of this chapter, we have been concerned with giving an idealized account of collaborative talk and with justifying our claim for its preeminence as a mode of teacher-learner interaction. However, we want to acknowledge immediately that the ideal conditions that we have assumed in the theoretical discussion are rarely encountered in reality. There are three main reasons for this. First, the sheer number of children who need to be supported, and the constraints imposed by the organization of the school day, mean that many interactions are cut short or interrupted. Second, since most of the children work in small groups rather than individually, there are issues of group collaboration to be addressed as well as the substantive issues raised by the tasks themselves. Third, there are limits to the resources of personal knowledge as well as of books, materials, and equipment that the teacher can draw on immediately in meeting the needs of particular children as they arise spontaneously in the course of the day. For all these reasons, the ideal can rarely, if ever, be achieved.

In turning to an examination of examples taken from one particular classroom, therefore, we wish to make it clear that our purpose is not to evaluate them, but rather to explore the potential of collaborative talk as it is conducted in practice. To do this we shall focus our discussion of the extracts on the following four questions:

- In what ways is the talk collaborative?
- What aspects of the task are addressed in the participant's talk?
- What aspects of learning are being enabled in the talk?
- How are the participants contingently responsive to each other?

"SO YOU'VE CHANGED YOUR TOPIC."

Let us return to João and Eric. In the extract below, they have not yet begun to construct their model. As the teacher joins them, the two boys in their enthusiasm both start speaking at once:

1 *J:* \<We're\> doing a model
2 *T: Wow*
3 *E: I know* what the model's going to be
(João and Eric both talk at once for eight seconds as they describe their intentions, so neither can be heard)
4 *T:* Hold it! I hear that you're making a model. I hear something about houses.
5 What's this going to be about? What's your topic?
6 *J:* Yukon
7 *E:* Yukon
8 *T:* You're making—
(João and Eric again speak together making the next few lines difficult to understand)
9 *J:* In the Yukon they have shops. I saw it in the *
10 *E:* You can make—you can make igloos
11 *J:* They say they have shops ** and it has a big mountain beside it
12 *E:* (to Richard, who has come to look) And we can do the other side **
13 *T: So you're* going to do a little town?
14 *J:* (nods)
15 *T:* Wow!
16 *J:* And we could make a big mountain and \<put those things\> on top
17 *T:* Uh-huh uh-huh
18 *J:* And then it would be covered with snow
19 *T:* Uh-huh
20 *J:* And then um—we could make a little shop here and park
21 *T:* What questions are you answering particularly?
22 *J:* Um— . . . Like "Where did they get the name from?" so we wanted—we wanted to do the model
23 *T:* So you—you've changed your topic a little bit
24 So you're making a model of the Yukon . showing a town?
25 *J:* Yeh
26 *T:* And some of the things you've learned about what it's like to live in the Yukon, is that it?
(During the next few turns Eric is trying to secure T's attention by calling her name. He has been left out of the preceding discussion)
27 *J:* But the mountain is small for the size of the town . like the mountain *—
28 *T: Which town* is this?
29 Is it a particular town?
30 D'you know the name of it?
31 *J:* It's the Yukon

32 *T:* That's the name—that's the name of the big territory
33 Can you find the name of a town?
34 *E:* We don't know
(T hands book to João and talks to Sandra briefly while João and Eric consult the book)
35 *T:* OK (turning back to boys)
36 This is a map that shows very few towns
37 There's one
38 *J:* I know. Whitehorse.
39 *E: Whitehorse*
40 *E:* Whitehorse . that's a famous . town in the Yukon
41 Uh-huh. *Whitehorse*
42 *J:* Is Alaska there too?
43 *T:* Pardon?
44 *J:* Alaska Alaska (pointing to two occurrences of the name on map)
45 *T:* This is the Alaska Highway—the Alaskan Highway
46 *J:* It's very complicated because it says United States and then the United—it's over there see
47 *T:* Yeh
48 *J:* The United States and *then United States*
49 *E:* **
50 *T:* OK . Why might it be like that?
51 Do you understand why?
52 *J:* Maybe . it's the \<shore's down that *\> too?
53 *T:* Yeh Alaska belongs to the United States
54 *J:* (who is on the edge of the group also looking at a map) I found it I found it
55 *T:* You did?
56 *E:* (looking at index) It says Yukon—Yukon's three things and ** you can find—you can look through every page . that has the Yukon on it
57 One of them might be a photograph of a town
58 *T:* That's true that's true

The first point to note is the teacher's "active listening," indicated in the opening lines by her "Wow!" and "I hear that you're making a model," etc. By echoing what the boys have said, she is assuring them that she has heard and is interested. She is also letting them know what she takes to be the salient points in what she has heard and indirectly inviting them to consider whether these are the points that they, too, judge to be the most important. At the same time, the particular phrasing of (4), "I hear something about houses," suggests that there is some problem about comprehensibility—a problem to which the solution might range from being more informative or explicit to speaking one at a time.

The teacher's first turn ends with a question about the issue that underlies their decision to make a model: "What's this going to be about? What's your topic?" (5). Although their first replies seem to provide some sort of answer, it is clear from what follows (9–20) that they have not really understood the purpose of her question. For the two boys continue to elaborate on the details of the model they want to make rather than considering the question to which their model is addressed. In spite of this, the teacher continues to listen and echo back to them (e.g., "So you're going to do a little town" [13]).

But interspersed with her expressions of support, she continues to address the problem of articulating a statement of inquiry by posing questions that might elicit the issue the boys are investigating: "What questions are you answering particularly?" (21), and "So you're making a model of the Yukon . showing a town? And some of the things you've learned about what it's like to live in the Yukon, is that it?" (24–26). This last question, it will be noted, also acts as a model of the sort of question which the boys' intention to construct a model could appropriately address.

By juxtaposing these two kinds of response, the teacher is making a critical distinction for the children between the action-goal, that of making a model, and the topic-goal, that is to say, the question that is directing their inquiry. This is clearly an important distinction for them to understand, for it is only when the two goals are brought into interaction with each other that an inquiry can be productive. Moreover, it is a distinction that is too often overlooked in discussions of goal setting with students, although it has begun to figure in recent research on writing (Freedman 1985).

That her concern is with the need for an articulation of a statement of inquiry rather than that they should stick to a previously agreed topic is corroborated by the teacher's ready acceptance of the change that has taken place: "So you—you've changed your topic a little bit" (23). At the same time, this observation also emphasizes the teacher's recognition of the boys' ownership of the task and her willingness to accept their decision to change their topic. In so doing, she also demonstrates another important feature of planning: that the setting and revising of goals and subgoals is an ongoing and recursive process as the various components interact with each other.

In fact, the following talk (28–61) exemplifies the revision of planning in operation, as the agreement that the model will be of a single town rather than of the whole Yukon Territory leads to a scaling down of the original intention and to the search for a specific town to be the subject of the model. With the help of the book provided by the teacher, Eric comes up with a strategy for solving the problem (56–57), and it is by using a photograph of Dawson City that they are able to form the specific plan that is being discussed in the extract with which this chapter opened.

"I THINK HE'S GOT A POINT."

During the next week, the model progressed apace and, by the time we meet João and Eric again, they are reaching the final stages.

1 *J:* We're going to—we're going to cover it with white tissue paper, Eric
2 *E:* <That's what we've got to do>
3 That's for when they have snow.
4 And after . by mistake it could avalanche on here (pointing to the base of the mountain on the model) and some houses will be crushed
5 *T:* I wonder if that's a danger here (pointing to the equivalent place on the photograph)
6 I think you're quite right about some *mountains*
7 *J: I thought* it was summer (in the photograph)
8 *E:* Yeh but in winter—but if it's in winter . .
9 *J:* Yeh . yeh the seasons could change
10 *T:* That's true
11 And they don't move their houses here . . do they?
12 *E:* **
13 Yeh they can't like lift it and go "ow ow" (miming lifting a very heavy weight) unless they just go "da da da da" (said in a sing-song voice, which seems to represent the use of magic)
(all laugh)
14 *T:* I don't think they're going to do that . .
15 Well if you have a look here . . (pointing to photo in book)
16 See where the houses are . along the river . and then .
17 What does this look like?
18 *J:* That's a mountain
19 *T:* Part of the mountain
20 *E:* (pointing to model) These are one of these mountains
21 *T:* uh-huh uh-huh
22 You know you don't have to have the same number of houses in here as in the photograph (pointing to book)

23 *E: I know*

24 *J: Yeh* but some of—like one or two over here would be OK (pointing to base of mountain on model)

25 *E:* Yeh but if we put one or two over next to the houses . we won't have room for the tissue paper

26 Here almost squashed even

27 *T:* Right . sounds like this is something you boys have to talk about a little more

28 You both have good points

29 *J:* Yeh I think he—he got a point because . if we put tissue paper over it . that—

30 *T:* Is that what you plan to do with these houses?

31 *E:* Yeh

32 *J:* And then we could put like . little—put it like little streets coming through here

33 *T:* Uh-huh . interesting

34 *E:* Yeh we could like er . if you still want to make the thing, right? we could make—you could put pine trees all around there

35 *J:* Around the mountains

36 *T:* Very good

37 *J:* OK, let's go

As is evident in this and the earlier extract, collaborative talk emphasizes both the personal and the social aspects of learning. The social is made important because successful completion of the task depends on the combined efforts and expertise of both participants; the personal, because each collaborator has his own resources, ideas, and approaches to the task. But most importantly, the commitment to collaborate obliges the participants to recognize the relevance of each other's expertise and, where necessary, to realign their own knowledge systems. It is this balancing of the social and the personal that enables learning to occur.

From a superficial reading of these transcripts, it might appear that, of the pair, it is João who plays the dominant role of knower/doer and that Eric is the helper. However, a closer examination of their talk, particularly the extract currently under consideration, makes it evident that each has his own ideas about the task of making a model of Dawson City. It is not surprising, therefore, that their differing perspectives should come into conflict when, as in this extract, they have to reach a practical decision on how to proceed. However, it is not their differences that are noteworthy. Rather, it is the way in which collaboration on the task to which they have committed themselves both brings out each child's differing abilities and makes it possible for each to enable the other's

learning in the joint thinking and doing that the task demands. As the teacher commented on reading the above extract, "These two boys have a fascinating style of working through their [mis]conceptions with a lot of talk that appears confusing on the surface but on reflection their logic is evident."

The nub of the problem is that João wants their model to be an accurate representation of the scene in the photograph from which they are working, while Eric is more concerned with achieving internal consistency within the model itself. The problem is brought into focus by the question as to whether they should add more houses to the model. Based on the number he can see in the photograph, João wishes to put some more at the foot of the mountain. But, following through the implications of João's plan to use tissue paper to represent snow on top of the mountains, Eric argues that, if an avalanche were to occur, houses placed at the foot of the mountain would be crushed (3–4). Although João accepts this objection, he does not abandon his plan for, a moment later, he again suggests adding more houses at the foot of the mountain (24). This time Eric counters with the objection that if the houses were too tightly packed together, there would not be room for the tissue paper that they intended to put on the roof of each house (25–26) and to this practical (i.e., constructional) objection João agrees and concedes that Eric has "got a point" (29). They could, however, represent streets going between the houses (32) and, in place of the houses at the foot of the mountain, Eric suggests, they could put pine trees (34). With this agreed, the practical João calls for a resumption of activities: "OK, let's go."

To this interaction, it is interesting to note, the teacher contributes very little by way of suggestion or new information. It is as if, as she herself put it in a subsequent discussion, her presence is sufficient to enable the two boys to listen to each other's perspectives and take account of the arguments behind them. And this is the impression one gains from examining her role in the discussion. She listens to what each of the boys has to say and, in her responses, implicitly accepts the validity of both points of view. "I wonder if that (i.e., an avalanche) is a danger here," she says to Eric (5), pointing to the foot of the mountain in the photograph—the spot that is in dispute as the site for additional houses on the model. But João's wish to achieve an accurate representation of the photograph is also recognized when she tells them that they don't have to have the same number of houses in the model as in the photograph (22), and she states "You both have good points" (28).

In this respect, her most interesting contribution to the discussion is line 11. Perhaps sensing that João has not fully appreciated the implications of Eric's argument, the teacher jokingly points out that people in the Dawson City shown in the photograph do not move their houses with the changing seasons and, therefore, by implication, that even if their model depicts a summer scene, they should take account of such a hypothetical winter catastrophe by not sitting houses in a position from which they would have to be removed if they were to change their model to represent the same scene in winter. It is not possible to tell from the ensuing remarks whether the two boys took in the full significance of this one utterance, the force of which depends on the initial "and" that makes connection with João's preceding concession that the seasons could change, and the "here" that contrasts the city in the photograph with the boys' representation of it in the model. The point we are making, however, is not that this utterance succeeded in convincing João, but rather that it illustrates very clearly the teacher's concern both to make her contributions contingently responsive to each of their perspectives and, at the same time, to encourage them to follow the incompatibility of their implications through to a logical conclusion. As she says a moment later, "Sounds like this is something you boys have to talk about a little more" (27).

CONCLUSION: ATTAINING LITERATE THINKING THROUGH TALK

The preceding analyses of the collaboration between João, Eric, and their teacher have illustrated the potentially empowering nature of collaborative talk and have highlighted the centrality of concerns such as problem solving, ownership, challenge, and intersubjectivity of understanding. If we now look at the list of characteristics that are intrinsic to the achievement of these concerns—such features as explicitness, connectivity, justification, and relevance—it will be seen that they are precisely the sort of attributes that are held to be particularly characteristic of written discourse (Chafe 1985). They are also attributes of thinking that are considered to develop as a consequence of becoming literate (Cole and Bruner 1971; Goody 1977). Since, however, we are dealing here with spoken language, it seems that we should reconsider the traditional defini-

tion of literacy and, in the present context, ask what "literate thinking" is and how it develops.

Until quite recently, answers to these questions would almost certainly have taken for granted that the linguistic-cognitive processes of reading and writing must be centrally involved (e.g., Olson 1977). However, as a result of further comparisons of spoken and written language, including cross-cultural studies (Scribner and Cole 1981; Heath 1983a; Tannen 1985), a more complex picture has begun to emerge. While it would probably still be agreed that literate thinking is most likely to occur in connection with reading and writing, it is now recognized that thinking that displays many of the same characteristics can occur in oral interaction between those who are literate when the purposes of the interaction demand it (Olson and Astington 1990). Langer (1987) cites the following example:

> When a group of people read one of the classics and then discuss the theme, motives, action and characters at a Great Books meeting, I would say they were using literate thinking skills. . . . Further, when those people see a movie and then discuss the motives and alternative actions and resolutions, I would again say they were using literate thinking skills even though they had neither read nor written. And if the people engaged in that very same conversation about a movie did not know how to read or write, I would still say they had engaged in literate thinking. (p. 3)

If we accept this argument, then we must also accept that the process of becoming literate can potentially take place through speech as well as through engagement with written language. For it is not the mode of language use that defines literate thinking, but rather the manner in which the language is employed. Thinking is literate when it exploits the symbolic potential of language to enable the thought processes themselves to become the object of thought. Under appropriate conditions, this can occur in either writing or speech.

Throughout this chapter, it has been assumed that the prime function of schooling is to develop effective thinking. We can now make this assumption more explicit by stating that what schools should be attempting to promote is the development of *literate* thinking. Elsewhere, we have argued for the preeminent role of writing in performing this function (Wells and Chang 1986), although we would have to concede that not all writing has this effect (Wells 1987). However, even when giving primacy to writing, we have also made a plea for the recognition of a similar role for talk, while recognizing that it is only certain types of talk that have these literate consequences. In this chapter, our aim has been to show that one type of talk that has this potential is what we have called collaborative talk. It now remains to show just how this can occur.

As an example, let us consider the discussion between João and Eric of their reasons for and against locating more houses at the foot of the mountain in their model of Dawson City. Both boys have to make their arguments explicit; they also have to make them relevant to their own position as well as to that adopted by the other. Although these requirements are reduced somewhat by the physical presence of the objects referred to, there is no doubt that they are felt and, within the children's capabilities, responded to as well. Decisions concerning relevance and presentation thus come into play, and these are certainly instances of literate thinking.

Another important aspect of literate thinking is the recognition of the need to consider alternatives and to justify them by appeal to systematic knowledge. This, too, is illustrated in the collaborative talk between João, Eric, and their teacher when each has to extrapolate from his or her knowledge about seasonal variation in climate, topography, land relief, and so on, in order to decide whether to site more houses at the foot of the mountain. Although the discussion is brief, it illustrates how the collaboration that is necessarily involved in a task such as making a model can lead children purposefully to access their mental dictionaries of knowing and understanding and, in the process, become more aware of them.

Reflecting on what one has done—questioning the outcome of one's efforts—and revising it, if necessary, is another important feature of literate thinking. For the testing of one's assumptions of knowing and not knowing may lead to, or at least call for, a realigning of or adding to one's existing knowledge systems. Although this kind of literate thinking is a common characteristic of expert performance, it is one that has to be deliberately acquired (Bereiter and Scardamalia 1987). Encouraging children to question their own efforts is one way of helping them to adopt this practice.

So far, we have drawn attention to the literate consequences of addressing the content of the task: the need to make one's intentions and one's understanding of the topic intelligible to another and at the same time to oneself. But we should also recognize the potential benefits that derive from the goal-oriented nature of collaborative talk. The tasks in relation to which the talk occurs make demands for planning and execution, which themselves may become the subject matter of talk. It is important to emphasize, however, that it is not the talking through of plans that is claimed to be advantageous in itself; rather, it is when planning and similar processes are raised to the level of conscious attention so that they may be brought under intentional control that such talk warrants being described as literate.

A good example of this conscious attention to goal-setting occurs when João and Eric are asked to formulate the question they are addressing in the making of their model. This episode qualifies as literate, we would argue, because in responding to the request to identify their question, João and Eric are developing self-regulatory procedures. They are learning to adopt a "What is my question?" and "Where am I going?" stance to the task they undertake.

Of course, thinking of the kind that we have characterized as literate does not only occur when activities are carried out collaboratively. It might also have occurred if the children in this classroom had been working on their own, although it would probably have been in an attenuated form. However, because they needed to achieve intersubjectivity about their intentions, which was essential if their joint efforts were to be productive, the children were encouraged to turn their thinking back upon itself—reflectively selecting and evaluating it—in order to construct an intelligible, coherent, and convincing verbal formulation. It is above all because it can foster the growth of this critical reflectiveness that collaborative talk has such important potential for the development of literate thinking.

In this article, we have only had space to consider two examples of collaborative talk, taken from recordings made in the course of one class project. . . . As a result, there is a danger that we have read more into what was said than the participants themselves were aware of. We must also admit that our claims about the potential benefit of collaborative talk may not have been realized in the learning that actually took place as a result of these particular interactions. On the other hand, although of limited significance when considered in isolation, the extracts that we have analyzed take on a different significance when they are seen as a small but representative sample of the many similar learning opportunities that each child enjoyed during the course of those two weeks.

However, it is with the teacher's comments that we should like to end. They are taken from a discussion that followed a viewing of that part of the recording that included the first discussion with João and Eric.

That part with João and Eric—it's just like that business that kids need time to talk about what they're going to write about, to work out their ideas, and then to do rough copies to find out what they really think, and then revise. . . . That really interested me. I kept seeing little parts where it's like João and Eric—that nudging them to make the connection between two ideas, asking them what their topic is. I mean it's the same as the writing process—having them tell you what they're doing, where they're going, what their questions are . . . and having them review the process and what they're doing.

Attending to the extracts that we had selected to analyze, the teacher has clearly made a very similar interpretation, understanding and knowing for herself the significance of the talk in which she had been involved. Although she does not use the term herself, there is little doubt that what has excited her about these examples, and others like them, is the potential for the development of literate thinking that is to be found in collaborative talk.

REFERENCES

Anderson, J. R. (1982). "Acquisition of cognitive skill." *Psychological Review, 89,* 369–406.

Barnes, D. (1992). *From communication to curriculum.* Portsmouth, NH: Boynton/Cook-Heinemann.

Beaugrande, R. de. (1984). *Text production: Toward a science of composition.* Norwood, NJ: Ablex.

Bereiter, C. & Scardamalia, M. (1989). "Intentional learning as a goal of instruction." In L. B. Resnick, ed. *Knowing, learning, and instruction: Essays in honor of Robert Glaser.* Hillsdale, NJ: Lawrence Erlbaum Associates.

Chafe, W. (1985). "Linguistic differences produced by differences between speaking and writing." In D. R. Olson., N. Torrance, and A. Hildeyard, eds. *Literacy, language, and learning.* Cambridge: Cambridge University Press.

Cole, M. & Bruner, J. S. (1971). "Cultural differences and inferences about psychological processes." *American Psychologist. 2:* 867–76.

Cross, T. G. (1978). "Mothers' speech and its association with rate of linguistic development in young children." In N. Waterson and C. Snow, eds. *The development of communication.* Chichester, UK: Wiley.

Donaldson, M. (1987). *"The having of wonderful ideas" and other essays on teaching and learning.* New York: Teachers College Press.

Flower, L. & Hayes, J. R. (1981). "A cognitive theory process of writing." *College Composition and Communication, 32* (4): 365–87.

Goody, J. (1977). *The domestication of the savage mind.* Cambridge: Cambridge University Press.

Heath, S. B. (1983). "Protean shapes in literacy events: Ever-shifting oral and literate traditions." In D. R. Olson, N. Torrance, and A. Hildeyard, eds. *Literacy, language, and learning.* Cambridge: Cambridge University Press.

Karmiloff-Smith, A. (1979). "Micro- and macro-developmental changes in language acquisition and other representational systems." *Cognitive Science, 3:* 91–118.

Langer, J. A. (1986). *Children reading and writing: Structures and strategies.* Norwood, NJ: Ablex.

Olson, D. R. (1977). "From utterance to text: The bias of language in speech and writing." *Harvard Educational Review, 47:* 245–81.

Olson, D. R. & Astington, J. W. (1990). "Talking about text: How literacy contributes to thought." *Journal of Pragmatics, 14:* 557–573.

Pascual-Leone, J. (1980). "Constructive problems for constructive theories: The current relevance of Piaget's work and a critique of information processing simulation psychology." In R. H. Klume and H. Spada, eds. *Developmental Models of Thinking.* New York: Academic Press.

Schaffer, H. R. (1977). "Early interactive development." In H. R. Schaffer, ed. *Studies in mother-infant interaction.* London: Academic Press.

Scribner, S. & Cole, M. (1981). *The psychology of literacy.* Cambridge: Harvard University Press.

Tannen, D. (1985). "Relative focus on involvement in oral and written discourse." In D. R. Olson, N. Torrance, and A. Hildeyard, eds. *Literacy, language, and learning.* Cambridge: Cambridge University Press.

Vygotsky, L. (1978). *Mind in Society.* Cambridge: Harvard University Press.

Wells, G. (1987). "Apprenticeship in literacy." *Interchange, 18* (1/2): 109–23.

Wells, G. (1986). *The meaning makers: Children learning language and using language to learn.* Portsmouth, NH: Heinemann.

Wells, G. (1985). *Language development in the pre-school years.* Cambridge: Cambridge University Press.

Wells, G. & Chang-Wells, G. L. (1986). "From speech to writing: Some evidence of the relationship between oracy and literacy." In A. Wilkinson, ed. *The writing of writing.* U.K.: Open University Press.

Wertsch, J. V. ed. (1981). *The concept of activity in Soviet psychology.* Armonk, NY: Sharpe, Inc.

Wittrock, M. C. (1974). "Learning as a generative process." *Educational Psychologist, 11:* 87–95.

Invitations to Reflect on Our Practice: A Conversation with Gordon Wells

by Ruth Shagoury Hubbard

Working in the field of language development, and exploring the role of language in education, Gordon Wells has had enormous impact on teachers' understanding how they can improve opportunities for learning within their classrooms. In his groundbreaking book, *The Meaning Makers* (Heinemann, 1986), he reported the results of a 15-year longitudinal study "Language at Home and School" in Bristol, England. In recent years, he has collaborated with teachers in Toronto, Canada, studying learning in multilingual schools. *Constructing Knowledge Together* (1992), coauthored with Gen Ling Chang, tells the story of the discovery these researchers made together—how the teachers found ways to create classrooms in which children used literacy not only as a tool for learning about topics that interested them, but also for sharing their understanding with others. Dr. Wells is a professor of education at Ontario Institute for Studies in Education in Toronto, where he continues to teach and research in the fields of language, literacy and learning.

This interview helped us both explore the new possibilities of e-mail and its effect on literate behavior. As you'll discover in the following pages, Gordon Wells is an innovator, and he invited me to experiment with him as we carried on a "conversation in slow-motion" through e-mail correspondence.

Ruth Hubbard: I think I'd like to start by going back a bit and discovering more about what inspired your interest in language development. I remember reading that Noam Chomsky's work intrigued you while your daughter was a young child, and you began to look carefully at the ways that she was using and developing language. Was this the start for you?

Gordon Wells: Who can say when in one's life certain interests start: a sixth form (grade 12) teacher who encouraged my interest in literature; a first degree at Cambridge which included translating poems from French to English; living in France and teaching English as an "assistant" in a lycee; my first class in England, where the 12-year-olds were better at "parsing" English sentences than I was, causing me to focus on syntactic analysis for the first time in my life; teaching English as a second language to young Ghanaians and encountering through their eyes the idiosyncrasies of the English language? All these, no doubt, had some bearing on my developing interest in language.

But *the* moment, I still believe, was in 1966 when—in preparation for starting a diploma in applied linguistics to equip me to "take responsibility for ESL" in a teacher training college—I first read Chomsky's "Aspects of the Theory of Syntax" (1965). I realized then that, although I might be required to become an ESL specialist (though I never did), what really interested me was how children learn *any* language to which they are exposed. As it happened, too, my first child, Katharine, was just learning to talk at that time, so I had a further reason for being interested in the incredible feat that all children perform, and with so little apparent effort.

RH: How did you go about studying your daughter's language? Did you follow her around with a tape recorder, or take notes in the form of a journal or diary? Can you say a little about any ways that studying her language led to the way you "bugged" the children's naturally occurring conversation in the Bristol study?

GW: With my first daughter, my interest was very amateur. I noticed some of the amusing things she said and marveled at her inventiveness; also the speed with which she learned—and not only language. At that time we were living in Ghana where I was housemaster in a boys' secondary school in a house attached to the boys' boarding house. I can still remember her toddling round the small garden, stark naked except for a sunhat, shouting, "Boys, come and see me!"

Serious study started with my second daughter, who turned two while I was studying linguistics at Edinburgh. I only had a large reel-to-reel tape recorder in those days, so I used to have to engage Deborah in play with her dolls close to the tape recorder and try to elicit sentences with positive and negative auxiliaries by manipulating the dolls and their surroundings. I recorded her in this way every week over a period of several months. When I had transcribed and analyzed the recordings, I was delighted to find that the "sequence of emergence" was as I had predicted: negative forms invariably emerged later than positive forms. Still better, the tags—such as "don't we?," "can I?"—appeared only after she was producing both interrogative and negative forms, just as the theory predicted. Subsequently, however, I discovered that there were almost as many children whose development supported the alternative hypothesis; so from this and similar findings about other linguistic systems, I came to recognize that children have differing strategies for learning—in rather general terms, "analytic" or "holistic."

But back to studying my daughters. Probably the most important thing I learned was that children do not produce their most advanced utterances to order. If you really want to get a clear picture of their language development, you have to observe them across as wide a range of situations as possible, and the possible ways of doing this are fairly limited. If you are studying a single child, you can either note down conversations as they occur, as Halliday did for his study of Nigel (Halliday, 1975) or you can use elaborate recording equipment, with a microphone in every room and a switching device to enable you to select the one in the child's location, as Ruth Clark did (Clark 1974). But both these approaches have limitations and they are simply not feasible with $n = 128$! Hence the development of the remotely controlled bugging technique.

In fact, the development of this technique extended over a couple of years and owed much to the skill and inventiveness of my late colleague, Bernard Chapman. At that time (1969–1971), the wireless microphone was a new invention and the prototypes were large, heavy and in no way designed for day-long wear by one-year-olds who spilled their food down their fronts with monotonous regularity. Electronic timers barely existed either, and it was Bernard who thought up a much cheaper mechanical version that was driven by an old-fashioned alarm clock.[1]

RH: I'd like to return to your earlier comment about the profound impact Chomsky's work had on your thinking. It sounds as if studying your daughters' language allowed you to find ways you agreed and disagreed with his work.

GW: Chomsky, of course, attributed children's incredible feat of learning language to a "language acquisition device"—a biologically provided "organ"—that could take whatever input that was available and construct a grammar of that language. However, as I quickly discovered when I started to research this issue empirically, there is much more to language learning than that. The "input," as Chomsky calls it, is not simply a corpus of more or less well-formed sentences of the target language but, much more importantly, the means whereby the child is enabled and encouraged to become a participant in an already existing community, for whom language is a means for interacting with other people, coordinating activity, and generally making sense of what is going on. What I also discovered was that, even for children growing up in the same linguistic community, the "input" is not identical—or even equivalent. Not only are some children talked with more frequently, but more importantly, the quality of the conversations in which they are involved differs in both the range of topics talked about and in the roles they are permitted and/or encouraged to take on in the development of those topics.

My dissatisfaction with Chomsky's account was initially theoretical: There is no such creature as the "ideal native speaker/hearer" and real language is always language being used to do something in a particular situation by particular individuals who have intentions, beliefs, and emotions. Children do not learn language for its own sake but in order to interact with their caregivers and siblings. Similarly, parents don't talk with their children to teach them the language but to engage them in shared activities and to socialize them into the family's and the culture's ways of

---

[1]Photographs of the apparatus, and of a child being dressed in the "harness," can be found in Wells (1985) *Language Development in the Pre-School Years*, Cambridge University Press, pp. 32–33. If there were time and space, I could tell many anecdotes about the trials and tribulations, as well as about the laughs and lucky breaks, that we experienced over the 15 years of this *long* longitudinal study. For those who are interested, though, this story is told in some detail in the Introduction to *Language Development in the Pre-School Years*.

acting and understanding. However, over the years that I was involved in the Bristol Study, following the 128 children's early language development by "bugging" their naturally occurring conversations at home, these views were fully confirmed by the recordings we made. From this empirical evidence, it was very clear that language learning takes place in and through situationally relevant conversations.

As I said earlier, the ease and speed of language learning seemed to depend on the quality of the conversations that the children experienced. So I attempted to tease out the characteristics of such "high quality" parent-child conversation and came up with a set of principles that I thought could be helpful to parents who asked for advice (Wells, 1986, p. 50). Since then, I have discovered that, although these principles characterized many of the conversations in which the rapidly developing children in our study took part, researchers studying very different communities have found that children's early conversational experience may be characterized by quite different principles (e.g. Heath, 1983; Ochs & Schieffelin, 1983). These findings are of particular relevance for teachers in today's classrooms, where a high proportion of children may come from cultures very different from the mainstream, white, middle-class communities that have until recently served as the reference point for assessing children's development and as the basis for planning classroom learning opportunities.

Although principles like those I enunciated certainly provide a route to success in school for many children, they may disenfranchise others whose early home experiences have been based on different and perhaps equally effective principles. In recent years, therefore, I have become very interested in exploring issues of language learning and learning through language in the much more culturally heterogeneous communities that are typical of schools in Toronto and other large urban centers: What activities and modes of discourse optimize opportunities for learning for *all* the members of such communities?

Of course there isn't going to be a single right answer, as all classroom communities are both unique and constantly becoming. So there is a real need for teachers to see their role as including that of asking this question, and trying to answer it with respect to the particular classrooms in which they are currently teaching. In fact, only yesterday, I was reading the wonderful answers that teacher-researcher Karen Gallas made with the children in her Grade 1 classroom. As she observes, whether we recognize it or not, "the teacher, by virtue of both verbal and non-verbal support or denial of a discourse, transmits a very clear message about the types of communication that are appropriate for school" (Gallas, 1994, p. 18).

RH: Are you aware of other language researchers who have affected your work?

GW: Undoubtedly the most important influence on my growing understanding of the essentially social nature of language learning and learning through language was the work of Lev Vygotsky and of more recent writers in the sociocultural tradition that he founded. I still remember the excitement with which I first read *Thought and Language* in 1967, the same year that I encountered Chomsky in print. On first reading Vygotsky, it was his characterization of thinking in terms of "inner speech" that most intrigued me; I also found support for my ideas about the importance of adults being "contingently responsive" to children's conversational initiations—of "leading from behind"—in his now well-known concept of teaching as working with the learner in his or her "zone of proximal development." However, during the intervening years, I have learned a lot more about Vygotsky's sociocultural theory and have come to see it as offering a comprehensive framework for thinking about education, and one that is empowering for teachers as well as for students. As a result, much of my recent researching, teaching, and writing has been concerned with exploring the practical implications of Vygotsky's ideas for learning and teaching in the classroom and also for teacher development.

This last September, I had the privilege of attending the first international conference on Vygotsky's work ever to have been held in Russia, and I am currently revising the paper that I gave there, which proposes some extensions and modifications of Vygotsky's ideas about the development of scientific concepts. In this and other recent papers, I have been trying to bring together the ideas of Vygotsky and Halliday on the role of language as the principal means for learning and teaching with Deweyan ideas on active, inquiry-based learning; happily, I am able to illustrate this "hands on, minds on, hearts on" approach to learning and teaching with transcripts of observations I have made in the classrooms of teacher colleagues. My aim is to develop a vision of education that is both relevant to the challenges of contemporary society and supportive of individual growth and development; one that, with an emphasis on the creation of communities of inquiry, in which meaning is co-constructed dialogically through speech, writing and other modes of action and communication, seeks to value the contributions of all participants in the shared search for understanding and the development of effective and responsible action.

RH: Like Shirley Brice Heath's work, your research helps point out the ways that there may be a mismatch between the typically "mainstream" school expectations and the language learning experiences of some children—which, though different, may be equally effective, as you point out. How do you think teachers can begin to turn the lens back on themselves, monitoring more consciously the ways they communicate so they can better meet the needs of the populations in their specific classrooms? I know you are working with many teacher researchers in Toronto who teach in ethnically diverse classrooms. How are they framing their studies and collecting their data? Can you give an example?

GW: One approach that two teachers explored a couple of years ago was the provision of opportunities for newly arrived children to tackle problems initially in their first language and, when they had arrived at a solution, to try to express it in whatever English they had at their disposal. Here is an excerpt from their account of their research with a small group of Polish-speaking children in a grade two class.

> The children listened to the story of *Curious George* read in English, and then were asked to explain and predict various events. They were encouraged to answer in Polish if they felt unable to answer in English. The positive results of this initiative can be seen in this example:

Ewa (Teacher):	What do you think George is going to do now?
Peter:	Maybe he . . . I don't know.
Ewa:	Powiedz po polsku. (Say it in Polish)
Peter:	On chyba zje te ciasto i pani bedzie sie gniewac na niego. (He'll probably eat the cake and the lady will be angry with him.)
Christina:	Albo sie zchowa gdzies. (Or he'll hide somewhere.)
Beata:	Eat. He eat cake.

In many of these exchanges during this session, students claimed that they did not know what to say, until Ewa told them that they could use Polish. It then became clear that they had understood much of the English text and were using personal experiences as well as making inferences from text and pictures to develop logical ideas which they could express coherently in their [first language]. (Orzechowska & Smieja, 1994, pp. 135–136)

These two teacher researchers were themselves native speakers of Polish but they argue that there are other ways of providing first language support:

We do not underestimate the practical difficulties of providing the kind of language support which we advocate for ESL students. However, even a monolingual class teacher without a bilingual assistant can find ways of incorporating ESL students' first language into some learning activities. The students can be paired up or grouped, and encouraged to work through problems and share ideas in their first language, before trying to do so in English. . . . The crucial step is for educators to acknowledge ESL students' need and right to use their first language for academic learning. When this idea becomes accepted, then the appropriate means of implementing bilingual support will be investigated by boards of education and schools. (Orzechowska & Smieja, 1994; pp. 149–150)

RH: How are you using e-mail to support the work of teacher researchers like Ewa and Anna? What are some of the benefits you are finding—and what are some of the problems you need to solve?

GW: It's interesting you should ask about my use of e-mail, as I find I have been spending an increasing amount of time on this form of communication over the last couple of years. I first discovered the value and the pleasure of taking part in this sort of conversation about four years ago when I was introduced to the XLCHC network, which is organized by Michael Cole at UCSD to discuss issues in sociocultural theory and its applications to education and other fields of activity. Gradually overcoming my fear of appearing ignorant and stupid, I began to make occasional contributions to discussions on issues of personal concern to me and discovered that this form of writing was an excellent way of clarifying my own ideas. In these discussions, I also learned about other people's work and picked up useful references for further reading. Over time, too, I began to feel that I was becoming a member of an academic community that, although separated in space, was united by a commitment to developing theory in order to act with understanding, and characterized by a generosity of spirit that is somewhat uncommon in academic life.

However, it was not until the summer of 1992 that I first began to use e-mail in my interactions with teachers and, even then, my motive for doing so was somewhat selfish. That summer, I taught a course in Vancouver, at UBC. Both the content and the mode of the course were a new departure for me, and so I decided to make it the occasion for engaging in teacher research myself. E-mail, I thought, would provide me with one source of evidence that I could draw on as I reflected on the course through subsequent writing. In the event, this did indeed prove to be the case, and I drew quite heavily on the voluminous record of our conversations that the computer amassed for me when I came to write about my action research. However, in the process, I discovered that e-mail had much more to offer, for it made a significant contribution to the course as a whole by encouraging all of us to be more systematically reflective.

I had in the past tried using dialogue journals but had always been dissatisfied with the inevitable delay between student entry and teacher response. By inviting the 28 teachers in my class to dialogue with me by e-mail, I made it possible for our exchanges to be more relevant to our immediate concerns. In addition, many of them found, as I had done, that writing an e-mail message that was certain of receiving a personal response encouraged them to attempt to clarify for themselves—in writing— issues that they would otherwise probably have left unexamined, or discussed orally and then forgotten.

I am a great believer in "writing to learn"—or, rather, in the increased understanding of a topic or issue that can occur in the course of writing and revising a text in order to communicate one's ideas clearly to an interested reader. E-mail has this advantage of producing a permanent record of one's thinking, to which one can return for further thinking; however, because of its dialogic form, it also has some of the immediacy of conversation, inviting response—but at a pace that allows that response to be considered before being sent.

The next step was to create a class network so that messages could be sent, if one chose, to all the other members of the class, inviting responses from anyone who wished to contribute. The network also allowed me to forward messages that I was receiving from the XLCHC network, for some of them, I thought, were of relevance to the topics that we were investigating through our own action, reading, writing, and talking. In sum, e-mail contributed significantly in all these ways to the creation of the community of inquiry that I hoped our class would become.

Back in Toronto, I began to use e-mail in all my classes, encouraging all class members who had access to a computer with a modem to give it a try. One of the chief advantages, as I saw it, was that they would be able to discuss their classroom research with me and with other course members as it progressed. I also hoped that, by gaining some facility with this new medium of communication themselves, some would experiment with the possibilities that computer-mediated communication opens up for linking their students with classes in other parts of Canada or even further afield. In the meantime, in collaboration with the Teacher Federations, the Ontario Ministry of Education has established a province-wide computer network for all teachers in Ontario, in an initiative called "Creating a Culture of Change." As a result, e-mail and various forms of computer conferencing are rapidly gaining popularity among teachers in this part of the world. In fact, when XTAR (the international teacher researchers' network on the Internet) was opened in October this year, Ontario teachers formed one of the largest regional groups of subscribers. (For information on how to join XTAR, see the end of this interview.)

Not surprisingly, therefore, I am particularly enthusiastic about the use of e-mail among the members of our research team. Our group consists of five classroom teachers, one graduate student, two professors, and one full-time research officer and, together, we share the direction of the project. The theme of our research is the relationship between modes of discourse and the opportunities for learning that they provide (or fail to provide). Within this theme, two types of inquiry are being undertaken: first, individual teachers are investigating topics of their own choosing with whatever degree of involvement by the university members that they request; second, video-recorded observations made in these teachers' classrooms, interviews with teachers and students, and samples of the students' work are being collected to enable a systematic study to be made of issues that are decided on by the team as a whole.

Because we work in quite widely separated locations, however, we are only able to meet face-to-face one evening a month. In this situation, e-mail enables us to keep in touch on a daily basis. In fact, because we are able to log on to the network at our own convenience and spend as much or as little time on any particular occasion as fits our overcrowded schedules, there is actually much more extended discussion of individual teachers' inquiries than would be possible if we always met in the same physical space.

In addition to these inquiry topics, other issues of general concern are also discussed at considerable length. This week is the time for reporting to parents and we have had a very constructive exchange concerning initiatives being taken in different schools and school boards to make this event, and the evaluation activities it necessarily entails, both more inclusive of students and parents and more genuinely a learning experience for all concerned. Earlier in the year, when two of our members were feeling somewhat overwhelmed by the challenges posed by new teaching assignments, there occurred a very rich discussion of community-building strategies.

You asked earlier about my contribution to this activity. The answer, I think, is that it is very similar to what I described in the context of that summer course two years ago. To some extent, I act as a mailman, forwarding messages that I think will be of interest from other networks, and mentioning books and articles that I have come across that I think may be helpful in relation to a particular inquiry. When I have spent time in one of the teachers' classrooms, I usually send a personal message, commenting on some of the interesting things I have observed from the point of view of our inquiry theme and perhaps offering a theoretical perspective or a suggestion about how we might proceed. But for much of the time I simply follow the discussion, learning from the rich experience of my teacher colleagues and marveling at the way in which this new medium of communication is enabling us all to grow.

RH: Perhaps as a wrap-up you would be willing to comment on the process of this interview itself—both the benefits and drawbacks? Have you seen the Ode to E-Mail from an op-ed piece that appeared in the Wall Street Journal suggesting that "E-mail someday will unite us all in a shared state of epistolary bliss. E-mail is ethereal; it consumes no paper, no ink, and only a misting of fossil fuels. E-mail is nearly instan-

taneous. Best of all e-mail combines the vacuity of phone talk with the potential per-
manence of letters. A fledgling still, e-mail promises to burgeon beyond anyone's cal-
culation. Maybe the letter's Golden Age isn't dead after all; it may be yet to come"
(Wall Street Journal, Nov. 9, 1994, p. A22).

GW: I really like this Ode—apart from the "vacuity of phone talk." E-mail may be
informal but it is not, in my experience, vacuous.

Thinking about the experience of taking part in this interview by e-mail, I am
reminded of Judith Newman's *Interwoven Conversations* (1991). Because this interview has extended over a whole week, it has indeed been interwoven with other
activities, and, as in any conversation, each contribution has been influenced by and
has influenced those on either side. Like Judith, I have been engaged in learning and
teaching and in reflecting critically on both. Since the experience has been particularly fruitful for me, I should like to describe it in more detail.

Yesterday, our research group presented a three-hour session at the Science Teachers of Ontario's Annual Conference; our chosen topic was "Inquiry in the Learning
and Teaching of Science." The principal speakers were two teacher colleagues who
were to talk about their own inquiries. Mary Ann Gianotti's inquiry was about how
she and another grade 2 teacher had learned to make their students' questions the driving force of their science program; her video excerpt, transcripts she had made of student discussion, and samples from their journals showed how, starting from some
hands-on activities that the teachers had arranged and with the support and guidance
they provided along the way, her seven-year-old students were able to arrive at some
quite sophisticated insights about the properties of air. One boy, for example, was able
to explain how the flight of a plane depends on the interaction of four forces: lift,
thrust, drag and gravity; his text was accompanied by an informative diagram.

Zoe Donoahue's inquiry, also conducted in part with a colleague, concerned her
attempt to make more meaningful for grade 3, 4, and 5 students the writing they
did in their science logbooks during and after practical work on technology. The key
to her considerable success was asking for her students' advice and suggestions as to
the changes to be made to her original plans. As a result of being invited to share in
defining the purpose for the writing and to contribute to a list of helpful sentence
starters, such as "One problem I had was. . . . ", "The way I solved it was. . . . ",
"What I learned was. . . . ", the children began to invest much more effort in their
writing and came to see that it played an important role in the understanding they
developed about the various structures they were designing and making.

My role in the session was to provide a brief introduction and during the week,
I was thinking about what were the most important points to make in providing a
framework within which the anticipated audience might interpret the teachers' presentations. At the same time, I was drafting a proposal for a presentation our group
plans to make at a conference of teacher researchers to be held next spring. Ideally,
of course, the drafting of the proposal should have been a joint activity, but because
of the pressure of school work—particularly report writing—the teacher members
of the group were not able to find the necessary time. So my problem in preparing
this proposal was to identify an aspect of our collaborative work that would: (a)

make a substantive—and hopefully productive—contribution to the conference; (b) be one to which all members of our group would have something they wanted to contribute; and (c) provide an occasion for all of us to deepen our understanding about various involvements in learning and teaching.

In both conference sessions, I knew I wanted to emphasize the essential similarity between learners, whether they be students in school classrooms, teachers among their colleagues, or teacher-educators and researchers in universities. And, since learning is an integral part of engaging in purposeful activities with others, I also wanted to emphasize the need to create communities of inquiry as an essential condition for effective learning to occur. However, simply to assert the importance of community-creating activities would not be sufficient, I felt. More effective would be to show communities of inquiry in action.

The solution to my problem came from the other conversations in which I was involved—ones that included students in my doctoral class, people on the XLCHC network, and an author whose work I was prompted to read as a result of what was being discussed in these other conversations (Wartofsky, 1979). In all three conversations, the question at issue could be formulated as: "What is the role of tools of various kinds in the activities that provide the occasions for learning?"

Let me quote what for me was the key sentence in the Wartofsky text.

> . . . our own perceptual and cognitive understanding of the world is in large part shaped and changed by the representational artifacts we ourselves create. We are, in effect, the products of our own activity, in this way; we transform our own perceptual and cognitive modes, our ways of seeing and of understanding, by means of the representations we make. (Wartofsky, 1979; p. xxiii)

This is a familiar theme in sociocultural theory. Many years earlier, Vygotsky had written: "The individual develops into what he/she is through what he/she produces for others. This is the process of the formation of the individual" (Vygotsky, 1981; p. 162). And so, while reading Wartofsky, all these ideas suddenly fell into place: I realized that artifacts and tools are the same things, but seen from different points in time in the ongoing process of productive activity. The text on which one is working is a semiotic *artifact*—a structure of meaning one is producing; later, when rereading and reflecting on this same text, it functions as a semiotic *tool*—it is a means for achieving a clearer perception and understanding of the topic about which one is writing and thinking. And what is true for texts is also true of the results of experiments, diagrams, models, stories, and discussions, and *all* the products of our activities.

Thinking about this, I understood more clearly the role of the various artifacts produced by the children that Mary Ann and Zoe were going to talk about; for they were also and equally the tools whereby they came to see and understand the principles at work in the flight of planes or the interlocking movement of gear wheels. At a different level, our e-mail discussions about the teachers' inquiries and the chapters in which they had written about them for the book we are planning were, equally, both artifacts and tools for achieving the increased understanding that was guiding the changes they were introducing in their classroom practices.

And, for me, this e-mail interview has served a similar function. The questions you have asked have invited me to reflect on *my* practice and, in some cases—as, for example, my use of e-mail—this has been the first time I have thought about the topic in such a reflective and critical manner. So the interview has been an important learning experience for me.

Many years ago, commenting on children's early development, I wrote:

> . . . although storying may have its roots in the biologically given human predisposition to construct stories in order to make sense of perceptual information, it very quickly becomes the means whereby we enter into a shared world, which is continually broadened and enriched by the exchange of stories with others. In this sense, the reality each one of us inhabits is to a very great extent a distillation of the stories we have shared. (Wells, 1986; p. 196)

This interview has given me a chance to share some of my stories and the stories of my colleagues and, in the process, to come to a deeper understanding of the role that all these kinds of semiotic artifacts play in the activity of learning and teaching. Perhaps we should all have the opportunity to learn through being invited to tell stories about our ways of making meaning.

REFERENCES

Bernstein, B. (1971). *Class, codes, and control* (Vol. 1). London: Routledge.

Chomsky, N. (1965). *Aspects of the theory of syntax*. Cambridge, MA: MIT Press.

Clark, R. (1975). Performing without competence. *Journal of Child Language 1*, 1–10.

Gallas, K. (1994). *The language of learning: How children talk, write, dance, draw and sing their understanding of the world*. New York: Teachers College Press.

Halliday, M. (1975). *Learning how to mean*. London: Arnold.

Newman, J. (1991). *Interwoven conversations*. Toronto: OISE Press and Portsmouth, NH: Heinemann.

Orzechowska, E., & Smieja, A. (1994). ESL learners talking and thinking in their first language. In G. Wells (Ed.), *Changing schools from within: Creating communities of inquiry* (pp. 130–154). Toronto: OISE Press and Portsmouth, NH: Heinemann.

Vygotsky, L. (1981). The genesis of higher mental functions. In J. V. Wertsch (Ed.), *The concept of activity in Soviet psychology* (pp. 156–181). Armonk, NY: Sharpe.

Wartofsky, M. W. (1979). *Models, representations, and scientific understanding*. Boston: Reidel.

ANNOUNCING "XTAR"
A NETWORK FOR TEACHER RESEARCHERS

XTAR is a telecommunications discussion intended to enable teacher researchers to share their inquiries—their questions and their findings, their insights, problems and suggestions—with colleagues in schools and universities all over the world. Anyone involved in classroom inquiry is welcome to participate and to encourage others to do so.

To subscribe to XTAR:
_____

Send a message to: listserv@lester.appstate.edu
Skip the Subject
In the body of the message write: Subscribe XTAR and your name, e.g.:

    Subscribe XTAR William E. Blanton

You will then receive a reply telling you that your subscription has been accepted and giving more information about the network. Please send a message introducing yourself and say a little about your interests.

If you have any questions, please address them to:

William E. Blanton   or   Gordon Wells
BlantonWE@conrad.appstate.edu   gwells@oise.on.ca

Extension: Talk in Schools

ALL THINKING IS SORTING: LENSES FOR LOOKING AT LANGUAGE

Analyzing language within the classroom is the key to understanding many of these language theories. You may choose to begin with your own students, although many teachers also find it practical to analyze talk from a colleague's classroom.

It is easy to become overwhelmed with all the possibilities for looking at language in a classroom. We've found it often helps teachers to start with a few simple activities that can indicate patterns of language use in their own classrooms. As you begin to analyze language in your classroom, find the questions or issues around language use that are intriguing to you; only then can you find a research or assessment question that will sustain your interest.

ANALYSIS THROUGH ANECDOTAL RECORDS

Analyzing talk can begin with something as simple as keeping consistent anecdotal records of oral exchanges in the classroom. One way to begin this is to choose a time to keep records in your classroom when there is a lot of peer interaction. Pat McLure does this during her daily small reading groups. She writes a brief, one-page analysis of the talk around the books children bring to share at these groups (See Figure II–1).

Pat's records are a large part of the language analyzed in *Listening In* by Tom Newkirk in this text. Keeping these records each day takes only a few minutes of Pat's time. More important, as Pat writes, the students spend less time looking to her as the teacher to mediate the talk and more time speaking with each other. By the end of the school year, Tom noted that Pat had more than 60 examples of each child's language in these records.

Name/Book	Comments	Date: 12/10/87
Caitlin The Terrible Thing That Happened At Our House	Caitlin summarizes the first part of the book. Kim says she is glad Mast Way Cafeteria isn't like *that*—it's nice and clean. Caitlin reads about ten pages, then stops (her favorite part). Kim: shows Caitlin her favorite part (big buildup of "No one cares, no one listens") Peter: I like the part where the dog ran into the table.	
Kim Funny Bones	Picks a favorite part. Reads well, much better than she read it when she first read it on Monday. Asks for help with four words. Pat: Why did you pick that as your favorite part? Kim: Because I could read it. And I also want to show you something. The book starts with almost the same words as it ends with (shows two pages). Pat: It comes back with the same words. Peter: I've heard that book before and I like the frighten part. Caitlin: I like when the dog bones and the "woofs" are all mixed up.	
Peter Caps for Sale	Reads this well. Explains other parts of the book as he reads. Talks about unusual arrangement of words on the page—"you have to move the book around to read it." Pat: I like the way the words and pictures are on the page in different spots. Peter: And they kinda make you guess, and the answer is on the next page.	
	[Group reads well, and is fairly attentive. Good questions; details pointed out.]	

Figure II-1
Pat's book-sharing conference form.

If you choose to keep records during informal or formal discussion periods in your classroom, try to be consistent. Set aside 10 minutes every day when you will note what is said and who says it. After you have a few weeks of notes, you will begin to notice patterns. You might look for who controls topics, what causes you to intercede, or when children seem to hold the floor longest. After you see these patterns emerge, you will have a sense of what you might want to explore in depth in your classroom.

TAPE ANALYSIS

Tape recording and analyzing one small piece of language in a classroom (rather than a series of conversations) is a good place to start in finding a focus for classroom language research. As we discussed in the extensions at the end of Part I, audio and video tapes are important resources for teachers. But even with a transcribing machine, tape transcription is time-consuming. We estimate it takes about one hour to transcribe every seven minutes of tape. (And the time you need for tape transcription multiplies if you don't have a transcribing machine.)

We encourage you to start with a tape recording of a one-half hour segment from your own classroom, or that of a colleague, with an analysis that *doesn't* involve transcription. After you have recorded the segment, listen to it two or three times without any transcription. (You can save time by listening to the tape in a car as you commute to work, or run errands.) As you listen to the tape, ask yourself, "What surprises me? What topics might I want to explore further?" After you've listened to the tape repeatedly and jotted down some of these initial reactions, you may want to try the "Thinking About Classroom Discourse" exercise developed by Elaine Furniss and Pamela Green [Furniss & Green. (1991). *The Literacy Agenda* (p. 87). Portsmouth, NH: Heinemann.]

Figure II–2 is a good beginning because it doesn't require a full transcription of the tape. You can work your way through the questions, making rough estimates of classroom talk ratios, and listening for examples of markers like "silence" or "negotiation." After you've completed the chart, you may want to star a few topics that are most interesting to you. For example, you might discover you're interested in looking further at your pattern of questioning students, or peer-to-peer talk.

Another starting point for analyzing language is an analysis of verbal and nonverbal behavior. Susan Pidhurney uses a "double entry" transcription strategy, which is both easy to do and can be adapted to an individual teacher's needs. Sue always puts a transcript on the left-hand side. Then, the right-hand side is sometimes used to note nonverbal behaviors, and sometimes is used for analysis (see Figure II–3).

Finally, you may want to try Gay Su Pinnell's "Functions of Language Observation Form" for analyzing the functions of talk in your classroom according to Halliday's categories (p. 151).

None of these activities is enormously time-consuming. By structuring your anecdotal records in new ways, charting verbal and nonverbal behaviors during discussion activities, or attempting focused analysis of one small sample of language from a classroom, you'll notice different patterns beginning to emerge—and you'll discover new questions as well. These questions will frame your continued language research agenda.

Thinking about classroom discourse

Questions to consider		Responses for my classroom
1 Purpose:	What was the purpose for talk in this session? In which context did it occur?	
2 Structure of the lesson:	Did the lesson follow the I) teacher initiation R) student response format? E) teacher evaluation Find some examples from your tape/transcript which show either this format or some alternatives.	
3 Talk ratio:	What was the ratio of teacher talk to student talk during the lesson? 75:25? 50:50? 25:75? How might this change?	
4 Elaboration:	Were there opportunities for more talk about the same topic for either students or the teacher: How was this made possible?	
5 Peer/peer talk:	What opportunities for students to talk to one another for specific purposes were actually set up by the teacher in the lesson?	
6 Silence:	Did any longish periods of silence occur in the lesson? What was the purpose of silence? Who cut it short? How long did it continue? How do you feel about silence between talk?	
7 Negotiations:	Was anything negotiated during the lesson? Procedures/meanings? Ideas? How did you know when agreement was reached? Or was it?	
8 Feedback:	Who gave whom feedback during the lesson? What form did it take? Was it effective? Could it have been more effective?	
9 Student reactions:	What form of talk did student reactions take? Did they have any role in structuring the way the talk occurred in the lesson?	
10 Differential treatment:	Did you treat students differently? What differences in talk can you find which are evidence of this? How might you change this?	
11 Talk as scaffold:	Can you find examples of teacher OR peer talk which acts as a temporary support for student learning? How can you provide opportunities for this to occur?	
Organization changes I could make to allow other comments for more effective classroom talk:		Other comments

Figure II–2

Thinking about classroom discourse chart.

Source: The Literacy Agenda (p. 33–34) by E. Furniss and P. Green, 1991, Portsmouth, NH: Heinemann.

Verbal	Nonverbal
Josiah: [raising hand] Mrs. Pidhurney?	
Mrs. P.: Josiah?	
Josiah: We could make a book.	
students: Yeah, we could make a book!	
Mrs. P.: A book?	
John: Yeah, our own creepy sheep book.	
Mrs. P.: How would we do that?	
Ethan: We could draw scary things.	
Megan: Scary things!	
Mrs. P.: OK. With sheep?	
some students: Yeah!	
some students: No!	
Linda: I don't know how to draw sheeps.	
Mrs. P.: We could look in the book.	
John: No, we could just make things that	*lots of wiggling*
scared them.	
Mrs. P.: OK. Who will read your book?	
Shannon: The morning class!	
Several students: Yeah! Yeah!	
Mrs. P.: OK, that sounds like something	
they would like. Where do we start?	
John: With a title.	
Mrs. P.: A title?	
Melissa: For the book.	
Mrs. P.: OK, any ideas?	
[chatter . . . chatter . . . chatter]	
: Any ideas?	
Josiah: It could be about scary things.	
John: Scaring kids!	
Shannon: Scaring everyone!	*all hands up*
Mrs. P.: Everyone?!	
Ethan: Mr. Shaw!	
Several students: Yeah! Scare Mr. Shaw!	*students out of their spot*
Shannon: How about scaring the teachers?!	*in circle, crowding around my*
Several voices: Yeah!	*chair, hands raised in cheers*
John: We'll scare 'em all!	
Josiah: We need paper.	
Ethan: And crayons.	
Shannon: Let's go.	*Everyone heads for work table.*

Figure II–3
Susan Pidhurney's double-entry manuscript.

PART

III

Sociocultural and Personal Perspectives

Literacy and the Oral Foundations of Education

KIERAN EGAN

Editor's introduction

What happens when children make the transition from *oral* language into *written* language? Kieran Egan believes we can come to understand the cognitive demands of this transition by the way children and nonliterate cultures make sense of their worlds through communication without literacy. Through his exploration of the ways that different cultures use sophisticated oral language forms, Egan demonstrates that orality needs to be appreciated as the foundation on which literacy can be built.

We have inherited from the ancient Greeks the notion of a deep-cutting distinction between rational and irrational thinking. The word they commonly used for "reason" was *logos*, which was also the term used for "word" or "speech." For the Greeks of the Platonic tradition, then, taking a rational view enabled one to give an articulate account of something: "We have a rational grasp of something when we can *articulate* it; that means, distinguish and lay out different features of the matter in perspicuous order" (Taylor, 1982, p. 90). Rationality entails trying to perceive things as they are, despite our hopes, fears, or intentions regarding them. One may achieve such a view by *theoria* (sight, speculation, contemplation): theoretical understanding results from taking a disengaged perspective. Only the knowledge that results from this kind of intellectual activity, Plato argued in *Timeus* and *The Republic*, is true knowledge. The manner in which Plato distinguished rational thinking and its product—true knowledge (*episteme*)—from irrational thinking and its various products—confusion, superficial plausibility, mere opinion (*doxa*)—involved setting up a number of enduring conceptual associations. Among these associated ideas, and of particular interest in this

article, was that of adulthood with the attainment of *episteme* and childhood with *doxa*.[1] This rational theoretic understanding, Plato and his pupil Aristotle argued, gives a superior view of reality. Those who violate the basic standards of the articulation of this theoretical understanding are, in this view, irrational, and they fail to articulate what is real and true.

With the "rediscovery" of classical Greece by nineteenth-century European scholars, and the growing sense of Greece's cultural superiority over the classical Roman models that had dominated European intellectual and artistic life during the previous century, the distinction between rational and irrational thinking began a new career. It proved a convenient tool for dismissing from serious comparison with Western forms of thought those forms of "primitive" thought that expanding colonial empires, early anthropological

---

[1]See the parable of the lion in *The Republic*, ed. Cornford, 1941, ch. 24. For a discussion of the sets of associations, see Simon (1978), pp. 164ff.

Source: Egan, Kieran, "Literacy and the Oral Foundations of Education," *Harvard Educational Review*, 57:4, pp. 445–472. Copyright (c) by the President and Fellows of Harvard College. All rights reserved.

studies, and travelers' tales were bringing increasingly to the attention of Europeans and North Americans (Jenkyns, 1980; Turner, 1981). When combined later in the century with the extensions of evolutionary theory, the distinction between "rational" and "irrational" thinking helped to generate theories about the development of human societies from irrational beginnings to the refined rationality of contemporary Western intellectual life. Frazer (1900), for example, argued that human thought always passes through a magical stage, to a religious stage, and finally to a rational scientific stage. This distinction has entered during this century into everyday language, finding varied, more or less casual, use in terms of approval or disparagement. At the same time, in the scholarly world, the distinction has come increasingly into question. Anthropologists such as E. E. Evans-Pritchard (1937), for example, have argued the rationality of witchcraft in particular cultural settings, and classicists such as E. R. Dodds (1951) have pointed to the irrationality of significant features of Greek life and thought. Vexed and problematic though the distinction is, it remains deeply embedded in Western cultural history and habits of thought (Hollis & Lukes, 1982; Putnam, 1981; Wilson, 1970).

The mental life of children has commonly been represented in terms influenced by this distinction. Children are assumed to begin life in irrational confusion and ignorance, and education is regarded as the process of inculcating both rationality and knowledge. In his allegory of the cave in *The Republic* Plato likens the process of education to unchaining prisoners in a dark cave; while chained, they can see on the cave wall only flickering shadows of what is happening outside, and, when released, they are led out to behold reality. Similarly, Christian ideas of education represented the child as beginning in sin and ignorance, able to progress only gradually and with great difficulty to virtue and knowledge.

Children and "savages" have often been assumed to lack access to certain forms of thought that are considered the hallmarks of rational adulthood. Attempts have been made to capture the perceived differences between the thought forms of people in oral cultures and those of literate Westerners in distinctions such as primitive/developed, irrational or prerational/rational, mythic/historical, simple/complex, mythopoeic/logico-empirical, "cold"/"hot," traditional/modern, and so on (see Goody, 1977; Hollis & Lukes, 1982). Relatively

recently, attempts have been made to break down these distinctions as applied wholesale to particular kinds of cultures. Jack Goody, for example, has argued that any distinction that suggests "two different modes of thought, approaches to knowledge, or forms of science" is inadequate, not the least because "both are present not only in the same societies but in the same individuals" (1977, p. 148). That is, whenever we try to define precisely some distinctive feature of "our" thinking, we find examples of it in "their" cultures, and whenever we identify a distinctive feature of "their" thinking, we find cases in "our" culture. Robin Horton has shown that what have been regarded as distinctive features of scientific thinking are common in traditional cultures in Africa (1970, 1982); and it has now, post-Freud, become a cliché that certain central features of mythic thinking are common in Western cultures (Blumenberg, 1985). (One wonders, for example, whether Bronislaw Malinowski's [1922] outrage at the wastefulness of piles of rotting yams in the Trobriand Islands would be equally directed at the "mountains" of dairy food and grains and "lakes" of wine that have accumulated in support of the farming policies of the European Economic Community.) "We" and "they" constantly exhibit thinking that is both rational and irrational, complex and simple, logico-mathematical and mythopoeic. We are "them" and they are "us." (See Lévi-Strauss, 1966; Goody, 1977.)

What about the evident differences, then, between modes of thinking used in oral societies and those used in complex industrial ones? While we may indeed recognize common features in forms of thought that were in the past considered entirely dissimilar, we need to recognize also that modern science, history, and mathematics are hardly identical with anything found in oral cultures. One can scarcely claim that differences do not exist. How do we account for them if we reject explanations involving "primitiveness" or deficiencies of mind or of language? And how do we characterize the dramatic changes in forms of thought and methods of inquiry made during the Greek classical period—changes that involved the birth of philosophy, critical history, and modern science? Goody (1977) maintains that the evident differences are best accounted for by technology, especially the technology of writing. His argument builds on and extends a growing body of work that is seeking to clarify how literacy affects strategies of thinking. The economy of the mind inclines us to theorize that members of oral cultures—in which what one knows is what one remembers—use particular mental strategies, and that some different mental strategies are used in literate cultures—in which various mental operations can be enormously enhanced by visual access to organized bodies of knowledge.

The path from orality to literacy is one that we want all children to take as they pass through our educational systems. Better understanding of what this movement entails might clarify some of our practical educational problems. It might, for example, help us find ways to reduce the rates of illiteracy in Western societies, and perhaps also to improve the quality and richness of literacy we can achieve. From the research that has so far drawn on our increasing knowledge of orality and of the transition to literacy, it is clear that any adequate conception of literacy must account for much more than simple encoding and decoding "skills" and must encompass significant features of rationality (Olsen, 1977, 1986). That is to say, even though there is considerable difficulty in characterizing rationality with precision, it is increasingly clear that the acquisition of literacy can have cognitive effects that have traditionally been considered features of rational thought—particularly those associated with "abstract" thinking. Considering oral cultures, then, may help us to understand better what is entailed in the transition of Western children from orality to literacy.

This is not to posit some mysterious evolutionary recapitulation process in the lives of our schoolchildren. There is a trivial sense in which an education involves the individual's recapitulating the development of his or her culture; in a matter of years we learn knowledge, skills, and ways of making sense of the world that were developed over millennia. Recapitulation theorists in Europe and North America have gone further, however, and have argued that the classroom curriculum should be designed so that children learn the central content of their cultures largely in the sequence in which that content was invented or discovered. Recapitulation schemes in schools have been based on notions of biological recapitulation, logical sequences in the development of knowledge, and/or psychological predispositions (Gould, 1977). In what follows, however, I will be considering the recapitulation of specific techniques used in thinking. By making children literate, for example, we are recreating, in each individual's case, the internalization of a technology that can have some quite profound and

precise effects on cognitive processes and modes of communication. As Walter Ong has observed, "Technologies are not mere exterior aids but also interior transformations of consciousness" (1982, p. 82), and "Writing is a technology that restructures thought" (1986, p. 23).

Technology is a slightly aggressive term to use for writing, and "tools for thinking" is a handy but tendentious metaphor. One is led to assume that spades and computers have similar transforming powers over our manual and cognitive functions. That they have transforming powers is beyond doubt, but that these are the same as, or akin to, what internalizing literacy produces needs further evidence. I prefer to use a less aggressive term, coined, as far as I am aware, by Lévi-Strauss. In discussing the structural categories underlying totemic classification, he debunked the notion that totemic species are chosen because of their economic or culinary value; he argued they are not so much "*bon à manger*" (good for eating) as "*bon à penser*" (good for thinking with) (Lévi-Strauss, 1962). Literacy is a set of strategies that are not only utilitarian, but also *bon à penser*.

One purpose of this article is to explore oral practices that are also "good for thinking with." Orality, we shall see, is not a condition of deficit—to be defined simply as the lack of literacy. Regarding orality only in terms of literacy is (in Ong's neat simile) like regarding horses as automobiles without wheels (1982, p. 12). Orality entails a set of powerful and effective mental strategies, some of which, to our cost, have become attenuated and undervalued in many aspects of our Western cultures and educational systems. In the following pages I shall explore some of the effective strategies of thinking used in oral cultures, and then consider their relevance to education.

A word of caution is required. Any simplistic assumption that equates the thinking of adults in oral cultures with that of children in literate societies will be undermined in two ways. First, adults have the accumulated experience and cognitive development that children necessarily lack. Second, most children in Western cultures live in environments that presuppose literacy and its associated forms of thought: constant adult interactions with young children assume conventions that depend on literacy, and preliterate children are constantly encouraged to adopt forms of thinking and expression that are more easily achieved as a product of literacy.

My purpose is to focus on forms of thought that are *bon à penser* if one is not literate. Consequently, I will be *seeking* comparisons between forms of thought used by members of oral cultures and those used by modern Western children. The basis of the comparison, however, is neither knowledge content nor psychological development, but techniques that are required by orality. Keeping this idea to the fore will, I hope, allow us to avoid the kind of deprecatory ethnocentrism criticized above.

I shall not try to establish an exhaustive inventory of the intellectual strategies common in oral cultures. Further, I do not consider that the purpose of education in Western cultures is to preserve and develop such strategies uncritically. We are not in the business of preparing children to live in an oral culture—though it may be worth reiterating that we are preparing them for a literate-and-oral culture. Indeed, we see fast developing around us features of what Ong (1982) has called "secondary orality." The electronic media are its most energetic promoters, but even newspapers and journals are explicitly, and somewhat paradoxically, relying less and less on strategies of communication that draw on the skills of "high literacy" and their associated forms of thought (Ong, 1977). Although orality is not the end of our educational development, we might consider whether it is a necessary constituent of it, and whether the study of orality might be *bon à penser*, as we attempt to construct both a richer primary school curriculum and a fuller sense of how children might effectively learn its contents.

A central theme of this article might be summed up in Lévi-Strauss's observation:

> I think there are some things we have lost, and we should perhaps try to regain them, [but] I am not sure that in the kind of world in which we are living and with the kind of scientific thinking we are bound to follow, we can regain these things exactly as if they had never been lost; but we can try to become aware of their existence and their importance. (1978, p. 5)

I shall begin with a brief account of some of the overlapping branches of research in classical studies and anthropology that have helped to clarify the kinds of thinking that have proven effective in cultures that do not have writing. Next, I shall discuss some prominent features of orality—the poetics of memory, participa-

tion and conservation, and classification and explanation—that have proved *bon à penser*. I shall conclude by discussing the possible implications of these features of orality for early childhood education. Central to this discussion is a reconsideration of what the foundations of education are when literacy and rationality are conceived as growing out of, rather than displacing, the oral culture of early childhood.

THE REDISCOVERY OF ORALITY

The relatively recent rediscovery of orality by Western scholars is connected with some problems presented by Homer's epic poems. Thinkers could easily apply the influential late-Victorian evolutionary paradigm to the development of science, which was seen as a positive progression from myth to rationality to empirical science. When applied more generally to human cultures, however, this paradigm encountered the anomaly of Homer's literacy achievements. Educated Victorians were more familiar with long-ago battles on the windy plains of Troy, the wooden horse, and the destruction of the topless towers of Ilium than with much of their own society. How, they asked, could such vividly powerful epics, with their richness of human insight, their technical sophistication and emotional force, and their overwhelming, engaging reality, be composed by and for what were in all other regards considered primitive people? "Primitive" mentality—supposedly a mess of irrationality and confusion—must, it would seem, have had the resources to create some great cultural achievements.

Two other complications arose. First, the story of the *Iliad*, long regarded as straightforward fiction, came to be seen as an account of events that actually occurred in the thirteenth century B.C. This historicity began to be established by Heinrich Schliemann's excavations at Troy and Mycaenae during the latter part of the nineteenth century and has gradually become fuller and clearer. (. . . A persuasive picture of the period has been pieced together in Michael Wood's popular television series and book *In Search of the Trojan War* [1985]).

The second complication was the growing evidence that Homer and other poets in his tradition of wandering "singers of tales" were illiterate. As Berkley Peabody put it, "Despite the implications of its name, literature does not seem to have been the invention of literate people" (1975, p. 1). The master poet Homer lived about five hundred years after the events of which he sang, long after the kingdoms whose ships sailed for Troy had themselves been destroyed. Yet growing knowledge of the spread of literacy in Greece made it increasingly difficult for nineteenth-century scholars to imagine Homer—by tradition blind in any case—sitting at a table *writing* his poems.

But how could such technically complex poems, many thousands of lines long, be composed without writing? Surely no illiterate bard could make up such supple hexameters in a matter of hours while he sang, and then recall them word for word? Virgil, that other great epic poet of the ancient world, labored for years writing his *Aeneid* by hand. We know (Suetonius, *De Poetis*) that he revised it constantly and on his deathbed asked that it be destroyed; the highly literate Virgil believed that he had struggled in vain to match the power, vividness, and quality of Homer's work.

The story of the rediscovery of the Homeric methods of composition is itself an epic of scholarly ingenuity. In the 1920s, Milman Parry (1928), following a number of earlier scholars (Wolf, 1795/1884; Vico, 1744/1970), contended in his doctoral dissertation that the structure and distinctive stylistic features of the Homeric poems reflect directly the requirements of oral methods of composition (Burke, 1985; Griffin, 1980). Parry's analyses of the *Iliad* and the *Odyssey* showed that they were composed largely of verbal formulae—repeated morphemic clusters—whose form was dictated by the metrical requirements of the hexameter line. For example, Homer used a large number of adjectival epithets for most of the recurring nouns in the poems—for wine, the sea, ships, the major characters, and so on. The epithet chosen at any point is not necessarily the most apposite for the meaning of the line, but is dictated instead by its fit into the line's meter (Kirk, 1965, ch. 1). One-fifth of Homer's lines are repeated almost verbatim elsewhere in his poems; in about 28,000 lines there are about 25,000 repeated phrases (Parry, 1928).

The poet who performed orally did not memorize the poems, as we would have to do. Rather, the singer learned—through a long, *non-literate* apprenticeship—the particular metrical form of his tradition, until it was absorbed like a somatic rhythm, which habitually accompanied and shaped his thought (Lord, 1964). The content of the song was held together first by the poet's clear grasp of the overall story, and the meter determined the pattern of sounds. As Albert B. Lord

wrote, "Man without writing thinks in terms of sound groups and not in words" (1964, p. 25). Traditional oral performance, then, does not involve repeated recitation of a memorized poem—the idea of a fixed text is a product of literacy. Rather, each performance is a new composition. It may be very like previous ones, and certain patterns will recur, but the singer is composing each time, not repeating something fixed in memory. It is, in Lord's words, "the preservation of tradition by the constant re-creation of it" (1964, p. 29).

These metrically arranged units of sound, then, accumulated line by line in the Homeric poems to repeat the heroic story. The poet "stitched" together the formulae to fit the metrical line, and the episodes to fit the story. The Greeks called singers "rhapsodes"—literally, "song-stitchers." It seems likely that Homer, as one of the greatest epic poets, represented the culmination of his tradition, and that he recited his poems to trained scribes.

In the early 1930s, Parry supplemented his arguments by studying methods of oral composition being used by contemporary singers of heroic tales in Yugoslavia. After his death, his work was supported and extended by Lord's studies (1964) of comparable singers in the Balkans. Lord has described in some detail the conditions of their intensive, and almost invariably non-literate, training, which cannot be very unlike Homer's (Lord, 1964, esp. ch. 2). This work has been further elaborated by Peabody's ingenious analysis of Hesiod's *Works and Days* (1975). Peabody has shown in still greater depth how the oral poet uses the techniques developed over uncountable generations to realize for the audience a kind of alternate reality. That is, the techniques of oral poetry are designed to discourage critical reflection on the stories and their contents, and instead to "enchant" the hearers, drawing them into the world of the story. I will describe these techniques below.

This process of enthralling the audience, of impressing upon them the reality of the story, is a central feature of education in oral cultures. Their social institutions are sustained in large part by sound, by what the spoken or sung word can do to commit individuals to particular beliefs, expectations, roles, and behaviors. Thus the techniques of fixing the crucial patterns of belief in the memory—rhyme, rhythm, formula, story, and so on—are vitally important. Education in oral cultures is largely a matter of constantly immersing the young in enchanting patterns of sound until their minds resonate to them, until they become in tune with the institutions of their culture.

The Homeric poems were called the educators of the pre-classical Greeks because they performed this social function. Poems were not listened to or learned solely because of their aesthetic value; that was incidental to their value as "a massive repository of useful knowledge, a sort of encyclopedia of ethics, politics, history, and technology which the effective citizen was required to learn as the core of his educational equipment" (Havelock, 1963, p. 29). In the process of such an education a substantial amount of mental energy is spent memorizing the chief messages of the culture, because they can exist and survive only in people's memories. According to Eric Havelock, little mental energy is left for reflection on those messages, or analysis of them, because such activities would interfere with the need to sink them unquestioningly into every mind.

Havelock further extended Parry's and Lord's work. His *Preface to Plato* (1963), *Origins of Western Literacy* (1976), and *The Muse Learns to Write* (1986) help clarify the achievements of the early literate Greek philosophers, by offering a better understanding of the oral poetic culture that preceded it. In particular, they highlight Plato's reasons for wishing to exclude poets from his ideal state. Havelock read Plato's *Republic* as a program for educating people to discard the residues of oral culture and to embrace forms of thinking made possible by full literacy. In Havelock's interpretation, Plato says that the mind need no longer be immersed in the oral tradition, memorizing and copying the paradigmatic structures and patterns of the Homeric poems, but can be freed to engage its proper objects—what we might call abstract concepts, and what he called Forms or Ideas. Plato characterized this mode of thinking as opposed to the Homeric tradition; the Platonic scheme of education, as he saw it, brought the mind to reality, while Homer's crippled the intellect through its seductive illusions and distortions of reality.

The new forms of thinking made possible by literacy, early in our educational discourse, were represented as enemies of the oral techniques that were *bon à penser*: "Plato's target was indeed an educational procedure and a whole way of life" (Havelock, 1963, p. 45). There are clear ambivalences in Plato's reflections on the oral tradition (see the *Phaedrus* and the possibly apocryphal *Seventh Letter*) and on Homer, but

in the end those earlier forms of thinking, education, and society had to be destroyed to make way for the new abstract forms of thought and whatever world they brought with them. Plato did not conceive his educational scheme as a structure built on the oral tradition, but as a replacement for it. His work, in Havelock's view, "announced the arrival of a completely new level of discourse which as it became perfected was to create in turn a new kind of experience of the world—the reflective, the scientific, the technological, the theological, the analytic. We can give it a dozen names" (1963, p. 267). Plato's influence is so strong in Western thought that it is extremely difficult for us now to imagine the kind of consciousness created in the oral tradition, and the kind of experience created for listeners by a singer of tales or teller of myths.

Havelock's description of the techniques of oral recitation in the ancient world shows that audiences received poems rather differently from the way we read the same texts today. A youth in an oral culture, whether Greek or Australian aborigine, needed to expend considerable mental resources to learn by listening to these foundations of his or her cultural institutions. But the messages of the professional singers were also repeated everywhere by their listeners. Proverbs and maxims and riddles uttered at meals, on rising or going to sleep, in the market or the field, are constantly repeated pieces of the great myths or epic poems of oral cultures. African children, for example, traditionally learn the practices and mores of their ethnic groups through riddles asked by their grandparents. In religious schools throughout the Muslim world, young students commit to memory phenomenally long passages of Koranic literature and law. It is likely that biblical stories were first repeated and handed on by singers and storytellers, as are the tales of African *griots* in many places today.

Learning the sustaining messages of an oral culture differs from the effort at accumulation of knowledge with which we are familiar in literate cultures. In oral cultures memorization is central, but it is not performed in the way that we might try to learn something by heart. For us memorization is usually an attempt to remember a text so that it is possible to repeat it verbatim on command; and our techniques are typically impoverished, involving largely repetition, some mnemonics perhaps, or saying words aloud with our eyes closed, and so on. In an oral culture, learning proceeds more somatically, with the whole body used to support the memorizing process. The Homeric singer, and singers throughout the world, usually use a simple stringed instrument, sometimes a drum, whose beat reinforces the rhythm of the telling and draws the hearer into the enchantment of the song. The audience does not so much listen to it, as we might listen to a play, as they are invited to live it. The acoustical rhythm created by the singer and his instrument is supported by the repetitive meter, rhythmic body movements, and by the pattern of formulae and the story, to set up conditions of enchantment that impress the message on the minds of the hearers. The techniques of the skilled performer generate a relaxed, half-hypnotized pleasure in the audience.[2]

This semi-hypnotized state is similar to that often described by anthropologists as the condition in which audiences receive the fundamental messages of their culture. Thus, Lévi-Strauss, in his study of mythology, aimed "to show, not how men think in myths, but how myths operate in men's minds without their being aware of the fact" (1969, p. 12). He preferred to compare this process to a musical performance rather than to linguistic forms or texts: "The myth and the musical work are like conductors of an orchestra, whose audience becomes the silent performers" (p. 17). While no Western educator would wish to replicate all aspects of this phenomenon in our schools, it seems important to understand the nature of this receptive state. Anyone familiar with children's rapt attention to television broadcasts may recognize Lévi-Strauss's descriptions.

Similarly, Edmund Leach (1967) argued that the structural patterns of myths and their underlying messages are communicated powerfully and unambiguously by oral performances, despite considerable variation in the surface stories and settings:

Whenever a corpus of mythology is recited in its religious setting, such structures are "felt" to be present, and convey meaning much as poetry conveys meaning. Even though the ordinary listener is not fully conscious of what has been communicated, the "message" is there in a quite objective sense. (Leach, 1967, p. 12)

According to Lévi-Bruhl, when a sacred myth is recited in the course of ritual settings or other situations characterized by heightened emotion, "what they [the participants] hear in it awakens a whole gamut of harmonies which do not exist for us" (1910/1985, p. 369). The written form of the myth that we can study "is but the inanimate corpse which remains after the vital spark has fled" (1910/1985, p. 369).

In his re-examination of orality, Goody (1977, 1986, 1987) has not only undermined traditional notions of the move from "primitive" to rational thought, and instead shown that the differences typically educed as evidence for such a shift are better understood as epiphenomena of the move from orality to literacy; he has also clarified some specific steps that accompanied the move from orality to literacy, and has detailed various consequences of literacy—for example, the development of Western scientific inquiry and abstract thought (Goody & Watt, 1968; Goody, 1986, 1987). (For the best current survey of this field, see Ong, 1982.)

In the following discussion of several techniques of oral expression common in non-literate cultures, my choice has been guided not by a desire to conduct a systematic survey, but primarily by educational relevance.

Oral Expressions: Bon à Penser

In listing certain features of oral cultures I do not mean to imply that such cultures are all alike; nor do I imply that they all use precisely the same sets of techniques for preserving their institutions. Clearly, there are enormous differences among the cultures of pre-classical Greeks and those of early twentieth-century Trobriand Islanders, Australian aborigines, and the indigenous peoples of the Americas before extensive contacts with literate peoples. In particular, their myths, and the range of techniques used to transmit them, differ significantly.

It is inevitably difficult for us to think of orality simply as a positive set of tactics that are *bon à penser*; the intellectual capacities and forms of communication that have been stimulated by literacy intrude upon our attempts to understand orally sustained forms of thought. But we need to see orality as an energetic and distinct set of ways of learning and communicating, not simply as an incomplete and imperfect use of the mind awaiting the invention of literacy. Orality is not at all the same as what we usually mean

---

[2] For a full discussion, see Havelock (1963), ch. 9, "The Psychology of Poetic Performance."

today by illiteracy in the Western cultural context. Illiteracy is perhaps best understood as a condition in which one has not acquired the positive capacities that either orality or literacy can provide.

Poetics of Memory

Let us begin considering orality by focusing on what seems to be the central reason it involves some different tactics of thinking from literacy: its need to rely on memory. If the preservation of the institutions of one's culture depends on the memories of its living members, then the techniques that most effectively impress the appropriate messages upon their minds and sustain them are vitally important. The Victorians, who judged members of oral cultures to be mentally "incapable" because of their supposed reluctance or inability to perform mental functions that are commonplace in literate Western cultures, often failed to recognize this fact at work in the intellectual "anomalies" of traditional societies they encountered. Lucien Lévi-Bruhl, writing in 1910, described various feats of memory that seemed to him prodigious, but to the oral peoples he studied, commonplace:

> This extraordinary development of memory, and a memory which faithfully reproduces the minutest details of sense-impressions in the correct order of their appearance, is shown moreover by the wealth of vocabulary and the grammatical complexity of the languages. Now the very men who speak these languages and possess this power of memory are (in Australia or Northern Brazil, for instance) incapable of counting beyond two and three. The slightest mental effort involving abstract reasoning, however rudimentary it may be, is so distasteful to them that they immediately declare themselves tired and give it up. (Lévi-Bruhl, 1910/1985, p. 115)

Lévi-Bruhl perceived there were no differences between his own capacities and those of his subjects on any simple scale of mental superiority or inferiority, but that the conditions of life in oral cultures stimulated different mental developments to deal with those conditions. The people he observed had a highly developed set of techniques for learning and remembering, and their apparent incapacity for "abstraction," as such, lay in the dissociation of the problems Lévi-Bruhl gave them from their lives. It may be helpful to

remember this as we investigate the development of our children's capacities for abstract thinking (Hayek, 1969; Egan, in press).

Goody's experience with the LoDogaa of Ghana (1977, pp. 12–13) makes this clear. When he asked some tribesmen to count for him, they responded with the—to them—obvious question, "Count what?" The LoDogaa have not only an abstract numerical system, but also several sophisticated forms of counting that are chosen according to what is being counted: their methods for counting cows and for counting cowrie shells differ. "Abstract reasoning" is beyond no human mind; but abstraction that is very heavily dependent on writing is not available to people who do not write or read.

In describing the apparent anomaly of prodigious mental feats executed by the supposedly mentally deficient, Lévi-Bruhl (1910/1985) perceived that there were no differences between purely oral and literate peoples on any simple scale of mental superiority/inferiority, but that the conditions of life in oral cultures stimulated a difference in mental developments to deal with those conditions. He located a wide range of those differences precisely. The uses of memory in oral cultures, Lévi-Bruhl concluded, "are quite different because its contents are of a different character. It is both very accurate and very emotional" (1910/1985, p. 110).

Oral cultures engage the emotions of their members by making the culturally important messages event-laden, by presenting characters and their emotions in conflict in developing narratives—in short, by building the messages into stories. Lévi-Strauss pointed out that "all myths tell a story" (1962, p. 26), and Lord concluded that the story provides the firm structure for the constant reconstruction of heroic songs. The various linguistic structures in the end "serve only one purpose. They provide a means for telling a story. . . . The tale's the thing" (Lord, 1964, p. 68). The story form is one of the few cultural universals—everyone, everywhere, has told and enjoyed stories. They are one of the greatest cultural inventions for catching and fixing meaning. Perhaps "discovery" is a more appropriate term than "invention": some enormously creative person or people discovered that messages shaped into the distinctive form of the story were those best remembered, and they carried a charge of emotional identification that greatly enhanced social cohesion and control.

Myth stories also, of course, have what we would consider aesthetic value. But whereas we distinguish aesthetic from utilitarian values, for members of oral cultures these are bound up together (Durkheim, 1915, ch. 4; Cassirer, 1946). The story form has been one of the most powerful and effective sustainers of cultures across the world. Its great power lies in its ability to fix affective responses to the messages it contains and to bind what is to be remembered with emotional associations. Our emotions, to put it simply, are most effective at sustaining, and helping in the recall of, memories of events (Bartlett, 1932). This should not be a surprise if we reflect on the events of our lives that are most memorable. Almost invariably we find that they are accompanied by vivid emotional associations, and retain quite clearly a particular emotional tone. Most of the world's cultures and its great religions have at their sacred core a story, and indeed we have difficulty keeping the facts of our history from being shaped constantly into stories. It is likely that the simplified histories sanctioned in the schools of most nation states (Ravitch, 1983) have at least as much in common with the origin myths of oral cultures as they do with the austere ideals of historiography. The story form also has important implications for schooling. Its survival among oral peoples as a technique for sustaining culture speaks to its appropriateness for education, despite our recent tendencies to neglect it. There are many ways in which we might use this most powerful of communicative media in education today, especially in the primary school (Egan, 1985, in press).

Rhyme, rhythm, meter, repetition of formulae, redundancy, the use of visual imagery—figures of speech used to create enchantment in oral cultures throughout the world—are also among the techniques used in Western poetry, and the state of mind they induce is close to what we describe as poetic. Like the singer of heroic tales or the reciter of myths, the literate poet shapes sound to create particular emotional effects and fix particular meanings. The shaping of sound finds one outlet in poetry and another in rhetoric. These two, along with music, are perhaps the most evident and direct manifestations of the oral tradition that have survived in the literate world.

Metaphor, metonymy, and synecdoche are important among the linguistic tools that are bon à penser. In oral cultures, thinking moves according to the complex logic of metaphor, more readily than it follows the sys-

tematic logic of rational inquiry. As Ernst Cassirer notes, "It is a familiar fact that all mythic thinking is governed and permeated by the principle [of metaphor]" (1946, p. 92; see also Lévi-Strauss, 1966, esp. ch. 7). Although the logic of mythic thinking, with its reliance on metaphor, has been difficult for some Westerners to make sense of, we should appreciate and find readily accessible this metaphoric power, for it suffuses all languages. It is one of the foundations of all our mental activity, upon which our systematic logics of rational inquiry also rest, or—a better metaphor—the soil out of which they grow. Both myth and our everyday language, then, are permeated with metaphor; as Cassirer concluded, "The same form of mental conception is operative in both. It is the form which one may denote as *metaphorical thinking*" (1945, p. 84). Or, as Lévi-Strauss observes, "metaphor . . . is not a later embellishment of language but is one of its fundamental modes—a primary form of discursive thought" (1962, p. 102; see also Cooper, 1986).

The characteristics of oral literature that I have mentioned are generated by a people's need to memorize and be committed to their cultural institutions. We find these techniques to a greater or lesser degree in all oral cultures: "At different periods and in different cultures there are close links between the techniques for mental recall, the inner organization of the faculty (of memory), the place it occupies in the system of the ego, and the ways that men picture memory to themselves" (Vernant, 1983, p. 75; see also Finnegan, 1970, 1977).

We remain familiar with these tactics that are *bon à penser*, but usually in a much attenuated or altered form. Rhyme, for example, seems little more than fun for us now, a part of children's games, anachronistic and therefore ironic in modern poetry. We would hardly consider its systematic use a matter of vital social importance. We can write, so we do not need rhyme to sustain the memory of our institutions. These survivors of orality—rhyme, rhythm, meter, story, metaphor—serve largely (I am tempted to write "merely") aesthetic purposes for us. While metaphor and story may still seem to us culturally important in some imprecise way, we tend to think of rhyme and rhythm as only causal cultural survivors, anachronisms serving merely to entertain the literate—like the lords and ladies of a defeated civilization made into clowns and dancers. But art has a utilitarian purpose when it supports faith—whether in gods, in the validity of one's cultural institutions, in one's society, in one's sense of oneself. The origins of any of the tools of spoken language invented to create and sustain memory lie in the remarkable human ambition "to liberate the soul from time and open up a path to immortality" (Vernant, 1983, p. 95). All the world's amazing cultural and technological achievements since the development of literacy have been built on the efficacy of these oral tools of communication and the intellectual space they once did, and can still, generate. We would do well, therefore, to consider carefully their actual and potential roles in early childhood education.

Participation and Conservation

An Ojibwa Indian observed: "The white man writes everything down in a book so that it will not be forgotten; but our ancestors married the animals, learned their ways, and passed on the knowledge from one generation to another" (Jenness, in Lévi-Strauss, 1966, p. 37). This sense of participation in the natural world, of having knowledge that is different from the kinds of propositions generated by rational inquiries, reflects a mental condition anthropologists have often tried to describe as a kind of oneness with nature; by comparison, our normal relationship with the natural world seems alienated. "The mainspring of the acts, thoughts, and feelings of early man was the conviction that the divine was immanent in nature, and nature intimately connected with society" (Frankfort, Wilson, & Jacobsen, 1949, p. 237). All the attempts to pinpoint the causes and character of this sense of participation in nature display a conviction that, despite their inadequacies when it comes to pragmatic control *over* the world, myth and consciousness in oral cultures somehow enable people to feel that they are comfortable participants *in* their life world. But it is not a simple condition, obviously, nor one we can feel unequivocally regretful of having largely lost. Ong describes it this way:

> The psyche of a culture innocent of writing knows by a kind of empathetic identification of knower and known, in which the object of knowledge and the total being of the knower enter into a kind of fusion, in a way which literate cultures would typically find unsatisfyingly vague and garbled and somehow too intense and participatory. (Ong, 1977, p. 18)

One of the cornerstones of Western rationality is knowing, as it were, where we end and the world begins: distinguishing the world from our feelings, hopes, fears, and so on. This form of thinking seems to be very largely a product of literacy. As Ong puts it, "Writing fosters abstractions that disengage knowledge from the arena where human beings struggle with one another" (1982, pp. 43–44), or, in Peabody's words: "The shift in medium from utterance to record affects the way such an institution works and tends to change what was an immediate, living, active agent into an increasingly distant, timeless, passive, authority" (1975, pp. 1, 2). In an oral culture the ear is most highly attuned to picking up cultural messages, supplemented by the eye. In our case it is usually the other way around.

Sound is alive and participatory. It is effective within only a short physical range. The hearer must be in the presence of the speaker—there are no carefully crafted memos from the president or manager. "The living word," as Socrates put it in Plato's *Phaedrus*, "has a soul . . . of which the written word is properly no more than an image" (Jowett, 1892, p. 279). The living word is the word in the arena of human interactions and conflicts. It is not the distanced and "cooled" word of the written text. Language use in an oral culture tends to be, in Ong's phrase, "agonistically toned" (1977, p. 113); it is charged with the direct energy of the speaker's body, and thus with the speaker's hopes, fears, wants, needs, and intentions. Oral heroic tales are full of bragging, elaborate abuse of adversaries, and exuberant praise of leaders or those from whom the speaker wants a favor. The tensions of daily struggles are felt face-to-face in an oral culture. These facts of oral life lead to a verbally highly polarized world, of good and evil, friends and enemies, fear and security. Ong points out that the mental life of oral cultures "is sure to carry a heavy load of praise and vituperation" (1977, p. 112), because "if one does not think formulary, mnemonically structured thoughts, how can one really know them, that is, be able to retrieve them, if the thoughts are even of moderate complexity?" (p. 104). Thus, because oral cultures "necessarily store knowledge largely in narrative concerned with interacting human or quasi-human figures" (1977, p. 112), there is a powerful pressure to polarize. The African Batomba, for instance, have two typically polarized paraphrasatic names for White foreigners: "The white man, honored by all, companion of our chiefs" or, as occasion may demand, the pointed expression "You do not touch the poisonous caterpillar" (Ong, 1977, p. 112). In such societies the forms of verbal play also tend to be "agonistically toned"—riddles, tricks, and jokes are often characterized by a playful competitiveness or even aggressiveness.

In an oral culture "the meaning of each word is ratified in a succession of concrete situations, accompanied by vocal inflections and physical gestures, all of which combine to particularize both its specific denotation and its accepted connotative uses" (Goody & Watt, 1968, p. 306). As a result, words typically are not themselves objects of reflection, and thus oral cultures have no epistemology as we might define it. When words are closely tied into their context of reference, philosophical problems do not arise. People in oral cultures do not dissociate words from things to the point where they might wonder how short the legs of a small table have to be for it to be considered a tray. This feature of their thinking has nothing to do with "defects" or "inadequacies" of the mind, but is rather a function of the uselessness of many of our forms and techniques of thought in the conditions of most oral cultures.

In nearly all oral cultures, for example, time is reckoned in terms of the significant daily activities of the social group. An "abstract" or dissociated system for measuring time, such as we employ, is useful only when it is necessary to coordinate a large number of quite diverse kinds of activities. Such diversity does not exist in most oral cultures, where time measurement reflects the sequence of activities that constitute the rhythms of daily life.

In his studies of non-literate peasants in remote areas of the Soviet Union, Alexander Luria (1976) posed to them apparently simple problems, such as "In the far north, where there is snow, all bears are white. Novaya Zemlya is in the far north and there is always snow there. What colors are the bears around Novaya Zemlya?" His subjects, no doubt politely wishing to play their part in the conversation, would reply that they had never been to Novaya Zemlya and so they didn't know, or that they had seen a black bear but never a white one, and so on. The rules and underlying forms of thought of the kind of conversation in which Luria tried to engage these non-literate people are familiar to us, but appeared bizarre to them. The point is not a concern with mental capacity, but with social utility, and the influence of the latter over cogni-

tion. Pragmatic thought in oral cultures participates more intimately in the life world; it does not treat the world and experience as objects distanced from people's emotional, aesthetic, and utilitarian needs. As such, it makes "no clear-cut distinction between subjective states and the properties of the cosmos" (Lévi-Strauss, 1969, p. 240).

Oral cultures have been described as being intellectually inclined toward homeostasis, conservatism, and stability in ways that our modern literate cultures are not (see Geertz, 1973, esp. ch. 5). Such cultures, of course, undergo changes of many kinds—migration, disaster, invasion, merging with other groups—but the mental forms dominant in oral cultures strive to maintain verbal accounts of the culture's life that assert continuity and stability.

One striking difference between oral and literate cultures is in their different attitudes to the past; literate peoples have and value accurate historical accounts; oral societies cultivate what J. A. Barnes has called "structural amnesia"—systematic procedures for "forgetting," or wiping out from the oral records of the culture's past (Goody & Watt, 1968, p. 309). Although oral cultures often preserve the memory of particular historical events in stories or in memorized genealogies of leading families, it usually turns out that the record kept does not reflect past reality with complete accuracy. Rather, it is faithful to present social conditions and statuses. As conditions change, so do the accounts or genealogy. Malinowski (1954) showed this process at work among the Trobriand Islanders. As changes occurred in the structure and power relationships of their society, the myths of origin changed to reflect the current social structure; that is, historical changes were gradually effaced. Malinowski concluded that "myths serve to cover certain inconsistencies created by historical events" (1954, p. 125). The oral record, then, ensures that "the individual has little perception of the past except in terms of the present" (Goody & Watt, 1968, p. 310).

We find it hard to think of this structural amnesia as anything other than an unawareness of history, another difficulty resulting from the lack of literacy. It seems merely a way of making the best of things, or the only strategy manageable if the society cannot keep written records. But the positive value of such structural amnesia is that it tends to preserve a sense of stability and clarity. The social structure and its prevailing institutions are constantly supported by whatever sanction is contained in the myths, whether of sacred ancestors or gods, and are constantly renewed: "time is recorded only biologically without being allowed to become 'history'—that is, without its corrosive action being able to exert itself upon consciousness by revealing the irreversibility of events" (Eliade, 1959, pp. 74–75). One technique constantly used to achieve this end is the assertion of continual rebirth—rebeginning as the first beginning. We preserve a vague shadow of this sense of birth in our New Year festivals. Even if we, like Malinowski (1954), discount other functions of myth, we ought not to disregard the sense of intellectual security conferred by sloughing off the memory of events that are no longer relevant or useful to present life. This is indeed another way in which orality is *bon à penser*. While direct comparisons are difficult to make, this process may have relevance as we consider preliterate children's conceptions of time and the implications this may have for developing a history curriculum based on the telling of stories. We may wish to make better use of the children's imaginative lives as vividly lived in the present moment.

This emphasis on the preservation of stability through selective memory of events relevant to present social conditions leads to what is often characterized as a conservative frame of mind. It is indeed conservative, but in a radical sense. The pressure to preserve in memory the institutions of one's culture does not invite innovation or experimentation. Although some oral cultures are undoubtedly more resilient in this regard than others, on the whole anthropologists attest to the powerful sanctions against change. "The most apparently trifling innovation may lead to danger, liberate hostile forces, and finally bring about the ruin of its instigator and all dependent upon him" (Lévi-Bruhl, 1910/1985, p. 42). The cultural institutions support a limited stock of archetypal forms of appropriate behavior for each member of the society, and the repetition of these alone is sanctioned and validated by the myths. These are believed to be the behaviors of sacred ancestors or gods, which it is the human task to imitate: "The inhibition against new invention, to avoid placing any possible strain on the memory, continually encourage[s] contemporary decisions to be framed as though they were the acts and words of the ancestors" (Havelock, 1963, p. 121) or, we might add, gods. As Mircea Eliade wrote, the individual in oral cultures "acknowledges no act which has

not been previously posited and lived by someone else, some other being who was not a man. What he does has been done before. His life is a ceaseless repetition of gestures initiated by others" (1959, p. 15.) In such a culture, "only the changeless is ultimately significant" (Frankfort, 1961, p. viii).

Although these generalizations may be somewhat less appropriate for some oral cultures than for others, they do point to further common ways in which their orality is, in their cultural context, *bon à penser*. The pressures against change and innovation serve stability, order, and intellectual security. One's familiar territory is intellectually mapped out, categorized, and under secure control. The resources of orality considered in this section help to provide intellectual security and a sense of persisting order in society despite historical changes. They also help to preserve a sense of participation in nature which users of literate forms of thought find somewhat alien. Not entirely alien, of course; attempts to recapture this sense of participation in nature find their most common literate expression in poetry. It is in the work of poets such as Wordsworth that the sense of participation in nature is most plausibly recaptured, and, significantly for my general argument about the cognitive effects of orality, it is in preliterate childhood that he most vividly locates it:

> Blest the infant Babe . . .
> No outcast he, bewildered and depressed.
> Along his infant veins are interfused
> The gravitation and the filial bond
> Of nature that connect him with the world.
> (*The Prelude*, Bk. II, 241–244)

Classification and Explanation

Members of oral cultures often have remarkably detailed knowledge of the flora and fauna of their environments, but their systems for classifying this knowledge tend to be very different from ours. Many anthropologists have commented on members of traditional societies who could give remarkably precise inventories of kinds of plants, trees, or weather conditions but had no words for "plant," "tree," or "weather." This phenomenon further supported their conclusions about such people's inability to "abstract."

Yet, indeed, some purely oral languages use abstractions where speakers of English would prefer concrete terms (see Boas, 1911). For example, the proposition "The bad man killed the poor child" is rendered in Chinook: "The man's badness killed the child's poverty" (Lévi-Strauss, 1966, p. 1). A major difference between oral cultures and our own lies not in their incapacity for abstraction, but in our dissociation from the life world. This kind of dissociation is a product of the techniques of writing, not some property that some human minds possess and others lack: "Writing, and more especially alphabetic literacy, made it possible to scrutinise discourse in a different kind of way . . . this scrutiny favoured the increase in scope of critical activity, and hence of rationality, skepticism, and logic" (Goody, 1977, p. 37).

Among the common basic techniques of classification in oral cultures is the use of what Lévi-Strauss called "binary opposites": "All classification," he wrote, "proceeds by pairs of contrasts" (1966, p. 139). These are not necessarily opposites in any precise logical or empirical sense, but become used as such by serving as the basis for further discriminations: "The substance of contradictions is much less important than the fact that they exist" (p. 95).

Lévi-Strauss began his four-volume analysis of myths by identifying sets of binary opposites on which each myth was built. Although many of his critics have regarded this as a rather arbitrary procedure, he presents a compelling argument by demonstrating the prevalence of such oppositions giving structure to the contents of myths.

Attempts at classification are fundamental to rational thought. It makes little sense to consider people who develop sophisticated taxonomic schemes "irrational" (Lévi-Strauss, 1966, p. 15). The differences between classifactory schemes in oral cultures and those in our scientific culture commonly rest on the qualities of phenomena used as the basis for classification. Lévi-Strauss's study of myth is, as he puts it, an attempt "to prove that there is a kind of logic in [the] tangible qualities" of the concrete phenomena of everyday life—of the raw and the cooked, honey and ashes, and so on (1969, p. 1). While our children's constant classifications of their universe are necessarily less sophisticated, an understanding of the logic they use in forming them may help us understand their development of literacy.

The kinds of explanations offered in oral cultures about natural and cosmological phenomena often seemed to Victorian intellectuals perverse or crazy, and were taken as clear evidence of oral peoples' infirmities of mind. Unfamiliar medical practices were considered bizarre (although today a growing body of anthropology literature elucidates the physical or psychological efficacy of many traditional practices). Lévi-Strauss, however, pointed out that the mistake of earlier interpreters of such explanations "was to think that natural phenomena are *what* myths seek to explain, when they are rather the *medium through which* myths try to explain facts which are themselves not of a natural but a logical order" (1966, p. 95). We must, he said, attend to the form as well as the content of such explanations if we are to understand them.

For us, explanation is a central part of our efforts both to understand and control nature, to have practical effects. But its main purpose in oral cultures "is not a practical one. It meets intellectual requirements rather than or instead of satisfying needs" (Lévi-Strauss, 1966, p. 9). In serving such intellectual purposes it does not, like our logic, tie itself to the ways the world in fact works; indeed the "savage" mind "does not bind itself down, as our thought does, to avoiding contradictions" (Lévi-Bruhl, 1910/1985, p. 78). Certainly in the myths and medical lore of oral cultures, the literate, rationalistic concern with non-contradiction is not a prominent structuring feature. Underlying the surface of explanations that may seem bizarre to Western observers, however, is a quest for order in diversity whose motive should be familiar to us from the similar motive that drives our science (see Horton, 1970, pp. 131–171).

The mode of thought that directs the approaches of various oral cultures to classification and explanation is closely linked with the modes of expression discussed earlier. Malinowski observed of the Trobriand Islanders: "They never explain in any sense of the word; they always state a precedent which constitutes an ideal and a warrant for its continuance, and sometimes practical directions for the procedure" (1954, p. 110). What seem like explanations in oral cultures do not focus only on the relevant relationships among content features, but they mix in the whole equipment of the psyche—the explanation, that is, is cast in the form of a narrative in which characters, events, motives, and emotions carry the idea forward—leading to what Goody calls the "personalization of theory" (1977, p. 42).

IMPLICATIONS FOR EARLY CHILDHOOD EDUCATION

The research on orality sketched above has a number of implications for early childhood education; here I will consider just two. The first concerns the early childhood curriculum; the second concerns methods of teaching.

The implications turn on the validity of the connections that can be established between characteristics of orality and the thinking of young children in modern literate cultures. I started by noting the need for caution in making such connections. First, psychological development connections seem particularly inappropriate. For example, the fact that adults in oral cultures commonly cannot perform intellectual tasks such as properly concluding "disembedded" syllogisms or successfully achieving Piagetian conservations (Ashton, 1975; Buck-Morss, 1982), does not mean that they are psychologically or developmentally equivalent to children in Western literate cultures, nor does the fact that adults in Western literate cultures can commonly perform such tasks make them psychologically superior or intellectually more fully developed. It means only that Western adults have adapted to a cultural environment shaped by centuries of elaboration of the thinking techniques made possible by literacy. Second, it is inappropriate to seek connections in the *content* of thoughts between adults in oral cultures and children in Western cultures; the concern here, is rather, what they think *with*. The connections I am focusing on are in certain formal characteristics of thought, in the strategies and resources the human mind has available and has developed over countless centuries in oral cultures. As young children in Western literate cultures themselves inhabit an oral culture, they have access to the intellectual resources of early orality until such a time as literacy is internalized.

There are two ways in which we might hope to establish relationships between the resources available to thought in oral cultures and those deployed by modern Western children. The first is analytic. This focuses on the necessary requirements of thought in oral conditions, and on what is entailed by the need to memorize when written recording is not available. Such analytic work obviously goes forward most

securely and fruitfully when combined with the second method, which is empirical. We can observe characteristic features of language and thought in oral cultures around the world, and see whether we find similar features in the language and thought of preliterate children in Western cultures; we may then be able to suggest some research issues that are worthy of further attention. The empirical observations alone can provide us only with correlations; it is the analytic work that can posit causal relationships between observed forms of language and the requirements of an oral environment.

The body of this article has outlined a variety of formal characteristics of thought inferred from observations in oral cultures. One obvious source of equivalent material about modern Western children is in ethnographic studies of their lore and language. Fortunately, there are a number of quite substantial studies of children's oral cultures, notably those made by the Opies (1959, 1969, 1985) in Britain, and the Knapps (1976) and Sutton-Smith (1981) in the United States.

Those techniques used in oral cultures to shape sound into more memorable forms we find also to be prominent in children's oral cultures. Rhyme, rhythm, meter, and the story form are ubiquitous. The prominence of rhyme in everyday speech will in all English-speaking countries elicit the response, "You're a poet and didn't know it" (Opie & Opie, 1959, p. 73). The strength of rhythm and meter is such that many children's songs are made up of parodies of well-known, usually solemn or sacred, songs carried on echoes of the same rhythms and meters. The Opies report variants of this practice all over Britain (1959, p. 108). A children's taunting rhyme recalls the lively competitiveness and moral core of many verbal games observed in oral cultures:

Liar, liar, pants on fire!
Nose as long as a telephone wire.
(Knapp & Knapp, 1976, p. 11)

Children's easy use of metaphoric thinking is evident in their ability to understand the kinds of metaphors that fill all languages—"It's bitter cold," "He feels bouncy today"—and their easy perception of the distinction between literal and metaphoric usage—"Mom killed that plan!" In what might be expected to be the constraining circumstances of constructed tasks, Gardner et al. (1975) report that nursery school children are much more likely than other children to use a metaphor to complete a sentence of the form, "He looks as gigantic as _____." This ready grasp of metaphor and punning is prerequisite to an understanding of the jokes that are common in children's oral culture: "What did the quarter say when it got stuck in the slot?" "Money's very tight these days"; "Why does Fred work in the bakery?" "I guess he kneads the dough," and so endlessly on.

Children's sense of the story form seems to exist very early in life; it is clearly evident in the language of many children by age two (Applebee, 1978; Pitcher & Prelinger, 1963). Themes framed as binary opposites, too, are evident as the most prominent structuring elements in the classic folktales (Bettelheim, 1976) and in children's invented stories (Paley, 1981). The stories are particularized versions of the struggles between such moral concepts as good and evil, bravery and cowardice, fear and security, hope and despair, and so on.

Rhyme, metaphor, and stories are, of course, found in adult cultures as well. This in no way undermines their identification as prominent features of orality. In literate Western cultures we do not move from orality to literacy, but rather from orality to a combination of literacy and orality. The techniques that are *bon à penser* for oral peoples do not disappear with the acquisition of literacy; they may be attenuated, but even the most highly literate people are also dependent in many circumstances of their lives on some aspects of orality. In addition, literate adults use techniques of thinking encouraged specifically by literacy; the Western forms of rational inquiry and the standard written forms for reporting their results have developed in part by their exclusion of the techniques of orality. Attempts were made in the past to reach accommodation between the two in the field of rhetoric (see Ong, 1971; Todorov, 1982, ch. 3), but their clear separation, institutionalized by the dominance of positivistic science, is evident in the commonly dismissive use of the phrase "mere rhetoric." Previously, mingling the features of orality and literacy was not considered odd. Orality tends to survive, however, only in the daily lives of literate peoples; it is attenuated to the point of near invisibility in the cultures of positivistic science and technology, and in the realms of the most refinedly "literate" scholarship.

It is possible to take each of the characteristics of orality indicated in the body of this paper and find clear analogies in the oral culture of modern Western children (Egan, forthcoming). That such empirical connections are unlikely to be merely coincidental is suggested by the analysis of orality and what it implies for linguistic forms and techniques of thinking—an analysis owed largely to the main authorities cited above; in particular, Goody, Havelock, and Ong. Let us provisionally assume that this kind of study of oral cultures throughout the world can yield a better understanding of orality and that an understanding of orality can help us better understand young children's minds in literate cultures.

Too often, I think, our perception of young children is clouded when we consider them illiterate and lacking in the skills of Western rationality. It is far better, I would argue, to regard them as oral in a positive sense: they have a distinctive culture of their own. While the image of young children as *tabulae rasae*, or empty vessels to be filled with knowledge, is no longer prominent in educational discourse, we persist in characterizing young children in terms of the absence of the development and knowledge that constitute the mature condition. Even otherwise liberating theories such as Piaget's, for example, represent the developmental process as the gradual accumulation of increasingly sophisticated capacities and their hierarchical integration (Inhelder & Piaget, 1969). Such theories, when used to reflect on education, focus attention on the sequence of capacities to be developed, helping further to define young children in terms of what they lack. In Piaget's scheme, for example, they are *pre*-operational. Developmental schemes focus on the acquisition of the forms of thought characteristic of literate cultures, such as Piaget's focus on logico-mathematical structures, show a gradually rising scale of achievements to adulthood. If we were to focus instead on the thinking techniques of oral peoples, we would surely produce a quite different "developmental" profile. If the techniques of orality are, as I suggested earlier, conducive to formation of the imagination, we might have cause to be very concerned about this.

Perhaps we need a *New Science* of childhood based on the insight that led Vico (1744/1970) towards a better understanding of the "irrational" thinking of early peoples: He argued that notions of irrationality were beside the point; rather, they were "poets who spoke in poetic characters. This discovery, which is the master key of this Science, has cost us the persistent research of almost all our literary life because with our civilized natures we cannot at all imagine and can understand only by great toil the poetic nature of these first men" (Vico, 1744/1970, p. 5).

Vico's thesis was that literacy and rational prose, and the forms of thought associated with them, which Westerners consider so fundamental to their "civilized natures," were late achievements in human thinking. He contended that they grew from, and on, our "poetic nature." If, instead of viewing children's transition from orality to literacy as unqualified progress, we were to view it as a trade-off made for obvious functional advantages in a literate culture, then we might gain a different view of what is entailed in early education. This might make us more wary of displacing orality with literacy, and more sensitive to how we might preserve some of the more valuable characteristics of orality. We cannot hope to preserve orality in children just as it existed before the achievement of literacy, with all its cultural consequences. But we can hope to preserve or regain some things we have been in danger of losing, or have lost, in the dominant conceptions of early childhood education. These conceptions, I would argue, focus primarily upon the absence of literacy and the skills of Western rationality, and fail to recognize the presence of positive orality.[3]

What are these valuable characteristics of orality, then, and how can we hope to preserve or regain them? They are the characteristics Vico summed up by calling people in oral cultures "poets"—in the sense of people whose culture relied on, and whose cultural environment stimulated the development of, the features of orality sketched above. (The poet in Western cultures is, of course, the person who most forcefully retains and deploys the resources of orality—the sensitivity to the sounds of words and their emotional effects, the precise use of metaphor, the arrangement of sound in metrical patterns, the use of rhyme, and so

on). The young child, as a "maker" of imaginative worlds, is a kind of poet, and is in command of some considerable intellectual resources developed and exercised by such imaginative work. It is worth remembering that in our attempts to create artificial intelligence in computers, the most refined mathematical and logical operations have proven the easiest to simulate, while we still have no idea how to simulate these sophisticated and complex "poetic" operations.

The need to remember led, in oral cultures, to the invention of particular techniques to convey and make memorable ideas and information. We saw as prominent among these techniques the story-shaping of narratives—myths—made up of vivid characters and events which carried those ideas and information. What we generally call the imagination is a mental capacity that is evoked, stimulated, and developed by the needs of orality. Its value for literate culture persists; yet we have been in danger of depreciating it. We would be wise to preserve it as fully as possible (Egan & Nadaner, in press). Valuable too is the fluent and flexible use of metaphor, as it is fundamental to language and thought, and is, along with the systematic logic of Western rationality, one of the tools of effective thinking (Cooper, 1986). In the education of modern children into literacy, then, we will want to ensure that fluency of metaphoric thinking is maintained and, if possible, increased. Similarly, the sense in which members of oral cultures see themselves as participants in nature, rather than as set off against it and "conquering" it, seems a valuable characteristic that we should try to preserve in children and regain for literate Western cultures. The development of this sensibility in some form may save us from destroying the natural world that sustains us.

What kinds of curricula will stimulate the development of young children's orality? Two main concerns will need to guide development of such programs. First, they must ensure the fullest possible development of the techniques of orality. This follows the recognition that associating literate/oral with the polarities of rational/irrational is inappropriate. Oral and literate are not opposites; rather, the development of orality is the necessary foundation for the later development of literacy. Second, it must be remembered that our school curricula are preparing children not for an oral culture, but for a literate one, with distinctive forms of thought and understanding. They must prepare children for particular kinds of scientific

---

[3]Referring to dominant conceptions in an area of such diversity as present educational discourse can leave some uncertainty about what is meant, and on what the impression of dominance is based. I mean here those conceptions of early childhood education that see the primary task as initiating the child into the basic skills of literacy and rational forms of inquiry, with little attention to the character and sophistication of children's orality and their imaginative lives. Such conceptions are evidenced in the practice of all too many classrooms, as reported, for example, in J. I. Goodlad's *A Place Called School* (1984). This bias may also be seen in curriculum guides in various subjects, in textbooks designed for pre-service and in-service teachers, and, perhaps most vividly, in textbooks designed for children's use. . . .

understanding, logic, and historical consciousness, among other things. During the early school years, children will also be learning to read and write with increasing sophistication. Stimulating orality is not incompatible with the early stages of acquiring the skills of literacy—indeed a sensitive program of instruction will use the child's oral cultural capacities to make reading and writing engaging and meaningful. I think one can plausibly argue that Western schools' relatively poor achievement in teaching literacy is due in significant part to the failure to recognize and stimulate the development of a rich orality in the first place, and then to use the capacities of orality to teach literacy. Following Ong (1982), I think the "transforming" effects of literacy do not begin to have significant impact on children's oral culture until literacy is fluently mastered, used for pleasure, and "internalized," a process that occurs around age seven or eight in most Western cultures.[4]

A useful guiding question for the curriculum developer considering how best to initiate children into science, logic and philosophy, or history would be, "What is the oral foundation of science, or of logic and philosophy, or of history?" Throughout, our focus has been not on knowledge content or psychological development, but on the *techniques* that are *bon à penser*. The question about oral foundations is not, therefore, about curriculum content; it does not lead us to magic, astrology, or myth, but to the forms of thought that undergird them. In history, for example, our aim is not to teach children myths, but to provide them with the foundations of historical understanding that underlie myth. This involves the sense of intellectual security that comes from knowing one's place in a wider context of human experience.

We might, for example, construct an early-childhood history curriculum that tells the story of Western culture as a struggle for freedom against tyranny, for peace against arbitrary violence, for knowledge against ignorance, for power against powerlessness, and so on. In the first year the overall story of Western culture, for example, might be taught as one such struggle of binary forces. In each of the next two or three years the overall story could be taught again using different binary organizers to illuminate further dimensions of the culture's history. In my view, such a curriculum

would be more engaging, meaningful, and educationally valuable than the typical content of the social studies curriculum. Such a presentation of historical content need not falsify history, though, like all historiography, it must simplify it. And its problems of ideological bias are no different in kind from those of any historiography (Egan, 1982).

What are the oral foundations of science? Among the characteristics of orality noted above are a sense of participation in nature and a sense of inquiry about it. In oral cultures those inquiries might lead to magic, witchcraft, and forms of classification that seem strange to Western science. Yet if our elementary curriculum is concerned with providing foundations that will remain constituents of scientific understanding, we might consider how to encourage respect and appreciation for the natural world and our place in it.

One part of our elementary science curriculum, then, might involve children in close and systematic observation of some particular natural object or process—a tree, rain, a spider's web, a patch of grass. Each child would have his or her own object. It might become usual, for example, to see young children observing that object at length—say, for twenty-minute intervals three times a week. They might break off other activities to observe how a tree moves in winds of different intensities, how the leaves hang in the sun, or how rain water drips down. This would not be a matter of "training in observation skills," with checklists and reports. Rather, the activity would have no end beyond itself; the child would be encouraged to share the life of the tree, let his or her imagination flow into it, feel its branches and stretch with it toward the light, let stories form about it, converse or commune with it. This brief example may indicate how our conception of the range of human characteristics that are appropriately addressed by the curriculum is changed by a focus on the oral foundations of education. Such efforts might reinforce the sense of participation in nature that scholars have seen as characteristic of oral cultures.

Another capacity that tends to be very largely ignored in present curricula is the sense of humor. The early stimulation and development of the sense of humor, and even the sense of the absurd, seem to me to be ways of setting in place the foundations of logic and philosophy. Recognition of the categories deployed in arguing and thinking, and fluency in analyzing them, are integral to those disciplines. One of the arenas of

---

[4] For a more extensive account of an "oral" curriculum, see Egan, in press.

oral culture in which fluency in manipulating categories occurs is the joke. Lewis Carroll was one logician who seemed keenly aware of this, and used such category-manipulating jokes extensively. His *Alice* adventures, which grew from stories invented aloud for children, contain many examples of the kinds of jokes that stimulate flexibility in the use of categories, and which highlight the limits of the grasp our categories have on reality. The beginning of logic and philosophy, then, might involve encouraging each child to "see" jokes and become jokesters. From there we could move on to more sophisticated jokes, like Zeno's paradoxes, and later to consideration of paradoxes in the nature of knowledge, morality, art, and so on.

What implications follow for teaching? I will focus briefly on some that seem to follow from the prominence of the story form in oral cultures. We might think of teaching the curriculum as telling young children the great stories of their culture. In the case of Western culture these involve the stories of their history, mathematics, logic, arts, and sciences. They *are* terrific stories. At present, teachers are encouraged to plan by organizing the curriculum into sets of objectives to be attained. If we were to think of lessons and units as good stories to be told rather than (or in addition to) objectives to be attained, we might be able to organize our content in ways that make it more accessible and engaging to young children.

If we consider just a few features of the story form, we should be able to develop a technique for the planning and teaching of lessons and units that would offer an alternative to the now dominant objectives-content-methods-evaluation schemes derived from R. Tyler's model (1949). The selection of content for the class or unit to be planned would be determined by identifying what binary opposites best catch and expose its most important themes. A unit on heat, for example, might be planned around the dichotomy of heat-as-helper/heat-as-destroyer. A class on the Vikings might use survival/destruction as central story themes. We might recreate the terror induced by a Viking raid on a monastic community. We would not have to *explain* the value of manuscripts or sacred vessels, but instead would *show* their value through the horror felt by the monks at their destruction. Then we could select the remaining content according to the related criteria provided by the central binary conflict, to elaborate and develop the story. The conclusion of the lesson, or unit, would come with the resolution or mediation of the

binary opposites whose conflict set the story in motion. Mediation might be sought, for example, by indicating the value of the constructive energy of the Vikings in the overall story of Western culture. Evaluation of such lessons or units might focus on children's understanding of the content in the context of the overall story, and on their coherent use of the content in stories of their own (Egan, 1985).

I recognize that the prominence of binary opposites here will seem a little odd to many people. Their use need not lead to extreme reductionism. My argument, made at length elsewhere (Egan, in press), is simply based on the prominence and utility of initially grasping the world in binary terms. Some (for example, Lévi-Strauss, 1966) argue that the use of binary opposites is simply a function of the structure of the human mind. I think one need not go so far in order to recognize their ubiquitousness in the forms of thought common in oral cultures and in the ways young children spontaneously make sense of the world and experience.

Some of the teaching and curriculum practices sketched above are, of course, already evident in some classrooms. If my description of orality is accurate and relevant to the education of young children, it would be surprising if many teachers had not shaped their lessons and teaching methods, in their own ways, to draw on some of the same observations about children—even though those observations might be articulated in different terms. I do not claim originality for these ideas on educational implications of orality; rather, I am concerned to establish a set of principles that might help us more systematically and routinely to achieve the kinds of successes that good teachers manage daily.

The most general implication of this brief exploration is that we should consider children when they come to school as already in possession of some features of orality that are *bon à penser*. Their ability to think and learn is, in general, sophisticated, but structured according to norms significantly different from those of literate adult cultures. Two corollaries follow. First, clear understanding of children's orality is essential if we are to make what we want to teach engaging and meaningful; second, orality entails valuable forms of thought that need to be developed as the foundation for a sophisticated literacy and Western rationality. If we see the educational task as simply to put literacy in place, we risk undermining the very foundations on which a rich literacy must rest. Stimulating children's imaginations, metaphoric fluency, and narrative sophistication can become more prominent aims of early education. Such a view might help to resolve what is often seen as a conflict in early education between the need to establish the "skills" of literacy and rational thought and the wish to encourage more varied experience and imaginative development. This brief exploration should have shown that these are not competitors; rather, the fullest achievement of literacy requires the fullest achievement of oral capacities as well.

REFERENCES

Applebee, A. N. (1978). *A child's concept of story*. Chicago: University of Chicago Press.

Ashton, P. T. (1975). Cross-cultural Piagetian research: An experimental perspective. *Harvard Educational Review, 45*, 475–506.

Bartlett, F. (1932). *Remembering, a study in experimental and social psychology*. New York: Cambridge University Press.

Bettelheim, B. (1976). *The uses of enchantment*. New York: Knopf.

Blumenberg, H. (1985). *Work on myth*. Cambridge: MIT Press.

Boas, F. (1911). *The mind of primitive man*. New York: Macmillan.

Broman, B. L. (1982). *The early years in early childhood education*. Boston: Houghton Mifflin.

Buck-Morss, S. (1982). Socio-economic bias in Piaget's theory and its implications for cross-cultural studies. In S. Modgil & C. Modgil (Eds.), *Jean Piaget: Consensus and controversy*. New York: Praeger.

Burke, P. (1985). *Vico*. New York: Oxford University Press.

Cassirer, E. (1946). *Language and myth* (S. K. Langer, trans.). New York: Harper.

Cooper, D. E. (1986). *Metaphor*. Oxford: Blackwell.

Cornford, F. M. (Ed.). (1941). *The Republic of Plato*. New York: Oxford University Press, ch. 26.

Dodds, E. R. (1951). *The Greeks and the irrational*. Berkeley and Los Angeles: University of California Press.

Douglas, M. (1966). *Purity and danger*. London: Routledge & Kegan Paul.

Durkheim, E. (1915). *The elementary forms of the religious life*. London: Allen & Unwin.

Egan, K. (1982, March). Teaching history to young children. *Phi Delta Kappan*, 439–441.

Egan, K. (1985). *Teaching as story-telling*. London, Ont.: The Althouse Press, and London: Methuen.

Egan, K. (in press). *Primary understanding*. London and New York: Routledge & Kegan Paul.

Egan, K., & Nadaner, D. (Eds.). (In press). *Imagination and education*. New York: Teachers College Press.

Eliade, M. (1959). *Cosmos and history*. New York: Harper & Row.

Evans-Pritchard, E. E. (1937). *Witchcraft, oracles and magic among the Azande*. New York: Oxford University Press.

Finnegan, R. (1970). *Oral literature in Africa*. New York: Oxford University Press.

Finnegan, R. (1977). *Oral poetry: Its nature, significance, and social context*. Cambridge: Cambridge University Press.

Frankfort, H. A. (1961). *Ancient Egyptian religion*. New York: Harper.

Frankfort, H. A., Wilson, J. A., & Jacobsen, T. (1949). *Before philosophy*. Harmondsworth, Egn.: Pelican.

Frazer, J. G. (1900). *The golden bough* (2nd ed.). London: Macmillan.

Gardner, H., Kircher, M., Winner, E., & Perkins, D. (1975). Children's metaphoric productions and preference. *Journal of Child Language, 2*, 125–141.

Geertz, C. (1973). *The interpretation of cultures*. New York: Basic Books.

Gega, P. C. (1986). *Science in elementary education*. New York: McGraw-Hill.

Goodlad, J. I. (1984). *A place called school*. New York: McGraw-Hill.

Goody, J. (1977). *The domestication of the savage mind*. New York: Cambridge University Press.

Goody, J. (1986). *The logic of writing and the organization of society*. Cambridge: Cambridge University Press.

Goody, J. (1987). *The interface between the written and the oral*. New York: Cambridge University Press.

Goody, J., & Watt, I. (1968). The consequences of literacy. In J. Goody (Ed.), *Literacy in traditional societies* (pp. 304–345). New York: Cambridge University Press.

Gould, S. J. (1977). *Ontogeny and phylogeny*. Cambridge: Harvard University Press.

Griffin, J. (1980). *Homer*. New York: Oxford University Press.

Havelock, E. A. (1963). *Preface to Plato*. Cambridge: Harvard University Press.

Havelock, E. A. (1976). *Origins of Western literacy*. Toronto: Ontario Institute for Studies in Education.

Havelock, E. A. (1986). *The muse learns to write*. New Haven: Yale University Press.

Hayek, F. A. (1969). The primacy of the abstract. In Arthur Koestler and J. R. Smythies (Eds.), *Beyond reductionism*. New York: Macmillan.

Heath, S. B. (1983). *Ways with words*. Cambridge: Cambridge University Press.

Hollis, M., & Lukes, S. (Eds.). (1982). *Rationality and relativism*. Cambridge: MIT Press.

Horton, R. (1970). African traditional thought and Western science. In B. Wilson (Ed.), *Rationality* (pp. 131–171). Oxford: Blackwell.

Horton, R. (1982). Tradition and modernity revisited. In M. Hollis & S. Lukes (Eds.), *Rationality and relativism*. Cambridge: MIT Press, 201–260.

Huizinga, J. (1949). *Homo ludens*. London: Routledge & Kegan Paul.

Inhelder, B., & Piaget, J. (1969). *The early growth of logic in the child*. New York: Norton.

Jenkyns, R. (1980). *The Victorians and ancient Greece*. Cambridge: Harvard University Press.

Jowett, B. (1982). *The dialogues of Plato*. London: Macmillan.

Kirk, G. S. (1965). *Homer and the epic*. New York: Cambridge University Press.

Knapp, M., & Knapp, H. (1976). *One potato, two potato*. New York: Norton.

Leach, E. (1967). Genesis as myth. In J. Middleton (Ed.), *Myth and cosmos* (pp. 1–13). New York: Natural History Press, 1–13.

Lévi-Bruhl, L. (1910/1985). *How natives think* (L. A. Clare, trans.; C. S. Littleton, Intro.). Princeton: Princeton University Press.

Lévi-Strauss, C. (1962). *Totemism*. New York: Merlin.

Lévi-Strauss, C. (1966). *The savage mind*. Chicago: University of Chicago Press.

Lévi-Strauss, C. (1969). *The raw and the cooked*. New York: Harper & Row.

Lévi-Strauss, C. (1978). *Myth and meaning*. Toronto: University of Toronto Press.

Lord, A. B. (1964). *The singer of tales*. Cambridge: Harvard University Press.

Luria, A. R. (1976). *Cognitive development: Its cultural and social foundations*. Cambridge: Harvard University Press.

Luria, A. R. (1979). *The making of mind*. Cambridge: Harvard University Press.

Malinowski, B. (1922). *Argonauts of the western Pacific*. London: Routledge & Kegan Paul.

Malinowski, B. (1954). *Magic, science and religion*. New York: Anchor.

Michaelis, J. (1985). *Social studies for children*. Englewood Cliffs, NJ: Prentice Hall.

Olsen, D. R. (1977). Oral and written language and the cognitive processes of children. *Journal of Communications, 17* (3), 10–26.

Olsen, D. R. (1986). Learning to mean what you say: Towards a psychology of literacy. In S. de Castell, A. Luke & K. Egan (Eds.), *Literacy, society and schooling*. New York: Cambridge University Press.

Ong, W. J. (1971). *Rhetoric, romance, and technology*. Ithaca: Cornell University Press.

Ong, W. J. (1977). *Interfaces of the world*. Ithaca: Cornell University Press.

Ong, W. J. (1982). *Orality and literacy*. New York: Methuen.

Ong, W. J. (1986). Writing is a technology that transforms thought. In G. Baumann (Ed.), *The written word: Literacy in transition* (pp. 23–50). Oxford: Clarenden Press.

Opie, I., & Opie, P. (1959). *The lore and language of school-children*. New York: Oxford University Press.

Opie, I., & Opie, P. (1969). *Children's games in street and playground*. New York: Oxford University Press.

Opie, I., & Opie, P. (1985). *The singing game*. New York: Oxford University Press.

Paley, V. G. (1981). *Wally's stories*. Cambridge: Harvard University Press.

Parry, M. (1928). *L'Epithète traditionelle dans Homère*. Paris: Socièté Editrice les Belles Lettres.

Parry, M. (1971). *The making of Homeric verse: The collected papers of Milman Parry* (A. Parry, Ed.). Oxford: Clarendon Press. (This includes the previous reference in English translation.)

Peabody, B. (1975). *The winged word*. Albany: State University of New York Press.

Pitcher, E. G., & Prelinger, E. (1963). *Children tell stories: An analysis of fantasy*. New York: International Universities Press.

Putnam, H. (1981). *Reason, truth and history*. New York: Cambridge University Press.

Ravitch, D. (1983). *The troubled crusade*. New York: Basic Books.

Shepherd, G. D, & Ragan, W. B. (1982). *Modern elementary curriculum*. New York: Holt, Rienhart & Winston.

Simon, B. (1978). *Mind and madness in ancient Greece: The classical roots of modern psychiatry*. Ithaca: Cornell University Press.

Spence, J. E. (1984). *The memory palace of Matteo Ricci*. New York: Viking Penguin.

Sutton-Smith, B. (1981). *The folkstories of children*. Philadelphia: University of Pennsylvania Press.

Taylor, C. (1982). Rationality. In M. Hollis & S. Lukes (Eds.), *Rationality and relativism (pp. 87–105)*.

Todorov, T. (1982). *Theories of the symbol* (C. Porter, trans.). Ithaca: Cornell University Press.

Troutman, A. P., & Lichtenberg, D. K. (1982). *Mathematics: A good beginning*. Monterey, CA: Brooks/Cole.

Turner, F. M. (1981). *The Greek heritage in Victorian Britain*. New Haven: Yale University Press.

Tyler, R. (1949). *Basic principles of curriculum and instruction*. Chicago: University of Chicago Press.

Vernant, J. P. (1983). *Myth and thought among the Greeks*. London: Routledge & Kegan Paul.

Vico, G. (1744/1970). *The new science* (T. G. Bergin & M. H. Fisch, trans.). Ithaca: Cornell University Press.

Wilson, B. R. (Ed.). (1970). *Rationality*. Oxford: Blackwell.

Wolf, F. A. (1795/1884). *Prolegomena ad Homerum*. Halle.

Wood, M. (1985). *In search of the Trojan War*. London: BBC.

Whose Standard? Teaching Standard English

LINDA CHRISTENSEN

- -

Editor's introduction

Language often functions as a gatekeeper in our society. High school teacher Linda Christensen explores ways to help her students understand the power of their own language patterns and also learn "the Standard" without humiliation. She takes them inside language so they understand its rules, examining social patterns at the same time they are studying English.

- - - - - - - - - - - -

When I was in the ninth grade, Mrs. Delaney, my English teacher wanted to demonstrate the correct and incorrect ways to pronounce the English language. She asked Helen Draper, whose father owned several clothing stores in town, to stand and say "lawyer." Then she asked me, whose father owned a bar, to stand and say "lawyer." Everyone burst into laughter at my pronunciation.

What did Mrs. Delaney accomplish? Did she make me pronounce lawyer correctly? No. I say attorney. I never say lawyer. In fact, I've found substitutes for every word my tongue can't get around and for all the rules I can't remember.

For years I've played word cop on myself. I stop what I'm saying to think, "Objective or subjective case? Do I need I or me here? Hmmmm. There's a lay coming up. What word can I substitute for it? Recline?"

And I've studied this stuff. After all, I've been an English teacher for almost 20 years. I've gone through all of the Warriner's workbook exercises. I even found a lie/lay computer program and kept it in my head until I needed it in speech and became confused again.

Thanks to Mrs. Delaney I learned early on that in our society language classifies me. Generosity, warmth, kindness, intelligence, good humor aren't enough—we need to speak correctly to make it. Mrs. Delaney taught me that the "melting pot" was an illusion. The real version of the melting pot is that people of diverse backgrounds are mixed together and when they come out they're supposed to look like Vanna White and sound like Dan Rather. The only diversity we celebrate is tacos and chop suey at the mall.

UNLEARNING "INFERIORITY"

It wasn't until a few years ago that I realized grammar was an indication of class and cultural background in the United States and that there is a bias against people who do not use language "correctly." Even the terminology "standard" and "nonstandard" reflects that one is less than the other. English teachers are urged to "correct" students who speak or write in their home language. A friend of mine, whose ancestors

Source: "Whose Standard? Teaching Standard English" by L. Christensen, 1994. In *Rethinking Our Classrooms* (pp. 142–145), B. Bigelow, L. Christensen, S. Karp, B. Miner & B. Peterson, Eds., Milwaukee: Rethinking Schools Limited.

came over on the Mayflower, never studied any of the grammar texts I keep by my side, but she can spot all of my errors because she grew up in a home where Standard English was spoken.

And I didn't, so I've trained myself to play language cop. The problem is that every time I pause, I stop the momentum of my thinking. I'm no longer pursuing content, no longer engaged in trying to persuade or entertain or clarify. Instead I'm pulling Warriner's or Mrs. Delaney out of my head and trying to figure out how to say something.

"Ah, but this is good," you might say. "You have the rules and Mrs. Delaney to go back to. This is what our students need."

But it doesn't happen that way. I try to remember the rule or the catchy phrase that is supposed to etch the rule in my mind forever like "people never get laid," but I'm still not sure if I used it correctly. These side trips cost a lot of velocity in my logic.

Over the years my English teachers pointed out all of my errors—the usage errors I inherited from my mother's Bandon, Oregon dialect, the spelling errors I overlooked, the fancy words I used incorrectly. They did this in good faith, in the same way, years later, I "corrected" my students' "errors" because I wanted them to know the rules. They were keys to a secret and wealthier society and I wanted them to be prepared to enter, just as my teachers wanted to help me.

And we should help kids. It would be misleading to suggest that people in our society will value my thoughts or my students' thoughts as readily in our home languages as in the "cash language" as Jesse Jackson calls it. Students need to know where to find help, and they need to understand what changes might be necessary, but they need to learn in a context that doesn't say, "The way you said this is wrong."

WHEN FEAR INTERFERES

English teachers must know when to correct and how to correct—and I use that word uneasily. Take Fred, for example. Fred entered my freshman class last year unwilling to write. Every day during writing time I'd find Fred doodling pictures of *Playboy* bunnies. When I sat down and asked him why he didn't write, he said he couldn't.

I explained to him that in this class his writing couldn't be wrong because we were just practicing our writing until we found a piece we wanted to polish, in

the same way that he practiced football every day after school, but only played games on Fridays. His resistance lasted for a couple of weeks. Around him, other students struggled with their writing, shared it with the class on occasion and heard positive comments. Certainly the writing of his fellow students was not intimidating.

On October 1st, after reading the story, "Raymond's Run" by Toni Cade Bambara, about trusting people in our lives, Fred wrote for the first time:

I remember my next door neighbor trusted me with some money that she owed my grandmother. She owed my grandmother about 25 dollars.

Fred didn't make a lot of errors. In the first piece of writing it looked like he had basic punctuation figured out. He didn't misspell any words. And he certainly didn't make any usage errors. Based on this sample, he appeared to be a competent writer.

However, the biggest problem with Fred's writing was the fact that he didn't make mistakes. This piece demonstrates his discomfort with writing. He wasn't taking any risks. Just as I avoid lawyer and lay, he wrote to avoid errors instead of writing to communicate or think on paper.

When more attention is paid to the way something is written or said than to what is said, students' words and thoughts become devalued. Students learn to be silent, to give as few words as possible for teacher criticism.

VALUING WHAT WE KNOW

Students must be taught to hold their own voices sacred, to ignore the teachers who have made them feel that what they've said is wrong or bad or stupid. Students must be taught how to listen to the knowledge they've stored up, but which they are seldom asked to relate.

Too often students feel alienated in schools. Knowledge is foreign. It's about other people in other times. At a conference I attended recently, a young woman whose mother was Puerto Rican and whose father was Haitian said, "I went through school wondering if anyone like me had ever done anything worthwhile or important. We kept reading and hearing about all of these famous people. I remember thinking, 'Don't we have anyone?' I walked out of the school that day feeling tiny, invisible, unimportant."

As teachers, we have daily opportunities to affirm that our students' lives and language are unique and important. We do that in the selections of literature we read, in the history we choose to teach, and we do it by giving legitimacy to our students' lives as a content worthy of study.

One way to encourage the reluctant writers who have been silenced and the not-so-reluctant writers who have found a safe and sterile voice is to encourage them to recount their experiences. I sometimes recruit former students to share their writing and their wisdom as a way of underscoring the importance of the voices and stories of teenagers. Rochelle, a student in my senior writing class, brought in a few of her stories and poems to read to my freshmen. Rochelle, like Zora Neale Hurston, blends her home language with Standard English in most pieces. She read the following piece to open up a discussion about how kids are sometimes treated as servants in their homes, but also to demonstrate the necessity of using the language she hears in her family to develop characters:

"I'm tired of washing dishes. Seems like every time our family gets together, they just got to eat and bring their millions of kids over to our house. And then we got to wash the dishes."

I listened sympathetically as my little sister mumbled these words.

"And how come we can't have ribs like the grownups? After all, ain't we grown?"

"Lord," I prayed, "seal her lips while the blood is still running warm in her veins."

Her bottom lip protruded farther and farther as she dipped each plate in the soapy water, then rinsed each side with cold water (about a two second process) until she felt the majority of suds were off.

"One minute we lazy women that can't keep the living room half clean. The next minute we just kids and gotta eat some funky chicken while they eat ribs."

. . . Suddenly it was quiet. All except my little sister who was still talking. I strained to hear a laugh or joke from the adults in the living room, a hint that all were well, full and ready to go home. Everyone was still sitting in their same spots, not making a move to leave.

"You ought to be thankful you got a choice."

Uh-oh. Now she got Aunt Macy started. . . .

After reading her work, Rochelle talked about listening to her family and friends tell their stories. She urged the freshmen to relate the tales of their own lives—the times they were caught doing something forbidden, the times they got stuck with the dishes, the funny/sad events that made their freshman year memorable. When Rochelle left, students wrote more easily. Some. Some were afraid of the stories because as Rance said, "It takes heart to tell the truth about your life."

But eventually they write. They write stories. They write poems. They write letters. They write essays. They learn how to switch in and out of the language of the powerful as Rochelle does so effortlessly in her "Tired of Chicken" piece.

SHARING LESSONS

And after we write, we listen to each other's stories in our read-around circle where everyone has the opportunity to share, to be heard, to learn that knowledge can be gained by examining our lives. . . . In the circle, we discover that many young women encounter sexual harassment, we learn that store clerks follow black students, especially males, more frequently than they follow white students, we find that many of our parents drink or use drugs, we learn that many of us are kept awake by the crack houses in our neighborhood.

Before we share, students often understand these incidents individually. They feel there's something wrong with them. If they were smarter, prettier, stronger, these things wouldn't have happened to them. When they hear other students' stories, they begin to realize that many of their problems aren't caused by a character defect. For example, in Literature in U.S. History, the class I teach with Bill Bigelow, a young man shared a passionate story about life with his mother who is a lesbian. He loved her, but felt embarrassed to bring his friends home. He was afraid his peers would think he was gay or reject him if they knew about his mother. After he read, the class was silent. Some students cried. One young woman told him that her father was gay and she'd experienced similar difficulties, but hadn't had the courage to tell people about it. She thanked him. Another student confided that his uncle had died from AIDS the year before. What had been a secret shame became an opportunity for students to discuss sexual diversity more openly. Students who were rigidly opposed to the idea of homosexuality gained insights into their own homophobia—especially when presented with the personal revelations from their classmates. Those with homosexual relatives found new allies with whom they could continue their discussion and find support.

Sharing also provides a "collective text" for us to examine the social roots of problems more closely: Where do men/women develop the ideas that women are sexual objects? Where do they learn that it's OK for men to follow women or make suggestive remarks? Where is it written that it's the woman's fault if a man leers at her? How did these roles develop? Who gains from them? Who loses? How could we make it different? Our lives become a window to examine society.

LEARNING THE "STANDARD" WITHOUT HUMILIATION

But the lessons can't stop there. Fred can write better now. He and his classmates can feel comfortable and safe sharing their lives or discussing literature and the world. They can even understand that they need to ask "Who benefits?" to get a better perspective on a problem. But still when they leave my class or this school, some people will judge them by how their subjects and verbs line up.

So I teach Fred the rules. It's the language of power in this country, and I would be cheating him if I pretended otherwise. I teach him this more effectively than Mrs. Delaney taught me because I don't humiliate him or put down his language. I'm also more effective because I don't rely on textbook drills; I use the text of Fred's writing. But I also teach Fred what Mrs. Delaney left out.

I teach Fred that language, like tracking, functions as part of a gatekeeping system in our country. Who gets managerial jobs, who works at banks and who works at fast food restaurants, who gets into what college and who gets into college at all, are decisions linked to the ability to use Standard English. So how do we teach kids to write with honesty and passion about their world and get them to study the rules of the cash language? We go back to our study of society. We ask: Who made the rules that govern how we speak and write? Did Ninh's family and Fred's family and LaShonda's family all sit down together and decide on these rules? Who already talks like this and writes like this? Who has to learn how to change the way they talk and write? Why?

We make up our own tests that speakers of Standard English would find difficult. We read articles, stories, poems written in Standard English and those written in home language. We listen to videotapes of people speaking. Most kids like the sound of their home language better. They like the energy, the poetry, and the rhythm of the language. We determine when and why people shift. We talk about why it might be necessary to learn Standard English.

Asking my students to memorize the rules without asking who makes the rules, who enforces the rules, who benefits from the rules, who loses from the rules, who uses the rules to keep some in and keep others out, legitimates a social system that devalues my students' knowledge and language. Teaching the rules without reflection also underscores that it's OK for others—"authorities"—to dictate something as fundamental and as personal as the way they speak. Further, the study of Standard English without critique encourages students to believe that if they fail, it is because they are not smart enough or didn't work hard enough. They learn to blame themselves. If they get poor SAT scores, low grades on term papers or essays because of language errors, fail teacher entrance exams, they will internalize the blame; they will believe they did not succeed because they are inferior instead of questioning the standard of measurement and those making the standards.

We must teach our students how to match subjects and verbs, how to pronounce lawyer, because they are the ones without power and, for the moment, have to use the language of the powerful to be heard. But, in addition, we need to equip them to question an educational system that devalues their life and their knowledge. If we don't, we condition them to a pedagogy of consumption where they will consume the knowledge, priorities, and products that have been decided and manufactured without them in mind.

It took me years to undo what Mrs. Delaney did to me. Years to discover that what I said was more important than how I said it. Years to understand that my words, my family's words, weren't wrong, weren't bad—they were just the words of the working class. For too long, I felt inferior when I spoke. I knew the voice of my childhood crept out, and I confused that with ignorance. It wasn't. I just didn't belong to the group who made the rules. I was an outsider, a foreigner in their world. My students won't be.

Language Prison

All day words
run past my tongue

words tumble and fall
and you catch
the wrong ones
and count them back to me

All day I watch
my tongue

for words
that slip
down the slope of my
neighborhood

words that separate
me from you

words that you catch
and hold against me

All day I watch
for words misshapen
or bent
around my too thick tongue

run-down at the heel words
thin soled words

words that slip
from my tongue

words that tell of mops
and beer
and bent backs

words that shape my world
against a different map
than yours

All day I watch my tongue
for words

—*Linda Christensen*

American Sign Language: "It's Not Mouth Stuff—It's Brain Stuff"

RICHARD WOLKOMIR

• •

Editor's introduction

In this article, Richard Wolkomir explains recent research on how deaf people communicate—the cultural and mental processes, body motions and facial expressions involved in American Sign Language. This work helps shed new light on the origins of language as well as the connections between language and culture.

• • • • • • • • • • • •

In a darkened laboratory at the Salk Institute in San Diego, a deaf woman is signing. Tiny lights attached to her sleeves and fingers trace the motions of her hands, while two special video cameras whir.

Computers will process her hands' videotaped arabesques and pirouettes into mathematically precise three-dimensional images. Neurologists and linguists will study these stunning patterns for insight into how the human brain produces language.

Sign has become a scientific hot button. Only in the past 20 years have linguists realized that signed languages are unique—a speech of the hand. They offer a new way to probe how the brain generates and understands language, and throw new light on an old scientific controversy: whether language, complete with grammar, is innate in our species, or whether it is a learned behavior. The current interest in sign language has roots in the pioneering work of one renegade teacher at Gallaudet University in Washington, D.C., the world's only liberal arts university for deaf people.

When Bill Stokoe went to Gallaudet to teach English, the school enrolled him in a course in signing. But Stokoe noticed something odd: among themselves, students signed differently from his classroom teacher.

"HAND TALK": A GENUINE LANGUAGE

Stokoe had been taught a sort of gestural code, each movement of the hands representing a word in English. At the time, American Sign Language (ASL) was thought to be no more than a form of pidgin English. But Stokoe believed the "hand talk" his students used looked richer. He wondered: Might deaf people actually have a genuine language? And could that language be unlike any other on Earth? It was 1955, when even deaf people dismissed their signing as "slang." Stokoe's idea was academic heresy.

It is 37 years later. Stokoe—now devoting his time to writing and editing books and journals and to producing video materials on ASL and the deaf culture—is having lunch at a café near the Gallaudet campus and explaining how he started a revolution. For decades educators fought his idea that signed languages are natural languages like English, French and

Source: "American Sign Language: 'It's Not Mouth Stuff—It's Brain Stuff'" by R. Wolkomir, 1992, *Smithsonian*, 25(4), pp. 30–41.

214

Japanese. They assumed language must be based on speech, the modulation of sound. But sign language is based on the movement of hands, the modulation of space. "What I said," Stokoe explains, "is that language is not mouth stuff—it's brain stuff."

It has been a long road, from the mouth to the brain. Linguists have had to redefine language. Deaf people's self-esteem has been at stake, and so has the ticklish issue of their education.

"My own contribution was to turn around the thinking of academics," says Stokoe. "When I came to Gallaudet, the teachers were trained with two books, and the jokers who wrote them gave only a paragraph to sign language, calling it a vague system of gestures that looked like the ideas they were supposed to represent."

Deaf education in the '50s irked him. "I didn't like to see how the hearing teachers treated their deaf pupils—their expectations were low," he says. "I was amazed at how many of my students were brilliant." Meanwhile, he was reading the work of anthropological linguists like George Trager and Henry Lee Smith Jr. "They said you couldn't study language without studying the culture, and when I had been at Gallaudet a short time, I realized that deaf people had a culture of their own."

When Stokoe analyzed his student's signing, he found it was like spoken languages, which combine bits of sound—each meaningless by itself—into meaningful words. Signers, following similar rules, combine individually meaningless hand and body movements into words. They choose from a palette of hand shapes, such as a fist or a pointing index finger. They also choose where to make a sign; for example, on the face or on the chest. They choose how to orient the hand and arm. And each sign has a movement—it might begin at the cheek and finish at the chin. A shaped hand executing a particular motion creates a word. A common underlying structure of both spoken and signed language is thus at the level of the smallest units that are linked to form words.

Stokoe explained his findings on the structure of ASL in a book published in 1960. "The faculty then had a special meeting and I got up and said my piece," he says. "Nobody threw eggs or old vegetables, but I was bombarded by hostility." Later, the university's president told Stokoe his research was "causing too much trouble" because his insistence that ASL was

indeed a *language* threatened the English-based system for teaching the deaf. But Stokoe persisted. Five years later he came out with the first dictionary of American Sign Language based on linguistic principles. And he's been slowly winning converts ever since.

"WHEREVER WE'VE FOUND DEAF PEOPLE, THERE'S SIGN"

Just as no one can pinpoint the origins of spoken language in prehistory, the roots of sign language remain hidden from view. What linguists do know is that sign languages have sprung up independently in many different places. Signing probably began with simple gestures, but then evolved into a true language with structured grammar. "In every place we've ever found deaf people, there's sign," says anthropological linguist Bob Johnson, "but it's not the same language. I went to a Mayan village where, out of 400 people, 13 were deaf, and they had their own Mayan Sign—I'd guess it's been maintained for thousands of years." Today at least 50 native sign languages are "spoken" worldwide, all mutually incomprehensible, from British and Israeli Sign to Chinese Sign.

Not until the 1700s, in France, did people who could hear pay serious attention to deaf people and their language. Religion had something to do with it. "They believed that without speech you couldn't go to heaven," says Johnson.

For the Abbé de l'Epée, a French priest born into a wealthy family in 1712, the issue was his own soul: he feared he would lose it unless he overcame the stigma of his privileged youth by devoting himself to the poor. In his history of the deaf, *When The Mind Hears*, Northeastern University psychologists Harlan Lane notes that, in his 50s, de l'Epée met two deaf girls on one of his forays into the Paris slums and decided to dedicate himself to their education.

The priest's problem was abstraction: he could show the girls a piece of bread and the printed French word for "bread." But how could he show them "God" or "goodness"? He decided to learn their sign language as a teaching medium. However, he attempted to impose French grammar onto the signs.

"Methodical signing," as de l'Epée called his invention, was an ugly hybrid. But he did teach his pupils to read French, opening the door to education, and today he is a hero to deaf people. As his pupils and disciples proliferated, satellite schools sprouted throughout Europe. De l'Epée died happily destitute in 1789 surrounded by his students in his Paris school, which became the National Institution for Deaf-Mutes under the new republic.

Other teachers kept de l'Epée's school alive. And one graduate, Laurent Clerc, brought the French method of teaching in sign to the United States. It was the early 1800s; in Hartford, Connecticut, the Rev. Thomas Hopkins Gallaudet was watching children at play. He noticed that one girl, Alice Cogswell, did not join in. She was deaf. Her father, a surgeon, persuaded Gallaudet to find a European teacher and create the first permanent school for the deaf in the United States. Gallaudet then traveled to England, where the "oral" method was supreme, the idea being to teach deaf children to speak. The method was almost cruel, since children born deaf—they heard no voices, including their own—could have no concept of speech. It rarely worked. Besides, the teachers said their method was "secret." And so Gallaudet visited the Institution for Deaf-Mutes in Paris and persuaded Laurent Clerc to come home with him.

During their 52-day voyage across the Atlantic, Gallaudet helped Clerc improve his English, and Clerc taught him French Sign Language. On April 15, 1817, in Hartford, they established a school that became the American School for the Deaf. Teaching in French Sign Language and a version of de l'Epée's methodical sign, Clerc trained many students who became teachers, too, and helped spread language across the country. Clerc's French Sign was to mingle with various "home" signs that had sprung up in other places. On Martha's Vineyard, Massachusetts, for example, a large portion of the population was genetically deaf, and virtually all the islanders used an indigenous sign language, the hearing switching back and forth between speech and sign with bilingual ease. Eventually, pure French Sign would blend with such local argots and evolve into today's American Sign Language.

After Clerc died, in 1869, much of the work done since the time of de l'Epée to teach the deaf in their own language crumbled under the weight of Victorian intolerance. Anti-Signers argued that ASL let the deaf "talk" only to the deaf; they must learn to speak and to lip-read. Pro-Signers pointed out that, through sign, the deaf learned to read and write English. The Pros also noted that lipreading is a skill that few master. (Studies estimate that 93 percent of deaf schoolchildren who were either born deaf or lost their hearing in early childhood can lip-read only one in ten everyday sentences in English). And Pros argue correctly that the arduous hours required to teach a deaf child to mimic speech should be spent on real education.

"Oralists" like Horace Mann lobbied to stop schools from teaching in ASL, then *the* method of instruction in all schools for the deaf. None was more fervent than Alexander Graham Bell, inventor of the telephone and husband of a woman who denied her own deafness. The president of the National Association of the Deaf called Bell the "most to be feared enemy of the American deaf." In 1880, at an international meeting of educators of the deaf in Milan, where deaf teachers were absent, the use of sign language in schools was proscribed.

After that, as deaf people see it, came the Dark Ages. Retired Gallaudet sociolinguist Barbara Kannapell, who is cofounder of Deafpride, a Washington, D.C. advocacy group, is the deaf daughter of deaf parents from Kentucky. Starting at age 4, she attended an "oral" school, where signing was outlawed. "Whenever the teacher turned her back to work on the blackboard, we'd sign," signs Kannapell. "If the teacher caught us using sign language, she'd use a ruler on our hands."

Kannapell has tried to see oralism from the viewpoint of hearing parents of deaf children. "They'll do anything to make their child like themselves," she signs. "But, from a deaf adult's perspective, I want *them* to learn sign, to communicate with their child."

In the 1970s, a new federal law mandated "mainstreaming." "That law was good for parents, because they could keep children home instead of sending them off to special boarding schools, but many public schools didn't know what to do with deaf kids," signs Kannapell. "Many of these children think they're the only deaf kids in the world."

Gallaudet's admissions director, James Tucker, an exuberant 32-year-old, is a product of the '70s mainstreaming. "I'd sit in the back, doing work the teacher gave me and minding my own business," he signs. "Did I like it? Hell no! I was lonely—for years I thought I was an introvert." Deaf children have a right to learn ASL and to live in an ASL-speaking community, he asserts. "We learn sign for obvious reasons—our eyes aren't broken," he signs. Tucker adds: "Deaf culture is a group of people sharing similar values, outlook and frustrations, and the main thing, of course, is sharing the same language."

Today, most teachers of deaf pupils are "hearies" who speak as they sign. "Simultaneous Communication," as it is called, is really signed English and not ASL. "It looks grotesque to the eye," signs Tucker, adding that it makes signs too "marked," a linguistic term meaning equally stressed. Hand movements can be exaggerated or poorly executed. As Tucker puts it: "We have zealous educators trying to impose weird hand shapes." Moreover, since the languages have entirely different sentence structures, the effect can be bewildering. It's like having Japanese spoken to English-speaking students with an interpreter shouting occasional English words at them.

New scientific findings support the efforts of linguists such as Bob Johnson, who are calling for an education system for deaf students based on ASL, starting in infancy. Research by Helen Neville, at the Salk Institute, shows that children *must* learn a language—any language—during their first five years or so, before the brain's neural connections are locked in place, or risk permanent linguistic impairment. "What suffers is the ability to learn grammar," she says. As children mature, their brain organization becomes increasingly rigid. By puberty, it is largely complete. This spells trouble because most deaf youngsters learn language late; their parents are hearing and do not know ASL, and the children have little or no contact with deaf people when young.

Bob Johnson notes that more than 90 percent of all deaf children have hearing parents. Unlike deaf children of deaf parents, who get ASL instruction early, they learn a language late and lag educationally. "The average deaf 12th-grader reads at the 4th-grade-level," says Johnson. He believes deaf children should start learning ASL in the crib, with schools teaching in ASL. English, he argues, should be a second language, for reading and writing: "All evidence says they'll learn English better." It's been an uphill battle. Of the several hundred school programs for the deaf in this country, only six are moving toward ASL-based instruction. And the vast majority of deaf students are still in mainstream schools where there are few teachers who are fluent in ASL.

Meanwhile, researchers are finding that ASL is a living language, still evolving. Sociolinguist James Woodward from Memphis, who has a black belt in karate, had planned to study Chinese dialects but switched to sign when he came to Gallaudet in 1969. "I spent every night for two years at the Rathskeller, a student hangout, learning by observing," he says. "I began to see great variation in the way people signed."

Woodward later concentrated on regional, social and ethnic dialects of ASL. Visiting deaf homes and social clubs in the South, he found that Southerners use older forms of ASL signs than Northerners do. Southern blacks use even more of the older signs. "From them, we can learn the history of the language," he says.

Over time, signs tend to change. For instance, "home" originally was the sign for "eat" (touching the mouth) combined with the sign for "sleep" (the palm pillowing the cheek). Now it has evolved into two taps on the cheek. Also, signs formerly made at the center of the face migrate toward its perimeter. One reason is that it is easier to see both signs and changes in facial expressions in this way, since deaf people focus on a signer's face—which provides crucial linguistic information—taking in the hands with peripheral vision.

Signers use certain facial expressions as grammatical markers. These linguistic expressions range from pursed lips to the expression that results from enunciating the sound "th." Linguist Scott Liddell, at Gallaudet, has noted that certain hand movements translate as "Bill drove to John's." If the signer tilts his head forward and raises his eyebrows while signing, he makes the sentence a question: "Did Bill drive to John's?" If he also makes the "th" expression as he signs, he modifies the verb with an adverb: "Did Bill drive to John's inattentively?"

Sociolinguists have investigated why this unique language was for so long virtually a secret. Partly, Woodward thinks, it was because deaf people wanted it that way. He says that when deaf people sign to the hearing, they switch to English-like signing. "It allows hearing people to be identified as outsiders and to be treated carefully before allowing any interaction that could have a negative effect on the deaf community," he says. By keeping ASL to themselves, deaf people—whom Woodward regards as an ethnic group—maintain "social identity and group solidarity."

A KEY LANGUAGE INGREDIENT: GRAMMAR

The "secret" nature of ASL is changing rapidly as it is being examined under the scientific microscope. At the Salk Institute, a futuristic complex of concrete labs poised on a San Diego cliff above the Pacific, pioneer ASL investigator Ursula Bellugi directs the Laboratory for Cognitive Neuroscience, where researchers use ASL to probe the brain's capacity for language. It was here that Bellugi and associates found that ASL has a key language ingredient: a grammar to regulate its flow. For example, in a conversation a signer might make the sign for "Joe" at an arbitrary spot in space. Now that spot stands for "Joe." By pointing to it, the signer creates the pronoun "he" or "him," meaning "Joe." A sign moving toward the spot means something done *to* "him." A sign moving away from the spot means an action *by* Joe, something "he" did.

In the 1970s, Bellugi's team concentrated on several key questions that have been of central concern ever since MIT professor Noam Chomsky's groundbreaking work of the 1950s. Is language capability innate, as Chomsky and his followers believe? Or is it acquired from our environments? The question gets to the basics of humanity since our language capacity is part of our unique endowment as a species. And language lets us accumulate lore and pass it on to succeeding generations. Bellugi's team reasoned that if ASL is a true language, unconnected to speech, then our penchant for language must be built in at birth, whether we express it with our tongue or hands. As Bellugi (above) puts it: "I had to keep asking myself, 'What does it mean to be a language?'"

A key issue was "iconicity." Linguistics has long held that one of the properties of all natural languages is that their words are arbitrary. In English, to illustrate, there is no relation between the sound of the word "cat" and a cat itself, and onomatopoeic words like "slurp" are few and far between. Similarly, if ASL follows the same principles, its words should not be pictures or mime. But ASL does have many words with transparent meanings. In ASL, "tree" is an arm upright from the elbow, representing a trunk, with the fingers spread to show the crown. In Danish Sign, the signer's two hands outline a tree in the air. Sign languages are rife with pantomimes. But Bellugi wondered: Do deaf people *perceive* such signs as iconic as they communicate in ASL?

One day a deaf mother visited the lab with her deaf daughter, not yet 2. At that age, hearing children fumble pronouns, which is why parents say, "Mommy is getting Tammy juice." The deaf child, equally confused by pronouns, signed "you" when she meant "I." But the sign for such pronouns is purely iconic: the signer points an index finger at his or her own torso to signify "I" or at the listener to signify "you." The mother corrected the child by turning her hand so that she pointed at herself. Nothing could be clearer. Yet, as the child chattered on, she continued to point to her mother when she meant "I."

Bellugi's work revealed that deaf toddlers have no trouble pointing. But a pointing finger in ASL is linguistic, not gestural. Deaf toddlers in the "don't-understand-pronouns" stage do not see a pointing finger. They see a confusing, abstract word. ASL's roots may be mimetic, but—embedded in the flow of language—the signs lose their iconicity.

By the 1980s, most linguists had accepted sign languages as natural languages on an equal footing with English, Italian, Hindi and others of the world. Signed languages like ASL were as powerful, subtle and intricately structured as spoken ones.

The parallels become especially striking in wordplay and poetry. Signers creatively combine hand shapes and movements to create puns and other humorous alterations of words. A typical pun in sign goes like this: a fist near the forehead and a flip of the index finger upward means that one understands. But if the little finger is flipped, it's a joke meaning one understands a little. Clayton Valli at Gallaudet has made an extensive study of poetry in ASL. He finds that maintenance or repetition of hand shape provides rhyming, while meter occurs in the timing and type of movement. Research with the American Theater of the Deaf reveals a variety of individual techniques and styles. Some performers create designs in space with a freer movement of the arms than in ordinary signing. With others, rhythm and tempo are more important than spatial considerations. Hands may be alternated so that there is a balance and symmetry in the structure. Or signs may be made to flow into one another, creating a lyricism in the passage. The possibilities for this new art form in sign seem bounded only by the imagination within the community itself.

The special nature of sign language provides unprecedented opportunities to observe how the brain is organized to generate and understand language. Spoken languages are produced by largely unobservable movements of the vocal apparatus and received through the brain's auditory system. Signed languages, by contrast, are delivered through highly visible movements of the arms, hands and face, and are received through the brain's visual system. Engagement of these different brain systems in language use makes it possible to test different ideas about the biological basis of language.

The prevailing view of neurologists is that the brain's left hemisphere is the seat of language, while the right controls our perception of visual space. But since signed languages are expressed spatially, it was unclear where they might be centered.

To find out, Bellugi and her colleagues studied life-long deaf signers who had suffered brain damage as adults. When the damage had occurred in their left hemisphere, the signers could shrug, point, shake their heads and make other gestures, but they lost the ability to sign. As happens with hearing people who suffer left-hemisphere damage, some of them lost words while others lost the ability to organize grammatical sentences, depending on precisely where the damage had occurred.

Conversely, signers with right-hemisphere damage signed as well as ever, but spatial arrangements confused them. One of Bellugi's right-hemisphere subjects could no longer perceive things to her left. Asked to describe a room, she reported all the furnishings as being on the right, leaving the room's left side a void. Yet she signed perfectly, including signs formed on the left side. She had lost her sense of *topographic* space, a right-hemisphere function, but her control of *linguistic* space, centered in the left hemisphere, was intact. All of these findings support the conclusion that language, whether visual or spoken, is under the control of the left hemisphere.

One of the Salk group's current efforts is to see if learning language in a particular modality changes the brain's ability to perform other kinds of tasks. Researchers showed children a moving light tracing a pattern in space, and then asked them to draw what they saw. "Deaf kids were way ahead of hearing kids," says Bellugi. Other tests, she adds, back up the finding that learning sign language improves the mind's ability to grasp patterns in space.

THINKING AND DREAMING IN SIGNS

Salk linguist Karen Emmorey says the lab also has found that deaf people are better at generating and manipulating mental images. "We found a striking difference in ability to generate mental images and to tell if one object is the same as another, but rotated in space, or is a mirror image of the first," she says, noting that signers seem to be better at discriminating between faces, too. As she puts it: "The question is, does the language you know affect your other cognitive abilities?"

Freda Norman, formerly an actress with the National Theater of the Deaf and now a Salk research associate, puts it like this: "English is very linear, but ASL lets you see everything at the same time."

"The deaf *think* in signs," says Bellugi. "They *dream* in signs. And little children sign to themselves."

At McGill University in Montreal, psychologist Laura Ann Petitto recently found that deaf babies of deaf parents babble in sign. Hearing infants create nonsense sounds like "bababababa," first attempts at language. So do deaf babies, but with their hands. Petitto watched deaf infants moving their hands and fingers in systematic ways that hearing children not exposed to sign never do. The movements, she says, were their way of exploring the linguistic units that will be the building blocks of language—their language.

Deaf children today face a brighter future than the generation of deaf children before them. Instruction in ASL, particularly in residential schools, should accelerate. New technologies, such as the TDD (Telecommunications Device for the Deaf) for communicating over telephones, relay services and video programs for language instruction, and the recent Americans with Disabilities Act all point the way to a more supportive environment. Deaf people are moving into professional jobs, such as law and accounting, and more recently into computer-related work. But it is not surprising that outside of their work, they prefer one another's company. Life can be especially rewarding for those within the ASL community. Here they form their own literary clubs, bowling leagues and gourmet groups.

As the Salk laboratory's Freda Normal signs: "I love to read books, but ASL is my first language." She adds, smiling: "Sometimes I forget that the hearing are different."

An Interview with Hang Nguyen

by Suzanne Stiel

Hang Nguyen came to the United States in 1983 as one of the "boat people" from Vietnam. Her family constructed their own boats and organized their own escape. Her father came in the first boat with seven of Hang's brothers and sisters. Hang came in the second boat with her sister, her husband, and her daughter who was four years old. Her mother and grandmother came to the United States in 1992. Hang's parents, grandmother, and nine brothers and sisters are living in Pennsylvania. She has one sister who escaped by boat to Australia and still lives there today. Hang and her family were immersed in a new language and culture when they fled Vietnam to seek sanctuary in the United States. She shares with Suzanne Stiel first-hand experiences they endured at school and the effect on her daughter's self-esteem when she was asked to make choices between the languages of home and school. Hang lives in Portland, Oregon, with her daughter Thu, and works as a multicultural specialist for Portland Public Schools.

Susanne Stiel interviewed her; Hang's comments follow.

There are many things that are disappointments. I guess the trend now is changing a little bit, more toward multiculturalism. I think the problem I faced then was that my daughter wasn't treated as if she was an entity, as if she was a person who could speak, who could learn, who could understand, because she didn't speak English. The teachers in school tended to treat parents of minority kids like they're stupid idiots, savage and uncivilized. So when they talk to you they are always patronizing, always give you a phrase like "You are very nice, and your daughter is very nice," but never any comment like "she's very smart," or "she's very quick," or "she's intelligent." Nothing! It's always "She's very nice in class and behaves." That's the thing that really bugged me all those years.

Another thing is when there was a fight in school because my daughter didn't speak English. She wanted to play, but she didn't know the rules and the other kids started getting mad and fighting. The teacher came out and pulled my daughter in and was pointing at her, "You behave yourself! You don't do this here! This is not Vietnam!" I thought that remark was really stupid! The town we lived in was very conservative. All white. It seemed like everything their way was fine, but my way was not.

First thing when my daughter came home she said "I'm not supposed to speak Vietnamese at home, Mom, because I have to learn English. My teacher said to go home and practice English." That was the message she got when she was five and six years old. And that is the thing that really made me angry. When she told me that I was just astounded. I was appalled. I asked her, "Who told you that?" And she said "My teacher did; she said that I'm supposed to go home and speak English, so I can get used to it and use it because I live here." That was the first disappointment that I got in this country.

After that every time I went to the conference I always heard "Oh, you are very nice," but never anything like "Do you need some help?" or "Do you think I can help you with anything?" or anything related to my daughter actually learning. They always made comments about how very nice I am, meaning I may be an idiot, but I'm smiling and I'm polite! When I asked pointed questions like "What about my daughter's math score? I want to know her score. I want to see her work," they tell me "She's doing fine, just fine," which means that they don't know if she's doing fine or not. But at the conference I am the parent and they have to treat me like other parents, but they don't want to bother. It had only been five minutes and they were saying "It was very nice to meet you. I have another parent waiting outside." That parent went in and I hung around to see, and that parent was there for half an hour and all kinds of work was brought out! Since that day, in my mind, I would not come to the conference unprepared, and I would not leave until I'd seen my daughter's work. After that I made my point clear to every teacher when I went in for a conference.

Another disappointment that is related to this is how my daughter changed. She refused to learn the cultural way, the family way. She refused to learn Vietnamese. She refused to speak Vietnamese at home. Her excuse was "If I speak Vietnamese and think in Vietnamese I am going to get confused and I will not be able to get ahead here." That's the message she's received since she was in first grade until now. It was a continual message. She was allowed in the ESL program for one year and then she had to be out in the mainstream classes. The worst thing that happened to my daughter is that she feels inferior, that she doesn't fit in. She tried very hard to belong, and she tried very hard to deny who she is. That attitude and that mentality were created the day she started school and continued until now. She just started coming around about six months ago saying "I want to know about the Vietnamese way," and "I will speak more Vietnamese at home now, Mom," and "I'm proud to be Vietnamese." But before, when I would go to the conference and would speak Vietnamese to her, she would say "Don't speak Vietnamese here." She would whisper in my ear. She was ashamed of it. Even when she was in seventh and eighth grade I would speak Vietnamese with her before we went into the conference and she would turn away. It was like she was saying "I don't know that language. Don't speak that language here because nobody speaks that language." Do you see how wrong it is to make a kid feel like she's not one of the group, and how wrong it is to make her turn away from her family? If they don't live the way the family lives how can they understand what is valuable and what is not? Do the parents have any way with them at all? When they say something, like disciplining them, the kids will not respect their parents because most parents don't speak English and don't live the American way. The kids go home and are disrespectful to their parents and totally ignore them. They don't see that their parents fit in with anything. They are ashamed. That's the problem.

My daughter has some friends who don't speak Vietnamese. They don't know how because they grew up here. I guess my daughter's interest in her culture started when I did the Asian Youth Leadership conference at Portland State University. I did one session called *Story of Who We Are*. I had a hundred kids in there and I was telling them a Vietnamese folktale. I read it in Vietnamese and then I read it in English, and then I asked them how they felt about it. Some understood it, and some didn't. Some remembered it, and some didn't. My message to them was to feel proud of who they are and where they're from, and not to forget that everyone has roots and traditions and culture. Then when it was in the newspaper I cut that section out and I showed it to my daughter. Some of her friends from school had gone to that conference and they told her how nice it was to hear that language, and to see, among millions of Americans, how suddenly your language was there and your story was told. I guess it gave my daughter an awakening call.

My daughter is bilingual, but only half bilingual because she doesn't know how to read and write. She only speaks Vietnamese. She can just guess. She can try to put words together and read them, but she is guessing, and she's not able to write them. She was four years old when we came over, and she started kindergarten early. So since she was five years old until just recently she has been continuously bombarded with the ideas "You live here. You have to speak the language. You have to learn the way to live here. Your language is not important. Your language is an embarrassment. If you learn your language you will not be able to learn English. English is the main language here." That's the message that she got. It was not always obvious, but she would be told "You need to go home and practice your English. You need this . . . you need that . . . ," and I think that was enough to poison her mind against what she stands for.

Sometimes my daughter asks me about Vietnam, and I tell her, but it doesn't seem to interest her at all. At some point maybe she will go back and ask for more details. I told her what happened, and how we came over here. She's just not interested. I think it's very difficult for parents coming here. They are too old. They're already rooted in the old culture and the old way of life, and the society was so different. You come over here and suddenly you see you are given rights, and there's no limit. And there's television, peers, the media, and all kinds of things that your kids are exposed to everyday.

Another hard thing for parents is they have to work. They cannot live on welfare. They cannot get charity. They've got too many kids. If they don't work they won't have anything. Because both parents have to work, sometimes long hours to get enough money, they don't have time for their kids at home. That very much affects how they grow up. They don't see their parents, and when they do their parents are so tired. They lie to their parents about this and that. The attitude of the parents is "I trust you. If you tell me you do so, then I believe that you do so." They were lying to get what they wanted. They were by themselves too much. When you're by yourself at a young age you want to explore. You won't stay home. Even though you want to please your parents, you would be gone when they're gone, and come back before they get home, so that you wouldn't make them feel bad. In the meantime you go out and explore.

And what do they explore? Things that they are never allowed to have at home, and are never allowed to do at home, such as smoking, drinking, going dancing and to the movies, hanging out and talking dirty, seeing this and that. That's what they're not allowed at home. So in between the times they see their parents, when the parents are absent, they will go do those things. In front of their parents they are very nice, so if anyone tries to tell their parents that their son or daughter are doing these things, they will not believe it. I may be wrong in my estimation, but I would say that a very high number of Vietnamese families here, maybe seventy-five to eighty percent, have this problem. Their kids will lie to them. They will turn away from them, and will do things that we would call rebellious. They rebel against their culture, and against the beliefs that the parents really stand for.

In Vietnam you have this, but you also have what we call a collective culture. You have your aunts and uncles, the whole family surrounding you. In Vietnam the biggest thing is the family pride. Whatever you do contributes to that pride. You don't do something and get credit for yourself. Your family, your parents, your grandparents get the credit. You will hear "Her grandson did this or that," and that makes the family feel proud because it gives them honor. Over here you don't see this. Over here, for example, if you graduated you would get the credit for that yourself, but over there people would be talking about so-and-so's granddaughter or so-and-so's niece graduating and it would reflect on every member of the family. The family reputation relies on every single member of the family. That's what keeps the kids in line. If you are shunned by your family because you have done something bad, no one would take you in because they are all protecting what I call the social order. If one family says that you're bad, your own family would disown you. You must be really bad. It's hard for kids over there to get out of line. It's also unfair in some ways. Families are too strict. But one thing compensates for another. Over here you take credit for what you do yourself. Your parents are in the background. Over there it's because of your parents that you are successful, because they have contributed, they've been supportive, everything. So when kids come over here they start seeing this.

First they go to school and say "I'm going to get all A's so my parents will be proud." Then when they get the awards and recognition, their name's up on the board, nothing is sent home to the parents. In Vietnam they would send everything home to the parents, and the parents would see the work of their child. Here, the child's name is on the board in school, and whose parent is going to see that? Only the other students are going to see that. It is very much individualized. That makes it very difficult for Vietnamese parents to reinforce the family tradition. My daughter saw it right away. In Vietnam I would not live so far away from my parents. I could have my own house, but very close to theirs. I would still go back and forth, and rely on them for help. Over here she can see it. We moved across the country and we're here by ourselves. Do I rely on my family? No. Does my family rely on me? No. Everybody has their own life to take care of. The young people see it right away. They have their own life. Especially when they are coming over at sixteen and seventeen, they know that in a year or two they are going to get out. So who's going to listen to their parents?

Narrative, Literacy, and Face in Interethnic Communication

RONALD SCOLLON AND SUZANNE SCOLLON

Editor's introduction

Ronald and Suzanne Scollon are researchers who have spent many years studying the language and culture of the Athabaskan Indians, a tribe located primarily in Alaska and the Northern Canadian territories. In this excerpt from their study, *Narrative, Literacy and Face in Interethnic Communication*, the Scollons consider the subtle ways differences in communication styles across cultures can cause misunderstanding.

THE DISTRIBUTION OF TALK

When two or more people talk together, it takes a lot of coordination to keep things going smoothly. Although it does not seem like it, in ordinary conversation the various speakers are careful not to talk all at once or to interrupt or to fail to answer if there is a question. This cooperation takes a good bit of work and common understanding. In interethnic communication there are often differences in the systems of the speakers, so that mistakes happen that lead to further misunderstandings. We will look in this section at how conversationalists decide who speaks first, how topics are controlled, how turns at talking are exchanged, and how conversations are ended.

Who Speaks First

When an Athabaskan and a speaker of English talk to each other, it is very likely that the English speaker will speak first. Many people have observed this. It is not hard to see why the English speaker will speak first if we consider what was said about the presentation of self. The Athabaskan will feel it is important to know the relationship between the two speakers

before speaking. The English speaker will feel talking is the best way to establish a relationship. While the Athabaskan is waiting to see what will happen between them, the English speaker will begin speaking, usually asking questions in fact, to find out what will happen. Only where there is a longstanding relationship and a deep understanding between the two speakers is it likely that the Athabaskan will initiate the conversation.

Control of Topic

It might not seem very important at first glance who speaks first in a conversation. Studies of conversation have shown, however, that the person who speaks first also controls the topic of conversation. Schegloff (1972) found that the person who spoke first took the role of the summoner. His speech in effect asks the other speaker for the right to talk. The second speaker

Source: Excerpt from *Narrative, Literacy, and Face in Interethnic Communication* (pp. 22–28) by R. Scollon and S. Scollon, 1983, Norwood, NJ: Ablex.

226

answers but in a very open way. The answer of the second speaker gives the first speaker the right to go ahead and talk. The first speaker then introduces the topic of the conversation to which the second must then reply. If the second speaker wants to introduce his own topic he must wait for a chance to introduce it later, after they have talked about the first speaker's topic.

These general rules seem so obvious and trivial that it is hard to believe how strictly we hold to them. It is easy to see how strong these rules are, though, by trying to break them. If someone calls on the phone (the phone ring is the first speaker), and if you answer by talking about what you want to talk about, both you and the caller will feel something very strange has happened. During their study, one of Schegloff's colleagues was being troubled by obscene phone calls. She found that if she picked up the phone but did not say anything, the caller would not go on to say any obscenities. He was following the conversational rules that would only allow him to speak after the second speaker answered. He followed conversational rules even though he was violating the moral rules of the same society.

In another study Scollon (1976) found that a one-year-old child learned these conversational rules before she was two years old. A one-year-old has very little she can say easily. The child in that study, Brenda, found that if she was the first speaker she could talk about what she wanted to talk about. She used one word, "here," as a summons. She would give a piece of paper or trash or almost anything to someone else and say, "here." The other person would take it and say "thank you." Then Brenda would say whatever she wanted to say.

Sometimes an adult would try to speak to Brenda first. She would refuse to answer. If the adult persisted she would say "here" and hand him something. That would make her the first speaker and ultimately give her the right to introduce her topic. Brenda had learned how to use speaking first to keep control of the topic of conversation by the time she was two years old.

We have said that in Athabaskan-English conversations the English speaker almost always speaks first. This has the consequence of allowing him to introduce his own topic and of making it very difficult for the Athabaskans to introduce any other topic. The general result of these two facts is that in interethnic communications between Athabaskans and English speakers

the topic of conversation is almost always the English speaker's topic, not the Athabaskan's.

Another complication is introduced by the fact that at least some Athabaskans use a conventional greeting that gives the answerer the right to introduce the topic. At Fort Chipewyan, Alberta, it is common to greet people with ?ɛdlánioen "what are you thinking?" The appropriate response is an open-ended introduction of the answerer's topic if he should choose to say something.

Here as before these discourse problems lead to stereotyping. The Athabaskan starts to feel that his ideas are always being ignored. At the same time he feels that the English speaker is either egocentric or ethnocentric. He feels that the English speaker only wants to talk about his own ideas. From the English speaker's point of view it seems either that the Athabaskan does not have any ideas of his own or that when they are introduced these ideas are off the topic. By putting together the assumptions about the presentation of self that Athabaskans and English speakers hold and a quite mechanical rule of conversational interchange, we get a situation in which one speaker is always in control of what the participants talk about.

The Exchange of Speaking Turns

We have said that at least in English conversation one speaker begins, a second answers, the first introduces the topic, and the second continues on that topic. Of course, conversations can be more complicated than that. There may be more than two speakers, for one thing. But to keep this discussion from getting too complex, we will just talk about two-person conversation.

As the conversation goes on the speakers continue to take turns in speaking. They do not normally both speak at the same time. In fact, simultaneous speech is usually a good sign that something has gone wrong. When the timing goes off so far that both speakers start speaking together it usually takes some time to smooth things out again. Usually after one speaker finishes the other can take a turn. If the other one does not say anything, then the first speaker can take another turn if he wishes. If the other comes in too soon it feels as if he is interrupting.

Problems start to come up when two speakers have different systems for pausing between turns. Generally speaking, Athabaskans allow a slightly longer pause between sentences than do English speakers. The difference is probably not more than half a second in length, but it has an important effect on interethnic communication. When an English speaker pauses he waits for the regular length of time (around one second or less), that is, *his* regular length of time, and if the Athabaskan does not say anything, the English speaker feels he is free to go on and say anything else he likes. At the same time the Athabaskan has been waiting his regular length of time before coming in. He does not want to interrupt the English speaker. This length of time we think is around one and one-half seconds. It is just enough longer that by the time the Athabaskan is ready to speak the English speaker is already speaking again. So the Athabaskan waits again for the next pause. Again, the English speaker begins just enough before the Athabaskan was going to speak. The net result is that the Athbaskan can never get a word in edgewise (an apt metaphor in this case), while the English speaker goes on and on.

The Athabaskan point of view is that it is difficult to make one's whole point. The length of pause that the Athabaskan takes while expecting to continue is just about the length of pause the English speaker takes in exchanging turns. If an Athabaskan has in mind a series of sentences to say, it is most likely that at the end of the first one the English speaker will think that he has finished because of the length of the pause and will begin speaking. The Athabaskan feels he has been interrupted and the English speaker feels the Athabaskan never makes sense, never says a whole coherent idea. Much of this misunderstanding is the result of something like a one-half second difference in the timing of conversational pauses, but it can result in strong stereotypical responses to the opposite ethnic group.

A second factor in the exchange of speaking turns that only increases the difficulty we are looking at here is that there are different expectations about how long a speaker should be allowed to speak at one turn. Generally Athabaskans expect that a speaker will take as long as necessary to develop an idea. The ideal situation is that of an older speaker, a person in a clear superordinate position, narrating a traditional story. Although this idea may not often be practiced, there is nevertheless an expectation that something like a monologue is the normal speaking turn. The role of other speakers is that of an audience that by frequent traffic signal responses indicates that it is following. English speakers, on the other hand, treat monologues as exceptions, with the norm being the dialogue in which speakers exchange more or less equal turns.

In Athabaskan-English interethnic communication, the expectation that English speakers have is rarely fulfilled. True dialogue rarely occurs. The reason for this has been given. The exchange of turns works toward the English speaker's continually regaining the floor and against the Athabaskan's being able to hold the floor for more than a brief speaking turn. Where an Athabaskan may expect to get his turn after a long English monologue, he rarely gets more than a brief statement before another English monologue begins. The result is again stereotyping of the English speaker as egocentric and the Athabaskan as having no ideas of his own.

Departure Formulas

It is safe to say that an Athabaskan-English conversation will usually begin with the English speaker speaking first. It is almost as certain that it will end with the Athabaskan making no formal close. On the surface the explanation seems simple enough. Most of the formulas for ending conversation refer to the future. Athabaskans feel it is bad luck to make predictions about the future. This applies even to such routine statements as "I'll see you later" or "I'll see you tomorrow." Where the English speakers feel these are simple closing statements, ways of saying "Now our talk is ended," they carry an overtone of bad luck for the Athabaskan and thus are avoided.

The impression of these closing formulas from the Athabaskan point of view again confirms the English speaker's bravado regarding his good luck and future. From the English speaker's point of view, the lack of closings gives a feeling that something has gone wrong in the communication. As we have reason to believe now, that is very likely to be true; but it may be misleading. The conversation may have been very compatible and yet leave the English speaker feeling that something went wrong because of the lack of a close.

We need to look a bit closer at departures to understand this problem. As Goffman (1974) has said, departures do much more than bring a conversation to a close. They set up the conditions for future conversations. English speakers feel it is essential at the end of each encounter to be clear just where you stand with the other speaker. The closing formula is the way this is done. Something as simple as "It's been nice talking to you" suggests that you expect to do more of it in the future. As we depart we prepare the future, and it is this aspect of the formula that for the English speaker fits in well with the general negotiation of intersubjective reality. The departure is the final check on where you have gotten to in the negotiation that has taken place. It cements this into place so that the negotiation can be resumed at the next opportunity.

This preparation of the future through the departure formula is directly contrary to the Athabaskan prohibition on speaking strongly of the future. If one enjoyed a conversation, it would be bad luck indeed to say so and that you hoped it would happen again. So in closing a conversation as in beginning it, the Athabaskan is careful not to display carelessness or to present himself in too favorable a light. The English speaker who has begun the conversation as a way of getting to know the other closes the conversation with an indirect but important summary of how things have gone. Perhaps the worst outcome from the English point of view is a complete rupture of the relationship. This would be shown by a violation of discourse conventions, including the convention of a formulated departure. The Athabaskans, being careful of courting bad luck, may quite unknowingly signal to the English speaker the worst possibility, that there is no hope of getting together again to speak.

The Importance of Discourse and Cultural Factors

In interethnic communication between English speakers and Athabaskans, talk is distributed so that the English speaker is favored as first speaker, as controller of topic, as principal speaker, and yet in the end he may not have any conclusive idea of what went on. For the Athabaskan speaker it is difficult to get the floor, to bring the conversation around to his own topic, and in the end to feel he has had much effect on the outcome. This situation is prepared by cultural expectations about the presentation of self. It works through the mechanics of a slight difference in pausing systems and the general mechanics of turn taking in human communication. The result is a considerable potential for difficulty in interethnic communication. It is important to point out now that we have not yet mentioned any factors that

have to do with the grammatical or lexical structure of language directly. The potential difficulties and misunderstandings that we have discussed are the same whether the communication is carried on in English, Athabaskan, so-called Village English, or any combination of these. As long as the discourse patterns and the presentation of self are clearly Athabaskan in origin on the one hand and English in origin on the other these possibilities of problems will arise.

At first it will seem ironic that the situation in which there is the greatest potential for problems is where the language being used by the two speakers is the most similar. We are so accustomed to thinking that communication is a matter of grammar and vocabulary that if the grammar and vocabulary are the same or similar for two speakers it is difficult to believe that there might be trouble. Yet, as we have said earlier, these discourse patterns and cultural expectations are learned very early in life and change slowly. Even where someone learns to speak a new language later in life, it is very likely that he will speak it using the discourse patterns of his early language training. In present-day Alaska and Canada, many people who do not speak any Athabaskan language have nevertheless learned Athabaskan discourse patterns which are essential for effective communication within the village, even though the language used may be English. We want to be careful then not to think that understanding will be automatic just because two speakers do not differ greatly in grammar or vocabulary. Assumptions about the presentation of self and the distribution of talk in interethnic communication lie at the bottom of many communicative conflicts.

REFERENCES

Goffman, E. (1974). *Frame analysis*. New York: Harper & Row.

Schegloff, E. (1972). Sequencing in conversational openings. J. Gumperz and D. Hymes (Eds.). *Directions in sociolinguistics*. New York: Holt, Rinehart and Winston.

Scollon, R. (1976). *Conversations with a one-year-old: A case study of the developmental foundation of syntax*. Honolulu: University Press of Hawaii.

Teasing: Verbal Play in Two Mexicano Homes

Ann R. Eisenberg

Editor's introduction

Cultural and social values are continually expressed through social interaction. Examining those interactions can provide important information about the relationship between language and culture. Teasing, for example, is regarded as a vital component of a child's developing communicative competence in many cultures. Ann Eisenberg examines some of the patterns of teasing in two Mexicano homes, showing how the verbal play is a respected linguistic skill and a way to interact for enjoyment, to reinforce relationships, and as a means of social control.

Teasing a child is behavior that seems specifically designed to create uncertainty in the recipient of the tease. Although the teaser does not actually intend the literal content of his or her utterance to be accepted as true, teasing creates the possibility that the child will believe the utterance to be true. According to Grice's (1975) maxim of quality, speakers should not say anything they believe to be untrue; yet in teasing children, adults intentionally violate this maxim. The question to be addressed in this chapter is why adults choose to tease children and thereby create this type of uncertainty in them.

Although descriptions of teasing are rare in the literature on interactions involving young children, there are enough data to indicate that explanations of teasing must focus on a particular cultural or subcultural group (Coles 1977; Heath 1981; Miller 1986; Schieffelin 1986; Simmons 1942). Teasing has been shown to vary across groups in its structural characteristics, assignment of roles permissible for children, and association with other speech forms, such as criticism, joking, and assertion. Thus, the specific focus of this chapter will be the teasing that occurred in the inter-

action of two Mexican immigrant families living in northern California.

The suggestion to be made is that while there are common characteristics shared by all teasing sequences, at any particular time the specific goal of the teaser may vary. Specifically, the adults in the current study teased for two primary, and sometimes overlapping, purposes: to control the behavior of children and to have fun with children. Some teasing sequences were simply for fun; others incorporated social messages into a playful context. Although these two forms were not entirely distinct, viewing teasing from these two perspectives provides a useful framework for understanding the complexity of the behavior.

Although adults primarily teased to have fun and to control children's behavior, teasing also emphasized the relationships existing between the parents

---

Source: "Teasing: Verbal Play in Two Mexicano Homes" by A. R. Eisenberg, 1986. In *Language Socialization Across Cultures* (pp. 182–198), B. B. Schieffelin & E. Ochs, Eds., Cambridge: Cambridge University Press.

involved in the interaction sequence. Those relationships were emphasized both by the verbal messages used in teasing and in the alignments created as teasing sequences evolved. Thus, in addition to asking why adults tease children, the paper also addresses the questions of what children may be learning within the context of such interaction. What were the children learning about the nature of talk and the way in which relationships were expressed through talk? In addition, how did the children learn to become active participants in teasing?

THE DATA BASE

The data were part of a study on the acquisition of communicative competence by two monolingual, Spanish-speaking girls living in the metropolitan area near Oakland, California. Both girls were born in the United States, but their parents were all immigrants from central Mexico who had lived in the United States for less than six years when the study began. All the adults spoke only Spanish at home. Both girls were first-born, each with a younger sister born during the course of the study.

The two girls, Nancy and Marisa, were audiotaped every three weeks in two two-hour sessions. Taping continued for approximately a year: from 21 to 32 months for Nancy and from 24 to 38 months for Marisa. The investigator made extensive contextual notes during each recording session, and transcriptions were made within two to four days. When it was unclear what was occurring in a recorded interaction sequence, portions of the transcripts were shown to the mothers and they were asked for their interpretations. The mothers were also frequently asked why they or their children had acted in a particular fashion.

The events recorded included a number of different situations and individuals. Most recordings were made in the home or outside in the yard or courtyard where the women of the neighborhood would often congregate. All the recording sessions included the mother, and most also included other relatives or neighbors. Nancy lived with her parents, infant sister, two maternal uncles, an aunt, and, for a few months, her grandfather and a male family friend. She also interacted on a daily basis with her 3-year-old neighbor Pablito, his family, and other slightly older cousins and neighbors. Marisa lived with her parents and

infant sister and, during the summer, her maternal grandmother and 12-year-old uncle. Next door lived her mother's sister, two uncles, and her 4-year-old cousin Laura, who was her constant playmate. Thus, the situations in which the girls were teased (or involved in teasing others) could also be compared with how older children and other adults were teased.

A teasing sequence was defined as any conversational sequence that opened with mock challenge, insult, or threat. A key feature of the teasing sequence was that the teaser did not intend the recipient to continue to believe the utterance was true, although he or she might intend the recipient to believe it initially. This is an important distinction, because teasers do often hope to "trick" their listeners into believing them so as to enjoy the results when the latter realize that they have been duped. Using the criterion of eventual intent is also useful in distinguishing teasing from another type of untrue utterance the adults often used when attempting to control the behavior of young children—namely, threatening them with the appearance of a witch or bogeyman (el CuCui) who would spirit them away. In teasing sequences, that the teaser did not intend the tease to be understood as true was always eventually made apparent, either by a disclaimer (for example, No lo creas 'Don't believe it'; Estoy jugando, no más, 'I'm just playing') or by the use of contextualization cues, such as exaggerated intonation, laughs, or winks, which signaled "This is play." No such cues accompanied threats that children were expected to believe.

Within teasing sequences, adults threatened to inflict bodily harm ("We're going to throw Marisa in the garbage!"), disrupt important relationships ("I'm going to take your baby away!"), and withhold affection ("I'm not going to love you any more!"). Affectional bonds between the child and someone else were also frequently threatened ("Nancy, Aunt Sonia says she doesn't love you!"). Valued abilities (e.g., singing, dancing) and attributes (e.g., attractiveness, sanity) were also attacked and adults used their knowledge of the children's fears, likes, and dislikes to threaten them playfully with events they knew would provoke dismay in the child ("I'm going to dress you as a witch for Halloween, right, Nancy?" said when the child was known to be afraid of witches).

The most common teasers were the girls' mothers, probably because they were most frequently with the children. After mothers, men—particularly uncles—were most likely to be teasers. Female relatives other than the mothers were much less likely to incorporate teasing into a relationship with a child. Hopper, Sims & Alberts (1983) have suggested that men are more likely to tease children than are women. Although this sex difference was not entirely supported in the current study, teasing did represent a larger proportion of men's conversations with young children. In one or two cases, nearly all of a specific uncle's interactions with a niece involved teasing and joking. In addition, men and women tended to tease in slightly different ways. Mothers were most likely to tease children about being crazy (or being locked up with the crazies) or with the withdrawal of love or disruption of a relationship (e.g., "I'm going to take your baby"), whereas uncles were more likely to tease girls about being ugly or to threaten them with bodily harm.

From a discourse standpoint, the typical teasing sequence began with the adult issuing a challenge directly to the child. At that point, the child could either defend herself or another adult could help the child with the defense. In other cases, the challenge was not actually addressed to the child, but was formed as a statement about the child and directed to a third party. Essentially, the teaser attempted to solicit the other individual's participation in teasing the child. In this type of sequence, the younger child could also be invited in as the co-teaser of another child or adult. In a similar type of sequence the very young child could also be given lines to repeat to help tease someone else. Most of the sequences in which the tease was directed to the child as addressee could be characterized as purely playful episodes. In contrast, while they incorporated elements of play, sequences in which the child's role was that of intended overhearer or invited co-teaser generally also involved a message about appropriate behavior.

TEASING AS PLAY

Telling jokes, describing comical situations, and teasing are important forms of fun and amusement in Mexican homes, and members of the culture place a high value on verbal playfulness. Humor is important because it is entertaining, serves as a time filler, and brings group members together (Castro 1982). Interpersonal relationships are important to Mexican peo-

ple, and a vital aspect of those relationships is humorous communication and verbal interplay.

Children become a part of these noisy times at a very early age. From infancy they are drawn into interactions with others. Mothers talk to infants as if they can understand and interpret their babbling, gestures, and cries for others. With the instruction *díle* 'say to him/her', they tell preverbal infants what to say to others, and the others respond as if the infants had repeated the parent's utterance. Once children begin to speak, they are expected to repeat what they are told to say and thus begin to use language to conduct interpersonal relationships (see Eisenberg 1982 for a more complete description of the use of *díle*). Conversations with young children are also highly routinized, allowing children to participate despite a lack of sophisticated linguistic resources. The content of such interactions is less important than simply having the interaction. The goal is simply to have children participate and to enjoy interacting with them.

Teasing provides another context in which adults and children can converse and thereby act out a social relationship, despite the limited linguistic resources of the child. Teases are uttered under circumstances and within relationships where it is most plausible for the antagonistic statement to be framed and understood as play (Bateson 1972; Goffman 1975). In the context of the study, many aspects of the situation in which teasing occurred suggested that, in its simplest form, teasing was a type of social play. First, teasing was most common when adults were taking a break from the routine chores of the day and were relaxing in the courtyard or sitting out front on the stoop. Teases also most commonly clustered together in discourse involving other playful forms, jokes, and laughter. The laughter and accompanying winks, play faces, provocative tones, deep sighs, and exaggerated or singsong intonation acted as "contextualization cues" (Gumperz 1977), signaling the playful nature of the attack.

In addition, the adults frequently repeated the same initiations over and over again so that the repetitiveness provided a background for interpreting the challenge as nonserious. Having participated in a very similar interaction before, the child knew what the outcome would be. Teasing also generally occurred in a context in which the child could feel safe. Teasers were almost always someone known to the child and someone who frequently engaged her in such interactions. Further evidence that the adults perceived teasing episodes as play was that when they were shown the sequences and asked what was going on, they would respond, "I was just playing." That children were allowed to talk back and challenge adults during teasing also marked the sequences as play, since speaking assertively was clearly inappropriate for children in other contexts. Children who challenged adults or were heard doing so with their young visitors were considered *malcriados* 'poorly raised' or *groseros* 'rude'.

Teasing "works" because of its inherent ambiguity. The recipient must decide whether the speaker is serious or whether he or she is "only joking." Once the teaser opens a teasing episode, a successful interaction can take two forms. In the first, the recipient immediately recognizes the tease and plays along, either defending himself or counterteasing. In the second, the recipient fails to understand that the teaser was not serious and thus becomes the "butt" of the tease. This second type of sequence is most successful when the recipient joins in the fun once he or she eventually realizes that the original statement was just a tease. The first type works because all the participants play together; the second works because someone's vulnerability is exposed.

The adults in the study began teasing a child to amuse themselves, but that amusement could either be shared with the child or be at the expense of the child. Although teasing could and did occur in dyadic situations, it was most common when three or more people were present, particularly when those other individuals were other adults. Within dyadic situations, adults used teasing to play *with* the child. Teasing initiations were highly ritualized and clearly accompanied by playful contextualization cues. The type of teasing initiation used in dyadic contexts was also quite easily responded to, making it simple for a child without sophisticated linguistic skills to play along.

Within triadic or multiparticipant contexts, however, there were many indications that teasing was intended to amuse the teaser and the audience rather than the teaser and the recipient of the tease (although eventually the recipient might join in the laughter at his or her own expense). Provoking an angry or confused response from a child was considered funny, particularly if another adult was present to share in the amusement over the child's anger or frustration. The teaser often played to the audience, signaling his or her expectation concerning the child's reaction with a smile or wink:

Example 1[1]

Nancy (N, 26 months) and her mother (M) are watching TV with the investigator (I) shortly before Halloween. They have just watched a commercial for Halloween candy and have discussed what Nancy will say when she goes trick-or-treating. Nancy's mother knows she is afraid of witches.

M: La voy a disfrazar de bruja, ¿verdad, hija?
(I'm going to dress her as a witch, right, honey?)
[Winks at I and speaks softly]
Le da miedo.
(It scares her.)
[To N] ¿Disfrazo de bruja?
(A witch costume?)

[N shrieks] no!/

M and I: [laugh]

In such situations, the adults responded with laughter to the child's anger or distress.

Because the adults often teased to amuse themselves and other adults, the joke was sometimes at a level of complexity that the child might not understand. In fact, it was often the child's nonresponse—the lack of awareness that someone was teasing—that amused the adults. The relationship between Nancy and her friend Pablito was the focus of this type of joking. The two were frequently teased about being boyfriend and girlfriend. Similarly, Marisa's father would tease her about the Anglo boy living upstairs, asking if she were going to kiss him and if she liked los hueros 'the fair ones'.[2] No matter how Marisa responded, he and her mother would laugh.

---

[1]Transcription conventions follow Bloom, Lightbown & Hood (1974). The child's speech appears in the right-hand column and the speech of all others on the left. Slashes (/) indicate the end of a child's utterance, and question marks in parentheses (?) indicate unclear or inaudible utterances. A colon indicates that the previous syllable of a word received exaggerated or unusually long intonation. All contextual information and nonverbal behavior is described in brackets on the left side of the page. Translations are meant to convey the gist of the conversation, although the English versions of the children's speech are closer to exact translation.
[2]The word huero often has the added connotation of "empty."

Children, as immature and unsophisticated speakers, were easy victims[3] of this type of tease. They were not, however, the only victims; ideal victims included both those who could not defend themselves and those who could be counted on to defend themselves well. Quick-witted adults frequently teased others who were less witty, including the investigator in the study, who was a nonnative speaker of Spanish and, like the young children, a less sophisticated speaker, who could therefore also be counted on to miss some of the nuances of the conversation.

The various adults in the study differed somewhat in the extent to which they felt upsetting a child through teasing was appropriate. Nancy was more likely than Marisa to be teased to the point of upset, particularly by her uncle Ramon, who was frequently criticized by Nancy's mother for angering the children. Ramon, it seems, was likely to go beyond the "bounds defined by custom" (Radcliffe-Brown 1940:186). Exactly when one "goes too far," however, seemed to be a situated accomplishment (Hopper, Sims & Alberts 1983): There were no general rules, although it was obvious that all participants knew when it had happened.

The multiparticipant context in which teasing most frequently occurred was also exploited in other ways. Teasing was "safe" when others were present because those others could help defend a child who could not yet defend herself. Alternatively, they could assure the child that the teaser was playing or that what he or she was saying was not true. Supporting the child in the interaction helped the child understand that teasing was a form of play and helped her learn to play along, enacting the role of self-defender. In the case of the youngest children, the second adult frequently gave the child the appropriate lines to repeat in response to the attack:

Example 2

[Marisa (M, 27 months) is having her hair braided by her Aunt Amalia (A) while her Uncle Carlos (C) looks on.]

C: [Wrinkling his nose and shaking his head] ¡Fea, fea!

(Ugly, ugly!)

A: "No es cierto," díle. "Soy bonita."
("That's not true," tell him. "I'm pretty.")

soy bonito/
(I'm pretty/)

C: [Imitates her speech] "No nonito."
¿No estás bonita?
(You're not pretty?)

A: "Sí," díle, "soy bonita."
("Yes," tell him, "I'm pretty.")

C: Estás fea.
("You're ugly.")

bonita/
(pretty/)

Throughout Ex. 2, Marisa's aunt gives her the appropriate reply to someone who accuses her of not being pretty—an important attribute for little girls. Telling Marisa what to say in response gave her the opportunity to assert important, positive characteristics about herself. In similar situations, Nancy's mother would tease her about her aunt not loving her and if Nancy became upset (rather than responding, for example, *No, a tí no te quiere* 'No, she doesn't love you'), her aunt would reassure her that she did love her. A secondary effect of the mother's challenge was that it put the aunt in the position of affirming the fact that a loving relationship existed between her and Nancy. Whatever the focus of the attack, the resolution of the episode almost always yielded a positive statement in response. "Yes, I am pretty" or "Yes, she does love me."

TEASING AS A SOCIAL CONTROL

While all of the teasing episodes were playful (by definition), many of them also seemed to involve something more than "just play." In many of the episodes, the adults' teasing also had an underlying message concerning the inappropriateness of someone's behavior. In these cases, the challenge was used as a subtle form of criticism to convey a message of disapproval when the offense did not seriously threaten the adult's authority. The most common offenses to provoke teasing were the child's silliness or failure to perform well, although minor offenses, such as refusing to greet someone, also led to teasing. These episodes of social control were similar to those described by Schieffelin (1986) in which Kaluli mothers in Papua New Guinea

---

[3]In general, the term "recipient" is used for the target of the tease. The term "victim" is reserved for the target of a tease that a teaser hopes will at least momentarily confuse the addressee.

teased children to shame them into behaving in accordance with their wishes.

Occasionally, the third party, often another child, was enlisted as co-teaser in the interaction. An utterance could be addressed to a third party, but the butt of the tease was the child, who was expected to overhear. Challenges were frequently issued to the third person, who was invited to agree about the shortcomings of the individual being teased: "Ah, Laura's crazy, isn't she?" or "We're not going to take Marisa to her grandpa's, right, Monica?" The adults manipulated the multiparticipant context to "gang up" on a child. The children were given the opportunity to play both the role of the indirect recipient of the tease and that of the individual asked to participate in the teasing.

The following sequence illustrates some of these discourse features:

Example 3

[Nancy (N, 24 months) and her mother (M) are sitting on the stoop with their neighbor, Ceci (C), an older woman. Nancy pulls away when Ceci tries to hug her.]

M: Oye, Nancy. Dále un besito a Ceci.
(Listen, Nancy. Give Ceci a kiss.)

[N whines and pulls away]

C: Un besito. [Sighs heavily, shaking head] Ah, pues, ya no te voy a querer.
(A kiss. Ah, then, I'm not going to love you anymore.)

M: [To C, shaking head, clicking tongue] No le de manzana ni nada lo que quiere.
(Don't give her an apple or anything she wants.)

C: [Shakes her head] Ya, no. Pues, porque ya no me quiere.
(Not any more. Because she doesn't love me any more.)

[To N] ¿Verdad que ya no me quieres?
(Isn't it true that you don't love me any more?)

Talking about the behavior of a child who was expected to overhear was common, both when the message was intended to be taken literally and when it was not. In their conversation with each other ("Don't give her an apple or anything she wants"; "No, not any more, because she doesn't love me anymore"), Doña Ceci and Nancy's mother were doing what Clark & Carlson (1982) called "talking laterally." In talking lat-

erally, the speaker does not appear to be speaking to the indirect addressee, an appearance that is often useful. There would, however, be no point in discussing not giving Nancy what she wants unless Nancy were there and intended to overhear. Similarly, when a teaser says to Erica, "Marisa's ugly, isn't she?"; he is not seeking confirmation of his statement for his own sake, but is doing so for the sake of Marisa, the third party. With the use of the tag question, the adult is not asking Erica the question, but is letting Marisa know she is asking Erica the question and inviting her to agree.

Yet the use of playful contextualization cues in Ex. 3—the exaggerated head-shaking and sighing and the clicking of tongues—also signaled that the adults did not intend these social-control messages to be taken too seriously. They did, however, intend to make Nancy uncertain about their intent. By teasing Nancy with the withholding of love, the two women were able to make a couple of points: that Nancy should give a kiss when asked for one; and that loving (and the giving of gifts that accompanies it) is contingent upon the child's demonstrations of affection.

In other related sequences, the young child was used as a foil to influence someone else. Older children who misbehaved also found themselves becoming the recipients of a group attack, as adults and other children joined together as attackers. Even other adults could be the recipients of a joint teasing venture, most commonly when one adult would give a young child lines to repeat to another adult. Having the child repeat lines to tease another individual enabled adults to communicate messages that might have been inappropriate to communicate directly. This type of teasing frequently involved potentially volatile issues, such as an uncle's laziness or a grandfather's drinking. As Abrahams (1962) pointed out, this form of verbal play is perilously close to real life. Having the child issue the challenge and invoking the teasing mode created a safe context for the communication of a potentially threatening message. By virtue of the communicative situation created, the recipient of the tease was in a position where it was difficult to respond as if the attack were actually serious. Becoming angry with the adult issuing the teasing statements was inappropriate because involving the child clearly signaled that the sequence was play—at least on the surface. Becoming angry with the child was even more inappropriate, because the child was clearly not the one issuing the challenges. This type of pointed teasing works for the teaser because he or she can always deny any intent to convey a message. Thus, the message is conveyed without fear of immediate retaliation.

TEASING AND RELATIONSHIPS

Thus far, teasing sequences have been discussed as examples of play with language and as attempts to control the behavior or young children. Yet at the same time the teasing sequences conveyed a number of underlying messages to children, especially messages concerning the nature of social relationships. Teasing sequences reinforced relationships both through the content of the episodes and through the structural relationships created as the sequences developed.

The content of teasing episodes addressed issues of relationships in many ways. Resolution and development of many of the sequences involved naming a series of family members who might protect, help, or defend a child in the face of an attack. For example, a teasing routine that Marisa and her mother frequently engaged in involved Marisa's mother threatening to leave Marisa behind when the family went to visit Grandpa in Mexicali. The episode would continue with Marisa listing individuals who might take her if Mama did not and her mother responding with reasons why those others would not or could not take her either. The theme of visiting Grandpa in Mexicali and the listing of relatives appeared in many other conversations as well and was an important strategy for scripting Marisa's interactions with her mother. Relationships with extended family members were extremely important to the families, and it was considered important for children to know who their relatives were and what those relationships involved (Eisenberg 1982).

The existence of important relationships was also emphasized through threats of those relationships. An important consequence of such threats was that the threat required a verbal statement acknowledging the existence of the relationship and often another verifying its continuation. For example, when an adult threatened to steal a baby sister, the child was supposed to counter, "No, mine!", stating that the baby was hers and could not be taken away. Similarly, in the following example, Nancy's mother placed Nancy's aunt Sonia in the position of affirming her love for Nancy:

Example 4

[Nancy (N, 27 months) wants Ana (A) to take her to the park, so her mother (M) tells her to ask Ana if she wants to go. Since "want" and "love" are the same verb in Spanish, Nancy misunderstands and asks if Ana loves her. Nancy's aunt Sonia (S) is also present.]

[To A] me llevas?/
(will you take me?/)

M: Díle a Ana, "Quieres?"
(Say to Ana, "Do you want to?"

me quieres?/
(do you love me?/)

A: Si.
(Yes)

M: Sonia no te quiere. Oye, Nancy, Sonia no te quiere. Quiere a Os:car, a la Bi:bi, y a Chape:tes.
(Sonia doesn't love you. Listen, Nancy, Sonia doesn't love you. She loves Oscar, Bibi, and Chapetes.)

[N screams angrily] cállate!/mensa!/
(shut up!/stupid!/)

M: [Shaking head sadly] No, Sonia no te quiere.
(No, Sonia doesn't love you.)

S: Nancy, sí te quiero.
(Nancy, I do love you.)

M: Oye, no te quiere, dice.
(Listen, she doesn't love you, she says.)

sí quiere a mi!/
(she does love me!/)

[M tells her not to tip the chair over]

Ex. 4 reinforces the relationship between Nancy and her aunt in two ways. First, the mother's challenge elicits the clear statement that Aunt Sonia does love Nancy, both from Nancy and her aunt. Second, the mother's challenge puts Nancy and her aunt in a position where they unite by both playing the role of contradictor to the mother's role as challenger.

Other messages about relationships concern the nature of specific relationships, particularly those between men and women. As Hopper et al. (1983) suggested, many of the themes that appear in teasing sequences involving father and uncles seem to involve issues related to courtship. Men tease about attractiveness or they threaten girls with restraint or injury, suggesting the ideas that girls must be attractive and perhaps also that females can expect males to restrict their movement. Within the context of the play frame, males may also threaten to withdraw affection or to trade affection or a favor for freedom from restraint. For example, typical teasing episodes involving Marisa and her uncle began with the challenge *Estás fea, ¿verdad?* 'You're ugly, right?', led Marisa's counterassertion that she was pretty, and concluded with the uncle's willingness to accept the counterassertion if she would "show him" she was pretty with a kiss.

Teasing also reinforced relationships through the alignments created within the episodes. Many times when an adult provoked a child by teasing, the outcome was an alignment between the child and her co-defender, as in Exx. 2 and 4. Mothers "forced" children into interacting with others by giving them lines to repeat in conversation with others or by teasing them so that the other person would help the child negotiate the resolution of the mock conflict. Adults also invited children into special relationships with them by using teasing to make another child (or adult) the "outsider." When teasing works—either because two people have fun with each other or because they share the enjoyment over frustrating someone else—the result is an increase in feelings of closeness and solidarity.

Successful teasing episodes remind one of Blount's (1972) description of the use of whispering among two Luo adults and children:

> Whispering, in time, comes to be an intensifier within the dyadic addressor—addressee relationship. Third parties are excluded from sharing the message, as indeed, one dimension of the message is that only one particular receiver is intended as the recipient. Furthermore, there is the implication that a special relationship holds between the two participants, and the shared knowledge of this relationship sanctions the appropriateness of the code. In one sense, the parent and child establish collusion, bracketing off their relationship from the remainder of the environment and thereby intensifying the interaction routine. (pp. 239–40)

In a similar fashion, teasing intensifies the relationship between those involved. That it is "safe" to tease a particular individual indicates that a special relationship exists. The knowledge that the relationship exists also "sanctions the appropriateness of the code." Teasing can also establish collusion by creating alignments; inviting a child to help tease creates a special and valued closeness between that child and the adult who invites her into the relationship. The other child must then work to gain entry into that relationship. In fact, the Mexican immigrant adults in the study also used whispering—the telling of secrets—to bracket off relationships. They would invite young children to come close with the statement *Te voy a decir una cosa* 'I'm going to tell you something', and would whisper something into the child's ear when she approached. Aunts were more likely to invite a child (and not the others) to share a secret; uncles were more likely to establish the special relationship by teasing.

CHILDREN'S PARTICIPATION IN TEASING

The remaining question concerns the children's own developing abilities to participate in teasing sequences. Over time both children became more adept at interpreting teasing as play and at participating in teasing sequences on their own. At first, however, neither child participated much in teasing sequences, unless supported in self-defense by another adult. Throughout the course of taping, most of their responses tended to be very simple, consisting of either a rapid denial ("No!") or, less frequently, the offer of an alternative to the threat or challenge.

Gradually, the girls began to recognize more different teasing initiations and to make more counterassertions. Rather than simply replying "No," they began rephrasing the challenge, changing the identity of the recipient of the tease. Thus, "Marisa's crazy," became "No, you" or "No, *Laura's* crazy." Over the year in which they were observed, each of the girls developed particular teasing routines with specific individuals and within those routinized sequences increased the extent to which they were able to participate. In the last few taping sessions, the girls also began to tease others, although their initiations were still infrequent, highly routinized, and usually occurred when they themselves had just been teased or had observed someone teasing someone else. Nancy, for example, would ask if someone wanted something she had, would hold it out, and then at the last minute would snatch it away, roaring with laughter. Marisa also made announcements that various people were crazy and would greet the sighting of every neighborhood dog with "Doggie, bite *X*!" uttered in singsong intonation.

As Miller (1986) indicated, singsong intonation was most important in determining whether a child recognized teasing as play and was the first of the contextualization cues the children learned. Even when the content of a child's retort was not quite appropriate, often the tone of the utterance was. Singsong intonation was not limited to teasing or responding to teasing, but appeared frequently in statements of possession, making those statements sound like taunts. From the adult standpoint, a singsong utterance like "I have playdoh, ah-ha, ah-ha!" may have been inappropriate or an overgeneralization, but for the child it may have been a way of determining when such taunts were appropriate and who was likely to respond to them. It may have been a means of learning which taunts and teases would work with adults and which would work with other children.

Toward the end of taping, Marisa was also able to manipulate singsong intonation and other contextualization cues associated with teasing to defuse the impact of a threat she had made—a threat that would have been inappropriate had it not been playful. In other words, Marisa could use the cues to say, "I was just playing":

Example 5

[Marisa (Ma, 34 months) protests when her father (F) teases her by offering her a taco with chile in it when he knows she does not like chile. Her mother (M) and grandmother (G) are also present.]

[Ma shakes her head] chile no, Papi/te pego, Papi/
(no chile, Daddy/I'll hit you, Daddy/)

F: [Sternly] ¿A quién le vas a pegar?
(Whom? Whom are you going to hit?)

[Ma laughs] mi mami/
(my Mommy/)

F: [Still stern] ¿Porqué?
(Why?)

M: [Laughs] ¡Mira!
(Look!)

mi Maya/
(my Grandma/)
[Ma laughs again]

F: [Laughs] ¿Porqué?
(Why?)

mi Tata 'lente/
(my Grandpa Valente/)

F: Oh tu tata Valente.
(Oh, your Grandpa Valente.)

M: [Laughs]

G: [Laughs] A tu Papa Valente ahorita no le alcanzas. Está muy lejos.
(Right now you can't reach your Papa Valente. He's very far away.)

[All laugh]

Marisa was probably not teasing when she first said, "I'll hit you," but once her father responded, she realized from his tone of voice that she should not have said that to him. Rather than pursue her original statement—and face punishment—she laughed to indicate that her threat was not serious and made it more outlandish (and hence, more playful) by adding her mother, grandmother, and grandfather to the list of those to be hit. (Listing the names of relatives is also an appropriate conversational theme no matter what the context.) Once her mother laughed, indicating that she accepted that Marisa was playing, her father accepted her threat as playful. Thus, Marisa was able to use teasing to get herself out of trouble.

Marisa's facility with teasing is even more interesting in view of the fact that, overall, Marisa's abilities lagged behind Nancy's. Although Nancy's knowledge of syntax was more sophisticated at 28 months than Marisa's was at 38 months, Marisa was more adept than Nancy both at responding to teasing and recognizing that teases were not serious. While Nancy continued to become angry when teased, Marisa could taunt back and work out exceptions to the challenges, as well as manipulate teasing to avoid punishment. Her facility with teasing, despite the limitations in her syntax and pronunciation, suggests that the acquisition of some speech genres may not be entirely dependent on grammatical development. The ability to distinguish between the surface meaning of an utterance and its intended meaning may not depend entirely on other linguistic abilities.

There are a number of possible explanations of why Marisa was more at ease with teasing than Nancy, despite her lack of grammatical sophistication. One is that the ability to recognize nonliteral meaning is more dependent on cognitive development that comes with age than are specific linguistic abilities. Thus, since Marisa was slightly older, she was somewhat better at participating in teasing. Another possible explanation may have to do with personality differences. Not all adults are equally good at teasing or at recognizing that they are being teased (hence, the sense that certain individuals make good victims), and this difference may first arise in early childhood as a result of temperamental or other factors.

Alternatively, differences in experiences with teasing may create these individual differences. Marisa's facility with teasing may have stemmed from having more experience with teasing, and in particular, more experience with the form of teasing that was fun for both participants. In Nancy's home, Nancy was more often the butt of the tease, and half the fun was upsetting her. In Marisa's family, however, teasing was not only more frequent but was more commonly marked with laughter. In addition, when Marisa was teased, she was given more help in responding to the teasing. Furthermore, Marisa's cousin, Laura, was the recipient of teasing as often as Marisa was, and the adults often invited Marisa to help tease Laura. Thus, Marisa received more practice and help both in responding to teasing and learning to tease others.

SUMMARY

A number of observations can be made about the use of teasing in these two Mexican immigrant homes. First, teasing was primarily a means of playing with a child, either for the amusement of the adult (or adults) or the adult and the child. Adults could tease children to establish or maintain an interaction with them when there was little information to share. Although the content of teasing often touched on important conversational themes (e.g., love, grandparents), the content was usually less important than simply having the interaction. Interpersonal relationships with intimates were extremely important in the families, and an important component of those relationships was verbal contact. Teasing was a way to interact—and to have fun with interaction—without being dependent on the exchange of information. Teasing also reinforced relationships in the alignments it created between individuals. When adults helped children respond to teasing or invited children to help them tease someone else, they created an additional close and special bond between themselves and the child.

Teasing could also be used as a means of social control. Although many of the adults' threats were not intended seriously (e.g., "I'm not going to love you any more"), there was a thin line between this type of empty threat and other empty threats that children were supposed to believe—or, at least, fear might be true. For example, the adults often warned the children that the police or a witch or the bogeyman might come take them away if they misbehaved.

Finally, teasing is also a linguistic skill that children may have to learn to manipulate to speak like the adult members of their particular cultural group. Learning to participate in teasing and to recognize that one is being teased requires sensitivity to nonverbal cues and an ability to go beyond the surface meaning of a message to determine the intentions of the speaker. Learning to tease without overstepping the boundaries of behavior appropriate for small children requires learning complex social rules. Children have to determine who can be teased and in what contexts. The differences between Marisa's and Nancy's ability to participate in teasing sequences suggest that the ability to play with language in this manner may not be closely related to the child's ability to discover the rules of syntax.

Language use is embedded in a complex system with culturally specific functions and meanings. In order to understand the meaning behind cultural variation in conversation and its effects on development, we must give careful attention to the ways of speaking across societies and the acquisition of both linguistic and sociocultural knowledge that is influenced by those ways of speaking. Since cultural and social values are continually expressed through social interaction, the examination of those interactions can furnish information about the relationship between language and culture and what children are being taught about them.

NOTES

The research for this paper was supported by grant NIE-G-81-0103 from the National Institute of Education. I would like to thank Shirley Brice Heath, Robert Hopper, Bambi Schieffelin, and Elinor Ochs for participating in many conversations about teasing, and Susan Ervin-Tripp and Dan Slobin for their comments on an earlier version of this paper.

The term "Mexicano" is the Spanish word for "Mexican" and was chosen over "Chicano" or "Mexican-American" because all members of the families still thought of themselves as Mexican and called themselves "Mexicano."

REFERENCES

Abrahams, R. D. 1962. Playing the dozens. *Journal of American Folklore* 75:209–220.

Bateson, G. 1972. *Steps to an ecology of mind*. New York: Ballantine.

Bloom, L. M., Lightbown, P. M., & Hood, L. 1974. *Conventions for transcriptions of child language recordings*. Unpublished manuscript. Columbia University.

Blount, B. 1972. Aspects of socialization among the Luo of Kenya. *Language in Society* 1:235–248.

Castro, R. 1982. Mexican women's sexual jokes. *Aztlan* 13:275–294.

Clark, H. H. & Carlson, T. B. 1982. Hearers and speech acts. *Language* 58:1–74.

Coles, R. 1977. *Eskimos, Chicanos, Indians*. Vol. 6 of *Children of crisis*. Boston: Little, Brown.

Eisenberg, A. R. 1982. Language acquisition in cultural perspective: talk in three Mexicano homes. Unpublished Ph.D. dissertation, University of California, Berkeley.

Goffman, E. 1975. *Frame analysis*. New York: Macmillan.

Grice, H. P. 1975. Logic in conversation. In P. Cole & J. P. Morgan, eds., *Syntax and semantics*, vol. 3: *Speech acts*. New York: Academic Press, pp. 41–58.

Gumperz, J. J. 1977. Sociocultural knowledge in conversational inference. In M. Saville-Troike, ed., *Linguistics and anthropology*. Georgetown University Round Table on Languages and Linguistics. Washington, D.C.: Georgetown University Press, pp. 191–212.

Heath, S. B. 1981. Teasing talk: strategies for language learning. Presented at the American Anthropology Association Meeting, Los Angeles, December.

Hopper, R., Sims, A. L., & Alberts, J. K. 1983. Teasing as Daddy's classroom. Presented at the Children Language Conference, Glasgow.

Miller, P. 1986. Teasing a language socialization and verbal play in a white working-class community. in B. Schieffelin & E. Ochs, eds., *Language socialization across cultures*. New York: Cambridge University Press, pp. 199–212.

Radcliffe-Brown, A. R. 1940. On joking relationships. *Africa* 13:195–210.

Schieffelin, B. 1986. Teasing and sharing in Kaluli children's interactions. In B. Schieffelin & E. Ochs, eds., *Language socialization across cultures*. New York: Cambridge University Press, pp. 165–181.

Simmons, L. W., ed. 1942. *Sun Chief: The autobiography of a Hopi Indian*. New Haven: Yale University Press.

English con Salsa

GINA VALDÉS

- -

Editor's introduction

Growing up bilingual often also means living two lives and learning the rules of two cultures. Gina Valdés' poem "English con Salsa" (on p. 242) celebrates the experiences, rhythms, and sounds of that double life.

- - - - - - - - - - -

GLOSSARY FOR "ENGLISH CON SALSA"

inglés con chile y cilantro: English with spice

Benito Juárez: President of Mexico from 1857 to 1863 and from 1867 to 1872

Xochicalco: small town in Mexico

dólares and dolores: dollars and pains

Teocaltiche: town in Mexico

English *refrito:* refried English

English *con sal y limón:* English with salt and lemon

requinto from Uruapán: small guitar from the town of Uruapán

mezcal from Juchitán: a strong liquor made from cactus, in this case from the city of Juchitán

amigos del sur: friends from the south

Zapotec: a specific tribe of Mexican Indians

Nahuatl: the Aztecan language

duendes: goblins or ghostly spirits

Santa Tristeza: Saint Sadness

Santa Alegría: Saint Happiness

Santo Todolopuede: Saint All-Powerful

pollo loco: literally, crazy chicken

chapulines: small children

Mixtec: an adjective describing something particular to the Mexican indigenous people known by the same name

la tierra: the earth

Source: "English con Salsa" by Gina Valdés is reprinted with permission from the publisher of *The Americas Review* Vol. 21 No. 1 (Houston: Arte Publico Press—University of Houston, 1994).

Welcome to ESL 100, English Surely Latinized,
inglés con chile y cilantro, English as American
as Benito Juárez. Welcome, muchachos from Xochicalco,
learn the language of dólares and dolores, of kings
and queens, of Donald Duck and Batman. Holy Toluca!
In four months you'll be speaking like George Washington,
in four weeks you can ask, More coffee? In two months
you can say, May I take your order? In one year you
can ask for a raise, cool as the Tuxpan River.

Welcome, muchachas from Teocaltiche, in this class
we speak English refrito, English con sal y limón,
English thick as mango juice, English poured from
a clay jug, English tuned like a requinto from Uruapán,
English lighted by Oaxacan dawns, English spiked
with mezcal from Juchitán, English with a red cactus
flower blooming in its heart.

Welcome, welcome, amigos del sur, bring your Zapotec
tongues, your Nahuatl tones, your patience of pyramids,
your red suns and golden moons, your guardian angels,
your duendes, your patron saint, Santa Tristeza,
Santa Alegría, Santo Todolopuede. We will sprinkle
holy water on pronouns, make the sign of the cross
on past participles, jump like fish from Lake Pátzcuaro
on gerunds, pour tequila from Jalisco on future perfects,
say shoes and shit, grab a cool verb and a pollo loco
and dance on the walls like chapulines.

When a teacher from La Jolla or a cowboy from Santee
asks you, Do you speak English? You'll answer, Sí,
yes, simón, of course. I love English!

                              And you'll hum
        a Mixtec chant that touches la tierra and the heavens.

Silencing in Public Schools

MICHELLE FINE

....

Editor's introduction

Other authors have explored what is possible when talk in schools is nurtured. Michelle Fine takes a look at the flip side, when adolescents' voices are silenced in schools. The following article looks closely at one of the findings from her disturbing high school ethnography. She examines what happens when students are excluded from the discussion and learn a passive role, burying their own voices.

• • • • • • • • • • • •

Lying is done with words and also with silence.

Adrienne Rich, *On Lies, Secrets and Silence.*

Demands for silencing signify a terror of words, a fear of talk. This essay examines these demands as they echoed through a comprehensive public high school in New York City. The silencing resounded in words and in their absence; the demands emanated from the New York City Board of Education, book publishers, corporate sponsors, religious institutions, administrators, teachers, parents, and students. In the odd study of *what's not said* in public schools, one must be curious about whom silencing protects, but vigilant about how silencing students and their communities undermines fundamentally the vision of education as empowerment (Freire 1985; Shor 1980).

This essay examines what doesn't get talked about in schools and how "undesirable" talk is subverted, appropriated, and exported. In this essay silencing constitutes a process of institutionalized policies and practices which obscure the very social, economic, and therefore experimental conditions of students' daily lives, and which expel from written, oral, and nonverbal expression substantive and critical "talk" about these conditions. Silencing orchestrates the paradoxi-

cal life of institutions such as schools, which are marked as *the* opportunity for mobility when indeed groups are unevenly "mobilized" by the same educational credential, and even more unevenly disabled by its absence. Further, in a city such as New York, dropouts from the wealthiest neighborhoods are systematically more likely to be employed than high school graduates from the poorest neighborhoods (Tobier 1984). Yet simple, seamless pronouncements of equal opportunity and educational credentials as the primary mode of mobility are woven through the curriculum and pedagogy of urban high school classes. Silencing constitutes the process by which contradictory evidence, ideologies, and experiences find themselves buried, camouflaged, and discredited.

While schools are replete with countertensions, including the voices of exposure and critique, the press

---

Source: "Silencing in Public Schools" by M. Fine, 1987, *Language Arts* 64 (2), pp. 157–174. Copyright 1987 by the National Council of Teachers of English. Reprinted with permission.

for silencing pervades low income urban schools. The centralized and tiered structure of educational administration, books used, curriculum generated, pedagogy applied, administrative withholding of data, "objective" mechanisms for evaluating teachers and students, and strategies for excluding parents/guardians and community activists compromise the means by which schools establish themselves as fortresses against low-income communities; students are subverted in their attempts to merge school and home, and conversations are aborted.

Silencing, I would guess, more intimately informs low-income, public schooling than relatively privileged situations. To question from above holds intellectual promise; to question from below forebodes danger. In low-income schools both the process of inquiry into students' lived experience, and the content to be unearthed are assumed to be, a priori, unsafe territory.

Silencing sustains the belief in schooling as the mechanism for social mobility, with contradictory evidence barred. And silencing diverts critique away from the economic, social, and educational institutions which organize class, race, and gender hierarchies. But the silencing process bears not only ideological or cosmetic consequence. These very demands permeate classroom life so primitively as to make irrelevant the lived experiences, passions, concerns, communities, and biographies of low-income, minority students. In the process the very voices of students and their communities that public education claims to nurture, shut down.

This essay focuses on silencing primarily at the level of classroom and school talk in a low-income, "low-skill" school. The corporate, institutional, and bureaucratic mandates from which demands for silencing derive, while acknowledged, remain relatively immune from the present analysis. This is not to locate blame inside classrooms nor with individual teachers, but merely to extract from these interactions the raw material for a critical view of silencing. The data derive from a year-long ethnography of a high school in Manhattan, attended by 3,200 students, predominantly low-income blacks and Hispanics from Central Harlem, and run primarily by black paraprofessionals and aides, white administrators and teachers, with some Hispanic paraprofessionals and teachers (see Fine 1985, 1986).

The analysis seems important for two reasons. First, there is substantial evidence that many students in this school, considered low in skill and motivation, were

eager to choreograph their own learning, to generate a curriculum of lived experience and to engage in a participatory pedagogy. Every attempt, intended or not, to undermine their educational autobiographizing, by teachers or administrators, sacrificed another chance to connect with students and their communities (Bastian, Fruchter, Gittell, Greer & Haskins 1985; Connell, Ashenden, Kessler & Dowsett 1984; Lightfoot 1978). While not overstating the academic energy spontaneously displayed by these adolescents, I would stress that those administrators, teachers, and paraprofessionals sufficiently interested and patient did generate classrooms of relatively "alive" participants. More overwhelming to the observer, however, silencing engulfed life inside the classrooms and administrative offices.

This loss of connection bears significant consequence for low-income, minority students who are fundamentally ambivalent about the educational process and its credentials (Carnoy & Levin 1985). As confident as they were that "you can't get nowhere without a diploma," most were also mindful that "the richest man in my neighborhood didn't graduate but from eighth grade." And, of course, they were not wrong. Each of these two beliefs withstands tests of empirical validity, measured in labor force statistics, as well as experiential validity, confirmed daily on their streets. "Within democratic society, . . . contradictions between the rhetoric of equality and the reality of domination must be obscured" (Cummins 1986, p. 25). And so the process of silencing camouflaged such contradictions, advancing ironically the cynicism of the latter student belief, eroding the idealism of the former.

The silencing process is but one aspect of what is often, for low-income students, an impoverished educational tradition. Infiltrating administrative "talk," curriculum development, and pedagogical technique, the means of silencing establish impenetrable barriers between the worlds of school and community life.

THE IMPULSE TO SILENCE: FEARS OF NAMING

In June of 1984 I decided to spend the following fall and spring conducting an ethnography inside this high school, watching specifically for the production and reproduction of high school graduates and dropouts, not yet interested in anything I would later consider silencing (see Fine 1985, 1986).[1] To my request for entree to his school, the principal greeted me as follows:

Field Note, June 1984.

Mr. Stein: Sure you can do your research on dropouts at this school. With one provision. You can not mention the words "dropping out" to the students.

MF: Why not?

Stein: I firmly believe that if you say it, you encourage them to do it.

My field notes continue, "When he said this, I thought, adults should be so lucky, that adolescents wait for us *to name* dropping out, or sex, for them to do it." From September through June I witnessed daily life inside classrooms, deans' and nurses' offices, the attendance room, and the lunchroom. Over time it struck me as even more naive that the school administrator would believe that what adults say engenders teenage compliance. With so little evidence that adult talk promotes any adolescent compliance, how could one continue to believe that if an authority says it, students will conform; that naming is dangerous and not naming is safe?

As the year transpired, what became apparent was not naivete but a systematic, school-based fear of talk; a special kind of talk which might be called *naming*. Naming gives license to critical conversation about social and economic arrangements, particularly inequitable distributions of power and resources, by which these students and their kin suffer disproportionately. The fear of naming provoked the move to silence.

One can only speculate on this inferred fear of naming. By no means universal, it was, by every measure, commonplace. Let us assume that urban teachers and administrators seek to believe that schooling can make a significant difference, collectively or individually, in the lives of these adolescents. Given that they have little authority to create what they might consider the necessary conditions (see Carnegie Forum on Education and the Economy 1986; Holmes Group 1986), "choices" are undoubtedly made about how to make sense of their work and their presumably limited effec-

tiveness. Not naming fits essentially with how one structures meaning of the work of public education.

With one strategy administrators and teachers viewed most of these students as unteachable, following the logic of social studies teacher Mr. Rosaldo, "If I reach 20 percent, if we save 20 percent, that's a miracle. Most of these kids don't have a chance." While the incidence of this belief remains to be documented, compelling correlational evidence suggests that those teachers who feel most disempowered in their institutions are also most likely to subscribe to such a notion, to agree that "These kids can't be helped" (Fine 1983). Perhaps these teachers have themselves been silenced over time. For them, *naming* social equities in the classroom could only expose social circumstances they believed to be basically self-imposed and diminish the distance between "them" and "us." When I presented the data to the faculty at the end of the year and suggested, for example, that the level of involuntary "discharges" processed through this school would never be tolerated in the schools attended by the faculty's children, I was reminded by a faculty member, "That's an absurd comparison. The schools my kids go to are nothing like this—the comparison is itself sensationalism!" The social distance between "them" and "us" was reified and naturalized.

Other teachers subscribed loyally to beliefs in a color-blind meritocracy. They merely dismissed the empirical data which would have had to inform the process of naming. Here they followed the logic of science teacher Ms. Tannenbaum, "If these students work hard, they can really become something. Especially today with Affirmative Action." They rejected or avoided counterevidence: e.g., that black high school graduates living in Harlem are still far less likely to be employed than white high school dropouts living in more elite sections of New York (Tobier 1984). Enormous energy must be required to sustain beliefs in equal opportunity and the color-blind power of credentials, and to silence nagging losses of faith when evidence to the contrary compels on a daily basis. Naming in such a case would only unmask, fundamentally disrupting or contradicting one's belief system.

But some educators did actively engage their students in lively, critical discourse about the complexities and inequities of prevailing economic and social relations. Often importing politics from other spheres of their lives, the feminist English teacher, the com-

---

[1]This research was made possible by a grant from the W. T. Grant Foundation, New York City, 1984 through 1985.

munity activist who taught grammar, or the Marxist historian wove critical analysis into their classrooms with little effort. These classrooms were permeated with the openness of naming, free of the musty tension which derives from conversations-not-had.

Most educators at this school, however, seemed to survive by not naming or analyzing social problems. They taught the curricula and pedagogical techniques they hoped would soothe students and smooth social contradictions. Many would probably have not considered conversation about social class, gender, or race politics relevant to their courses, or easily integrated into their curricula. One could have assumed, therefore, that they had benignly neglected these topics.

Evidence of *fear*, however, rather than neglect, grew salient when students (activated by curiosity or rebellion) raised topics which were rapidly shut down. A systemic expulsion of dangerous topics permeated the room. I would posit that, to examine power differentials, the very conditions which contribute to insidious social class, racial, ethnic, and gender divisions in the U.S., when the teacher is relatively privileged by class usually and race often, introduces for educators fantasies of danger. Such conversations *problematize* what seem like 'natural' social distinctions, such as the distinction between where one teaches and where one sends one's children to be taught. Such conversations threaten to erode teachers' authority. While usually not by conscious choice, teachers and administrators engaged in diverse strategies to preempt, detour, or ghettoize such conversations. *Not naming*, as a particular form of silencing, was accomplished creatively. Often with good intentions, not naming bore equally devastating consequences.

Naming may indeed be dangerous to beliefs often promoted in public schools; it is for that very reason *essential* to the creation of an empowered and critical constituency of educated social participants (Aronowitz & Giroux 1985). To *not name* bears consequences for all students, but more so for low-income, minority youths. To not name is to systematically alienate, cut off from home, from heritage and from lived experience, and ultimately to sever from their educational process. Following the lead of Adrienne Rich in the opening quote, silencing is examined below through what was said and what was not said in this public school across the academic year 1984–1985, beginning with the obvious, if redundant occurrence of administrative silencing.

ADMINISTRATIVE SILENCING: WHITE NOISE

Field Note: September 1985
We are proud to say that 80 percent of our high school graduates go on to college.
Principal, Parents' Association meeting, September 1985

At the first Parent's Association meeting, Mr. Stein, the principal, boasted an 80 percent "college-bound" rate. Almost all graduates of this inner city high school head for college; a comforting claim oft repeated by urban school administrators in the 1980s. While accurate, the pronouncement fundamentally detoured the conversation away from the fact that in this school, as in others, only 20 percent of incoming ninth graders of 1978–1979 were headed for college by 1985. The "white noise" promoted by the administration reverberated silence in the audience. Not named, and therefore not problematized, was retention. No questions were asked.

Not naming signifies an administrative craft. The New York City Board of Education, for example, refuses to monitor retention, promotion, and educational achievement statistics by race and ethnicity for fear of "appearing racist" (Personal Communication 1984).[2] As a result huge discrepancies in educational advancement, by race and ethnicity, remain undocumented in Board publications. Likewise dropout calculations may include students on register when they have not been seen for months; may presume that students who enroll in GED programs are not dropouts, or that those who produce "working papers" are about to embark on careers (which involves a letter, for example, from a Chicken Delight clerk assuring that José has a job, so that he can leave school at sixteen). Such procedures insidiously contribute to not naming the density of the dropout problem.

While administrative silencing is unfortunately almost a redundant notion, the concerns of this essay are primarily focused on classroom- and school-based activities of silencing. Examining the processes of not naming pedagogically and within the public school cur-

---

[2]Personal communication with employee in the High Schools' Division, New York City Board of Education, in response to inquiry about why New York City does not maintain race/ethnicity-sensitive statistics on dropping out and school achievement.

riculum, the essay ends with the most dramatic embodiment of silencing, the academically mute bodies of those young black teenage girls who say nothing all day, who have perfected the mask of being silenced, who are never identified as a problem.

The remainder of the essay moves from pedagogy to curriculum to discipline as discrete moments in the silencing process.

CLOSING DOWN CONVERSATIONS

Field Note: October 17, Business Class

White teacher: What's EOE?

Black male student: Equal over time.

White teacher: Not quite. Anyone else?

Black female student: Equal Opportunity Employer.

Teacher: That's right.

Black male student (2): What does that mean?

Teacher: That means that an employer can't discriminate on the basis of sex, age, marital status, or race.

Black male student (2): But wait, sometimes white people only hire white people.

Teacher: No, they're not supposed to if they say EOE in their ads. Now take out your homework.

Later that day:

MF: Why don't you discuss racism in your class?

Teacher: It would demoralize the students, they need to feel positive and optimistic—like they have a chance. Racism is just an excuse they use not to try harder.

What enables some teachers to act as if students benefit from such smoothing over (Wexler 1983)? For whose good are the roots, the scars and the structures of class, race, and gender inequity obscured by teachers, texts and tests (Anyon 1983)? Are not the "fears of demoralizing" a projection by teachers of their own silenced loss of faith in public education, and their own fears of unmasking or freeing a conversation about social inequities?

At the level of curriculum, texts, and conversation in classrooms, school talk and knowledge were radically severed from the daily realities of adolescents' lives and more systematically allied with the lives of teachers (McNeil 1981). Routinely discouraged from critically examining the conditions of their lives, dissuaded from creating their own curriculum, built of

what they know, students were often encouraged to disparage the circumstances in which they live, warned by their teachers: "You act like that, and you'll end up on welfare!" Most were or have been surviving on some form of federal, state or city assistance.

"Good students" managed these dual/duel worlds by learning to speak standard English dialect, whether they originally spoke black English, Spanish, or Creole. And more poignant still, they trained themselves to speak and produce in two voices. One's "own" voice alternated with an "academic" voice which denied class, gender, and race conflict; reproduced ideologies about hard work, success, and their "natural" sequence; and stifled the desire to disrupt.

In a study conducted in 1981, it was found that the group of South Bronx students who were "successes"—those who remained in high school—when compared to dropouts, were significantly *more* depressed, *less* politically aware, *less* likely to be assertive in the classroom if they were undergraded, and *more* conformist (Fine 1983)! A moderate level of depression, an absence of political awareness, the presence of self-blame, low-assertiveness, and high conformity may tragically have constituted evidence of the "good" urban students at this high school. They learned not to raise, and indeed to help shut down, "dangerous" conversation. The price of "success" may have been muting one's own voice.

Other students from this school resolved the "two voices" tension with creative, if ultimately self-defeating, strategies. Cheray reflected on this moment of hegemony after she dropped out: "In school we learned Columbus Avenue stuff and *I* had to translate it into Harlem. They think livin' up here is unsafe and our lives are so bad. That we should want to move out and get away. That's what you're supposed to learn."[3]

Tony thoroughly challenged the academic voice as ineffective pedagogy: "I never got math when I was in school. Then I started sellin' dope and runnin' numbers and I picked it up right away. They should teach the way it matters."

Alicia accepted the academic voice as the standard, while disparaging with faint praise what *she* knew: "I'm *wise*, not *smart*. There's a difference. I can walk into a

---

[3]Columbus Avenue, on the upper West Side, has recently become a rapidly gentrified, elite neighborhood in Manhattan, displacing many low-income, particularly black and Hispanic residents.

room and I knows what people be thinkin' and what's goin' down. But not what he be talkin' about in history."

Finally many saw the academic voice as exclusively legitimate, if inaccessible. Monique, after two months out of school, admitted, "I'm scared to go out lookin' for a job. They be usin' words in the interview like in school. Words I don't know. I can't be askin' them for a dictionary. It's like in school. You ask and you feel like a dummy."

By segregating the academic voice from one's own, schools contribute to controversy not only linguistic in form (Zorn 1982). The intellectual, social, and emotional substance which constitutes minority students' lives was routinely treated as irrelevant, to be displaced and silenced. Their responses, spanning acquiescence to resistance, bore serious consequence.

CONTRADICTIONS FOLDED: THE PEDAGOGICAL CREATION OF DICHOTOMIES

If "lived talk" was actively expelled on the basis of content, contradictory talk was basically rendered impossible. Social contradictions were folded into dichotomous choices. Again, one can only speculate on whom this accommodates, but the creation of dichotomies and the reification of single truths does much to bolster educators' control, enforcing an explicit distance between those who *know* and those who don't; discrediting often those who *think* (McNeil 1981).

In early spring, a social studies teacher structured an in-class debate on Bernard Goetz—New York City's "subway vigilante." She invited "those students who agree with Goetz to sit on one side of the room, and those who think he was wrong to sit on the other side." To the large residual group who remained midroom the teacher remarked, "Don't be lazy. You have to make a decision. Like at work, you can't be passive." A few wandered over to the "pro-Goetz" side. About six remained in the center. Somewhat angry, the teacher continued: "Ok, first we'll hear the pro-Goetz side and then the anti-Goetz side. Those of you who have no opinion, who haven't even thought about the issue, you won't get to talk unless we have time."

Deidre, a black senior, bright and always quick to raise contradictions otherwise obscured, advocated the legitimacy of the middle group. "It's not that I have no opinions. I don't like Goetz shootin' up people who look like my brother, but I don't like feelin' unsafe in

the projects or in my neighborhood either. I got lots of opinions. I ain't bein' quiet 'cause I can't decide if he's right or wrong. I'm talkin'."

Deidre's comment legitimized for herself and others the right to hold complex, perhaps even contradictory positions on a complex situation. Such legitimacy was rarely granted by faculty—with clear and important exceptions including activist faculty and paraprofessionals who lived in central Harlem with the kids, who understood and respected much about their lives.

Among the chorus of voices heard within this high school, then, lay little room for Gramsci's (1971) contradictory consciousness. Artificial dichotomies were understood as received and natural: right and wrong answers, good and bad behavior, moral and immoral people, dumb and smart students, responsible and irresponsible parents, good and bad neighbors. Contradiction and ambivalence, forced underground, were experienced often, if only expressed rarely.

I asked Ronald, a student in remedial reading class, why he stayed in school. He responded with the sophistication and complexity the question deserved, "Reason I stay in school is 'cause every time I get on the subway I see this drunk and I think 'not me.' But then I think 'bet he has a high school degree.'" The power of his statement lies in its honesty, as well as the infrequency with which such comments were voiced. Ronald explained that he expected support for his position neither on the street nor in the school. School talk filled youths with promises that few believed, but many repeated: the promises of hard work, education, and success; warnings about welfare. Street talk belied another reality, described by Shondra, "They be sayin, 'What you doin' in school? Could be out here scramblin' [selling drugs] and makin' money now. That degree ain't gonna get you nothing better.'"

When black adolescent high school graduates, in the October following graduation, suffered a 56 percent unemployment rate and black adolescent high school dropouts suffered a 70 percent unemployment rate, the very contradictions which remained unspoken within school were amplified in the minds and worries of these young men and women (Young 1983).

CONVERSATIONS PSYCHOLOGIZED: THE CURRICULUM SPLITS THE PERSONAL AND THE SOCIAL

Some conversations within the schools were closed; others were dichotomized. Yet a few conversations, indeed those most relevant to socioeconomic arrangements and inequities, remained psychologized. The topics were managed exclusively as personal problems inside the offices of school psychologists or counselors. The lived experiences of *all* adolescents, and particularly those surviving city life in poverty, place their physical and mental well-being as well as that of their kin in constant jeopardy. And yet conversations about these were conditions of life, about alcoholism, drug abuse, domestic violence, environmental hazards, gentrification, and poor health—to the extent that they happened at all—remained confined to individual sessions with counselors (for those lucky enough to gain hearing with a counselor in the 800–1 ratio, and gutsy enough to raise the issue) or, if made academic, were raised in hygiene class (for those fortunate enough to have made it to twelfth grade when hygiene was offered). A biology teacher, one of the few black teachers in the school, actually integrated creative writing assignments such as "My life as an alcoholic" and "My life as the child of an alcoholic" into her biology class curriculum. Her department chairman reprimanded her severely for introducing "extraneous materials" into her classroom. Teachers, too, were silenced.

The prevalence of health and social problems experienced by these adolescents, and their curricular marginalization, exemplified a rigid academic unwillingness to address these concerns, in social studies, science, English, or even math. A harsh resistance to name the lived experiences of these teens paralleled the unwillingness to integrate these experiences as the substance of learning. Issues to be avoided at all costs, they were addressed only once they dramatically pierced the life of an adolescent who sought help.

The offices of school psychologists or counselors therefore became the primary sites for addressing what were indeed social concerns, should have been academic concerns, and were most likely to be managed as personal and private concerns. The curricular privatizing and psychologizing of public and political issues served to reinforce the alienation of students' lives from their educational experiences, made worse only by those conversations never had.

CONVERSATIONS NEVER HAD

A mechanistic view of teachers terrorized of naming and students passively accommodating could not be further from the daily realities of life inside a public high school. Many teachers name and critique, although most don't. Some students passively shut down, but most remain alive and even resistant. Classrooms are filled with students wearing Walkmans, conversing among themselves and with friends in the halls, and some even persistently challenging the experiences and expertise of their teachers. But the typical classroom still values silence, control, and quiet, as John Goodlad (1984), Theodore Sizer (1985), Jean Anyon (1983), and others have documented. The insidious push toward silence in low-income schools became most clear sometime after my interview with Eartha, a sixteen-year-old high school dropout.

> MF: Eartha, when you were a kid, did you participate a lot in school?
> *Eartha:* Not me, I was a good kid. Made no trouble.

I asked this question of fifty-five high school dropouts. After the third responded as Eartha did, I realized that for me, participation was encouraged, delighted in, and a measure of the "good student." For these adolescents, given their contexts of schooling, "participation" signified poor discipline and rude classroom behavior.

Students learned the dangers of talk, the codes of participating and not, and they learned, in more nuanced ways, which conversations were never to be initiated. In Philadelphia a young high school student explained to me: "We ain't allowed to talk about abortion. They tell us we can't discuss it no way." When I asked a School District Administrator about this policy, she qualified: "It's not that they can't talk about it. The teacher, if the topic is raised by a student, can define abortion, just not discuss it beyond that." This distinction between *define* and *discuss* makes sense only if education signifies teacher authority, and control implies silence. Perhaps this is why classroom control often feels so fragile. Control through omission *is* fragile, fully contingent on students' willingness to collude and "play" at not naming. While it ostensibly postures teacher authority, it actually betrays a plea for student compliance.

Silence comes in many forms. Conversations can be closed by teachers, or forestalled by student compliance. But other conversations are expressly subverted, never had. A policy of enforced silencing was applied to information about the severe economic and social consequences of dropping out of high school. This information was systematically withheld from students who are being discharged. When students were discharged in New York State—a "choice" available to few middle-class, particularly white students—they were guaranteed an exit interview, which, in most cases, involved an attendance officer who asked students what they planned to do, and then requested a meeting with a parent/guardian to sign official documents. The officer handed the student a list of GED/outreach programs. The student left, often eager to find work, get a GED, go to a private business school, or join the military. Informed conversations about the consequences of the students' decision are not legally mandated. As they left, these adolescents *did not learn:*

- that over 50 percent of black high school dropouts suffer unemployment in cities like New York City (U.S. Commission on Civil Rights 1982);

- that 48 percent of New Yorkers who sit for the Graduate Equivalency Diploma test fail (New York State Department of Education 1985);

- that private trade schools, including cosmetology, beautician, and business schools have been charged with unethical recruitment practices, exploitation of students, earning more from students who drop out than those who stay, not providing promised jobs and having, on average, a 70 percent dropout rate (see Fine 1986);

- that the military, during "peacetime," refuses to accept females with no high school degree, and only reluctantly accepts such males, who suffer an extremely high rate of less-than-honorable discharge within six months of enlistment (Militarism Resource Project 1985).

Students were thereby denied informed consent if they left high school prior to graduation. These conversations-not-had failed to correct and therefore nurtured powerful beliefs that "the GED is no sweat, a piece of cake"; that "you can get jobs, they promise, after goin' to Sutton or ABI"; or that "in the Army I can get me a GED, skills, travel, benefits. . . . "

MAINTAINING SILENCE THROUGH DEMOCRACY AND DISCIPLINE

Means of maintaining silences and assuring no dangerous disruptions know few bounds. One institutionalized strategy involves the appropriation of internal dissent, framed as democracy for parents and students. This strategy is increasingly popular in this era of rhetorical "empowerment."

At this school the Parents' Association executive board was comprised of ten parents: eight black women, one black man, and one white woman. Eight no longer had children attending the school. At about midyear teachers were demanding smaller class size. So too was the President of the Parents' Association at this Executive meeting with the Principal.

President: I'm concerned about class size. Carol Bellamy (City Council President) notified us that you received monies earmarked to reduce class size and yet what have you done?

Mr. Stein: Quinones (Schools Chancellor) promised no high school class greater than 34 by February. That's impossible! What he is asking I can't guarantee unless *you* tell me how to do it. If I reduce class size, I must eliminate all specialized classes, all electives. Even then I can't guarantee. To accede to Quinones, that classes be less than 34, we must eliminate the elective in English, in social studies, all art classes, eleventh year math, physics, accounting, wordprocessing. We were going to offer a Haitian Patois bilingual program, fourth year French, a museums program, bio-pre-med, health careers, coop and pre-coop, choreography and advanced ballet. The nature of the school will be changed fundamentally.

We won't be able to call this an academic high school, only a program for slow learners.

Woman (1): Those are very important classes.

Stein: I am willing to keep these classes. Parents want me to keep these classes. That's where I'm at.

Woman (2): What is the average?

Stein: Thirty-three.

Woman (1): Are any classes over forty?

Stein: No, except if it's a *Singleton* class—the only one offered. If these courses weren't important, we wouldn't keep them. You know we always work together. If it's your feeling we should not eliminate all electives and maintain things, OK! Any comments?

Woman (1): I think continue. Youngsters aren't getting enough now. And the teachers will not any more.

Woman (3): You have our unanimous consent and support.

Stein: When I talk to the Board of Education, I'll say I'm talking for the parents.

Woman (4): I think it's impossible to teach forty.

Stein: We have a space problem. Any other issues?

An equally conciliatory student council was constituted to decide on student activities, prom arrangements, and student fees. They were largely pleased to meet in the principal's office.

At the level of critique, silence was guaranteed by the selection of and then democratic participation of individuals within "constituency-based groups."

If dissent was appropriated through mechanisms of democracy, it was exported through mechanisms of discipline. The most effective procedure for silencing was to banish the source of dissent, tallied in the school's dropout rate. As indicated by the South Bronx study referred to above (Fine 1983), and the research of others (Elliott, Voss & Wendling 1966; Felice 1981; Fine & Rosenberg 1983), it is often the academic critic resisting the intellectual and verbal girdles of schooling who "drops out" or is pushed out of low-income schools. Extraordinary rates of suspensions, expulsions, and discharges experienced by black and Hispanic youths speak to this form of silencing (Advocates for Children 1985). Estimates of urban dropout rates range from approximately 42 percent for New York City, Boston, and Chicago Boards of Education to 68–80 percent from Aspira, an educational advocacy organization (1983).

At the school which served as the site for this ethnographic research, a 66 percent dropout rate was calculated. Two-thirds of the students who began ninth grade in 1978–79 did not receive diplomas nor degrees by June 1985. I presented these findings to a collection of deans, advisors, counselors, administrators, and teachers, many of whom were the sponsors and executors of the discharge process. At first I met with total silence. A dean then explained, "These kids need to be out. It's unfair to the rest. My job is like a pilot on a hijacked plane. My job is to throw the hijacker overboard." The one black woman in the room, a guidance counselor, followed: "What Michelle is saying is true. We do throw students out of here and deny them their education. Black kids especially." Two white male administrators interrupted, chiding the "liberal tendencies" of guidance counselors, who, as they put it, "don't see how really dangerous these kids are." The meeting ended.

Dissent was institutionally "democraticized," exported, trivialized, or bureaucratized. These mechanisms made it unlikely for change or challenge to be given a serious hearing.

WHISPERS OF RESISTANCE: THE SILENCED SPEAK

In non-elite public high schools organized around control through silence, the student, teacher, or paraprofessional who talks, who tells or who wants to speak, transforms rapidly into the subversive, the trouble maker. The speaking student, unless she or he spoke in an honors class or affected the academic mode of imputing nondangerous topics and benign words, unless protected by wealth, influential parents, or an unusual capacity to be both critic *and* good student, emerged as provocateur. Depending on school, circumstance, and style, the students' response to silence varied. She may have buried herself in mute isolation. He may have been promoted to resist or organize other students. But most of these youths, for complex reasons, were ultimately propelled to flee prior to graduation. Some then sought "alternative contexts" in which their strengths, their competencies, and their voices could flourish on their own terms:

[Hector's a subway graffiti artist:] It's like an experience you never get. You're on the subway tracks. It's 3:00 A.M., dark, cold and scary. You're trying to create your best. The cops can come to bust you, or you could fall on the electric third rail. My friend died when he dropped his spray paint on that rail. It exploded. He died and I watched. It's awesome, intense. A peak moment when you can't concentrate on nothin', no problems, just creation. And it's like a family. When Michael Stewart [graffiti artist] was killed by cops, you know he was a graffiti man, we all came out of retirement to mourn him. Even me, I stopped 'cause my girl said it was dangerous. We came out and painted funeral scenes and cemeteries on the #1 and the N [subway lines]. For Michael. We know each other, you know an artist when you see him: It's a family. Belonging. They want me in, not out like at school.

Carmen pursued the Job Corps when she left school: You ever try plastering, Michelle? It's great. You see holes in walls. You see a problem and you fix it. Job Corps lost its money when I was in it, in Albany. I had to come home, back to Harlem. I felt better there than ever in my school. Now I do nothin'. It's a shame. Never felt as good as then.

Monique got pregnant and then dropped out: I wasn't never good at nothing. In school I felt stupid and older than the rest. But I'm a great mother to Chita. Catholic schools for my baby, and maybe a house in New Jersey.

Carlos, who left school at age twenty, after a frustrating five years since he and his parents exiled illegally from Mexico hopes to join the military: I don't want to kill nobody. Just, you know how they advertise, the Marines. I never been one of the Few and the Proud. I'm always 'shamed of myself. So I'd like to try it.

In an uninviting economy, these adolescents responded to the silences transmitted through public schooling by pursuing what they considered to be creative alternatives. But let us understand that for such low-income youths, these alternatives generally *replaced* formal schooling. Creative alternatives for middle-class adolescents, an after-school art class or music lessons, privately afforded by parents, generally *supplement* formal schooling.

Whereas school-imposed silence may be an *initiation* to adulthood for the middle-class adolescent about to embark on a life of participation and agency, school-imposed silence more typically represents the *orientation* to adulthood for the low-income or working-class adolescent about to embark on a life of work at McDonald's, in a factory, as a domestic or clerk, or on Aid to Families with Dependent Children. For the low-income student, the imposed silence of high school cannot be ignored as a necessary means to an end. They are the present *and* they are likely to be the future (Ogbu 1978).

Some teachers, paraprofessionals, and students expressly devoted their time, energy, and classes to exposing silences institutionally imposed. One reading teacher prepared original grammar worksheets, including items such as "Most women in Puerto Rico (is, are) oppressed." A history teacher dramatically presented his autobiography to his class, woven with details on the life of Paul Robeson. An English teacher formed a writers' collective of her multilingual "remedial" writing students. A paraprofessional spoke openly with students who decided not to report the prime suspect in a local murder to the police, but to clergy instead. She recognized that their lives would be in jeopardy, despite "what the administrators who go home to the suburbs preach." But these voices of naming were weak, individual, and isolated.

What if these voices, along with the chorus of dropouts, were allowed expression? If they were not whispered, isolated, or drowned out in disparagement, what would happen if these stories were solicited, celebrated, and woven into a curriculum? What if the history of schooling were written by those high school critics who remained in school and those who dropped out? What if the "dropout problem" were studied in school as a collective critique by consumers of public education?

Dropping out instead is viewed by educators, policy makers, teachers, and often students as an individual act, an expression of incompetence or self-sabotage. As alive, motivated, and critical as they were at age seventeen, most of the interviewed dropouts were silenced, withdrawn, and depressed by age twenty-two. They had tried the private trade schools, been in and out of the military, failed the GED exam once more, had too many children to care for, too many bills to pay, and only self-blaming regrets, seeking private solutions to public problems. Muting by the larger society had ultimately succeeded, even for those who fled initially with resistance, energy, and vision (Apple 1982).

I'll end with an image which occurred throughout the year, repeated across classrooms and across urban public high schools. As familiar as it is haunting, the portrait most dramatically captures the physical embodiment of silencing in the urban schools.

Field Note: February 16

Patrice is a young black female, in eleventh grade. She says nothing all day in school. She sits perfectly mute. No need to coerce her into silence. She often wears her coat in class. Sometimes she lays her head on her desk. She never disrupts. Never disobeys. Never speaks. And is never identified as a problem. Is she the student who couldn't develop two voices and so silenced both? Is she so filled with anger, she fears to speak? Or so filled with depression she knows not what to say?

Whose problem is Patrice?

POSTSCRIPT ON RESEARCH AS EXPOSING

The process of conducting research within schools to identify words that could have been said, talk that should have been nurtured, and information that needed to be announced, suffers from voyeurism and perhaps the worst of post hoc arrogance. The researcher's sadistic pleasure of spotting another teacher's collapsed contradiction, aborted analysis, or silencing sentence was moderated only by the ever-present knowledge that similar analytic surgery could easily be performed on my own classes.

And yet it is the very 'naturalness' of not naming, of shutting down or marginalizing conversations for the 'sake of getting on with learning' that demands educators' attention. Particularly so for low-income youths highly ambivalent about the worth of a diploma, desperately desirous of and at the same time discouraged from its achievement.

If the process of education is to allow children, adolescents, and adults their voices—to read, write, create, critique, and transform—how can we justify the insitutionalizing of silence at the level of policies which obscure systemic problems behind a rhetoric of "excellence" and "progress," a curriculum bereft of the lived experiences of students themselves, a pedagogy organized around control and not conversation, and a thoroughgoing psychologizing of social issues which enables Patrice to bury herself in silence and not be noticed?

A self-critical analysis of the fundamental ways in which we teach children to betray their own voices is crucial.

REFERENCES

Advocates for Children. *Report of the New York Hearings on the Crisis in Public Education.* New York, 1985.

Anyon, J. "Intersections of Gender and Class: Accommodation and Resistance by Working Class and Affluent Females to Contradictory Sex Role Ideologies." In *Gender, Class and Education,* edited by S. Walker and L. Barton. London: Falmer Press.

Anyon, J. "School Curriculum: Political and Economic Structure and Social Change." *Social Practice,* (1980): 96–108.

Apple, M. *Cultural and Economic Reproduction in Education.* Boston: Routledge & Kegan Paul, 1982.

Aronowitz, S., & Giroux, H. *Education under Siege.* South Hadley, Massachusetts: Bergin & Garvey, Inc., 1985.

Aspira, *Racial and Ethnic High School Dropout Rates in New York City: A Summary Report.* New York, New York, 1983.

Bastian, A., Fruchter, N., Gittell, M., Greer, C., and Haskins, K. "Choosing Equality: The Case for Democratic Schooling." *Social Policy,* (1985): 35–51.

Carnegie Forum on Education and the Economy. *A Nation Prepared: Teachers for the 21st Century.* New York: Carnegie Foundation, 1986.

Carnoy, M., and Levin, H. *Schooling and Work in the Democratic State.* Stanford: Stanford University Press, 1985.

Connell, R., Ashenden, D., Kessler, S., & Dawsett, G. *Making the Difference.* Sydney, Australia: George Allen & Unwin, 1982.

Cummins, J. "Empowering Minority Students: A Framework for Intervention." *Harvard Education Review,* 56 (1986).

Elliott, D., Voss, H., & Wendling, A. "Capable Dropouts and the Social Milieu of High School." *Journal of Educational Research,* 60 (1966): 180–186.

Felice, L. "Black Student Dropout Behaviors: Disengagement from School Rejection and Racial Discrimination." *Journal of Negro Education,* 50 (1981): 415–424.

Fine, M. "Perspectives on Inequity: Voices from Urban Schools." In *Applied Social Psychology Annual IV,* edited by L. Bickman. Beverly Hills: Sage, 1983.

Fine, M. "Dropping out of High School: An Inside Look." *Social Policy,* (1985): 43–50.

Fine, M. "Why Urban Adolescents Drop into and out of Public High School." *Teachers College Record,* 87 (1986).

Fine, M., & Rosenberg, P. "Dropping Out of High School: The Ideology of School and Work." *Journal of Education,* 165 (1983): 257–272.

Freire, P. *The Politics of Education.* South Hadley, Massachusetts: Bergin & Garvey Publishers, 1985.

Goodlad, J. *A Place called School: Prospects for the Future.* New York: McGraw Hill, 1984.

Gramsci, A. *Selections from Prison Notebooks.* New York: International, 1971.

Holmes Group. *Tomorrow's Teachers.* East Lansing, Michigan, 1986.

Lightfoot, S. *Worlds Apart.* New York. Basic Books, 1978.

McNeil, L. "Negotiating Classroom Knowledge: Beyond Achievement and Socialization." *Curriculum Studies,* 13 (1981): 313–328.

Militarism Resource Project. *High School Military Recruiting: Recent Developments.* Philadelphia, PA, 1985.

New York State Department of Education. Memo from Dennis Hughes, State Administrator on High School Equivalency Programs. December 4, 1985. Albany, NY.

Ogbu, J. *Minority Education and Caste: The American System in Cross-cultural Perspective.* New York: Academic Press, 1978.

Rich, A. *On Lies, Secrets and Silence.* New York. Norton Books, 1979.

Shor, I. *Critical Teaching and Everyday Life.* Boston: South End Press, 1980.

Sizer, T. *Horaces Compromise: The Dilemma of the American High School.* Boston: Houghton Mifflin, 1985.

Tobier, E. *The Changing Face of Poverty: Trends in New York City's Population in Poverty, 1960–1990*. New York, New York: Community Service Society, 1984.

U.S. Commission on Civil Rights. *Unemployment and Underemployment among Blacks, Hispanics and Women*. Washington, D.C., 1982.

U.S. Department of Labor. *Time of Change: 1983 Handbook of Women Workers*. Washington, D.C., 1983.

Wexler, P. *Critical Social Psychology*. Boston: Routledge & Kegan Paul, 1983.

Young, A. Youth Labor Force Marked Turning Point in 1982. U.S. Department of Labor. Bureau of Labor Statistics, Washington, DC., 1983.

Zorn, J. "Black English and the King Decision." *College English*, 44 (1982).

Black Students, Language, and Classroom Teachers

Darwin Turner   *University of Iowa, Iowa City*

Editor's introduction

Darwin Turner examines the resolutions passed by language organizations to affirm the right of students to use their own language without penalty in their classrooms. He contends that teachers who wish to put this resolution into practice must understand some basic facts about black English. In this article, he imparts those important facts, shares compelling anecdotes—and explodes a few myths along the way.

Since the late 1960s, linguists and teachers have focused increased attention on a dialect which has been labeled "black English." During the middle 1970s, the Conference on College Composition and Communication (CCCC) and the National Council of Teachers of English (NCTE) passed resolutions affirming the right of students to use their own language without penalty in the classroom. In 1980–81, the document again received attention. Many teachers assume the cause-and-effect relationship of the first two statements to be greater than it is. Such teachers forget the many NCTE meetings during which a white, and sometimes isolated, linguist—James Sledd—berated those who would require a southern white child—or any child—to change a language pattern learned in the home. Many more teachers are confused by the issues and even more by the rhetoric with which the issues have been debated. I wish to discuss these matters briefly and anecdotally with minimal documentation.

Although I began by linking the resolution on the students' right to their own language with the topic of black English, I must separate them in order to sum- marize each clearly. For those of you who may have forgotten, the resolution reads:

> We affirm the students' right to their own patterns and varieties of language—the dialects of their nurture or whatever dialects in which they find their own identity and style. Language scholars long ago denied that the myth of a standard American dialect has any validity. The claim that any one dialect is unacceptable amounts to an attempt of one social group to exert its dominance over another. Such a claim leads to false advice for speakers and writers, and immoral advice for humans. A nation proud of its diverse heritage and its cultural and racial variety will preserve its heritage and dialects. We affirm strongly that teachers

Source: "Black Students, Language and Classroom Teachers" by D. T. Turner, 1985. In *Tapping Potential: English and Language Arts for the Black Learner* (pp. 30–40), C. K. Brooks, Ed., Urbana, IL: NCTE. Copyright 1985 by the National Council of Teachers of English. Reprinted with permission.

must have the experiences and training that will enable them to respect diversity and uphold the right of students to their own language (Committee on CCCC Language Statement 1974, 2–3).

Despite my own memories of Sledd's urgings, I must admit that I suspect that most English teachers who supported the resolution believed it applied only to Blacks, Chicanos, and Puerto Ricans. It is also true that black teachers endorsed the resolution. Essentially, I believe these teachers came from two groups. One group consisted of a number of blacks who, gaining self-esteem during the 1960s, sought to strengthen that identity by basing it on a language of black people, a language different from that of the Anglo-American oppressor. While some blacks sought to learn African languages, other blacks, dismayed by the impossibility of determining which African tongue identified their ancestors, established their relationships with the Afro-American masses by affirming the language of the ghetto, the language of the masses—even before they had fully determined the characteristics of that language or dialect. The desire was laudable; a people should have a language, and Afro-Americans are the only American people who cannot point to a language, dialect, or brogue as that of their ancestors.

Convinced that racism permeates education and cynically convinced that most teachers have no interest in teaching, a second group contended that most English teachers do not improve the writing of students. They merely pass the students from grade to grade. If white students are treated so cavalierly, the argument continued, then why should black students be failed merely because their illiteracy is different from the illiteracy of white students who pass? Although I have not yet descended to this level of cynicism about English teachers (I am fairly far down but not quite there), I see again a validity in the argument. Certainly, every time Henry Kissinger mispronounces English words, I shudder to think how English teachers would evaluate the intelligence of a black student who mispronounced the language so badly.

Even though I joined these groups finally to vote for the resolution, I worried then, and worry now, whether it might not cause more harm than good for black students. I suspected that most teachers would not read or remember the generally thoughtful background statement on which the resolution was based.

THE FORGOTTEN PASSAGES

Let me remind you of a few passages that I feared most teachers would never read.

American schools and colleges have, in the last decade, been forced to take a stand on a basic educational question: what should the schools do about the language habits of students who come from a wide variety of social, economic, and cultural backgrounds? The question is not new. Differences in language have always existed, and the schools have always wrestled with them, but the social upheavals of the 1960s, and the insistence of submerged minorities on a greater share in American society, have posed the question more insistently and have suggested the need for a shift in emphasis in providing answers. Should the schools try to uphold language variety, or to modify it, or to eradicate it?

. . . . The training of most English teachers has concentrated on the appreciation and analysis of literature, rather than on an understanding of the nature of language, and many teachers are, in consequence, forced to take a position on an aspect of their discipline about which they have little real information.

And if teachers are often uninformed, or misinformed, on the subject of language, the general public is even more ignorant. Lack of reliable information, however, seldom prevents people from discussing language questions with an air of absolute authority. Historians, mathematicians, and nurses all hold decided views on just what English teachers should be requiring. And through their representatives on Boards of Education and Boards of Regents, businessmen, politicians, parents, and the students themselves insist that the values taught by the schools must reflect the prejudices held by the public. The English profession, then, faces a dilemma: until public attitudes can be changed—and it is worth remembering that the past teaching in English classes has been largely responsible for those attitudes—shall we place our emphasis on what the vocal elements of the public think it wants or on what the actual available linguistic evidence indicates we should emphasize? Shall we blame the business world by saying, "Well, we realize that human beings use language in a wide variety of ways, but employers demand a single variety"?

. . . . We need to know whether "standard English" is or is not in some sense a myth. We have ignored, many of us, the distinction between speech and writing and have taught the language as though the *talk* in any region, even the talk of speakers with prestige and power, were identical to edited *written* English.

. . . . We need to ask ourselves whether our rejection of students who do not adopt the dialect most familiar to us is based on any real merit in our dialect or whether we are actually rejecting the students themselves, rejecting them because of their racial, social, and cultural origins.

. . . . An employer may have a southern drawl and pronounce "think" like "thank," but he will write *think*. He may say "y'all" and be considered charming for his quaint southernisms, but he will write *you*. He may even in a "down home" moment ask, "Now how come th' mail orda d'partment d'nt orda fo' cases steada five?" But he'll write the question in EAE [Edited American English]. Therefore it is necessary that we inform those students who are preparing themselves for occupations that demand formal writing that they will be expected to write EAE. But it is one thing to help a student achieve proficiency in a written dialect and another thing to punish him for using variant expressions of that dialect.

Students who want to write EAE will have to learn the forms identified with that dialect as additional options to the forms they already control (Committee on CCCC Language Statement 1974, 1–15).

I suspected that many teachers would use the resolution merely as an excuse for abdicating the responsibility of teaching black students anything about language. (Perhaps, like the second group of blacks, I am sufficiently cynical that I suspect that many white teachers do not care whether black students learn.)

Let me illustrate by quoting a white teacher. Disregard the content. Merely consider the vocabulary, construction, and such.

My first quarrel with such a program is that it does not develop the ability of a person to use language which I would further define as performance capability in a variety of social contexts on a variety of subject matter. Instead, we utilize valuable time to set up drill exercises which are designed to get the individual to replace socially stigmatized forms with socially preferred ones. I cannot endorse as valid a program that sacrifices individual language growth in exchange for some nebulous and highly problematic "social security." The child comes to us with some ability to play the horn and no ability to play the piano. This type of program presumes that a mediocre ability to play the piano is to be preferred to a better than average ability to play the horn. I cannot accept this thesis.

The author expresses his disbelief that there is any value in teaching blacks to use standard English. But I strongly doubt that the author emerged from his mother's womb writing language on the level of the passage that I have quoted. Nor do I believe that he taught himself entirely. Someone taught him. If students are to be permitted to use their own language, teachers, as the NCTE resolution says, must have a knowledge of the students' dialect so that they can help students improve communication.

The idea that teachers should learn more than one dialect was regarded as heresy by some of the linguists in NCTE. They felt that teachers need to know only standard English. Obviously they had paid no attention to the young white teacher who, after a brief term of teaching black students, complained that she could not understand them: " . . . Their language was not so different from mine, but their inflections, intonations, expressions, and lack of what is referred to as standard English threw me."

The CCC background statement asserts, correctly or incorrectly,

. . . when speakers of a dialect of American English claim not to understand speakers of another dialect of the same language, the impediments are likely to be attitudinal. What is really the hearer's resistance to any unfamiliar form may be interpreted as the speaker's fault . . . When asked to respond to the content, they may be unable to do so and may accuse the speaker of being impossible to understand (Committee on CCCC Language Statement, 1974, 4).

Whether or not the teacher resisted for psychological reasons, the fact is that she did not understand the language being used by the children. Furthermore, she arrogantly assumed that they understood her dialect; she even believed, I suppose, that they would understand that, when she said "threw me," she meant "confused me."

I would suggest that such a teacher cannot help students improve in their own dialect. Without such knowledge, this teacher, if she adopts the resolution, will be merely ignoring the black students because she is persuaded that they cannot learn English, or she will be assuring herself that they—unlike most human beings—come to the first grade writing and speaking their English flawlessly. (Does it not impress anyone as strange that, while one group of Americans led by Shockley and Jensen still seeks to define blacks as intellectually inferior, another group unintentionally implies that they have a phenomenal mastery of their language?)

Since I contend that teachers who wish to adopt the CCCC/NCTE resolution must understand some basic facts about black English, let me focus the remainder of my discussion on a few facts and myths about that dialect.

For a description of "black English," I refer you cautiously to J. L. Dillard's *Black English* (1973), and even more cautiously to *Black Language Reader*, edited by Robert Bentley and Samuel Crawford (1973). Both books suffer from weaknesses. The essays in the second book range from insight to asininity. Nevertheless, both provide a description of such deviations from edited American English as eliding medial consonants in pronunciation ("tied" for "tired"), omitting the present tense verb from sentences ("He heah now"), using the verb "be" to indicate a continuing state ("He be workin' on his lessons for four years"), omitting the verbal affixes *s*, *ed*, and so on.

In brief digression, let me say that I strongly doubt that many black Americans exhibit *all* of the variations identified with black English. Hence, the teacher looking for a perfect example of the black-English user may be disillusioned or may create one. There is, however, a more serious problem in identifying users of black English.

I started to begin this part of the discussion in the following manner: "I glad I here, but I be real confuse bout this subjick—black English—dat evuhbody be talkin bout." By delivering a few words in what I hope is an approximation of the so-called black English, I hope that I have shown that I am not trying to evade my racial identity, pretend to be middle-class, or

whatever it is that black people are supposed to be doing when they do not speak black English. Now that I have affirmed my identity as a black, please excuse me if I continue the remainder of this discussion in that language which I learned first from my mother who, a college graduate, was black inside as well as outside; that language which I learned also from two black adults who sometimes tended me during the day. Although they were rural and southern-born, they did not speak "black" English—probably because they did not know that they were expected to.

I would have begun in this somewhat bizarre manner because I am well aware that some people are so convinced that black English is the native voice of all blacks that they often hurl four allegations into the faces of blacks who protest against that assumption: The first allegation is that, as even Dillard states, eighty percent of the black people in the country use black English. (I do not know how he arrived at this figure, since I strongly doubt that even pollsters have interviewed eighty percent of black America.) The second allegation is that, since four-fifths of black Americans speak black English, any who do not have educated themselves away from their black heritage in an effort to become middle-class Americans. The third is that, since the first two allegations are true, any black American who denies them must be defensively trying to guard blacks against the assumption that their intellectual inferiority is evidenced by their language. The fourth is that, if the unconvinced black is sincere, he or she is a middle-class black who is separated from other blacks, or she or he lacks the linguists' facility for listening to speech.

I warned you that I would be anecdotal; I must also be personal. Most of these allegations, which have been printed in professional journals and books, are made by white scholars and teachers who know so little about blacks that these scholars and teachers make sense only to other equally unknowledgeable people.

Let us consider the four allegations in terms of my own experience as a black person who has lived in this country almost one-half century and who can talk about personal relationships with other blacks who date back another half-century: I have already questioned the first allegation—that four-fifths of black Americans speak and must write black English. I have never taught in high school, but I have taught more than a quarter of a century in black colleges in Georgia, Florida, North Carolina, and Maryland; and have taught black college students reared in many different states. Of the four characteristics I have echoed as distinctive of black language, the only one which I have found significant in teaching composition is the failure to affix *s* and *ed*. (Most of the sentence fragments that I have seen in students' writing do not result from the omission of a verb but from another cause.)

The second allegation—that blacks who do not speak black English are trying to be middle-class or to evade their racial identity—undoubtedly characterizes some blacks. Almost any statement about human beings characterizes some blacks. In my own life, however, I recall that in college I tried to be more colloquial and imprecise in English so that I would not embarrass my white classmates who did not use English as effectively. (Incidentally, until I entered the ninth grade, all of my teachers and classmates were black.)

The third allegation is that blacks who are conservative about black English are being defensive. Maybe some are. Most are not. The fourth is that, if sincere, they do not know other blacks. Can you imagine how absurd this allegation is when it comes from a white who has probably had minimal contact with blacks and who fails to comprehend how America's apartheid forces all classes of blacks into a single setting? Again, let me use myself as an example. I cannot, would not, deny that I was born into a middle-class family. But I attended school—grades one to six—in an all-black school in the heart of the inner-city ghetto: even in such a "northern" city as Cincinnati, segregation was practiced in schools as it is in Boston, Detroit, Chicago, and other cities today. My classmates were not middle-class. For grades seven and eight, I attended another all-black school, which graduated some of its students into reformatories. After four years of high school, college, and graduate education in predominantly white institutions, I taught in Georgia at a private college, where many of the black students fell short of rural southern standards of the middle-class. If they had been more "middle-class," their parents might have chosen to enroll them in a college more expensive than the one at which I taught. In Maryland, while teaching in a college, I was forced for economic reasons to live in a settlement of soldiers and factory workers. (There were three college instructors in the complex of more than three hundred homes.) While working on a doctorate, I supported myself by working among blacks in a steel mill, by clerking in a drugstore in Chicago's south side, and

by waiting tables. My experiences are not unique among middle-class black males. Yet teachers who publish articles in professional journals would inform me that the black middle class is too isolated from black common people to know how they speak. How arrogant can the ignorant be?

The point of this tirade is simple. Teachers who wish to practice the policy of the resolution on the students' right to language must not assume that a brown or black face means that the teacher has no need to educate that child in language. The teacher must determine who the child is and what language the child speaks.

AN ALLEGATION WORTH CONSIDERING

A different allegation, which is true, is that many black people who insist that black children must learn to read and write "standard" English (EAE or edited American English) are concerned that blacks have opportunity in the job market. Two strong forces oppose this view: nationalistic blacks and idealists (call them liberals if you will). The nationalistic blacks argue that employers should be compelled to respect black dialect; the liberals, echoing that idea, point to the whites who have gained position without effective command of standard English and to the blacks who are restricted despite their language proficiency.

Both the nationalists and the liberals see America with idealistic eyes. In time, America *may* become color blind. At present it is not. Although use of language may not matter in menial jobs, it does matter for the better paying jobs (and for entrance to the professional schools), where employers sometimes are seeking documentable reasons for rejecting blacks. Once, when I expressed this idea, a white acquaintance cited former Mayor Daley of Chicago as an example of the fact that failure to command standard English does not prevent a person from attaining high position. But I asked him and I ask you, outside the artificial worlds of entertainment and athletics, how many blacks without a command of English have whites appointed or elected to significant positions?

Remember, in addition, that the CCCC Background Statement does not say that students need not learn to write standard English. The statement reads, "It is necessary that we inform those students who are preparing themselves for occupations that demand formal writing that they will be expected to write edited American English" (1974, 15). It would be tragic if that statement were to be forgotten.

I do not deny that many blacks who write English effectively will not necessarily prosper in a white racist society: standard English will not necessarily earn jobs for them. But I am raising the alternative question, How restricted is the opportunity for blacks who do not command such language skills? Are idealists (black or white) imprisoning blacks in menial jobs with a naive hope that a white-oriented society will respond favorably to black differences tomorrow after a three-century record of continuing effort to prove the intellectual inferiority of blacks? Blacks can learn to write standard English. As the CCCC background paper states, if speakers of a great variety of American dialects do master EAE—from Senator Sam Ervin to Senator Edward Kennedy, from Ernest Hemingway to William Faulkner—there is no reason to assume that dialects such as urban Black and Chicano impede the child's ability to learn to write EAE while countless others do not (1974, 8).

There are at least three other myths which must be ignored by the teacher who wishes to teach language effectively to black children.

One, promulgated in professional journals, is that black English and other dialects lack the vocabulary for precise thinking and precise expression. Unfortunately, this nonsensical idea, disseminated often by university professors who are seeking self-esteem, is widespread. I have heard it in faculty meetings where the university professors spoke the imprecise jargon all too characteristic of such meetings. I have heard it expressed by a frequently quoted linguist, who stated that young black children could not think. (When challenged, he admitted, for that moment, that he meant that teachers speaking a different dialect could not follow or understand the thought processes of some black children.) Such attitudes are arrogantly ignorant. The mode of language has little to do with precision of thought. When particular snobbisms are eliminated, the mode of expression has little to do with clarity. For example, when my older son was a child, he often spoke (and still writes) a variation of black English. But, long before he reached his teens, I had learned to admire his capacity for effective reasoning and clear expression. Even while we teachers encourage students to avoid using localisms, we must not delude ourselves that they cannot match our capa-bility for thinking or that they cannot communicate. (If I were cynical, I might say that, having little else respected by a capitalistic society, we academics delude ourselves that we have the power of precise communication when, in fact, we may be failing to communicate with anyone outside our circle. Who are the demented—those inside, or those outside?)

A second myth arises among those teachers who have recently learned that blacks give such names as "shucking" and "dozens" to their word games. With the pomposity of anthropologists serenely confident that none are alive to dispute their discoveries, some teachers explain such word play in a way to distinguish it from communication by any other group. For example, I read, in a professional journal, an essay in which a young white scholar tried to explain how black students' rhetoric affects their written compositions. In addition to confusing the meanings of "the dozens" and "signifying," peer-group games which relatively knowledgeable black students would rarely use in English composition classes, the anthropological teacher explained "shucking" to his fellow whites in such a way that he implied that blacks are the only ones who have ever lied to extricate themselves from difficult situations. (I read some of these professional essays with fascination. If I were not black, I might be impressed; because I am, I do not know whether to laugh or cry. I now sympathize with those emerging nations that have restricted the entrance of anthropologists because they are tired of being studied.)

At another extreme is a third myth which would distinguish blacks from other Americans. One college instructor has shared with other teachers her presumption that black students hear in black English. (Notice the generalization about all blacks.) Therefore, she says, they spell in black English. Let us apply that reasoning to whites: Bostonians hear in Bostonian; therefore they spell *Boston* "Baston." Southerners hear southern; therefore, they spell *honor* "honah." Furthermore, that teacher, who tells other teachers to follow her practice of requiring students to spell words as she pronounces them, ignores the probability that she has some kind of dialect. Finally I would be pleased to learn how her word drills help students distinguish the spellings of "proceed," "precede," "supersede," and other such familiar examples of the refusal of American English to be a language which can be spelled accordingly to sound.

In this brief comment, perhaps I have told you little. Perhaps I have entertained some of you or annoyed others. I certainly have done little to provide you with a methodology for instructing all black children. I have not even taken a firm stand on the question of whether to adopt the resolution or whether to teach standard English or whether to urge bidialectalism. But, if I have persuaded you that no single methodology is suitable for teaching all black children, I have attained one goal. Educationists talk about the need to teach children as individuals. I ask you to remember that black children are children too. Look at them as individuals. And before you abandon them in their own language because of your humanitarian motives, ask yourself whether you have learned what language they are using and whether there is anything you can do to help them improve in language. Finally, I ask you to test cautiously whatever you hear about blacks and our language. Anthropologists and linguists

sometimes err. As you think about my remarks, please remember, as I stated earlier, I am a black using the words and grammar—the language—of my black mother and father and the language—as far as I know—of their parents. Should not this be considered "black English"?

REFERENCES

Bentley, Robert H., and Samuel D. Crawford. *Black Language Reader*. Glenview, Ill.: Scott, Foresman & Co., 1973.

Committee on Conference on College Composition and Communication Language Statement. "Students' Right to Their Own Language." *College Composition and Communication* 25 (Fall 1974).

Dillard, J. L. *Black English: Its History and Usage*. New York: Vintage, 1973.

It Begins at the Beginning

DEBORAH TANNEN

Editor's introduction

Analyzing everyday conversations and investigating their effects on relationships has been the focus of Deborah Tannen's work as a sociolinguist. In *You Just Don't Understand*, she explores the ways conversation patterns for men and women develop differently, making conversation between the genders often seem like cross-cultural communication. This brief excerpt serves as an introduction to Tannen's influential work.

Even if they grow up in the same neighborhood, on the same block, or in the same house, girls and boys grow up in different worlds of words. Others talk to them differently and expect and accept different ways of talking from them. Most important, children learn how to talk, how to have conversations, not only from their parents but from their peers. After all, if their parents have a foreign or regional accent, children do not emulate it; they learn to speak with the pronunciation of the region where they grow up. Anthropologists Daniel Maltz and Ruth Borker summarize research showing that boys and girls have very different ways of talking to their friends. Although they often play together, boys and girls spend most of their time playing in same-sex groups. And, although some of the activities they play at are similar, their favorite games are different, and their ways of using language in their games are separated by a world of difference.

Boys tend to play outside, in large groups that are hierarchically structured. Their groups have a leader who tells others what to do and how to do it, and resists doing what other boys propose. It is by giving orders and making them stick that high status is nego-

tiated. Another way boys achieve status is to take center stage by telling stories and jokes, and by sidetracking or challenging the stories and jokes of others. Boys' games have winners and losers and elaborate systems of rules that are frequently the subjects of arguments. Finally, boys are frequently heard to boast of their skill and argue about who is best at what.

Girls, on the other hand, play in small groups or in pairs; the center of a girl's social life is a best friend. Within the group, intimacy is key: Differentiation is measured by relative closeness. In their most frequent games, such as jump rope and hopscotch, Nick and Sue tried to get what they wanted by involving a third child; the alignments they created with the third child, and the dynamics they set in motion, were fundamentally different. Sue appealed to Mary to fulfill someone else's desire; rather than saying that *she*

Source: Excerpt from *You Just Don't Understand* (pp. 43–47) by Deborah Tannen, 1990. New York: William Morrow and Company. Copyright 1990 by Deborah Tannen, Ph.D. Used by permission of William Morrow & Company, Inc.

wanted the pickle, she claimed that Lisa wanted it. Nick asserted his own desire for the pickle, and when he couldn't get it on his own, he appealed to Joe to get it for him. Joe then tried to get the pickle by force. In both these scenarios, the children were enacting complex lines of affiliation.

Joe's strong-arm tactics were undertaken not on his own behalf, but chivalrously, on behalf of Nick. By making an appeal in a whining voice, Nick positioned himself as one-down in a hierarchical structure, framing himself as someone in need of protection. When Sue appealed to Mary to relinquish her pickle, she wanted to take the one-up position of serving food. She was fighting not for the right to *have* the pickle, but for the right to *serve* it. (This reminded me of the women who said they'd become professors in order to teach.) But to accomplish her goal, Sue was depending on Mary's desire to fulfill others' needs.

This study suggests that boys and girls both want to get their way, but they tend to do so differently. Though social norms encourage boys to be openly competitive and girls to be openly cooperative, different situations and activities can result in different ways of behaving. Marjorie Harness Goodwin compared boys and girls engaged in two task-oriented activities: The boys were making slingshots in preparation for a fight, and the girls were making rings. She found that the boys' group was hierarchical: The leader told the others what to do and how to do it. The girls' group was egalitarian: Everyone made suggestions and tended to accept the suggestions of others. But observing the girls in a different activity—playing house—Goodwin found that they too adopted hierarchical structures: The girls who played mothers issued orders to the girls playing children, who in turn sought permission from their play-mothers. Moveover, a girl who was a play-mother was also a kind of manager of the game. This study shows that girls know how to issue orders and operate in a hierarchical structure, but they don't find that mode of behavior appropriate when they engage in task activities with their peers. They do find it appropriate in parent-child relationships, which they enjoy practicing in the form of play.

These worlds of play shed light on the world views of women and men in relationships. The boys' play illuminates why men would be on the lookout for signs they are being put down or told what to do. The chief commodity that is bartered in the boys' hierarchical world is status, and the way to achieve and maintain status is to give orders and get others to follow them. A boy in a low-status position finds himself being pushed around. So boys monitor their relations for subtle shifts in status by keeping track of who's giving orders and who's taking them.

These dynamics are not the ones that drive girls' play. The chief commodity that is bartered in the girls' community is intimacy. Girls monitor their friendships for subtle shifts in alliance, and they seek to be friends with popular girls. Popularity is a kind of status, but it is founded on connection. It also places popular girls in a bind. By doing field work in a junior high school, Donna Eder found that popular girls were paradoxically—and inevitably—disliked. Many girls want to befriend popular girls, but girls' friendships must necessarily be limited, since they entail intimacy rather than large group activities. So a popular girl must reject the overtures of most of the girls who seek her out—with the result that she is branded "stuck up."

A Love of Language, a Love of Research, and a Love of Teaching: A Conversation with Deborah Tannen

by Ruth Shagoury Hubbard

Deborah Tannen has brought her original and complex analyses of language to a wider public, helping spark national debates about communication—and miscommunication—between the sexes, cross-culturally, in the workplace, and in the home. University Professor and Professor of Linguistics at Georgetown University, Dr. Tannen is the author of *That's Not What I Meant!: How Conversational Style Makes or Breaks Relationships*; *You Just Don't Understand: Women and Men in Conversation*; and, most recently, *Talking from 9 to 5: How Women's and Men's Conversational Styles Affect Who Gets Heard, Who Gets Credit, and What Gets Done at Work*, as well as many other articles and scholarly books.

In our conversation, Deborah Tannen shared how her love of language merges into all her work, from her teaching to her research, to the many kinds of writing that fill her life. Besides her nonfiction work, Tannen is a poet and playwright currently putting the final touches on a new play which will be produced this spring in Washington, D.C.

At the core of her rich life is her teaching, which she emphasized to me is her foundation and her mooring. Her profound respect for her students shines through in this interview, providing inspiration for all of us as we sort out the complicated conversation patterns in our classrooms.

Ruth Hubbard: Could you begin by sharing a little about what got you started studying language?

Deborah Tannen: There are always so many different possible answers to a question like that, and they would all be true. I would have to say that I have always been a lover of language, fascinated by language. I think that's true of a lot of people. I wrote from the time I was very young; at 6 or 7, I was already writing stories and poems at home.

RH: Was that encouraged by your family?

DT: I think they were indifferent. My father encouraged me to read, but I don't recall being urged to write. They were very impressed and supportive when I did it, but I don't think it was especially encouraged. My parents were born in Europe. My mother graduated from high school and that's all. My father is a lawyer, but never graduated from high school. You could do it back then. He came to this country when he was 12 and he had no father; he had a mother and a sister and as soon as he was able to go to work and support them, he did. He quit high school after one year and went to work full time to support the family—while constantly dodging the truant officer. But he was very smart. He took high school equivalency tests and went right into law school, which you could do at the time. He went to St. John's Law School at night. It was designed for this kind of student. So, he held down a full time job, went to law school, and got both a law degree and a master's degree in law.

RH: So, your parents spoke English as a first language?

DT: No, my father was born in Poland and grew up speaking Polish and Yiddish and my mother was born in Russia and grew up speaking Yiddish. They were apparently speaking fluent English in six months or so.

RH: Certainly, a facility with languages is in your family.

DT: Yes, my father had an aptitude for language, definitely. An interest in language, a love of language, an aptitude for it. I suppose I could say I picked it up from him. I always remember him reading and commenting on how people spoke and using "big" words.

RH: Did you grow up speaking or understanding either Polish or Yiddish?

DT: No.

RH: It's kind of sad, isn't it?

DT: I think so, and I gave my parents a real argument at one point. They said, "Well, who thought about it?"

RH: It's sad to me, too. My dad is Syrian and English is a second language for him, but I never learned to speak Arabic, and it was never encouraged for us. And I feel sort of cheated for not having that background.

DT: I feel the same way. I suppose our parents were part of the same era when immigrants wanted to become Americans and didn't think of the native language as anything really necessary. So, that was that.

RH: Did you start right out in college knowing that you were going to major in linguistics or study language?

DT: I came to linguistics late. I was almost 30 when I went back to graduate school. But English was always my love. I got a B.A. in English literature and then I went off and lived in Greece for a couple of years, and I think that had a lot to do with my interest in cross-cultural communication.

RH: I think your love of literature comes through in the way you write: You write like a novelist, and there are so many stories within, and also the wonderful references that you make to short stories and to novels.

DT: Which some people love and some people are irritated by. I do think that the fact that I studied literature and write fiction and poetry myself probably does come through.

RH: So, before you went back to school, were you teaching?

DT: Yes, I went to Greece where I taught English as a second language. I taught ESL in Greece for about a year and a half. Then I came back to the States, got a masters in English at Wayne State, and taught ESL there while working on my masters. Then I got a job at Mercer County Community College in Trenton, NJ, which I had for a year. I taught ESL there because by this time I was an experienced ESL teacher and nobody else had much experience at that time. I even developed an ESL program for them. Then I got a job at Lehman College of the City in New York, where I taught remedial writing for three years. After a summer linguistic institute in 1973, I decided to study linguistics. I went to Berkeley, where I got a Ph.D. in linguistics, and supported myself by teaching ESL at Berkeley.

RH: You have a pretty strong background in teaching English as a second language. It sounds like teaching is an important part of your life.

DT: I love teaching. That's the simple answer. It's also my foundation, my mooring. I miss it when I don't teach. In fact, I have had quite a bit of leave in the last few years. Right after the publication of *You Just Don't Understand*, of course, my whole life turned upside down. And I had a year and a half where I didn't teach, and I really missed it. I never feel that I do very well when I'm not teaching. This term, I will be teaching my two courses in linguistics.

RH: Do you find that you are able to merge your life and your research interests into your classroom work?

DT: Yes, I always do. When I did the research on gender, it made me look at my classroom differently. One class I taught was in analyzing conversation, so it was natural to turn the classroom into a lab. I had the class break down into small groups, which I often did, but I had the added element that I varied the groups according to conversational style and gender and then had them look at their interaction in the various groups and take field notes on it. It was fascinating. And the results were very enlightening for me and the students. It was back and forth between the teaching and the research, then going back to the classroom and doing more research.

RH: Which ends up really enriching your teaching, and when your students are involved in it with you, it invites them to try on the lenses of researchers, too.

DT: Yes, and I always try to do that. It's a natural because I teach analyzing talk and what we do in class is talk. So, it is a natural thing for the class talk to be the object of analysis also.

RH: Do you have any advice for some of the beginning teacher researchers who are just starting to analyze the language in their classrooms? What are some of the things that would help them get started?

DT: I think tape recording is a very helpful aid, if they feel comfortable and if their students feel comfortable. I think it's important to involve the students as researchers as well. And it's important to keeping running field notes. I would emphasize note-taking and tape recording, because if you just try to notice what's going on, and write it down later, you're apt to miss a lot. I'd invite the students to be observers and keep running field notes of observations about classroom interactions. Sometimes students are in a better position to notice things—for example, someone's hand is up and hasn't been called on. Whose topics become the basis for further discussion? Whose questions are answered more fully?

The question of what you're actually going to look at is a vexing one, because there's always so much one could look at. I tell my students you can start by looking for things that trouble you because they don't sit right and you think there's a problem, or you can start by trying to understand things that really go well. You might think, "This was just a great moment; this was a wonderful conversation we were having here." You could look at that and see what it was that made it so great.

RH: So, either a tension or something that you know is working well, but you don't know why.

DT: You can always, too, think about something you've read and test that in your own classroom. I know there's so much work done now about gender equity in the classroom. You could look at your own speaking patterns in the classroom along those lines. But it's very important not to become simple-minded about this. I get discouraged when I see people do things like just count features or words.

RH: Right. As your research has shown, if you just count interruptions, that's not going to really tell you what kind of interruptions, or if they are interruptions that people are comfortable with.

DT: Exactly. So, even if you count something, you need to look at it closely and ask what's being done here. What's the intent and what's the effect?

RH: As I was reading your most recent book, Talking from 9 to 5, *I kept thinking of your workplace findings in terms of the group work that so many of us do in our classrooms, and how maybe some of the same problems with negotiation are going on. It seems a more in-depth look at the impact gendered conversation styles might be having in schools could be helpful. Much more than just the straight counting.*

DT: Yes, I think that in many ways a classroom is a lot like a workplace, from the perspective that you're being judged. This is one of the key things that came out when I was looking at the workplace as compared to private conversation. The same thing goes for a classroom. On the one hand, you say things in class—both the teacher and the students—because you want the information out, but you're also going to be evaluated. Anything you say becomes the basis for judging you.

RH: And there's certainly the same hierarchy with the teachers having so much power.

DT: Anthropologists write about the participant structure which reflects the hierarchy. In schools, the teacher is the person who determines who speaks when—and often, physically, the teacher is up at the front, and the students look up at the teacher. All kinds of things like that. And there are hierarchies among the students, of course—the high-status kids and the low-status kids. A lot of which the teachers don't even know about.

Also, the organization of the classroom is really closer to the participant structure of boys' social groups than girls' because girls tend to talk one on one or in small groups. The boys' groups tend to be larger, and self-display is expected of boys so that they can get high status in the group. This is a lot closer to what they are usually expected to do in classrooms: show what they are good at and know, take center stage—all things that girls are resistant to do in the girls' social group, because maybe the other girls won't like them: "She's bossy. Who does she think she is?"

RH: Do you think of any other suggestions for teacher-researchers?

DT: I want to stress again that students really enjoy taping and transcribing. Transcribing makes you listen in a new way. I think the power of narrative is very useful. Kids are already very skilled at telling stories and that is something they can do—transcribe stories that are told in conversation and compare them to written stories and discover their structure. I'd also stress again the power of keeping field notes, which encourages people to be researchers.

RH: And having that written record helps you see patterns you wouldn't see otherwise.

DT: I think so, and also keeping a written record allows you to see how much you've learned: what you didn't know last week and you do know this week. It can feel like you always knew what you know now.

RH: Can you name some of the linguists or researchers or writers who have been important to you?

DT: Well, in the field, it would be three people I worked with at Berkeley: Robin Lakoff, Wallace Chafe, and John Gumperz. I also mention often Alton Becker—he's a professor emeritus at Michigan, a linguist. I got into linguistics that first summer in 1973 at the Linguistic Institute and I was lucky; I had Introduction to Linguistics with him. I managed to stay in touch with him for the rest of my career and now I count him as one of my closest friends. His approach to linguistics is very humanistic, and he writes about the aesthetics of language. He's quite anthropological, and has really helped me very much.

RH: His approach has clearly had an effect on you.

DT: Yes, first it resonated with interests that were there, but having his support has been very important. In addition, as colleagues, Fred Erickson and Shirley Brice Heath, whose work I respect enormously.

RH: What's next for you in your research?

DT: Believe it or not, what I'm actually doing right now is writing plays.

RH: That seems like a perfect tie-in: dialogue, conversation . . .

DT: Right. I'll need to finish the play I'm working on now very soon. Actually, I've written a first and a second draft and it's in the hands of the director. The play will be produced in the spring.

RH: What's it about?

DT: Well, it's about my family. Last fall, I had written a short play that was about my father and his childhood in Poland and the trip we made together to Poland. This spring they decided to give it a full production, but requested a second one to go with it. So, I wrote another one that leads up to the trip to Poland that I made with my father. I'm trying to get away from the completely autobiographical approach, but it is still largely based on my experiences. I guess it's about the sense in which parents are often completely different parents to each child. Although each child is born into the same family, it's quite a different family for each one. The play also explores each of our relationships to Judaism. That's what I've been doing most recently.

RH: What a change for you, but how much fun it must have been!

DT: I love it, yes. Of course, the last big project was *Talking from 9 to 5*, which I finished pretty recently. I'm not yet sure what my next big project will be.

RH: There is certainly a lot of current debate around the issues of language standards and the place of different languages, cultures, and dialects in the classroom. What do you believe teachers need to know or do in terms of these issues in their classrooms?

DT: That is so complicated. Of course, as a sociolinguist, I'm inclined to say all language is a dialect, makes sense, and serves a purpose. I'm aware of the history of this particular conflict. There was a movement, perhaps largely sparked by sociolinguists, that defended certain dialects: One example would be Black English, as it was then called, the language of African-Americans in cities. Teachers were told that they should understand the structure of the language that the kids were using and that they would likely even learn better if they were taught in their own language. And I know that that was interpreted by many African-American parents as, "You're trying to hold my kids back." "You wouldn't let your kids talk that way; how come it's all right for my kids?" So, I know that all these things are very complicated. I suppose realistically, one has to accept what those black parents were getting at: If a certain "standard English" is what is expected for advancement in the world, and you want schools to give kids the best chance, then ideally, they should give kids the tools to speak standard English.

But it's hard to say to kids, "Well, it's really okay for you to talk as you do, only I'm going to teach you a different way for different situations." They hear it as, "It's not okay." As I say, I think it's pretty complicated.

RH: Any suggestions for teachers to help them deal with it better?

DT: I would hope that teachers would not speak in terms of right and wrong. There's certainly no point in telling kids the way they are speaking is "wrong" when they know this is an effective way to speak. I think awareness would certainly be helpful. Robin Lakoff has commented that Oprah Winfrey, for example, uses vernacular Black English very effectively. She switches into it. She'll be speaking a variation of standard English, then slip in expressions in Black English, and it's very effective. So, maybe that's another way that kids could be researchers—watch Oprah, and notice how she does that.

RH: And, I suppose, notice how they do it themselves, that we all speak differently in different situations and to different people.

DT: So, maybe the general principle that I think everybody would recognize is that you don't talk the same way to everybody just as you don't dress the same way in every situation. It would be useful to think of it in those terms rather than this is the right way, this is the wrong way. Also, I hope that teachers would always speak to children with respect, and respect their ways of speaking as well as everything else about their cultures.

Life As We Know It

MICHAEL BERUBE

● ●

Editor's introduction

In his very personal essay, Michael Berube tells the story of the early years of his son James, born with Down's Syndrome. Berube eloquently explores what he calls a "crucial characteristic" of our common humanity: the desire to communicate, to understand and to be understood.

● ● ● ● ● ● ● ● ● ● ● ●

In my line of work I don't think very often about carbon or potassium, much less about polypeptides or transfer RNA. I teach American and African-American literature; Janet Lyon, my legal spouse and general partner, teaches modern British literature and women's studies. Nothing about our jobs requires us to be aware of the biochemical processes that made us—and, more recently, our children—into conscious beings. But in 1985–86, when Janet was pregnant with our first child, Nicholas, I would lie awake for hours, wondering how the baseball-size clump of cells in her uterus was really going to form something living, let alone something capable of thought. I knew that the physical processes that form dogs and drosophilas are more or less as intricate, on the molecular level, as those that form humans; but puppies and fruit flies don't go around asking how they got here or how (another version of the same question) DNA base-pair sequences code for various amino acids. And though humans have been amazed and puzzled by human gestation for quite a while now, it wasn't until a few nanoseconds ago (in geological time) that their wonder began to focus on the chemical minutiae that somehow differentiate living matter from "mere" matter. The fact that self-replicating molecules had eventually come up with a life-form that could actually pick apart the workings of self-replicating molecules . . . well, let's just say I found this line of thought something of a distraction. At the time, I thought that I would never again devote so much attention to such ideas. I figured the miracle of human birth, like that of humans landing on the moon, would be more routine than miracle the second time around. It wasn't.

Five years later, in September 1991, Janet was pregnant again, another fall semester was beginning, and I was up late writing. At 2:00 A.M., Janet asked when I was coming to bed. At 4:00 A.M., she asked again. "Soon," I said. "Well, you should probably stop working now," she replied, "because I think I'm going into labor." At which point she presented me with an early birthday present, a watch with a second hand.

That was the first unexpected thing: James wasn't due for another two weeks. Then came more unexpected things in rapid succession.

Eight hours later, in the middle of labor, Janet spotted a dangerous arrhythmia on her heart monitor. The only other person in the room was an obstetrics staff nurse; Janet turned to her and barked, "That's V-tach. We need a cardiologist in here. Get a bolus of lidocaine ready, and get the crash cart." (Being an ex-cardiac-intensive-care nurse comes in handy sometimes.) Pounding on her chest and forcing herself to cough she broke out of what was possibly a lethal heart rhythm. Labor stalled. Janet and I stared at each other for an hour. Suddenly, at a strange moment when she and I were the only people in the room, James's head presented. I hollered down the hall for help. James appeared within minutes, an unmoving baby of a deep, rich, purple hue, tangled in his umbilical cord. "He looks Downsy around the eyes," I heard. Downsy? He looks stillborn, I thought. They unwrapped the cord, cut it, gave him oxygen. Quickly, incredibly, he revived. No cry, but who cared? They gave him an Apgar score of 7, on a scale of 1 to 10. I remember feeling an immense relief. My wife was alive, my second child was alive. At the end of a teeth-grating hour during which I'd wondered if either of them would see the end of the day, Down syndrome somehow seemed like a reprieve.

Over the next half hour, as the nurses worked on James, and Janet and I tried to collect our thoughts, I realized I didn't know very much about Down's, other than that it meant James had an extra chromosome and would be mentally retarded. I knew I'd have some homework to do.

But what kind of homework were we talking about? Would we ever have normal lives again? We'd struggled for eight years on salaries that left us able to peer at the poverty line only if one of us stood on the other's shoulders. A mere three weeks earlier, the university had hired Janet, thus making us one of the extremely rare dual-career academic couples working in the same department; we knew how lucky we were, and we thought we were finally going to be "comfortable." But now were we going to spend the rest of our days caring for a severely disabled child? Would we have even an hour to ourselves? Christ, we'd only just finished paying off the bills two months earlier for *Nick's* birth, and now were we facing the kind of catastrophic medical debt that fills the op-ed pages? These were selfish thoughts, and the understanding that such thoughts are "natural" didn't make them any less bitter or insistent.

We went over the past few months. The pregnancy had been occasionally odd but not exactly scary. We'd decided against getting an amniocentesis, on the

grounds that a sonogram would pick up nearly any serious problems with the fetus *except* Down syndrome, and the chances of having a child with Down syndrome at Janet's age, thirty-six, were roughly equal to the chances of an amniocentesis-induced miscarriage (1 in 225 and 1 in 200, respectively). Later, there were some hitches: reduced fetal movements, disproportionate fetal measurements on sonograms, low weight gain, and so on. Our worries were vague but persistent.

Back in the present, over on his table in the birthing room, James wasn't doing very well. He still wasn't moving, he had no sucking reflex, and he was getting bluer. It turned out that the fetal opening in his heart hadn't closed fully. You and I had the same arrangement until around the time of birth, when our heart's ventricles sealed themselves off in order to get us ready to start conducting oxygen from our lungs into our bloodstream. But James still had a hole where no hole should be, and wasn't oxygenating properly.

There was more. Along with his patent ductus arteriosus and his trisomy 21, there was laryngomalacia (floppy larynx), jaundice, polycythemia (an abnormal increase in red blood cells), torticollis, vertebral anomaly, scoliosis, hypotonia (low muscle tone), and (not least of these) feeding problems. That's a lot of text to wade through to get to your kid.

Basically, James was in danger. If he made it through the night he would still be a candidate, in the morning, for open-heart surgery *and* a tracheostomy. Because of the laryngomalacia, which isn't related to Down's, he couldn't coordinate sucking, swallowing, and breathing, and his air supply would close off if he slept on the wrong side. The vertebral problems, we learned, occur in roughly one of six kids with Down's; his first three vertebrae were malformed, his spinal cord vulnerable. And his neck muscles were abnormally tight (that's the torticollis), leaving him with a 20-degree head tilt to the left. He was being fed intravenously and had tubes not only in his arm but in his stomach as well, run neatly through his umbilical artery, still viable from the delivery. Our first Polaroid of him shows a little fleshy thing under a clear plastic basin, lost in machinery and wires. I remember thinking, it's all right that they do all this to him now because he'll never remember it. But it can't be a pleasant introduction to the world.

Within days things got better, and one anxiety after another peeled away: Jamie's duct closed, and as I entered the intensive-care unit one morning I found that the staff had erased from his chart the phone number of the emergency helicopter service that would have flown him to Peoria for heart surgery. His blood-oxygen levels reached the high 90s and stayed there, even as he was weaned from 100 percent oxygen to a level just above the atmospheric norm. A tracheoscopy (that is, a viewing of his throat with an eyepiece at the end of a tube) confirmed that he didn't need a tracheostomy. He still wasn't feeding, but he was opening an eye now and then and looking out at his brother and his parents.

I got hold of everything I could on genetics, reproduction, and "abnormal" human development, dusting off college textbooks I hadn't touched since before Nick was born. At one point a staff nurse was sent in to check on *our* mental health; she found us babbling about meiosis and monoploids, wondering anew that Jamie had "gotten" Down syndrome the second he became a zygote. When the nurse inadvertently left behind her notes, Janet sneaked a peek. "Parents seem to be intellectualizing," we read. "Well," Janet shrugged, "that seems accurate enough."

Looking over the fossil record, I really don't see any compelling logic behind humans' existence on the planet. I'm told that intelligence has obvious survival value, since organisms with a talent for information processing "naturally" beat out their competitors for food, water, and condos, but human history doesn't convince me that *our* brand of intelligence is just what the world was waiting for. Thus I've never believed we were supposed to survive the Ice Age, or that some cosmic design mandated the cataclysmic collision in the late Cretaceous period that gave us an iridium layer in our soil and may have ended the dinosaurs' reign. Bacteria and horseshoe crabs unmodified for aeons are still with us, but what has become of *Eusthenopteron*, introduced to me by then-five-year-old Nicholas as the fish that could walk on land? If you were fighting for survival 350 million years ago, you'd think you'd have had a leg up on the competition if you developed small bones in your fins, enabling you to shimmy onto shore. But you'd be wrong: these days, *Eusthenopteron* is nothing more than a card in Nick's "prehistoric animals" collection, alongside the Ankylosaur, the mastodon, and the jessehelms. I figured we were here thanks to dumb luck, and though we have managed to understand our own biochemical origins and take neat close-up pictures from the far side of Saturn, we also spend much of our time exterminating ourselves and

most other species we meet. And nothing in Nick's cards says we too won't wind up in nature's deck of "prehistoric" animals.

Still, it wasn't until I got to college and started thinking about sex and drugs in rather immediate ways that I began to realize that the workings of chance on the molecular level are even more terrifying than on the evolutionary plane. Of course, the molecular and the evolutionary have everything to do with each other; it's just the minutiae of mitosis are more awe-inspiring to me than the thought of random rocks slamming into my home planet every couple of hundred million years. For those who don't feel like cracking open old textbooks, Richard Power's novel *The Gold Bug Variations* offers some idea of what's involved in cell division: "seven feet of aperiodic crystal unzips, finds complements of each of its billion constituents, integrates them perfectly without tearing or entangling, then winds up again into a fraction of a millimeter, all in two minutes." And this is just the ordinary stuff your cells are doing every moment. Sex, as always, is a little more complicated.

So let's talk about sex. Of the 15 percent of pregnancies that end in miscarriage, more than half are the result of chromosomal abnormalities, and half of these are caused by trisomy—three chromosomes where two should be. Of the myriad possible genetic mistransmissions in human reproduction, excluding anomalies in the sex chromosomes, it appears that only three kinds of trisomies make it to term: people with three thirteenth chromosomes (Patau's syndrome), three eighteenth chromosomes (Edwards' syndrome), and three twenty-first chromosomes (Down syndrome). About one in four or five zygotes with Down's winds up getting born, and since Down's accounts for one of every 600 to 800 live births, it would appear that trisomy 21 happens quite often, maybe on the order of once in every 150 to 250 fertilizations. Kids with Edwards' or Patau's syndrome are born severely deformed and profoundly retarded; they normally don't live more than a few months. That's what I would expect of genetic anomaly, whatever the size of the autosome: though the twenty-first chromosome is the smallest we have, James still has extra genetic material in every single cell. You'd think the effects of such a basic transcription error would make themselves felt pretty clearly.

But what's odd about Down's is how extraordinarily subtle it can be. Mental retardation is one well-known effect, and it can sometimes be severe, but anyone who's watched Chris Burke in TV's *Life Goes On* or "Mike" in McDonald's commercials knows that the extent of such retardation can be next to negligible. The *real* story of Down's lies not in intelligence tests but in developmental delays across the board, and for the first two years of James's life the most important of these were physical rather than mental (though thanks to James I've come to see how interdependent the mental and physical really are). His muscles are weaker than those of most children his age, his nasal passages imperceptibly narrower. His tongue is slightly thicker; one ear is crinkly. His fingers would be shorter and stubbier but for the fact that his mother's are long, thin, and elegant. His face is a few degrees flatter through the middle, his nose delicate.

Down's doesn't cut all children to one mold; the relations between James's genotype and phenotype are lacy and intricate. It's sort of like what happens in Ray Bradbury's short story "A Sound of Thunder," in which a time traveler accidentally steps on a butterfly while hunting dinosaurs 65 million years ago and returns home to find that he's changed the conventions of English spelling and the outcome of the previous day's election. As he hit the age of two, James was very pleased to find himself capable of walking; by three, he had learned to say the names of colors, to count to ten, and to claim that he would *really* be turning four. Of all our genetic nondisjunctions (with the possible exception of hermaphroditism), only Down syndrome produces so nuanced, so finely articulated a variation on "normal" reproduction. James is less mobile and more susceptible to colds than his peers, but—as his grandparents have often attested—you could play with him for hours and never see anything "wrong."

And then there's a variant form of Down's, called mosaicism, which results from the failure of the chromosome to divide not *before* fertilization but immediately *after*, during the early stages of cell division. Only one in a hundred people with Down's are mosaics, but it's possible for such folks to have some normal cells and some with trisomy 21; there's something about the twenty-first, then, that produces anomalies during either meiosis *or* mitosis. Now, that's truly weird. There's also translocation, in which the twenty-first chromosome splits off and joins the fourteenth or fifteenth, producing people who can be called "carriers"; they can give birth to more translocation carriers, nor-

mal children, or translocation kids with Down's. And although everyone knows that the incidence of Down's increases with maternal age, almost no one knows that three quarters of all such children are born to mothers under thirty-five, or that fathers are genetically "responsible" for about one fifth of them. *Parents seem to be intellectualizing.* And why not?

There has never been a better time than now to be born with Down syndrome—and that's really saying something, since it has recently been reported in chimpanzees and gorillas. Because our branch of the evolutionary tree split off from the apes' around 15 to 20 million years ago, these reports would seem to suggest that we've produced offspring with Down syndrome with great regularity at every point in our history as hominids—even though it's a genetic anomaly that's not transmitted hereditarily (except in extremely rare instances) and has no obvious survival value. The statistical incidence of Down's in the current human population is no less staggering: there may be 10 million people with Down's worldwide, or just about one on every other street corner.

But although *Homo sapiens* (as well as our immediate ancestors) has always experienced some difficulty dividing its chromosomes, it wasn't until 1866 that British physician J. Langdon Down diagnosed it as "mongolism" (because it produced children with almond-shaped eyes reminiscent, to at least one nineteenth-century British mind, of central Asian faces). At the time, the average life expectancy of children with Down's was under ten. And for a hundred years thereafter—during which the discovery of antibiotics lengthened the life span of Down's kids to around twenty—Down syndrome was formally known as "mongoloid idiocy."

The 1980 edition of my college genetics textbook, *The Science of Genetics: An Introduction to Heredity,* opens its segment on Down's with the words, "An important and tragic instance of trisomy in humans involves Down's syndrome, or mongoloid idiocy." It includes a picture of a "mongoloid idiot" along with a karyotype of his chromosomes and the information that most people with Down's have IQs in the low 40s. The presentation is objective, dispassionate, and strictly "factual," as it should be. But reading it again in 1991, I began to wonder: is there a connection between the official textual representation of Down syndrome and the social policies by which people with Down's are understood and misunderstood?

You bet your life there is. Anyone who has paid attention to the "political correctness" wars on American campuses knows how stupid the academic left can be: we're always talking about language instead of reality, whining about "lookism" and "differently abled persons" instead of changing the world the way the real he-man left *used* to do. But you know, there really is a difference between calling someone "a mongoloid idiot" and calling him or her "a person with Down syndrome." There's even a difference between calling people "retarded" and calling them "delayed." Though these words may appear to mean the same damn thing when you look them up in Webster's, I remember full well from my days as an American male adolescent that I never taunted my peers by calling them "delayed." Even from those of us who were shocked at the frequency with which "homo" and "nigger" were thrown around in our fancy Catholic high school, "retard" aroused no comment, no protest. In other words, a retarded person is just a retard. But *delayed* persons will get where they're going eventually, if you'll only have some patience.

One night I said something like this to one of the leaders of what I usually think of as the other side in the academic culture wars. Being a humane fellow, he replied that although epithets like "mongoloid idiot" were undoubtedly used in a more benighted time, there have always been persons of goodwill who resisted such phraseology. A nice thought, but it just ain't so. Right through the 1970s, "mongoloid idiot" wasn't an epithet; it was a *diagnosis*. It wasn't uttered by callow, ignorant persons fearful of "difference" and central Asian eyes; it was pronounced by the best-trained medical practitioners in the world, who told families of kids with Down's that their children would never be able to dress themselves, recognize their parents, or live "meaningful" lives. Best to have the child institutionalized and tell one's friends that the baby died at birth. Only the most stubborn, intransigent, or inspired parents resisted such advice from their trusted experts. Who could reasonably expect otherwise?

It's impossible to say how deeply we're indebted to those parents, children, teachers, and medical personnel who insisted on treating people with Down's as if they *could* learn, as if they *could* lead "meaningful" lives. In bygone eras, parents who didn't take their children home didn't really have the "option" of doing so; you can't talk about "options" (in any substantial sense of the word) in an ideological current so strong.

But in the early 1970s, some parents did bring their children home, worked with them, held them, provided them physical therapy and "special learning" environments. These parents are saints and sages. They have, in the broadest sense of the phrase, uplifted the race. In the 15-million-year history of Down syndrome, they've allowed us to believe that we're finally getting somewhere.

Of course, the phrase "mongoloid idiocy" did not cause Down syndrome any more than the word "homo" magically induces same-sex desire. But words and phrases are the devices by which we beings signify what homosexuality, or Down syndrome, or anything else, will mean. There surely were, and are, the most intimate possible relations between the language in which we spoke of Down's and the social practices by which we understood it—or refused to understand it. You don't have to be a poststructuralist or a postmodernist or a post-*anything* to get this; all you have to do is meet a parent of a child with Down syndrome. Not long ago, we lived next door to people whose youngest child had Down's. After James was born, they told us of going to the library to find out more about their baby's prospects and wading through page after page of outdated information, ignorant generalizations, and pictures of people in mental institutions, face down in their feeding trays. These parents demanded the library get some better material and throw out the garbage they had on their shelves. Was this a "politically correct" thing for them to do? Damn straight it was. That garbage has had its effects *for generations*. It may look like words, but perhaps the fragile little neonates whose lives were thwarted and impeded by the policies and conditions of institutionalization can testify in some celestial court to the power of mere language, to the intimate links between words and social policies.

Some of my friends tell me this sounds too much like "strict social constructionism"—that is, too much like the proposition that culture is everything and biology is only what we decide to make (of) it. But although James is pretty solid proof that human biology "exists" independently of our understanding of it, every morning when he gets up, smiling and babbling to his family, I can see for myself how much of his life depends on our social practices. On one of those mornings I turned to my mother-in-law and said, "He's always so full of mischief, he's always so glad to see us—the only thought I can't face is the idea of this little guy waking up each day in a state mental hospital." To which my mother-in-law replied, "Well, Michael, if he were waking up every day in a state mental hospital he wouldn't *be* this little guy."

As it happens, my mother-in-law doesn't subscribe to any strict social constructionist newsletters; she was just passing along what she took to be good common sense. But every so often I wonder how common that sense really is. Every ten minutes we hear that the genetic basis of something has been "discovered," and we rush madly to the newsweeklies: Disease is genetic! Homosexuality is genetic! Infidelity, addiction, obsession with mystery novels—all genetic! Such discourses, it would seem, bring out the hidden determinist in more of us than will admit it. Sure, there's a baseline sense in which our genes "determine" who we are: we can't play the tune unless the score is written down somewhere in the genome. But one does not need or require a biochemical explanation for literary taste, or voguing, or faithless lovers. In these as in all things human, including Down's, the genome is but a template for a vaster and more significant range of social and historical variation. Figuring out even the most rudimentary of relations between the genome and the immune system (something of great relevance to us wheezing asthmatics) involves so many trillions of variables that a decent answer will win you an all-expenses-paid trip to Stockholm.

I'm not saying we can eradicate Down's—or its myriad effects—simply by talking about it more nicely. I'm only saying that James's intelligence is doing better than it would in an institution, and people who try to deny this don't strike me as being among the geniuses of the species. And every time I hear some self-styled "realist" tell me that my logic licenses the kind of maniacal social engineering that produced Auschwitz, I do a reality check: the people who brought us Auschwitz weren't "social constructionists." They were eugenicists. They thought they knew the "immutable laws" of genetics and the "fixed purpose" of evolution, and they were less interested in "improving" folks like Jamie than in exterminating them. I'll take my chances with the people who believe in chance.

And yet there's something very seductive about the notion that Down syndrome wouldn't have been so prevalent in humans for so long without good reason. Indeed, there are days when, despite everything I know and profess, I catch myself believing that people

with Down syndrome are here for a specific purpose—perhaps to teach us patience, or humility, or compassion, or mere joy. A great deal can go wrong with us in utero, but under the heading of what goes wrong, Down syndrome is among the most basic, the most fundamental, the most common, *and* the most innocuous, leavening the species with children who are somewhat slower, and usually somewhat gentler, than the rest of the human brood. It speaks to us strongly of design, if design may govern in a thing so small.

After seventeen days in the ICU, James was scheduled for release. We would be equipped with the materials necessary for his care, including oxygen tanks and an apnea monitor that would beep if his heart slowed, became extremely irregular, or stopped. To compensate for his inability to take food orally, James would have a gastrostomy tube surgically introduced through his abdominal wall into his stomach. Janet and I balked. James had recently made progress in his bottle feeding; why do preemptive surgery? We nixed the gastrostomy tube, saying we'd prefer to augment his bottle feedings with a nasal tube and we'd do it ourselves. James stayed three more days in the ICU, and came home to a house full of flowers and homemade dinners from our colleagues.

For the most part, I've repressed the details of that autumn. But every once in a while, rummaging through the medicine closet for Ace bandages or heating pads, I come across the Hypafix adhesive tape with which we attached James's feeding tube to the bridge of his nose, or the strap we wrapped around his tiny chest for his apnea monitor. It's like discovering evidence of another life, dim but indelible, and you realize that once upon a time you could cope with practically anything. Running a small tube through your baby's nose to his stomach is the worst kind of counterintuitive practice. You have to do it carefully, measuring your length of tubing accurately and listening with a stethoscope to make sure you haven't entered the lung. Whenever James pulled out his tubes, we had to do the whole thing over again, in the other nostril this time, lubricating and marking and holding the tube while fumbling with the world's stickiest tape. It's a four-handed job, and I don't blame the staff doctors for assuming we wouldn't undertake such an enterprise alone.

But slowly we got James to bottle feed. After all, for our purposes, Jamie's nasal tube, like unto a thermonuclear weapon, was there precisely so that we *wouldn't* use it. Each week a visiting nurse would set a minimum daily amount for Jamie's milk intake, and whatever he didn't get by bottle would have to go in by tube. So you can see the incentive at work here. Within a month we began to see glimpses of what James would look like sans tube. Then we stopped giving him oxygen during the night, and gradually his tiny nostrils found themselves a lot less encumbered. He still didn't have a voice, but he was clearly interested in his new home and very trusting of his parents and brother.

In the midst of that winter James began physical therapy and massages. We stretched his neck every night, and whenever we could afford it we took him to a local masseuse who played ambient music, relaxed us all, and worked on James for an hour. His physical therapist showed us how everything about James was connected to everything else: His neck, if left uncorrected, would reshape the bones of his face. The straighter his neck, the sooner he'd sit up, the sooner he'd walk. If he could handle simple solid foods with equal facility in both sides of his mouth, he could center himself more easily; and the sooner he could move around by himself, the more he'd be able to explore and learn. In other words, his eating would affect his ability to walk, and his thighs and torso would impinge upon his ability to talk. I suppose that's what it means to be an organism.

Not only did we realize the profound interdependence of human hearts and minds; we also discovered (and had to reconfigure) our relations to a vast array of social practices and institutions. "Developmental" turns out to be a buzzword for a sprawling nexus of agencies, state organizations, and human disabilities. Likewise, "special needs" isn't a euphemism; it's a very specific marker. We're learning about the differences between "mainstreaming" and "inclusion," and we'll be figuring out the Americans with Disabilities Act for the rest of our lives. Above all else, we know that James is extremely lucky to be so well provided for; when every employer is as flexible as ours, when parental leave is the law of the land, when private insurers can't drop families from the rolls because of "high risk" children, when every child can be fed, clothed, and cared for—*then* we can start talking about what kind of a choice "life" might be.

Because, after all he's been through, James is thriving. He's thrilled to be here and takes a visible, palpable delight in seeing his reflection in the oven door as he toddles across the kitchen, or hearing his parents address him in the voices of the *Sesame Street* regulars,

or winging a Nerf ball to his brother on the couch. He knows perfectly well when he's doing something we've never seen before, like riding his toddler bicycle down the hall into the laundry room or calling out "Georgia" and "Hawaii" as he flips through Nick's book of the fifty states. He's been a bibliophile from the moment he learned to turn pages. His current favorite is Maurice Sendak's classic *Where the Wild Things Are*, surely a Great Book by any standard; he began by identifying with Max and then, in one of those "oscillations" described by reader-response criticism and feminist film theory, switched over to identifying with the wild things themselves—roaring his terrible roar and showing his terrible claws.

He has his maternal aunts' large deep eyes, and a beautiful smile that somehow involves his whole body. He's not only an independent cuss, but he also has an attention span of about twenty minutes—eighteen minutes longer than the average American political pundit. He's blessed with a preternaturally patient, sensitive brother in Nick, who, upon hearing one of his classmates' parents gasp "Oh my God" at the news that Jamie had Down's, turned to her and said with a fine mixture of reassurance and annoyance, "He's perfectly all *right*." Like Nick, James has a keen sense of humor; the two of them can be set agiggle by pratfalls, radical incongruities, and mere sidelong looks. He's just now old enough to be curious about what he was like as a baby: as he puts it, all he could do was go "waaah" (holding his fists to his eyes). Barring all the contingencies that can never be barred, James can expect a life span of anywhere from thirty-five to fifty-five years. For tomorrow, he can expect to see his friends at day care, to put all his shapes in his shapes box, and to sing along with Raffi as he shakes his sillies out and wiggles his waggles away.

Before James was born I frankly didn't think very highly of appeals to our "common humanity." I thought such appeals were well intentioned but basically inconsequential. Clearly, Muslim and Christian do not bond over their common ancestor in *Australopithecus*. Rwandan Hutu and Rwandan Tutsi do not toast to the distinctive size of their cerebral cortices. The rape of Bosnia, and Bosnian women, does not stop once Serbian soldiers realize that they too will pass from earth.

And yet we possess one crucial characteristic: the desire to communicate, to understand, to put ourselves in some mutual, reciprocal form of contact with one another. This desire hasn't proven any better at disarming warheads than any of the weaker commonalities enumerated above, but it stands a better chance nonetheless. For among the most amazing and hopeful things about us is that we show up, from our day of birth, programmed to receive and transmit even in the most difficult circumstances; the ability to imagine mutual communicative relations is embedded in our material bodies, woven through our double-stranded fibers. Granted, it's only one variable among trillions, and it's not even "fundamentally" human—for all we know, dolphins are much better at communication than we are. And the sociohistorical variables of human communication will always be more significant and numerous than any genetic determinism can admit. All the same, it's in our software somewhere, and, better still, it's a program that teaches itself how to operate each time we use it.

Whether you want to consider reciprocal communication a constant or a variable, though, the point remains that it's a human attribute requiring other people if it's going to work. Among the talents we have, it's one we could stand to develop more fully. It's only natural: among our deepest, strongest impulses is the impulse to mutual cuing. Nothing will delight James so much as the realization that you have understood him—except the realization that he has understood *you*, and recursively understood his own understanding and yours. Perhaps I could have realized our human stake in mutual realization without James's aid; any number of other humans would have been willing to help me out. But now that I get it, I get it for good. Communication is itself self-replicating. Sign unto others as you'd have them sign unto you. Pass it on.

Extension: Sociocultural and Personal Perspectives

Rarely is it possible to study all the instructions to a game before beginning to play, or to memorize the manual before turning on the computer. We can carry on the process of learning in everything we do, like a mother balancing her child on one hip as she goes about her work with the other hand or uses it to open the door of the unknown. Learning and living, we become ambidextrous. Mary Catherine Bateson[1]

BUILDING AN UNDERSTANDING OF LANGUAGE FROM THE STORIES IN OUR CLASSROOMS

We hope the end of this book marks a new beginning for you, that you will use it to help you open the door into a study of language in your classroom, school, and community. The tools of teacher research can help you balance the learning, living, and teaching that make up the daily fabric of teachers' worlds. The starting points for research into language in the context of your classroom are as varied as the readers of this book. Here is a sample of the range of questions teachers we know are pursuing as language researchers. Consider them as possible starting points for your language research:

What is my language pattern in talking with students?

How is the classroom talk during a science experiment different than the talk during a literature circle?

Where do students choose to sit during writing workshop and how does that affect the talk that takes place?

---

[1] From *Peripheral Visions: Learning Along the Way* (p. 9) by Mary Catherine Bateson, 1994, New York: Harper Collins.

What is this particular student's language with peers? How does it affect her socially?

How does my students' language change as they move from the classroom to the playground to the cafeteria?

What happens when students investigate their own register changes in different contexts?

What are the differences in talk in small groups between same-sex groups and mixed-sex groups? What are the benefits and drawbacks for each gender?

How do my students' questions change over the course of the year?

Once you have narrowed your focus to one specific question that reflects your language needs and interests, the starting point for your research may be as simple as making a commitment to look closely at students for 10 minutes a day in your classroom, thinking carefully about the issue. Keep in mind Deborah Tannen's suggestions, too, to start by looking for tensions you'd like to explore further, or trying to understand things that are going well. You might also find it helpful to write in a log or teaching journal about what you're noticing for a few minutes each day.

In the earlier extensions, we've shown you different ways to do language research and analysis in your classroom. Over the years, we've worked with many teachers who have sustained their interest in language in their classrooms—and many who have not. We thought it would be useful to close with what we have learned from the teachers who have been able to sustain an enthusiasm for language research over many years. The following principles guide the work of teachers who are able to build an understanding of language in their classrooms over time:

1. *Remember, you are the research instrument*. It's easy to get caught up in equipment and analysis constraints. Not having a quality tape recorder, or the time to record, becomes an excuse for not considering how language patterns are developing in your classroom. Keep Shirley Brice Heath's advice in mind: You are the research instrument, and you must learn to keep the instrument on all the time.

2. *Begin small and build*. Too many teachers leave a graduate course with grand plans of how they will systematically collect masses of data in their classrooms. All of us have developed ambitious plans, only to have them dissolve in the dailiness of teaching—the literature corner that needs to be rearranged, the report cards that need to be sent, and so on.

Good teachers are adept at finding teachable moments, and they can develop the ability to see researchable moments as well. Look for those small details—the way a head is turned during a whole-class discussion, the instant a child is able to change the topic of conversation with peers—and think about how you might look more closely at the issues those moments raise.

Carry Courtney Cazden's questions with you as you watch students talk. What kinds of thinking and talk do you want around this subject matter? Is there evidence of learners having a chance to do this kind of talk? What's the distribution of participation? Who's getting a turn? Who's not? Who's silenced? Much teaching is not systematic; it is a series of small interventions and shifts in thinking that happen in the midst of students. The same can be true of language research.

3. *Integrate the research into what you are already doing in your classroom and school.* Additional responsibilities are always hard to fit into the school day. Think about your professional goals and try to find some way to incorporate language analysis into these goals. For example, if you are going to add an oral language component to your oral assessment system, develop a language analysis agenda that will lead to new assessment tools. If you are changing from a basal to a literature-based reading program, you might choose to analyze the talk that takes place in literature discussion groups, comparing it to the kinds of written chatter that appear in students' response journals.

4. *Enlist colleagues and students as coresearchers.* Interest in language issues can only be sustained if you have colleagues who share your enthusiasm. It is clear from reading the interviews that these lifetime enthusiasts are all part of a network of teacher researchers. These networks can be close to home, in your school, your district, your classroom—and can also be national and international communities. Gordon Wells stresses the importance of his local group of teacher research colleagues, and the learning he is able to share and pursue through XTAR and other worldwide networks. An added benefit of being involved in these larger internet communities is the ability to use written communication as a tool for helping us learn and make sense of what we are exploring.

We also encourage you to reclaim some of the required in-service days in your district as research discussion days. In work with different school districts, we have found administrators are almost always excited when teachers want to try new things in their classrooms. Teachers who work with their colleagues developing a plan for investigation in their classrooms are often surprised at administrators' willingness to allow teachers to use in-service days to continue their work. As part of your plan, you will need to decide upon collective readings and discussions for the group, as well as research activities. You may want to read one of the articles from this collection and discuss it. Your group might also decide to do one of the initial language analysis activities from Part II. For example, you might do the "Thinking about Classroom Discourse" chart (p. 184) for 20 minutes in your individual classrooms, and then discuss your findings at a research meeting. You may want to take turns bringing in a tape excerpt to listen to and analyze together. It is important for these meetings to have a clear focus and agreed upon tasks, so that they don't wander too far away from the group's language research goals.

Knowing the theories and practices of the researchers and teachers in this collection provides opportunities for us all. As James Britton writes:

There are great opportunities for us, provided we see that interactive learning applies to teachers as well as to those we teach; provided we see our role as helping each other to theorize from our own experience, and build our own rationale and convictions. For it is only when we are theorizing from our own experiences that we can, selectively, take and use other people's theories. (From "English Teaching: Retrospect and Prospect" by J. Britton, 1982. In *Prospect and Retrospect: The Essays of James Britton* (p. 214), Gordon Pradl, Ed., Montclair, NJ: Boynton Cook.)

We hope the studies and stories in this collection come alive as you work with colleagues and students to make sense of them through your own experience. The root word of theory is the Greek word *theoria*, which means "to see and contemplate." The visions of language in this book can provide many new insights into your students and your teaching, but only as you test them out in your classroom, and talk about what you are seeing with the colleagues around you. Then, language can serve in new ways as a window into the thinking and learning going on in and out of your classroom.

Name Index

285

Subject Index